PERSONALIZED FOR

PATRICK GERALD

Gordon Wood

John Carver
NOV 2001

Pat taught me
more about coaching
than any other coach
in the world. He
helped me be successful.

COACH

of the

CENTURY

AN AUTOBIOGRAPHY

COLLECTORS SIGNATURE COPY

FIRST EDITION

HARD TIMES
CATTLE COMPANY
PUBLISHING

PUBLISHED BY
Hard Times Cattle Company Publishing

No part of this book may be reproduced in any form or
by any means without permission in writing from
Hard Times Cattle Company Publishing

Book Design and Editor: Renee Baker

All inquiries for volume purchases of this book
should be addressed to Hard Times Cattle Company Publishing at
P.O. Box 941792, Plano, Texas 75094

Telephone inquiries may be made by calling:
972-669-0707 or FAX 972-669-0894
e-mail: Fntngreen@aol.com

To Katharine—
the most caring and
unselfish person in the world.
She's the real hero of
Gordon Wood's story.

Also by John Carver

WINNING
a novel about small town
high school football

HARDBALL FEVER
a mystery novel played against a
backdrop of minor league baseball

SPECIAL ACKNOWLEDGMENT

Special thanks to:

GLENNA BROWNLEE
of Brownwood
for proofreading the manuscript

and to

my daughter
RENEE BAKER
for editing the manuscript and the photographs
and for helping with the thousand meticulous
details that are so important in publishing a book.

PREFACE

I'd never met Gordon Wood when I called to ask if he would consider endorsing my first novel *Winning*. At first he told me he was too busy to read my book, telling me he had a book of his own he was trying to promote. After a little persuasion, though, he agreed to thumb through my book. We agreed if he didn't like the story, he could pitch the book in the trash, and there would be no ill feelings. Three days later, Coach Wood called me at my office in Dallas.

"Carver, you need to put a warning on that darn book!" Coach told me. "That thing is hazardous to your health!"

As you probably guessed, Coach liked my novel about Texas high school football. According to Coach Wood, he'd been going to bed promptly at ten o'clock every night since he retired. He said he started to browse though my book, and before he realized it, it was 2:30 in the morning. That was the beginning of a mutual admiration which gradually evolved into friendship. Coach called me the next summer and invited me to come to Brownwood. He wanted to talk to me about helping him with an autobiography.

A conscientious author never passes up an opportunity to sell a few books, so I used Coach Wood's invitation as an excuse to schedule a booksigning in Brownwood. To promote my book-signing,, I arranged to do a couple of morning radio shows—one with Cathy Marie Hail on KXYL and one with Barry Rose on KOXE. Then I called *Brownwood Bulletin* sports editor Bill Crist to ask if he would mention my booksigning in his sports column. Bill had heard about my book and enthusiastically consented. When I told Crist I was also planning to visit with Coach Wood, he cautioned me about Gordon's coffee drinking pals.

"Be sure you roll up your britches before you meet those guys at the coffee shop, John. It gets pretty deep in there," Bill warned.

Since Brownwood rolls out of bed early, I finished both radio shows by 8:30 A.M. A few minutes after nine, Coach Wood met me at the Bennett Building where he maintains an office. We'd hardly shook hands when Herman Bennett stuck his head through the door.

"You fellows about ready for coffee?" Herman asked.

Ignoring the sports editor's warning, I accepted Coach Wood's invitation to join him and his pals for coffee, and as predicted, the B.S. did get rather deep. What surprised me, though, was how easily the men accepted a stranger into their group. I should've suspected I would truly like every one of Gordon Wood's friends. You see, both my parents were born in Comanche County, so growing up, I spent a lot of time in Comanche and Sidney. Brownwood is right next door, and the people there are every bit as warm and genuine—like most folks who live in West Texas.

Before the day was out, I had met many of Brownwood's Legends—Herman Bennett, Calvin Fryar, Bill Jamar, Groner Pitts, Morris Southall and Kenneth West. I even got to meet Steve Freeman, Brownwood High's current football coach.

Wouldn't you know, though. Coach saved the best for last. I would get to meet Katharine a few trips later. She is a very special lady.

The thing that intrigued me most was Gordon Wood's ability to produce winning football teams every where he coached. As I listened to story after story, winning season after winning season, a simple explanation didn't immediately surface. When I pushed Coach Wood for a specific reason, he credited his success to his assistant coaches Morris Southall and Kenneth West. That's partially true, but I knew there was more to it than that. Gordon Wood won at Roscoe, at Winters, and at Stamford—without the help of Coach Southall and Coach West, and the quality of his assistants was sometimes pretty sad.

During interviews with Morris Southall and Kenneth West, I asked the same question. What one thing made Gordon Wood teams so different and so successful? Neither Morris nor Kenneth had a ready-made answer. Coach Southall believed Warren Woodson's winged-T offense played a major role in his and Gordon's coaching success. Coach West told me the innovative "Illinois Defense" was the key to Brownwood's football prosperity.

With several different answers to such an elementary question, I began to believe there was no simple answer. Then one day I called Bob Reily, hoping he could clarify a question about one of Stamford's football games. Bob coached at Colorado City High back in the fifties. He still lives in Colorado City. Coach Reily's Wolves provided Stamford's Bulldog squads with some of their stiffest competition. Bob told me Coach Wood's success lay in the fact that he always had his football team ready to play at game time—not the day before, and not the next day.

Kenneth Lowe attended Southern Methodist University in the fifties when I was there. While I was solving math equations, Ken was snagging interceptions as a starter in the Pony defensive secondary and backing up Don Meredith at quarterback. Ken participated in perhaps the best Gordon Wood story of all—the catfish whistling story at Stamford. When I called him to verify a point about Stamford football, I discovered he also had an opinion about Gordon Wood's success. Ken believes Coach Wood won because he coached at schools where he had total control over his players—cities where football was so important that a phone call to a parent, a teacher or a school board member would solve almost any coaching problem. Ken's theory is at least partially validated by Coach Wood's experience at Victoria where football wasn't the most important game in town.

In a *Sports Illustrated* article featuring Brownwood High football, Carlton Stowers once wrote that Gordon Wood possessed the amazing ability to convince teenage football players that they were just a notch below superman. I can personally testify that this is true because Coach Wood convinced me I could write his biography, which is now finished. I can also testify that writing this biography is the hardest thing I have ever done. However, if you enjoy the story of Gordon Wood's life, that effort is entirely justified.

Even after all the interviews and all my research, I never did find a simple answer to my question—why Gordon Wood always won. If you think you know, call me. I'd really like to know.

—John Carver

COACH

of the

CENTURY

AN AUTOBIOGRAPHY

by
Gordon Wood

as told to
John Carver

1975—300th Coaching Victory. (credit: Wood Family Collection)

1978—Ex-governor John Connally presents Gordon with game ball following Brownwood's sixth state championship. (credit: Brownwood Bulletin)

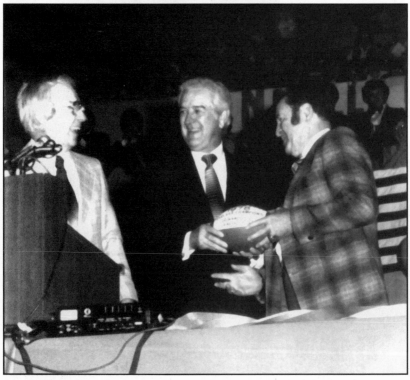

Gordon Wood's
Coaching Record
School by School

Rule High School

1940–41   5 Wins   11 Losses   2 Ties

Haskell High School

1942   1 Wins   0 Losses   0 Ties

U.S. Navy

1942–44   World War II Duty

Roscoe High School

1945–46   16 Wins   2 Losses   2 Ties
One District Championship

Seminole High School

1947–49   19 Wins   9 Losses   3 Ties
One District Championship

Winters High School

1950   6 Wins   4 Losses   0 Ties

Stamford High School

1951   9 Wins   1 Loss   0 Ties
1952   *13 Wins   1 Loss   0 Ties
*(*Includes forfeit victory over Colorado City.)*
Lost to Terrell 20–0, State Semifinals
1953   11 Wins   1 Loss   0 Ties
Lost to Phillips 20–14, State Quarterfinals

1954	9 Wins	1 Loss	0 Ties
1955	15 Wins	0 Losses	0 Ties

Beat Hillsboro 34–7, State Championship

1956	15 Wins	0 Losses	0 Ties

Beat Brady 26–13, State Championship

1957	8 Wins	2 Losses	0 Ties

Victoria High School

1958	6 Wins	4 Losses	0 Ties
1959	6 Wins	3 Losses	1 Tie

Brownwood High School

1960	13 Wins	1 Loss	0 Ties

Beat Port Lavaca 26–6, State Championship

1961	8 Wins	1 Loss	1 Tie
1962	11 Wins	1 Loss	0 Ties

Lost to Dumas 36–18, State Quarterfinals

1963	8 Wins	2 Losses	0 Ties
1964	7 Wins	2 Losses	1 Tie
1965	14 Wins	0 Losses	0 Ties

Beat Bridge City 14–0, State Championship

1966	8 Wins	2 Losses	0 Ties
1967	12 Wins	1 Loss	1 Tie

Beat El Campo 36–12, State Championship

1968	9 Wins	3 Losses	0 Tie

Lost to Lubbock Estacado 49–8, Bi-District

1969	11 Wins	3 Losses	0 Ties

Beat West Columbia 34–16,
State Championship

1970	12 Wins	1 Loss	1 Tie

Beat Cuero 14–0, State Championship

1971	10 Wins	3 Losses	0 Ties

Lost to Plano 10–8, State Semifinals

1972	6 Wins	4 Losses	0 Ties
1973	9 Wins	1 Loss	0 Ties
1974	11 Wins	1 Loss	1 Tie

*Tied Gainesville 20–20 in State Semifinals
but lost on first downs 18–16*

| 1975 | 8 Wins | 2 Losses | 0 Ties |
| 1976 | 10 Wins | 2 Losses | 0 Ties |

Lost to Perryton 13–0, State Quarterfinals

| 1977 | 13 Wins | 1 Loss | 0 Ties |

Lost to Dickinson 40–28, State Final Game

| 1978 | *15 Wins | 0 Losses | 0 Ties |

*(*Includes forfeit victory over Abilene Cooper.)
Beat Gainesville 21–12,
State Championship*

| 1979 | 10 Wins | 3 Losses | 0 Ties |

*Lost to Beaumont-Hebert 15–11
in State Semifinals*

| 1980 | 8 Wins | 3 Losses | 1 Tie |

*Lost to Lubbock Estacado 14–0
in State Quarterfinals*

| 1981 | 13 Wins | 1 Loss | 0 Ties |

*Beat Fort Bend Willowridge 14–9,
State Championship*

| 1982 | 9 Wins | 3 Losses | 0 Ties |

Lost to Gainesville 14–12, Bi-District

| 1983 | 8 Wins | 4 Losses | 0 Ties |

Lost to Vernon 11–6, Bi-District

| 1984 | 6 Wins | 3 Losses | 1 Tie |
| 1985 | 8 Wins | 4 Losses | 0 Ties |

*Lost to Lubbock Estacado 29–7
in State Quarterfinals*

TOTAL   **396 Wins**   **91 Losses**   **15 Ties**

*1967—Emory Bellard inducts Gordon into Texas High School
Coaches Hall of Honor. (credit: Wood Family Collection)*

*1983—Bum Phillips welcomes Gordon into Texas Sports Hall of Fame.
(credit: Wood Family Collection)*

CHAPTER ONE
The Early Years
(1914–1934)

I'M NOT SURE WHEN I decided to become a coach, but I do know when I decided not to be a dry land cotton farmer like my father. It was the summer of 1926 when my dad hauled me and my two brothers Troy and Garland up to Lamesa and hired us out to pick cotton. Ordinarily we would've been busy harvesting our own cotton, but the boll weevils and the weather had conspired to wipe out my family's crop. My dad left the three of us boys there on a huge cotton farm, camped out in the middle of nowhere. We slept in a tent, ate our meals out of tin cans, and picked cotton from sunup until sundown.

Four weeks later, after we'd finished picking that farmer's fields, my father came back, loaded us into his Dodge sedan and drove us to Artesia, New Mexico, where he'd cut a deal with another farmer to pick his cotton.

My brothers and I stayed in Artesia until my father returned the second week of November. He drove us back to Lamesa to the same farm we'd worked earlier. All the cotton had been picked, but now, our job was to pull the cotton—which means stripping the bolls from cotton stalks to harvest the last locks of cotton missed by the first pick. Fifteen hundred pounds of picked cotton make a bale, but it takes two thousand pounds of pulled cotton, called "bollies," to make a bale.

My brothers and I completed the task in three weeks, sometimes working in weather so miserable and so cold our frozen fingers would hardly hold onto the cotton. We returned home and started to school the first week in December.

I never minded the hard work, nor the aching back and

pricked fingers that went with picking cotton. Heck no, working with my brothers was fun. We made a game out of who could pick the most cotton—a game I never lost. Actually, we enjoyed the adventure, the opportunity to see the countryside and to be out on our own. What bothered me was watching my family struggle so desperately and never get ahead. I understood all along dad was only doing what he had to do to keep our family from starving. While Troy, Garland and I were humping it down those long cotton rows out west, dad and my older brother Dick were back at our home place doing the work all five of us would normally do. Nevertheless, when my dad finally brought us home, I began praying, hoping the Lord would show me a way to get off that farm. I'd made up my mind. Whatever profession I picked, I wanted a steady income. I didn't want to be dependent on something as unpredictable as the weather.

Instead, I chose a profession where a 6–4 season will get you fired, and your wins depend on the attention span of fifteen-, sixteen- and seventeen-year-old boys. I've never regretted my choice, not for a single minute. Even without the success I've enjoyed on the playing field, I could not have chosen a more rewarding career. My association with my players, my assistant coaches, school administrators, teachers and even my players' parents have given me enormous satisfaction. Watching the players I've coached become mature, responsible citizens fills me with a tremendous sense of pride.

And the good friends. A man couldn't ask for better friends than I've made because of my coaching associations.

Coaching definitely has its rewards. I'm not talking about monetary reward. A man can make more money working a whole lot less hours. But given a choice between coaching and some other job, I'd choose coaching every time. Coaching is an honorable profession. It darn sure beats farming for a living.

◆ ◆ ◆

MY FATHER, A.V. Wood, was working for my grandfather Sam Little when he married my mother Katherine. She was fourteen. The news upset my grandfather so much he grabbed his gun and went looking for my father. According to my Uncle John, Granddad Little's anger was about equally divided over his daughter getting married so young and his losing his best field hand. Anyway, not much time passed before my father lit out for Jones County to work on a farm near Anson, Texas.

My mother stayed behind in Austin with her parents, but the following spring, my father returned to Austin and brought her to West Texas to live with him. This time they settled a few miles south of Abilene in Taylor County on a few acres of land dad had arranged to share-crop. My folks traveled by wagon. Took them thirty-one days to make the trip.

Many years later, dad told me he and mother drove through Brown County during their trip from Austin to Abilene. Said all he remembered about Brownwood was the streets were crooked. Of course, they still are.

◆　◆　◆

FOR THE NEXT several years mom and dad moved from one rented farm to another. In those days tenants split the farm income with their landlord. Generally, the tenant received either a third or a fourth of the crop proceeds. Eventually my parents wound up on a piece of land near what is now the Wylie community. However, at that time the tiny settlement had no name.

Evidently the Little family thought dad had found his pot of gold, because shortly thereafter, right after the turn of the century, my Grandfather Little sold his Austin properties and moved his family to Taylor County. In 1903, my uncle and aunt, John and Florence Vance, arrived. Florence was my father's sister.

Wylie was originally called Sambo, named after my grand-father Sam Little. Sam was essentially a farmer, but he was also handy with tools. He and his son built a home for the Vance family. Then, attached to the new house, they constructed the community's first store. The store sold groceries and other essentials and was operated by my uncle.

With so many people moving to the community, Uncle John decided to open a post office in his store. Because of his close relationship with my grandfather, he anointed the post office with the name Samuel, but the name was rejected by Washington. Texas already had a town named Samuel. Eventually, a "Bo" was added to my grandfather's given name "Sam" and the post office was officially christened "Sambo." On December 19, 1904, the post office opened for business, with J.H. Vance as its first post master.

In 1917, John Vance became Taylor County's Tax Assessor-Collector. Uncle John was truly a remarkable character. You see, he was totally blind.

◆　◆　◆

PERHAPS IT GOT too crowded in Sambo. I'm not sure why, but along about 1912, my mother and father bought a farm in south Taylor County, picked up stakes and moved their family to Guion. That's where my brother Garland and I were born. I'm the youngest of eight children. Four boys—Dick, Troy, Garland and myself. Four girls—Deloria, Lucille, Alvina, and Marie. In those days large families were the fashion. Most people earned their living farming the land. Children made cheap and reliable help.

So many things were different back then. My family had a garden, naturally, but my father purchased our other food from a community store in Guion—on credit and with no interest. The woman who owned the store simply kept a running tab, and dad paid it off after his crop was harvested. You wouldn't believe the prices—three cents for a loaf of bread, eighteen cents for a twenty-pound sack of flour.

I was three when my father ran into financial difficulties. Dad was a smart farmer and a hard worker, but a sparse cotton crop and low prices did him in. Even though our farm was half paid off, he couldn't keep up the loan payments. Dad let the farm go back to the lender, and our family moved back to Sambo, which by that time had changed its name to Wylie.

◆　◆　◆

MY BROTHERS, MY SISTERS, and I grew up in a happy world. We were poor, but we thoroughly enjoyed each other's company. My dad loved farming, and he loved to sing. Many days I've sat on the back porch, watching my father walk along behind our two mules, plowing and singing at the top of his lungs. In those days a pair of good mules would bring three hundred dollars—half the price of a new automobile. Some of dad's happiest times were spent in the company of his mules.

One of my earliest memories was when I was five. My

brothers were off swimming in the creek below our house. A man came to our house asking to borrow some gas. His car had stalled out maybe a mile up the road.

My mother told him, "We'll be glad to loan you some gas, mister. This boy will show you where our car's parked." Mom handed the man a can and a hose and said, "You're welcome to siphon out whatever you need to get you back to town."

As I walked alongside the man toward our car, he seemed anxious. Finally, he said to me, "Son, I'm not sure I know how to siphon gasoline. You reckon you could do it for me?"

"Sure. I can get you all the gas you want," I replied confidently. Actually, I'd never siphoned gas before either, but I had watched my brothers. It looked easy. I was proud of myself for knowing something a grown man didn't know.

When we reached our car, I removed the gas cap and inserted the hose. I stuck the hose inside my mouth, clamped my lips, and sucked hard—the way I'd seen my brothers do. Instantly, I realized I'd done something wrong because gasoline filled my mouth. I swallowed a mouthful before I jerked back.

Dizzily, I staggered, reeling, my head spinning. My legs began to wobble. My shoulder hit the rear end of the car as I passed out and collapsed to the ground.

When I woke up, I was in bed. The man had carried me back to our house. I was lying there, half awake, half unconscious, and unable to move, when my brothers came back from swimming. My brother Garland was wearing a funny looking swim suit. I kept asking him over and over where he got it.

I was delirious, of course. The boy wearing the bathing suit wasn't Garland. As soon as my dad arrived, he and mother drove me into Abilene. I spent four days in the Abilene hospital. Doctor Jack Estes, who examined me, told my parents it was a miracle I didn't die.

◆　◆　◆

MY FATHER never had much use for higher education. Dad told me many times, "If you can get through the third grade, learn to read and write and do arithmetic so you can figure stuff, that's all you'll need. If you get too educated, you'll wind up a teacher or a preacher. Then most likely, you'll starve to death."

Perhaps that's why I didn't attend school until I was seven.

Even then I didn't start until December, after our cotton crop was harvested.

Pleasant Hill School was a wood frame building built in 1920, constructed with two intersecting gable roofs, ship-lap exterior wood siding and a painted wood floor. Inside was one large room which could be divided into two separate study areas by a roll-away curtain. Like many public facilities in those days, the building was used for classes during the week. On evenings and weekends the school often served as a town hall for community meetings and social events.

The school house was located near Caps Road on land which is now part of Dyess Air Force Base. The walk from our house to the Pleasant Hill School was a good two miles, but my folks never considered transporting us children to school in our wagon. That would wear out the mules, and dad had more important things to do than haul younguns.

Pleasant Hill was a two-teacher school. Students were separated into three classifications—primary, low-intermediate and high-inter-mediate which were equivalent to grades one through seven. I didn't learn much—except how easy it was to get in trouble.

Gordon's first class at Pleasant Hill School. (credit: Wood Family Collection)

I'd been attending school about a month when a group of older girls locked me and another boy out of our classroom. That made us mad, so we banged on the door and hollered at the girls, trying to make them let us in. Later, the girls went to the principal and told him we cussed at them. This wasn't true. We really didn't cuss the girls. Not that we couldn't have because I sure knew how. I was raised on a farm with three older brothers, and I'd been around cotton pickers all my life. Even at seven years old, I knew my fair share of curse words.

As punishment, the principal kept me and the other boy inside during recess. He told us to try and remember exactly what we'd said, but there wasn't anything to think about. We had told the truth.

The two of us were sitting there looking out the window, watching the other kids play in the schoolyard. That's when this older boy sneaked into the room to talk with us. He was a sixth grader, and I knew him from somewhere. Probably, he was a friend of my brothers. The sixth grader's name was Hobert Graham.

"Did y'all cuss at those girls?" Hobert asked.

"No, we never cussed nobody," I answered resentfully.

"What are you doing in here then? If I was to put a chair under that window, I'll bet you could climb out and go home, if you wanted to." Hobert pulled a chair up against the wall and opened the window.

That was all the encouragement I needed. I climbed out the window and headed home. I was halfway across the schoolyard when the principal saw me. He quickly enlisted several older boys to run me down and bring me back. They tried to catch me, but I was too fast. I didn't go back to school that year.

◆　◆　◆

BEFORE SCHOOL began the following year, my family moved to a farm north of Abilene, so I never had to face the Pleasant Hill principal again or pay a penalty for leaving school without his permission. I was eight years old before I actually attended school regularly.

For the next five years I attended North Park Elementary which was located a few blocks north of what was then called Simmons College. At the time, North Park was classified as a rural school because it was located outside Abilene's city limits. When we moved back to Pleasant Hill, I was starting sixth grade. That's the year I developed a taste for sports. I learned to play basketball.

Much to my relief, Pleasant Hill had a new principal named Parmenter. He was a Church of Christ minister who didn't know a thing about sports, but Mr. Parmenter's interest in his students had a tremendous influence on my life. He cared enough to hire a student athlete from McMurry College to come teach us basketball. About all we learned in those few short weeks was how to dribble, how to pivot, and shoot the basketball, but for a bunch of snotty-nosed farm kids who'd never seen a basketball game, it was a fantastic learning experience.

The principal's gesture constituted quite a sacrifice. Although his teacher's salary couldn't have been more than seventy dollars a month, Mr. Parmenter paid our student coach out of his own pocket.

After we learned enough basketball to compete, Mr. Parmenter arranged for us to play against other schools. We played maybe three actual games, but those games introduced me to competitive sports, and I loved it.

◆　◆　◆

HARD TIMES hit my family again in 1928. A hot, dry summer ruined our cotton crop, and my brother Dick injured his back. Dick's injury was so serious not a doctor in Abilene would operate on him. Eventually, my parents located a back specialist in Tyler, Texas, who agreed to perform the operation. When Dick came home, he was in a cast from his knees to his arm pits.

Money got so tight my mother decided to move into Abilene where she could take in other peoples' laundry. My father and my brother Troy stayed in Wylie to farm while mother, my sister Marie, my brothers Dick and Garland, and I moved into a house not far from the old Abilene High School. Our temporary home was so large mother was able to sublet half the house to another couple.

Those were difficult days for my family, and it broke my heart to see my mother work so hard. My older sister Deloria was married and had four young children. Both Deloria and her husband had jobs, so mother took care of their kids. At night mother did laundry. Many a night I crawled out of bed to go to the bathroom and discovered mother still awake and washing clothes.

In addition to all her other responsibilities, mother cared for

Dick who was in a cast. On weekends, my father and Troy left the farm and came to Abilene to be with us. During the year we lived in Abilene, I doubt my mother averaged four hours of sleep a night. Put simply, my mother was an amazing person. By example, she taught me many valuable lessons, about perseverance, about loyalty, about the importance of family.

Despite my family's troubles, a few positive things happened. That year I discovered football. Garland and I enrolled at Central Elementary. We were both in seventh grade. Garland was a year older, but by that time, I'd caught up with him. The second week after school started, my seventh-grade team played a football game. My coach decided I'd make a good defensive end.

Before that first game my school held a pep rally. I'd never seen a football game before, but at the pep rally, the cheerleaders kept yelling and talking about fighting and winning. Well, I was darn good at that. I'd been fighting with my older brothers as far back as I could remember.

During the game I don't remember making a single tackle, but I beat up on the poor kid playing opposite me something terrible. The player on the opposing team was Gene Estes. Gene was related to Doctor Jack Estes, the doctor who had helped me survive swallowing the mouthful of gasoline. Gene was crying and bawling and bleeding so bad his coach finally took him out. I beat up on the kid who replaced Gene just as bad. My team ended up losing, but I did a fine job of fighting. Man, I sure did like football.

When basketball season rolled around, I started every game. My grades were never straight A's, but in sports, I'd found something I was really good at.

Somehow mother earned enough money to pay off Dick's hospital bills and get the family back on its feet. The summer after Garland and I finished seventh grade, we moved back to Wylie.

◆　◆　◆

MY LOVE FOR FOOTBALL caused hard feelings between my father and me the year I entered tenth grade. I had decided I wanted to play football, but dad was against it. He thought football was a waste of time. Wylie High School didn't have a football team, so I went behind dad's back and talked my mother into transferring me to Abilene High School.

That was the beginning of the confrontation—a confrontation I was bound to lose. Don't get me wrong. My father was a great guy—a hard worker, a good provider, an honest man. His word was as good as money in the bank, but dad had strong convictions. Since I wouldn't be home to help with the other chores, dad insisted I handle all the milking, every morning and every evening.

From the beginning, I knew it wouldn't be easy. Transportation was a problem, but I knew a fellow named Pug Cox who lived about thirteen miles south of Wylie at Buffalo Gap. Cox was an all-state guard for Abilene High. On his way to school Pug drove through Wylie every morning and every afternoon on his way home. Each morning after I milked the cows, I'd walk the mile and a half to Wylie and catch a ride with Pug.

Dewey Mahew was the football coach at Abilene High, and he was partial to prolonged workouts. Many days Coach Mahew kept us on the practice field until after dark. Frequently, it was eight o'clock by the time Pug dropped me off at Wylie. I'd walk home, and there would be all those cows to milk. I lasted eight weeks before I quit the Abilene football squad and transferred back to Wylie High.

My father made his point. I never played another down of football all through high school.

◆　◆　◆

AT WYLIE HIGH SCHOOL, basketball was the number one sport, and we usually fielded a good team. We took on anyone who was willing. We played freshman teams from Abilene Christian College, Simmons College, McMurry College, and a JV team from New Mexico State. We played Abilene High several times each year. Each season Wylie High would play between forty and fifty basketball games.

Our basketball squad traveled to tournaments all over West Texas—Jayton, Sweetwater, Colorado City. Wylie was a poor school, so there was never any money budgeted for travel. Our basketball team traveled in automobiles, five players to a car. When we played out of town, we stayed overnight in private homes.

One winter, all five of us Wylie starters were crammed inside a four-door Ford driven by my brother-in-law. We were on our way to a tournament at Colorado City, traveling down U.S. Highway 80 which in those days was barely wide enough for two cars to pass. The weather was cold and nasty with sleet coming down so hard we could barely see the road. About a mile past Trent, Texas, our vehicle hit a slick spot, slid off the road and rolled over. None of us were hurt particularly, but we were all a little bruised and definitely shook up.

Our game was scheduled to begin in less than an hour, so we decided to hitch a ride and come back later for the car. We flagged down a passing car and hopped in. We'd traveled a mile or so when the driver asked where we were headed. We told him Colorado City.

Turned out, we were headed in the wrong direction. The automobile we'd flagged down was headed for Abilene. In the bitter cold and all the confusion we got our directions mixed up. We jumped out and highwayed it on back toward Colorado City where we trounced an all-star team from St. Joseph and beat Big Spring. Our basketball team advanced all the way to the tournament final before we lost to Colorado City.

◆　◆　◆

IN THE SPRING I ran track. I could outrun every speedster in Taylor County except for John Hamner who ran for Trent High School and Jack Patterson from Merkel. My best race was the half-mile, but I also ran the hurdles. My senior year I won five events in the county track meet. I won both the high and low hurdles despite practicing at a slight disadvantage. Wylie High School only owned one hurdle, which I personally built using scrap lumber from the school shop.

It was at that track meet I caught the eye of Les "Fats" Cranfill. He's the coach who recruited me and offered me an athletic scholarship. My scholarship was for basketball, track and football—even though I hadn't played football since tenth grade.

CHAPTER TWO
_____

The College Years
(1934–1938)

AS I ENTERED COLLEGE in the fall of 1934, a dark cloud hung over the entire nation. History books tell us the Great Depression lasted eleven years, from 1929 until 1940, but for the farming community in Taylor County, those years weren't much different than many others. For the Wood family, boll weevils, droughts, sand storms, too much rain, and low crop prices were equally devastating, and we'd endured calamities like that since before I was born.

In 1933, Congress approved the Agricultural Adjustment Act which saved many Taylor County cotton farmers from bankruptcy. Prior to the advent of the AAA Program, cotton prices had drifted down to less than six cents a pound. With an average yield of twenty-five ginned bales on a hundred-acre field, this worked out to an annual income of $7.50 per acre, not nearly enough for even a hard-working, self-sufficient family like mine to survive on.

The purpose of the AAA was to take half the acreage devoted to cotton out of production by plowing it up. Farmers were given the choice of accepting $11 for each acre plowed up, or taking one half in cash and the other half in cotton certificates to be drawn against existing cotton stockpiles. The money Taylor County cotton farmers received from this program was considered "manna from heaven." Somehow it didn't seem right. It certainly wasn't logical. How could my father make more money by *not* farming than he did by farming?

In 1933, Taylor County had 137,000 acres planted in cotton. The next year, under the acreage reduction program, only eighty-five thousand acres were planted. By the end of 1934, cotton prices had more than doubled.

The depression of the thirties did, however, severely affect many others. Simmons College, where I planned to attend on athletic scholarship, was on the brink of financial default. Teachers and administrators were owed more than forty thousand dollars in back salaries. Both my academic and athletic future seemed grim until Mr. and Mrs. John G. Hardin of Burkburnett, Texas, stepped forth, pledging $935,000 to guarantee the continued operation of the Baptist institution. The Hardins were cattle people who had been unexpectedly showered with immense wealth when oil was discovered underneath their enormous ranch. Shortly thereafter, the school trustees gratefully voted to change the college's name to Hardin-Simmons University.

The 1935 Bronco yearbook was the first official publication to identify the college as Hardin-Simmons. Seniors who graduated that year were the first to have Hardin-Simmons University imprinted on their diplomas.

◆　◆　◆

MOST OF THE UNMARRIED athletes were housed in on-campus dormitories, but my first year at Hardin-Simmons, I lived on the bubble. Mine was a partial scholarship which only paid fees and tuition. Room and board were not included. Whether I might be offered a full scholarship depended on how well I played and if the coaches were satisfied with my performance.

Since my family was well acquainted with half the population of Abilene, finding a place to live wasn't much of a problem. My father arranged for me to board with a woman who lived near the university. To compensate the woman, my dad hauled a cow into town and left it with her. The deal was I would tend the cow and give the milk to my landlady in return for my room and board.

Football practice began even before I got settled into my new quarters. Surprisingly, more than sixty freshman players reported for football. Since I hadn't played the game since tenth grade, I was worried I might be one of the first men cut, but after our freshman coaches, J.B. Neely and Guy Creighton, whittled the squad down to twenty, I was still onboard.

That season our yearling football squad played four actual games. I started all four at an end position. Our freshman club tried hard, but we played terrible, losing to North Texas Agricultural

College, Weatherford Junior College and the Texas Tech freshmen. The only team we beat was a group of so-called all-stars from Burkburnett.

Hardin-Simmons 1934–35 Freshman Basketball Squad.
Top row: Dennis Bivens, Chink Newberry, Junnell, Buel Ellison, Coach Jimmy Neely.
Bottom row: Larry Munday, "Babe" Wood, Jack Izard, Cagle Hunt, Bud Reeves.
(credit: Wood Family Collection)

FRESHMAN BASKETBALL was an entirely different story. Our two best players were Dennis Bivens and Ollie "Bud" Reeves. We played a total of ten games, winning eight and losing twice to Lamesa High School, a team loaded with talent. Lamesa went on to win their district championship, advancing to the state finals before they lost.

Our freshman basketball coach was Jimmy Neely, a former all-conference center at Hardin-Simmons. In 1932, Neely's average of 15.9 points per game broke the Texas Conference scoring record.

Near the end of basketball season, a Catholic high school from San Antonio contacted Coach Neely. They wanted to send their basketball team to Abilene to play our freshman squad. Neely agreed, and we played the San Antonio team a few nights later. I can't remember which team won, but after the game, Mose Simms, the Catholic school's coach, approached three of us on the Hardin-Simmons club and invited us to play with his team in the Catholic high school state tournament.

His offer sounded like great fun, so we went to Coach Frank Kimbrough who had replaced Les Cranfill as athletic director. Coach Kimbrough wasn't nearly so enthusiastic. He flat refused to let us go. Since I was living on the scholarship bubble, I decided not to go, but Ollie Reeves and Dennis Bivens disregarded Kimbrough's orders and went anyway. With Ollie and Dennis playing every minute of every game, the San Antonio school won the state meet.

Several days after his team won the state tournament, an article quoting Mose Simms appeared in the Abilene paper. Simms advised he'd decided against entering the Catholics' national meet because their rules were a bit stricter.

◆　◆　◆

COACH LESLIE "FATS" CRANFILL was a good man—admired by his players, adored by university basketball fans, loved by his associates and respected by his peers. From 1930 through 1933, Cranfill's basketball squads won four consecutive conference championships. In 1935, his basketball team ripped through the Texas Conference undefeated, earning an invitation to the national AAU tournament in Denver, Colorado.

Coach Cranfill was an absolutely amazing basketball coach, but in Texas where football is king, that don't swing much weight. Cranfill's football teams won only five games in 1933 and 1934, losing twelve with two ties. In Texas, particularly West Texas, a record like that simply won't cut the mustard. So despite his success on the basketball court, Cranfill was replaced as Hardin-Simmons' athletic director in the spring of 1935.

Coach Cranfill's successor was Frank Kimbrough, the brother of Texas A&M all-American John Kimbrough. Frank Kimbrough was the meanest, toughest, most intimidating individual I've ever known. For the next three years I lived in constant fear of the man.

◆　◆　◆

DESPITE A UNIVERSITY rule which required athletes to pass twenty-one hours each year to remain eligible for sports, academics were never a priority for either Coach Cranfill or Coach

Kimbrough, nor for any of the other coaches for that matter. If you flunked, you flunked. In the four years I attended Hardin-Simmons University, I can't remember any coach ever asking how I was doing in class. If a player wanted to maintain his scholarship, he was expected to pass without any assistance from the coaches. Pass or fail, it was left strictly up to the individual.

As a green freshman, with no one encouraging me to study, I hardly opened a book my first semester. Since I was on scholarship and important to the sports program, I figured my coaches would wave a magic wand at my professors, and somehow I would automatically pass. I found out different.

My first semester I passed one three-hour course. I failed every other subject. That meant I had to pass eighteen hours my second semester, and I had to do it while I played basketball, worked out for football, and ran track.

That spring I studied harder than I'd ever studied in my life. I couldn't take a chance on losing my scholarship. I had discovered attending college beat the heck out of working on that dang farm.

After my disastrous first semester, I only flunked one other course. That was a required physics class I was forced to take during my junior year and which most of the other football players failed too.

◆ ◆ ◆

IN ADDITION to football, basketball and track, I also boxed in college. I'd always been a good fighter, and with me being left-handed, I often held a distinct ring advantage. Not many amateur boxers could handle a hard hitting southpaw.

While I attended Hardin-Simmons, I fought for a boxing club sponsored and promoted by local boxing enthusiast Ray Crowell, an Abilene jeweler. I boxed in thirty-four fights. I won thirty of those matches, but the best fighter in Abilene was Truett Fulcher who won the heavy weight golden gloves championship in 1935. I had often thought about entering the golden gloves competition, but during the winter months when the tournament came around, I was too involved with basketball.

My sophomore year, our boxing team traveled to Port Arthur to compete in the Texas Amateur Athletic Federation State Tournament. I fought in the light-heavy division—161 to 176 pounds, making it all the way to the finals before losing to Buster Burrell.

Buster and I beat up on one another something awful. After three rounds, the ring judges ruled the fight a draw, so we were forced to fight a fourth. When the bout finally ended, neither of us could lift our gloves above our waists. Our faces were bloody and swollen. We were both so exhausted we could hardly stand.

In the summer of 1937, our boxing club again competed in the TAAF State Tournament. The meet was held in Abilene that year. I knew Buster Burrell would be coming, and I didn't want to face him again, so I trained hard, dieting and losing weight so I could drop down and fight in the middleweight division.

Imagine my surprise—Burrell was also hoping to avoid facing me. He had lost weight too. We both wound up in the middleweight division and found ourselves pitted against one another in the semi-finals. Our second skirmish was even bloodier than the previous year. This time I won, but I took a horrible beating.

Several hours after the fight I was still punch drunk, dizzy, and sick to my stomach. At four o'clock in the morning, I drove into Abilene, rousted a chiropractor out of bed and had him work me over. He cracked my joints, popped my back and stretched my limbs. I felt better when he finished, but I was still in no shape to box. Nonetheless, the next evening I fought Elton Jones in the finals. Jones attended McMurry College. He was an aggressive fighter, a hard slugger with a deadly left jab. Elton won the bout, but I lost mostly because of the dreadful flogging I'd taken the night before.

◆　◆　◆

KIMBROUGH'S COACHING genius began to take effect late in the football season of 1935. After losing to Texas Tech, Baylor and SMU, and with only one victory over lowly St. Edwards University, our Cowboy club began to gather momentum. With Vestal Newberry scoring on a sixty-yard run, we slid by Sul Ross 15–9. A week later Bedford Russell and Burns McKinney were the heroes, each scoring on long runs as we pasted Texas A&I 34–0.

The highlight of our football season, though, was defeating Howard Payne who had dominated Hardin-Simmons for years. Early in the game a crushing quarterback sack delivered by Otis Crowell caused the Yellowjackets' passer to fumble. The ball rolled into the end zone where Crowell pounced on it for a Cowboy touchdown. Final score: 14–0.

A 46–0 win over Texas School of Mines in the final game of the season earned us an invitation to play New Mexico in the Sun Bowl on New Years Day. The invitation was a really big deal, because in those days there weren't many bowl games.

The Sun Bowl battle ended in a 14–14 tie, but Gordon Wood wasn't invited to the party. Basketball season was underway, and Coach Kimbrough left me in Abilene. In Kimbrough's eyes I was a basketball player and nothing more than a blocking dummy for his football squad. That was okay by me. With several of our basketball regulars in El Paso with the football team, I logged in some valuable playing time.

That season our basketball team won eighteen and lost six, beating Texas Tech four times and finishing second in the Texas Conference. Our fans immediately noticed the aggressive change in our playing style. Under Frank Kimbrough's tutorage, Hardin-Simmons players were frequently ejected for physical contact. Local sportswriters accused us of playing basketball like a pack of oil patch roughnecks. Personal fouls were partially responsible for losses to Sul Ross and West Texas State which cost us the conference title. Playing basketball for Coach Kimbrough was sure different.

◆　◆　◆

FRANK KIMBROUGH loved football. In fact, he was a football wizard, way ahead of his time, but he didn't have much use for basketball. He simply put up with basketball. I've seen him sit on our bench and diagram football plays while his basketball team was in the midst of a gut-wrenching, down-to-the-wire game.

Many of the Hardin-Simmons athletes attended on multi-sport scholarships, like mine. For instance, during my junior year, three starters on the basketball squad were also starters on the football team. That may have irked Coach Kimbrough, but there was never any doubt in anyone's mind which sport was most important to our athletic mentor. The minute basketball season was over, he'd suit us up for spring training.

Every year I played for Coach Kimbrough, spring training went on for weeks and weeks. Generally, practice would begin about 2:30 in the afternoon and lasted until after dark. Playing football for Frank Kimbrough was a full time job.

Kimbrough's long, drawn-out practices often put him at odds with the cafeteria staff. Our cafeteria employees were congenial and conscientious, but like most people, they had private lives. In the evenings they were anxious to get the students fed and leave for home. Of course they couldn't. They had to stay on duty until Coach Kimbrough's football players straggled in from practice.

Now myself, I was scared to death of Coach Kimbrough, but some of the better players weren't. About ten of my teammates persuaded the cafeteria staff to furnish them with sack lunches. Supposedly, the snacks were to help tide the men through Kimbrough's extended workouts, but they also represented a back-handed display of labor rebellion.

Our standard practice routine was to scrimmage hard for forty-five minutes, take a break, then work for another forty-five minutes and take another break. Along about six o'clock, when any sensible coach would be home eating dinner with his family, Ed Cherry, Burns McKinney, Pete Tyler and several of the other older players fished out their sack lunches and began to snack.

Kimbrough's face turned beet red. You could tell he was mad as hell. He didn't say a word, but he got the message. A few days later Coach Kimbrough shortened our practice sessions. By six o'clock the football team was usually in line at the cafeteria.

◆　◆　◆

BEING A NAIVE country boy, I never dreamed the other athletes were being paid for their participation. I was perfectly happy to play three sports and work out four hours a day—all for the privilege of having the university provide my tuition, books, and room and board.

On weekends and in our free hours, Hardin-Simmons athletes were frequently required to do odd jobs. We policed the campus, watered the lawns, cleaned up the grandstands, even sanitized the stadium rest rooms. One Saturday in April, the entire football squad was assigned to yard maintenance at the football stadium. We worked hard all afternoon, weeding flower beds, mowing grass, mending fences and trimming the sidewalks. Otis Crowell, Ed Cherry, Malcolm Bridges and I had been assigned to work together. Using hand slings, we had leveled a field of high grass behind the stadium. When we finished, we were rather proud of the work we'd done.

"Man, we sure earned our keep today, didn't we?" Otis Crowell declared, breathing hard as he wiped at his sweaty face.

"Yep, that and the extra fifty dollars a month they pay you for opening those gigantic holes for Ed to run through," Bridges proclaimed. Like myself, Malcolm was a rag-knot scrub who was struggling to maintain his scholarship. His rash comment was prompted more by envy than admiration.

I was shocked by his disclosure. This was the first I had heard of players receiving any kind of monetary compensation.

Ed Cherry took exception to Bridges' spiteful remark. Ed was our fullback. In 1937, he had been named honorable mention all-American by the Associated Press. If Otis was being paid fifty a month, I'm sure Ed was receiving at least that much, maybe more.

"Malcolm, if you're worth room, board, tuition and fees, then Otis is worth that, plus the fifty dollars and a whole lot more."

Until that very day, I swear I never even suspected Hardin-Simmons athletes were being paid in hard cash for their services.

◆　◆　◆

ONCE DURING SPRING TRAINING, I was sitting on the sideline bench, watching intently as the first-string offense scrimmaged our defense. Otis Crowell had been injured on the previous play, and he came limping off the practice field. Otis was the best lineman on our team. He'd been selected to Jerry Mann's all-Texas team the season before. Otis was also a prankster, always cutting up, goosing his teammates, hiding their equipment, anything to get a laugh. When Otis sat down beside me, he nudged me hard, using an elbow to knock me off the end of the bench.

In retaliation, I leaped up and pushed back at the oversized lineman. That was a mistake, because Coach Kimbrough was watching. Coach didn't put up with horsing around. We both knew we were in for it as Kimbrough came striding toward the sideline.

"Crowell, you and Wood climb off your butts and take two laps!"

I was upset and mad at Otis. He had started the shoving match. I saw no reason I should be punished. Still, I was too afraid of Frank Kimbrough to speak up in my defense. When we stood up to run, Otis began to limp. Possibly his crippled movements reminded Coach Kimbrough why Otis was on the bench.

"Crowell, you go back and sit down! Wood, you do four laps!" Kimbrough commanded decisively. In Frank Kimbrough's mind I was nothing but cannon fodder. Having me run Crowell's laps was totally justified.

◆　◆　◆

COACH KIMBROUGH always looked out for his best players—sometimes to the chagrin of us team members who weren't so good. To supplement Otis Crowell's income, Coach Kimbrough arranged for him to work an after hours janitorial job. In the evenings after practice, Otis would dump the trash cans, clean the rest rooms and sweep the floors for an oil company which officed in a building about six blocks from the campus.

Otis lived in Matador, Texas, which is located in the high plains area about a hundred and fifty miles northwest of Abilene. When Otis went home for the Christmas holidays, Coach Kimbrough was worried Otis might lose his job. Kimbrough called me to his office.

"Wood, don't your folks live somewhere around Abilene?"

"Yes sir, out near Wylie."

"I understand you and Otis Crowell are good friends."

"Yes sir. Otis and I get along okay."

"Fine. Here's the key to the Magnolia Oil building. You take care of the janitorial work there until Otis comes back from the holidays. Make sure you do a good job now. We wouldn't want Otis to get fired on account of you, would we?"

Every evening for the next two weeks, I cleaned that building for Otis. I don't know whether my teammate got paid by the hour or by the week, but I never saw a dime of his pay.

◆　◆　◆

IN 1936, MY JUNIOR YEAR, Hardin-Simmons fielded a tremendous football team. During the regular season we posted eight wins and two losses—good enough to win us an invitation to play in the Sun Bowl for a second consecutive year.

Seven members of the football squad, including myself, also played basketball. Naturally, Coach Kimbrough's main interest was winning the bowl game, so in December, during the transition from football to basketball season, we basketballers shouldered a heavy load. Monday through Friday, we worked out for basketball in the morning and practiced football that afternoon. Three nights, sometimes as many as five nights a week, we played a basketball game.

In those first weeks of basketball season, we looked forward to Wednesdays with great anticipation. Wednesday was prayer meeting night. Baptist schools don't play basketball games on prayer meeting nights.

During the Christmas holidays, as our basketball schedule kicked into high gear, our basketball squad endured one of the most trying, and at the same time, most rewarding sports experiences I have ever been privileged to share.

On Monday and Tuesday evenings we played Baylor. At that time Baylor occupied second place in the Southwest conference. We won both games rather handily. Now remember, these games were played *after* we finished football practice.

The next night we didn't play because it was Wednesday, prayer meeting night. On Thursday and Friday evenings we took on SMU. The scores were close, 29–27, and 27–22, but we won both games. SMU was in first place and went on to win the Southwest Conference that year.

On Saturday, we played TCU and won that game. The score was 21–18. Sunday afternoon the football team departed for the Sun Bowl, taking starters F.O. Scroggins, Billy Harris and Carroll Benson. Coach Kimbrough also took Alton Terry, Blackie Calloway and Bud Reeves, leaving the basketball squad with an assistant coach and only six players. Only two of the players left behind were regular starters, so our basketball team consisted of two starters—Sam McCollum and Bob Glover, two second-stringers—Vernon Payne and myself, and two reserve players—Melvin Bivens and Cagle Hunt.

Monday night we played TCU again. Using only six players, we outscored the Horned Frogs 27–19. Actually, it was an easy game. Our depleted squad had fresh legs from top to bottom. With the football team in El Paso, we had no reason to practice football Monday afternoon.

On New Year's Day our football team blasted El Paso School of Mines 34–6.

Our basketball team finished the regular season with a perfect record—fifteen wins and no losses. After totally dominating our Texas Conference, we advanced to the Texas AAU Tournament in Dallas where we trounced Louisiana Sulfur before losing to an all-star team from Slaton.

◆　◆　◆

DURING MY FOUR YEARS at Hardin-Simmons, I was never a star in any sport. Matter of fact, compared to the talented athletes I played with and against, I wasn't very good. But I learned so much about sports and coaching strategy. The impact of my experiences at Hardin-Simmons shaped my life and helped me decide on a career. I wanted to be a coach. Watching my coaches at Hardin-Simmons helped me decide the kind of coach I wanted to be.

◆　◆　◆

A FEW YEARS AGO I boarded an airplane coming back from Washington, D.C. and ran into Frank Kimbrough. After he left Hardin-Simmons, Kimbrough coached at Baylor. He later coached football at West Texas State and eventually became their athletic director.

Some Hardin-Simmons football players believed in Coach Kimbrough like he was a second coming, but those who admired him most were generally the star players. Kimbrough cottoned up to his best athletes, but he had little use for players with mediocre ability. I never played for or worked under any coach I feared more than Frank Kimbrough. I wasn't alone. Every second line player he coached was afraid of him, and that's what I told him on the plane that day. Coach Kimbrough was truly surprised, but what I said was true. When he yelled at us, we'd go crazy.

Frank Kimbrough was a great football coach—a genius at football strategy, light years ahead of his time, but he was too hard, too aloof, too critical. Many of his players were afraid of him, and because of this, they didn't always play their best. I know I didn't. With more encouragement, and less fear, I know I could've been a better player and contributed more.

You look at successful coaches today. You'll see they take an interest in all their players—talking to them, communicating, encouraging their kids. You seldom see a winning coach who plays favorites or who bullies his players.

Hardin-Simmons graduate Gordon "Babe" Wood— Spring of 1938. (credit: Wood Family Collection)

I GRADUATED from Hardin-Simmons in the spring of 1938 with B.A. degrees in both History and Physical Education and a minor in Mathematics, but long before I received my diploma, I had definitely decided I wanted to be a coach.

I signed up with a teacher placement agency in Abilene. They found me my first coaching job—in Spur, Texas.

CHAPTER THREE

Learning the Ropes

(1938–1942)

IN 1938, THERE WERE three West Texas cities I considered to be choice coaching jobs—Ballinger, Stamford and Spur. Imagine my delight when the Abilene placement agency found me a coaching position at Spur High School. Spur boasted a population of perhaps twenty-three hundred people, but it was the principal economic center for all the ranch country between Abilene and Lubbock. A rail line operated by the Fort Worth and Denver Railroad made the community a major shipping point for cotton, cattle and wheat. Spur was served by two bus lines, Greyhound and Texas Central. The largest hotel between Lubbock and Abilene was also located in Spur—The Spur Inn.

For nine hundred dollars a year, seventy-five a month, I coached the basketball team, the track team and acted as assistant football coach. Since I obtained the job through a teacher placement agency, five percent of my first year's salary went to pay their fee. After deductions for teacher retirement and the placement agency fee, my first monthly paycheck, which I immediately cashed, amounted to $69.65. As I strolled out of the bank, I was all smiles. Stashed inside my front pants pocket was the most folding money I'd ever possessed at one time.

Being single, financially strapped, and short on transportation, I roomed in a house located a block from the high school, so I could walk back and forth. My room rented for eighteen dollars a month which included both room and board. My landlady served three meals a day, and she was a fantastic cook. The food she served was delicious and plentiful. I accumulated several extra pounds that first year.

The head football coach at Spur High School was Blackie

Wadzeck, a graduate of McMurry College where he was an all-conference football player. Blackie played football for Spur High School in the early thirties when coaches regularly recruited players from outside their district. The Spur football team Blackie played for in 1930 scored 748 points in fifteen games, beating Lorenzo 186–0 and Estelline 142–0. Blackie told me the Lorenzo players were so embarrassed by the outrageous score that they pitched their uniforms out the bus windows as they drove out of town. Spur also took on the Texas Tech varsity in the fall of 1930, hammering the Lubbock college kids 72–6.

Wadzeck's football teams operated from both single wing and double wing offensive formations which most coaches subscribed to at that time. Spur's district included Paducah, Flomot, Matador, Ralls, Crosbyton, and Lockney.

Spur opened the season with an easy victory over Roby. We were rocking along undefeated and with an excellent chance of capturing the district title when our Bulldogs collided with "Red" Amonette and his maroon and white Flomot Longhorns.

◆　◆　◆

ON THE FRIDAY prior to our Flomot game, Coach Wadzeck instructed me to go to Flomot and scout their game against

Football Stadium at Spur, Texas.
(credit: Herman Bennett)

Matador. That night Flomot ran all over Matador, mostly because of a light-footed gazelle named "Red" Amonette. Amonette was an absolutely amazing athlete. Seemed like every time the shifty ball-carrier touched the football, he broke for a touchdown. Saturday morning, I reported back to my head coach.

"Blackie, that Amonette kid is fast and dangerous. He's easily the best running back I've ever seen. No way we can keep him out of our end zone. To beat Flomot, we'll have to score at least forty points."

"That's the same old bull I heard last year," Wadzeck chided, rejecting my scouting advice. "No one thought we could stop Amonette then either, but our defense shut him down completely. Don't you worry, Babe. We'll do it again this year."

"I'm sorry, Coach Wadzeck, but I don't see how. Maybe you got lucky last year, but there's no way anyone's gonna shut "Red" Amonette down, not this year."

Our Bulldogs played a solid, mistake-free football game, but we lost to Flomot, something like 28–21. Amonette broke for four long runs, each of which led to a Flomot touchdown. The loss to Flomot cost Spur the district championship.

◆　◆　◆

SINCE SPUR HIGH SCHOOL didn't have a gymnasium, my basketball squad was forced to practice in the schoolyard. All our games were played on the opposing team's court. In my very first game as head basketball coach, my team got clobbered by McAdoo. The final score was 66–6. I was devastated. I knew if my boys didn't improve, I'd be looking for another job.

Melvin Bivens, a teammate of mine at Hardin-Simmons, was coaching at Dickens High School. Dickens is the county seat of Dickens County and is located twelve miles north of Spur. The day after that disastrous first game, I drove to Dickens. The purpose of my trip was to ask Melvin and the Dickens school superintendent if they would allow my basketball squad to practice in their gym. We would work out after Melvin's team finished their practice. Two hours later, when I headed back to Spur, I had their blessing.

The next day I approached O.C. Thomas, Spur's school superintendent. I needed transportation, and I had my eye on an old bus which belonged to the school district. When I told him I wanted to use the bus to transport my roundball squad back and forth from Spur to Dickens every afternoon, my boss wasn't necessarily negative. He was sympathetic to my team's predicament, but he didn't agree right away. Superintendent Thomas told me he wanted to think about it.

Several days later the superintendent called me to his office and gave me permission to use the bus. His consent, however, included one condition which put a grievous strain on my finances. He insisted I buy the gasoline. Undaunted, I quickly accepted his deal.

The old school bus turned out to be a gas guzzler. By season's end my pocketbook was a great deal lighter. Nonetheless, I've never made an investment which provided me with more satisfaction. Having a gym to practice in turned our season around.

At the end of each basketball season, no matter their size, all the high schools in Dickens County competed in one tournament. The tournament winner then advanced to the state playoffs. My basketball team played McAdoo again in the county tournament, and we beat them handily.

◆　◆　◆

DURING THE NIGHT before April Fool's Day, someone sneaked a milk cow into the high school. When teachers and students arrived the following morning, the hallways were littered with fresh cow droppings. Talk about stink—the entire school smelled like a barnyard. O.C. Thomas was furious. He called me to his office and asked if I could find out who was responsible.

Looking back, I'm not sure I would respond now the way I did then. But remember, I was an inexperienced young coach. This was my first job, and I was anxious to please. I assured the superintendent I could.

The best athlete on our football squad was a big strapping boy named Pete Wilhoit. This guy possessed more natural strength than any player who ever played for me. Pete was unbelievably strong and rail tough, but he had one weakness. The sight of blood caused him to faint dead away. On the football field blood is a frequent guest, so we used a lot of smelling salt reviving Pete.

Since Wilhoit was often the instigator of locker room shenanigans, I was fairly certain he had a hand in the cow incident. That afternoon after football practice I cornered him.

"Pete," I inquired, "were you the one who put the cow inside the school building?"

"Yes sir, it was me. I did it," Pete replied honestly, looking me straight in the eye. Pete wasn't the least bit remorseful. As a matter of fact, he seemed proud of himself for pulling off the stunt.

"Well, we need to get this thing straightened out," I told him. "I need to know who else was with you."

After Pete revealed the names of the other boys involved, I went directly to Superintendent Thomas and told him. The superintendent immediately telephoned Johnny Coonsman, the county sheriff. Sheriff Coonsman's response was swift. He apprehended the boys involved and brought them to the school building. The sheriff gave the boys two options. They could go to jail, or they could clean up the cow dookie, sand down the wood and varnish the floors. All this was to be done at the boys' expense. The school wasn't to pay one cent toward the floor repairs.

The other boys complained about not having enough money to rent a sander and pay for the paint, but Wilhoit didn't seem worried.

"I can't do it, Sheriff Coonsman. My family won't help, and I don't have a dime. I reckon you can't get blood out of a turnip," Pete stated defiantly.

"Naw, but I can throw those turnips so far back in the county jail we'll have to shoot food to 'em with a peashooter," the sheriff responded.

The sheriff's mandate dramatically changed the boys' attitudes. In less than a week the floor job was completed.

After he graduated from Spur High School, Pete Wilhoit attended Texas Tech on a football scholarship. Pete made an outstanding college football player.

◆ ◆ ◆

TO SUPPLEMENT MY INCOME, I managed Spur's municipal pool during the summer. The city furnished the water, the chemicals and the insurance. To compensate me for my services, I was allowed to keep the gate receipts. The pool was open for three months—June, July and August. Our admission receipts amounted to approximately a hundred dollars a month. I used the extra money to purchase an almost new '38 Ford. The car cost me $595. My monthly payments were $50 a month.

Being the city's center of youth activity, we kept the swimming pool open seven days a week. Monday through Saturday we opened at ten in the morning and closed at ten that night. Sundays, we opened from one until five. Leonard King, the high school band director, served as my assistant. I hired two eagle scouts to serve as life guards.

One Friday near the middle of July, I decided to drive to Abilene and visit my parents for the weekend. I left Leonard in charge.

Saturday morning I woke up with an uneasy feeling. I began to worry about the swimming pool situation. By Saturday afternoon I was convinced something bad was about to happen, so I cut my visit short and headed back to Spur. It was almost dark when I arrived back at the swimming pool. The minute I saw Leonard's face I knew something was wrong.

Leonard told me two boys named Simmons and McComb had been horsing around on the high diving board. After reaching the top of the ladder, the Simmons kid chickened out and decided not to dive. Climbing back down, the boy missed a step and lost his balance. As he fell, a ring the boy was wearing caught on a bolt. The youngster's ring finger had been jerked off at the big knuckle.

Leonard's news shook me. I was so distraught and upset I was ready to shut the pool down, but Leonard talked me out of it. He convinced me the kid's injury was a freak accident which would probably never happen again, and besides, the harm was already done. Shutting the pool down would only call more attention to the libelous situation.

Monday morning I made a point of going by to check on the Simmons boy. The city carried pool accident insurance, so I brought along the paperwork needed to make a claim.

To my surprise, Mr. Simmons refused to sign the papers, telling me, "We're not planning to make a claim."

"But why not? Our insurance will pay all the doctor bills," I explained. The father's attitude shocked me. His son was badly injured. I expected him to be fighting mad.

"Because the injury was an accident. It wasn't anybody's fault. We're not blaming anyone for what happened to our boy."

We argued for a few minutes. Finally, I insisted, "Mister Simmons, this is the second summer I've run that swimming pool.

Every month we pay for insurance to cover a situation like this, but we've never filed one single claim. Now I want you to sign this paper. We want to pay your doctor bills."

Simmons eventually agreed. Nowadays, a conversation like that would never take place. The chain of events would be automatic. By Monday, the boy's family would have hired a hungry lawyer. Before the week was out, the lawyer would have filed a million dollar lawsuit.

Here's an interesting footnote to this story. The other kid horsing around on the diving board with the Simmons boy that afternoon was Billy Joe "Red" McComb. McComb was twelve years old that summer. He lived in Spur until his junior year in high school when his family moved to Corpus Christi. Years later, "Red" McComb purchased the San Antonio Spurs. These days he owns the Minnesota Vikings. McComb is a lifelong and close friend.

◆   ◆   ◆

AFTER THE FOOTBALL SEASON ended in the fall of 1939, Blackie Wadzeck was promoted to high school principal. His promotion left the head coaching job vacant. Several months later during the second semester, Spur's school board voted to reward me with the head football coaching job. I was ecstatic. The board's affirmative action meant a substantial pay raise. Only two years out of college and I was already a head football coach. My joy wouldn't last long.

◆   ◆   ◆

BECAUSE OF THE COW INCIDENT on April Fool's Day the previous year, Superintendent Thomas asked me to arrange a day of activity. The purpose was to keep our students occupied and hopefully curtail the foolish pranks of prior years. I accepted the task with great enthusiasm. On April 1, I planned and supervised foot races, basketball games, volleyball games, and a host of other entertaining contests. My April Fool's agenda included both our elementary and high school pupils. The kids loved being outdoors, and my program worked out great.

On my way home that evening, I was feeling quite satisfied with myself. My April Fool's games were a bona fide success.

My second year at Spur, I rented a room in a fine old rock home occupied by the McGee family. Mr. McGee was deeply involved in community affairs. He was also a member of the school board. I knew something was wrong the second I stepped through the front door. Mr. McGee's leathery face was shrouded with sadness.

"Coach, I'm afraid I have some bad news for you," McGee told me. Tears filled his eyes as he spoke.

"What's that?" I asked. Seeing my landlord's grieved expression, my happy, self-satisfied demeanor was slipping away fast.

"The school board met this afternoon. They changed their mind about giving you the head coaching job. Instead, they voted to hire a fellow named Duckworth."

Mr. McGee's news devastated me. I didn't sleep a wink that night. The next day I found out the ugly details:

Woodrow Duckworth was a TCU graduate and one of the finest all-around athletes to ever play for the Horned Frogs. While he was at TCU, Woodrow earned thirteen letters in various sports—football, basketball, baseball, track, even tennis. TCU's head football coach was Dutch Meyer, one of the most successful coaches in the nation and a legend in southwest football circles. Naturally, Duckworth was one of Coach Meyer's favorites.

That afternoon while I was busy with the April Fool games, Dutch Meyer met with Spur's school board and convinced the trustees to hire Duckworth as their head coach. The whole episode was nothing but politics, and I was the victim.

◆　◆　◆

BECAUSE OF THE DISTASTEFUL situation at Spur, I immediately began to search for another job. No way I could work with Woodrow Duckworth. My harsh feelings were too strong. It wasn't his doing, but I'd been treated badly.

By the end of the school year I located another job—as head football coach at Rule, Texas, a small farming community located about sixty miles north of Abilene. Rule High School was in the midst of a 19-game losing streak when I took the reins.

The following fall Rule lost three more games, stretching the losing streak to twenty-two before the football team finally won. For me, that first season at Rule High was a colossal struggle. However, my team did break out of its losing streak, and prospects for the future seemed brighter. Most of my players were under-classmen who would be returning.

The next spring I was still simmering over the Spur coaching job and the way I'd been treated. I had a point to prove, so I drove to Spur and confronted Woodrow Duckworth. When I asked if he'd be willing to add Rule to his football schedule, Woodrow almost fell out of his chair laughing. Rule High School was less than half the size of Spur and owned a well-deserved reputation as the whipping boy for the area schools. If a coach wanted a sure win and a breather for his football squad, he included Rule's Bobcats on his schedule.

Woodrow eventually agreed to play my Rule team, and we signed a two-year contract.

◆　◆　◆

MY BEST TWO PLAYERS at Rule were Vernon Townsend and a rabbit-quick running back named Homer Turner. Vernon was my first-string quarterback. He would later become an outstanding football coach. The Townsend family lived right across the street from me. One afternoon near the end of the spring semester, Vernon knocked on my door and told me three of my football players—Wesley Almond, J.R. Barbee and Van Laughlin—were on the verge of failing. The boys were sophomores, all excellent football players—kids I was counting on to help me win the next fall.

The following day I checked out the three players' grades, and sure enough, they were each about to fail. My discovery unnerved me. I had been working night and day trying to turn the football program around. Without those three sophomores, my team's prospects were greatly diminished.

Thinking I could rectify the situation, I took my problem to Frank Hill, Rule's school superintendent. At first the superin-tendent was reluctant to intercede. It was only after I lost my temper and threatened to resign that he agreed to talk to the boys' teachers.

A few days later Superintendent Hill called me to his office and told me he'd worked things out with my players' teachers. He assured me the boys would all pass and be eligible for football the following fall. As I was leaving the superintendent's office, I met Vernon Townsend in the school hallway.

"Hey, Coach, what'd you find out about Almond, Barbee and Laughlin?"

"Everything's under control. I talked to the school superintendent. Looks like all three are gonna pass."

"That's great. Laughlin told me not to worry. He said if this school didn't think enough about his football to keep him eligible, they deserved to lose."

Suddenly I didn't feel so good about what I'd done. I realized I had been a party to blackmail—trading athletic ability for grades. I whirled around and marched straight back into the superintendent's office. I told Superintendent Hill if any one of those youngsters passed, I was leaving. All three boys wound up failing, but I learned a valuable lesson.

The three boys must've learned something too, because that next year their grades improved dramatically.

◆ ◆ ◆

IN THE FALL of 1941, my varsity consisted of eighteen players. Our uniforms were ragged, our equipment was old, and my boys were scrawny. When my kids took the football field before a game, their bedraggled appearance often prompted laughter among opposing fans. My team looked terrible, but we weren't nearly as bad as we looked. We opened our season by traveling to Spur to take on Woodrow Duckworth and his Bulldog football team.

Our bus arrived early Friday afternoon, and we checked into the Spur hotel. Woodrow was so confident he would win he invited my team to attend their pep rally held that afternoon. Electing not to show all my cards, I only brought fifteen members of my football squad to the rally, leaving my three largest players behind at the hotel.

More than a thousand Spur supporters attended the pep rally. Bulldog boosters were excited and enthusiastic. They yelled and screamed for more than an hour, mostly for our benefit. Every person there was totally convinced their blue and gold team would thrash my Bobcats soundly that evening. After the yell session broke up, one of the Bulldog halfbacks arrogantly strutted up to me.

"I'm gonna score a touchdown tonight, Coach Wood."

"That's fine, son. I hope you do," I answered calmly, faking a smile.

"But before I score, Coach, before I cross the goal line, I'm gonna turn around and trot right by your bench. Then I'll run back and score."

"That'll be fine, son. You do that. That ought to really please your daddy." I already had plenty of reasons to make me want to see my ballclub stomp the living daylights out of Woodrow Duckworth's Bulldogs, but now, my blood was boiling.

A few minutes before the opening kickoff, Woodrow casually strolled into our dressing room. Pitifully, he shook my hand. Then he climbed up on a stool to address my ill-dressed and anxious troops.

"Men," Woodrow advised, so full of himself that every button on his shirt was at risk of popping off, "I want you fellows to go out there tonight and play the best you know how. Don't ever quit. We're suiting out fifty players, and I plan to play every man. So don't worry about being embarrassed or about my team running up the score. You fellows hang in there and do the very best you can."

My football team surprised everyone that night, including me. At the end of the third quarter, Spur hadn't made a single first down. When I removed my best players from the game and subbed in several younger boys, Rule was leading by a score of 27–0. My starters were begging me to let them go back in when Blackie Wadzeck, Spur's high school principal, ambled up to our bench.

"Go ahead, Babe. Put your best players back in the game. Maybe if you score two or three more touchdowns, these dimwits will realize what a mistake they made."

The final score was 34–0. Spur made only three first downs. The Bulldogs never crossed the fifty-yard line. For me, that victory was one of the most satisfying of my entire coaching career.

Woodrow Duckworth was a good man, but not a successful coach. He knew all about football and football strategy, but he never understood motivation. Great natural athletes seldom make great coaches, possibly because success in sports often comes too easy for them. Woodrow eventually wound up selling sporting goods.

Several years later Blackie Wadzeck accepted a position as principal at Lamesa High School. He finished his career at San Angelo where he was superintendent of schools. While Blackie was superintendent, a delegation from Soviet Russia visited San Angelo. The Russians were touring U.S. schools. When their tour was finished, they said San Angelo had the finest school system in the United States.

Rule's football schedule included games against much larger schools; Anson, Baird, Hamlin, Spur, Stamford and Throckmorton. But despite the stiff competition, my Bobcat football team ended the 1941 season with a record of 3-3-2. With a majority of my varsity players returning and a fine group of outstanding athletes from an undefeated "B" team in my varsity pipeline, I harbored great expectations for the upcoming season.

◆ ◆ ◆

IT WAS SUNDAY MORNING. I was leisurely soaking in my bathtub, listening to the radio and day dreaming about basketball season when I heard the news. The date was December 7,—the day the Japanese attacked Pearl Harbor.

CHAPTER FOUR

The War Years

(1942–1945)

LESS THAN A WEEK after the attack on Pearl Harbor, I signed up to join the navy. Assuming I'd be called up immediately, I quit my coaching job at Rule and moved back to Abilene to live with my parents while I waited to be inducted.

In mid-January, C.B. Downing, the superintendent of schools at Albany, called me. He was short on teachers and asked if I'd come work on a day to day basis. I hadn't heard from the navy, and I needed money to live on, so I accepted the superintendent's offer. I had no idea I'd still be teaching in Albany when the school year ended.

◆ ◆ ◆

COACHING AT ALBANY was almost painful. Their sports program seemed in disarray, totally disorganized. Neither the coaches nor the players showed much enthusiasm for spring training— at least they didn't get after it the way I was accustomed to practicing football.

Exasperated with the situation, I approached Connie Smith, the head football coach. "How about letting me manage spring training for the seventh- and eighth-grade kids?" I asked.

"You'd just be wasting your time, Babe. Those young kids aren't interested in football. I doubt if you can find enough players to scrimmage," Coach Smith counseled.

"You let me worry about players. All I want from you is your permission," I countered confidently. Any West Texas coach who can't find twenty-two junior high boys who want to play football should apply for an administrative job.

"Well, okay. But don't expect any help from me or the other

coaches. We already have our hands full. You'll be strictly on your own."

I quickly agreed. Actually, I was relieved none of the other coaches wanted to help. I wasn't particularly impressed with their negative teaching methods anyway. I went to work recruiting, and when I was done, my spring football practice included almost every single boy in seventh and eight grade.

Near the end of April, I divided the youngsters into two teams and played a real game with officials, first-down chains, and a lighted scoreboard. More than three hundred of the boys' parents, grandparents and friends attended. To enter through the front gate and watch the game, we charged each person a bar of soap.

The navy ended my Albany coaching experience by calling me in July, but when I left, the school system at Albany had plenty of soap—enough to last for years.

◆　◆　◆

THE NAVY ASSIGNED me to officer's candidate school at Columbia University in New York, along with fifteen hundred other college graduates. The competition was fierce. Many of my fellow hopefuls had completed pre-naval courses in college. Many of the prospective navy officers hailed from Florida and the East Coast and knew about ships. I'd grown up in West Texas, and until that day I arrived in New York, I'd never even seen a ship.

Even though I worked harder, tried harder, and studied harder than any human being attending that school, my mind couldn't grasp the unusual subjects they were teaching. I wasn't the only one who had trouble. Two hundred of my classmates dropped out during the first three weeks. Another hundred were gone before graduation.

Four weeks from graduation, I washed out. My final downfall was astronomy. I should have been devastated, because in all my life I had never failed at anything I'd set my mind to. But to tell the truth, when it was over, I was totally and absolutely relieved.

◆　◆　◆

AFTER I WASHED OUT of officer's candidate school, I was like a fish out of water, flopping around without any sense of direction. The navy's usual policy was to immediately discharge the men who flunked out of officer's school. Then they would ship the men home where they could be drafted. However, the officer who handled my discharge suggested I go to Washington, D.C. and apply for officer's school in the Marine Corps.

I tried that, but changed my mind when I discovered I'd have to endure another rigorous study session. My experience at Columbia University had soured me on military education. I also considered signing on with the Coast Guard, but they wanted to send me back to school too.

Finally, I discovered a plan called the "Gene Tunney Program" which was designed for athletes holding a college degree. These people promised to put me on the navy's payroll and send me home until their next training session started. I couldn't believe my good fortune, but my luck got even better.

While I was back home in Abilene, the school superintendent at Haskell called and invited me to coach their high school football team until my travel orders arrived. I accepted the superintendent's offer, grateful for the extra pay and for a break from military service. I installed a new offense, then moved their starting running back to quarterback and the quarterback to running back. Haskell won two games, beating Albany and Stamford before I had to leave.

◆ ◆ ◆

WHEN MY TRAVEL ORDERS arrived, they included a train travel voucher and instructions to pick up a Tom Tinker in Fort Worth and accompany him to Norfolk, Virginia. Tinker was a graduate of Texas A&M and a former captain of their basketball team. We immediately became good friends.

We changed trains in Dallas, and ten hours later, we were only halfway to Norfolk. Butt weary and bored silly, I decided to walk through the train, thinking I might run into someone I knew in one of the other cars. Two cars back, I discovered a shirtless male about my age. I'd never seen anyone like this fellow. He was wearing sunglasses and reading a newspaper. He was six-foot-two, 225 pounds, and without an ounce of fat on his body. His arms and chest simply rippled with huge, bulging muscles. I ran back to get Tom Tinker. Tom had to see this.

The muscular man's name was Denutchio. Like us, he was headed for the Norfolk Naval Station. When Tom and I introduced ourselves, Denutchio told us he was a movie star and a stand-in for

Johnny Weissmuller in the Tarzan movies. Later, we verified this to be true because we actually saw him in a couple of Tarzan films shown on base.

In spite of his magnificent body, Denutchio turned out to be an obnoxious chap and rather stuck on himself. At first, we laughed when he swung through the barrack rafters and yelled like Tarzan, but after a while we tired of his weird behavior and zany antics. He was easily the most unpopular chief petty officer in our entire company.

One Saturday afternoon Denutchio was bragging about his swimming ability. Now, I considered myself a pretty good swimmer. I started swimming when I was four and could outswim almost anyone who wasn't trained to swim competitively.

Eventually, Denutchio got carried away with his boasting, saying he'd bet ten dollars he could swim faster than any man in the room. When I accepted his challenge, he wanted to raise the stakes to twenty dollars. I instantly agreed.

During the few weeks we'd been stationed at Norfolk, I had become close friends with Creed McClure. McClure was from Tennessee. Creed agreed to accompany us and act as judge. Outside, the snow was three feet deep, and the base swimming pool was eight hundred yards away, so just getting to the pool took some effort.

Ten minutes later we hit the water. We had agreed to a fifty-yard race. In a twenty-five-yard pool, that's down and back. I swam as hard as I could, but as we approached the opposite end and turned, Denutchio was a yard ahead. I lowered my head and swam even harder. Halfway back I pulled even.

To be perfectly honest, I think we both hit the end of the pool at the same time, but Creed said I won. The fellow running the pool said Denutchio won. Denutchio wanted to race again, but I told him we had picked our judge before the race started, and back in Texas, we never changed officials once a game got underway.

Creed and I took the twenty bucks and went into Norfolk where we ate the biggest and best meal we could find. Several months later Creed and I would both be stationed in California, and we would become even better friends.

In seven short weeks the navy taught me everything I needed to know to be a chief petty officer. In the regular navy, they referred to us as "slick arms." Graduation from the Gene Tunney Program earned me a two-week furlough and duty as a basic training instructor in San Diego.

◆　◆　◆

MY JOB at the San Diego Naval Base was to teach new recruits some basic military skills and ship them overseas or to special training schools. Many of the men assigned to training duty were former coaches. Early on, the navy discovered that ex-coaches and men who played sports have a special knack for organizing and training other men.

When I arrived, each company consisted of one hundred and twenty men, with one chief petty officer and two assistant instructors assigned to each company. With manpower in short supply, it wasn't long before the navy trimmed our training crews to a petty officer and only one assistant. In the beginning, a training session lasted eight weeks, but before the war ended, our basic training sessions were whittled down to three weeks with one hundred and eighty men in each company. The navy also decided one good petty officer could get the job done without any assistants.

◆　◆　◆

AFTER OUR RECRUITS completed basic training, the navy's policy was to have a chief petty officer accompany the sailors to their next duty—to Norman, Oklahoma, for electronic school; Gulfport, Mississippi, for radio and communication school; and College Station, Texas, for signal school. For the petty officers, escort duty was a choice assignment. Usually after the men were safely delivered, the instructor traveling with them could squeeze out three or four days for personal business, often arranging to route himself back through his hometown to visit with friends and family. According to base policy, the chief petty officers chosen were selected as a reward for doing a good job.

Even though I consistently turned out award winning companies, my name was never among those posted for travel duty. However, I noticed Bill White's name was almost always on the escort list. I'd known Bill before the war when he coached at Baird, Texas. I figured he knew something I didn't, so I looked him up one evening.

"Bill, the base officers keep telling me if I do a good job, I'll be rewarded with travel duty. But that's not working. I've put companies through here that've won every award possible. That don't seem to swing much weight because you're the one they always pick. I wanna know why."

Bill grinned sheepishly and pulled me aside, keeping his voice low so no one would hear. "You gotta grease the right palms, Babe. If you'll promise not to tell anyone else, I'll tell you how I do it."

"Alright, I promise. I won't tell another soul," I replied, frustrated because there had to be a gimmick to receiving the reward I clearly deserved. Nonetheless, if there was some secret formula, I wanted in on it.

"First, there's something you need to know. That Captain up there at headquarters with the scrambled eggs on his cap, he don't run this man's navy. It's the yeoman who works for him who makes all the decisions. He's the one you need to butter up. Tell you what. I'll arrange for the three of us to go out and eat, and you pick up the tab. You treat that yeoman right, and he'll take good care of you."

Gordon with his father and mother on leave from navy in Abilene.
(credit: Wood Family Collection)

Sure enough, I did exactly like Bill advised, and after the very next training session, I was assigned to escort duty. I discovered the yeoman liked whiskey, so after every trip, I brought him a bottle of liquor. From that date forward, I enjoyed a favored status. After every training session the base commander selected me to travel with our graduates.

◆　◆　◆

FOR ALMOST A YEAR, I also taught boxing. My instructions were to teach my students just enough to know the basics. That was fine with me. Many days my boxing classes would only last a few hours. Then I'd be free to do whatever I pleased.

Still, I wanted to do a good job, so I wrote out a lesson plan for boxing instructors. The navy liked my plan so much they published it. Perhaps I did too good a job, because a few months after the boxing booklet was published, I began to have more men assigned to my classes than I could handle. My free time disappeared. All day I'd teach at the boxing center, then in the evenings, I was ordered to go to another part of the base and lead company recruits through thirty minutes of vigorous calisthenics.

In the navy I learned one thing about boxing. A man's head isn't built to take the constant hammering it takes in the ring. After a year of teaching boxing, a continuous ringing sound affected my hearing. Every morning I'd wake up sick to my stomach and so dizzy I could hardly roll out of my bunk. When I began to vomit regularly for no apparent reason, I gave up my boxing job. I got my fill of boxing in the service, and I've had zero interest since.

◆ ◆ ◆

WAR IS HELL. Even for men like myself who didn't fight in actual combat, the war uprooted our careers and changed our lives. Everyone who participated in World War II came home with a different perspective—on career, on family, on life.

One of the few good things that happened to me during those horrible years was meeting my wife Katharine. Creed McClure, my good friend from Tennessee, was with me that evening. Like most of our nights on the town, we were alone—two single guys cruising the downtown bars in San Diego. It was the ninth of November, and the first time we'd been off the base in weeks. Our first stop was at a nightclub in the basement of the U.S. Grant Hotel. We found a table and were about to order drinks when a fellow we'd never seen before approached us. The man wasn't wearing a uniform. He was obviously a civilian.

"You guys here alone?" the civilian asked.

"Yeah, what's it to ya?" Creed answered, thinking the man wanted to join us.

"Nothing, but I'm here with three girls. One of the girls is from Kansas. We're celebrating her birthday. Thought you two might want to join us."

"Whatta they look like?" I asked, suspicious of the man's motives. Why would a fellow with three women want to share their company with two sailors?

"Not bad. They're sitting at the table on the other side of the dance floor. Take a look and judge for yourselves."

One glance and we could see the girls were okay. Most likely we would have accepted his offer no matter what the girls looked like. Single women were scarce, and in San Diego, there were ten lonesome sailors for every available female.

Not waiting for a second invitation, Creed and I hastily joined the birthday party. During the introductions we discovered it was Katharine's birthday. The other two girls were co-workers who shared quarters with her at a women's boarding club.

Katharine was a beauty. Creed and I were both immediately smitten with the birthday girl who reluctantly admitted she was from Waverly, Kansas. She had followed her older sisters, Fern and Betty, to San Diego to work in the war effort.

At first, Katharine was shy, probably categorizing me as just another serviceman on the prowl, but after we danced and talked, she opened up. Katharine was a terrific dancer, so graceful, so warm and soft. We were gliding easily across the dance floor to a popular Glenn Miller tune when I told her I was a football coach.

"Is that right? Well, I've always wanted to marry a football coach," she giggled and snuggled up closer. We danced and talked and laughed until the wee hours.

◆　◆　◆

OURS WAS A WHIRLWIND COURTSHIP. With the world at war, young people like Katharine and I were in a hurry. Not knowing whether we'd survive, or even if our country would survive, we snatched at happiness whenever we could.

I was busy teaching men to be sailors, training young boys to become the fighting men our country desperately needed to man our ships and win the fierce battles raging in Europe and across the Pacific. Every eight weeks a company of my troops had to be trained and ready to ship out. Katharine worked at Consolidated Vought Aircraft, a company which would later merge into General Dynamics. Her duties essentially involved clerical work, but during the war years, every job associated with the production of war materials was vitally important.

Even though our free time was limited, we managed to squeeze out a few hours to spend together. On most dates we simply went to a picture show where we held hands in the dark. On a couple of occasions we attended parties given by my naval base petty officers, but our favorite getaway was visiting Leonard and Beth King.

Leonard and I met and became good friends while I coached at Spur High School. After the war started, he was one of the first to enlist. Leonard was stationed at San Diego's North Island Naval Base. While he waited for orders to ship out, Leonard, Beth, and their daughter Ann had taken residence in a grand old hotel on Coronado Island. Leonard was a talented musician, and his wife Beth played the piano like no one I've ever known.

After Katharine and I began dating, Leonard and Beth were the first of my Texas friends I introduced her to. Katharine thoroughly enjoyed their company, but years later, she would declare, "Gordon took me there to have the Kings look me over and get their approval, because his immediate family was back in Texas."

One Sunday evening, Katharine and I had been visiting the Kings. We were on our way back to San Diego when a tire blew out. My ancient '29 Dodge coupe, which I had frugally purchased for fifty dollars, didn't carry a spare. It was late, so I called Leonard to come get us and drive us to the dock where we caught the ferry. When Katharine and I arrived on the opposite side of the bay, we flagged a taxi.

Maybe I was upset over my car. I can't remember the exact details, but during the ride home we quarreled over something. I left in a huff, telling Katharine it was a good thing I had orders to escort a fresh batch of troops to Norman, Oklahoma, because that would give us time to think things over. When I climbed aboard the train leaving for Norman a few days later, we still hadn't made up.

The return leg of my trip I had managed to route back through Abilene where I planned to spend a couple of days with my parents before heading back to California. It was in Texas I began to regret my senseless argument with Katharine. I wanted to call her, to hear her voice, and explain how I felt, but the women's club where she lived had no telephone. So instead of calling, I night-wired

Katharine a telegram, telling her I missed her and asking her to marry me. I wouldn't know her answer until I arrived back in San Diego, but the following day I borrowed my dad's pickup, drove into Abilene, and picked out a ring.

Happily, Katharine accepted my marriage proposal, her only condition being we marry in a church. On the fourteenth of January, in a small Presbyterian church, two months and five days after we met, we exchanged wedding vows. Leonard King was my best man.

Since neither the naval base barracks nor the women's club were suitable for a married couple, the next order of business was finding a place to live. That wasn't an easy task. Most San Diego landlords were reluctant to rent to servicemen because we were usually in limbo—in and out, sometimes in a matter of weeks.

While we searched high and low for decent living quarters, Katharine and I shared a small two-story house with another family. They lived upstairs. We lived downstairs. That arrangement wasn't real bad, but the house only had one bathroom. Every morning I had to wait in line.

We eventually located a garage apartment behind the home of a Portuguese couple. It was the perfect spot for a young married couple. The apartment was near my naval base and set atop a hill on Point Loma. Our bedroom window overlooked San Diego Bay. Many nights we went to bed with the harbor full of ships only to find it empty when we awoke the next morning. Katharine and I were as happy as two young people could be in those anxious days.

A few weeks after we married, Katharine discovered she was pregnant. One day I was a footloose West Texas football coach. Then, without warning, I was whisked away to a strange place to teach men how to fight a war. Now I was married and expecting a family. My life was moving fast, much too fast.

◆　◆　◆

IN SPITE of my full schedule, I found time for my first love—basketball. With the base captain's consent, we formed a basketball team and scheduled games with other nearby bases. With men shipping out every few weeks, I was always on the lookout for new talent for my basketball squad. Some days as many as two thousand fresh recruits arrived at our base. As the men filed off their busses,

San Diego Naval Base Basketball Team. Jack Stone is #21.
(credit: Wood Family Collection)

I'd get on the loudspeaker and inquire if anyone had played college basketball. If a fellow answered yes, I would usher him to the base gym and try him out.

One day I had picked up three recruits who seemed like good prospects. Then I noticed a lanky, burr-headed kid. He acted like he wanted to say something but was too shy. I instructed the men to wait while I hurried back to check out this tall fellow.

"You ever play college basketball, son?" I asked.

"No sir, I never went to college. Only finished high school. But I played semi-pro on a corporate team."

"Who'd you play for?" I inquired. I'd heard about corporate-sponsored clubs which traveled around the country playing basketball, but I'd never met anyone who actually played for one. I was intrigued with the youngster. He certainly looked like a player.

"Carroll Shamrock Corporation," the young man replied. "We won the national championship last year."

The recruit's name was Jack Stone. He turned out to be far and away the best player who ever played on my San Diego roundball squad. Before he shipped out two months later, I asked Jack to get in touch with me after the war, promising I could get him a basketball scholarship to Texas University.

Several years later I picked up the *Abilene Reporter-News*, and there was Jack Stone's clean-shaven mug looking back at me. He was playing for Kansas State University.

When Katharine and I drove to Kansas that December for our annual Christmas visit with her parents, we were able to watch Jack Stone and his Wildcat team play in a Big Eight tournament held at Kansas City. His senior year, Jack was the team captain. In 1951, his K-State team lost to Kentucky 68–58 in the NCAA National Championship game. Jack scored twelve points and grabbed six rebounds.

◆　◆　◆

WHILE I SERVED in the navy, my brother Garland served in the army. Garland was involved in actual combat and participated in the North Africa, Sicily and Italy campaigns. My brother didn't fare as well as me. He came back from the war partially disabled and a completely different person.

Garland, Alvina, and Gordon.
(credit: Wood Family Collection)

◆　◆　◆

WORLD WAR II officially ended on September 2, 1945. With so many men in the service, a serious teacher shortage prevailed back on the home front. To address this problem, the government initiated a policy of early discharge for members of the armed forces who could show they had a teacher's job waiting.

Ted Edwards was the school superintendent at Roscoe, Texas, a tiny, but prosperous, farming community about twelve miles west of Sweetwater. On September 10, acting on a recommendation from Hal Sayles, a sportswriter for the Abilene newspaper, Superintendent Edwards contacted me and offered me a job as high school principal and head football coach. The salary he proposed was twenty-seven hundred a year, three times the pay of my first coaching job at Spur. His terms were explicit. School had already started. If I wanted the job and an early release, he wanted me at Roscoe High on the twelfth. Otherwise, he intended to hire someone else.

My daughter Patricia was born on the fifth of September. She was seven days old, and Katharine was barely out of the hospital the day I departed for Texas.

CHAPTER FIVE

Starting Over
(1945–1947)

WORKING AT ROSCOE HIGH SCHOOL was one of the most enjoyable experiences of my coaching career. The town's people were wonderful, the teachers supportive, and the school administrative staff helpful and efficient. That was so important because I was a very busy man. In addition to my duties as high school principal and football coach, I taught three math classes and drove the morning school bus. When football season was over, I coached the basketball and track teams.

Even though I was busier than a barefoot boy in a red ant bed, those first weeks in Roscoe were lonely. Saturdays and Sundays were the worst. Before the war I had enjoyed my bachelor's life, but in Roscoe, after the euphoria of our Friday night football game wore off, heartache would set in. I called Katharine every Sunday afternoon, but our brief telephone conversations only served to make me miss her more.

I'd been a civilian and on the job six weeks before Katharine was able to travel. When Leonard King's wife suggested she fly, Katharine was petrified. Even though she worked in an aircraft factory before we married, Katharine had never flown in an airplane. Her exact words were, "I wouldn't get on an airplane with my baby for love nor money."

Eventually we did convince her to fly. The flight from San Diego to Abilene took eight hours, whereas by train it was a torturous two day trip. When she and our baby daughter Patricia arrived at the Abilene municipal airport via an American Airlines twin engine prop, I was a relieved and happy man.

◆ ◆ ◆

IN 1945, the population of Roscoe approached fourteen hundred. One hundred and thirteen students, grades nine through twelve, attended Roscoe High. Eighteen boys suited out for football that fall. Thirteen of those boys were not only good players; they were exceptional.

Prior to my joining the navy, my football teams had run strictly from a straight "T" formation, but now I wanted to try a fresh approach. At Roscoe, I began experimenting with a winged-T offense, but I didn't limit my offense to one formation. My players were cooperative and quick to learn, so I tried lots of ideas. Many times my team broke from their huddle, lined up in a winged-T, and shifted into a single wing formation. Sometimes we would line up in a winged-T with an unbalanced line and put a man in motion. Included in our offensive arsenal were more than twenty passing plays. I've always believed in an aggressive aerial game. My football team's offensive formations were so deceptive and so unpredictable we drove opposing coaches nuts.

Many of the formations and shifts I employed originated from Clyde "Bulldog" Turner, a teammate of mine at Hardin-Simmons who later played for the Chicago Bears in the National Football League. Adjusting to so many talented players, I also changed my defense, generally using a 5–4–2, five men on the line, four linebackers and two deep backs. Our defensive ends played like corner backs do in the pros today. A majority of the time we only rushed the three middle linemen. Occasionally, we rushed all five linemen plus two linebackers. Years later when Bud Wilkerson used the same defense at Oklahoma, it became known as the Oklahoma five.

◆ ◆ ◆

BY THE TIME Katharine and Patricia arrived, my Roscoe football team had won six games in a row, defeating teams from much larger schools like Hamlin, Stamford, Hobbs, Sweetwater, Colorado City and Rotan. My Plowboys had scored two hundred and four points while allowing only thirteen. We were well on our way to capturing Roscoe's first district title in six years. Only three teams stood in our way—Merkel, Loraine and Snyder. Merkel was a must win contest. The

Badgers had been regional champs the previous year, and they were next on our schedule.

◆ ◆ ◆

OUR GAME AGAINST MERKEL was played on their field on a cold, windy Friday evening. Before the game began my senior players gathered in a tight circle to clasp hands and dedicate themselves to victory.

Don Witherspoon took the opening kickoff, tucked the ball under his arm and scampered to his left. Halfway across the field Witherspoon handed off to Walter Maloney who was going in the opposite direction. Maloney slipped through the grasp of one Badger and hip faked another. Galloping up the right sideline, he shifted into overdrive. Grunts and sharp popping sounds resonated across the playing field as Plowboy linemen Lynn Williamson, Douglas Buckner and Bobby Emerson leveled Badger defenders with bone-crushing side-body blocks. When Maloney crossed the goal line following an 85-yard return, Roscoe fans went berserk.

Our fake kick on the point after attempt caught the Badgers completely by surprise. Maloney carried the ball in for the extra point.

Merkel roared right back, scoring a touchdown on a long, time-consuming drive. Despite an outstanding goal line stand by my staunch Plowboy defense, the Badgers scored again right before the half to take the lead 12–7. It was the first time my team had been behind in a game that season.

During the second half the momentum seesawed back and forth. Merkel would drive into Roscoe's territory and stall out. Then my Plowboys would pound their way back onto Merkel's end of the field. When Alton Green broke through for a twenty-yard run near the end of the fourth quarter, fans on both sides were completely exhausted from yelling. Three plays later Maloney scored his second touchdown of the night on a draw play, and absolute pandemonium rocked the stadium. On the extra point try we tried another fake field goal. This time Maloney took the ball and fired a short pass to Witherspoon in the end zone.

The game ended with Merkel on our thirty-five, driving for a touchdown.

Final score: Merkel 12, Roscoe 14.

In the following weeks, we wrapped up the title, beating

Loraine 55–0, and Snyder 44–0, but our victory over Merkel actually determined the district champ.

My Roscoe squad was loaded with talent. Probably any coach in Texas could have won with the same players, but I'm convinced that changing my mind set, being willing to experiment with a new offense, marked the beginning of my future coaching success.

◆　◆　◆

WE PLAYED at home the Friday night my football team defeated Snyder. After the scoreboard clock ticked off the final second, Plowboy boosters stood and clapped and cheered and stomped their feet for more than ten minutes. For my players it was a wonderful expression of appreciation. For me, it was an exhilarating and gratifying show of support.

Sometime during the Snyder game, Roscoe fans passed a hat around the grandstands. The following Monday, Clyde Jay, Roscoe's bank president, exchanged the miscellaneous donations for twenty-dollar bills and brought the money to Katharine in an envelope. The cash-filled envelope contained two hundred dollars—ten crisp, brand-new twenties. Katharine and I were both overwhelmed by the town's generosity. My wife told the banker that was the most money she had ever possessed at one time.

Included inside the envelope were the names of each person and the exact amount he contributed. Many people gave fifty cents, some a dollar, not many kicked in more than a dollar. Katharine still has that list of names. Every now and then we pull it out to remind us how generous people have been to us. We know each of those dollars were hard earned, so they were gifts given straight from the heart.

◆　◆　◆

AFTER MY PLOWBOYS wrapped up the district championship, I made one of the dumbest coaching decisions of my career. With a two-week gap between our final game of the regular season and our upcoming bi-district tilt, I was worried my team might lose its edge. That's why I agreed to play an extra game with Anson in Abilene. The game meant nothing. The Tigers had won their district and had an off week before their bi-district game. Anson had an excellent ballclub and was expected to go a long way in the playoffs. I was determined to show them how good we were. That led to my undoing.

Early in the contest the Tigers set the tone for rough play. After almost every play some sort of extracurricular fisticuffs or shoving took place. In the trenches a lot of nasty name calling went back and forth. That didn't bother me because my Plowboys rushed out to a seven-point lead. I was confident we would win. At least I was until my best player Walter Maloney broke loose for a long gain. An Anson linebacker named Fry caught Walter from behind, grabbed him by his shoulder pads and wrestled him to the ground. As Maloney went down, he tore an Achilles tendon.

Roscoe won 14–0, but with my star player hurt and a bi-district contest scheduled for the next Saturday, I was hardly in a mood to smile.

◆　◆　◆

EVERY COACH has days that make his hair fall out. Sometimes, no matter how hard you try, no matter how meticulously you plan, or how well you prepare, circumstances beyond your control conspire against you. My Plowboys had sailed through the football season undefeated, winning ten consecutive games, and scoring three hundred and thirty points while allowing only twenty-five. We were scheduled to play the Monahans Loboes on Saturday for bi-district. How could so many things go wrong so fast?

Monday morning, my running back Walter Maloney, who had been a solid starter for four years, showed up for school on crutches. Maloney had torn an Achilles tendon in the Anson game. Believing I could speed up the healing process, I tried every treatment I could think of. At the suggestion of Joe Bailey Chaney, an Abilene sporting goods salesman who once coached football at Howard Payne, I doused Walter's injured foot with kerosene, wrapped it in a wool blanket and ironed it with a hot iron. This didn't help a bit. What I discovered is what the Dallas Cowboys discovered many years later. It takes seven to eight weeks for an Achilles tendon to heel, and there's not a darn thing a desperate coach can do to accelerate the process.

Monday evening, two other key players, Alton Green and J.T. Lyday, were involved in a head-on car collision. Green was my fullback, and at 190 pounds, he was tough as nails. Lyday weighed 270 pounds, and coming off a three-point stance, he was rattlesnake-quick. Lyday and Maloney were my co-captains. In the accident, Green tore up a knee. Lyday came to school the next day with nine stitches over one eye. Neither was in any condition to workout for football.

On Tuesday, a flu epidemic hit Roscoe, affecting half the student body, including several members of my football squad. Wednesday afternoon, only eight boys suited out for football practice.

Saturday afternoon, I had twelve players in uniform for our Monahans game. With so many walking wounded, my sideline resembled a war zone. The Loboes scored in the final seconds to squeeze out a 7–6 win and eliminate my previously unbeaten Plowboys from the state playoffs.

◆　◆　◆

FOR ME, THE BIGGEST ADJUSTMENT that first year in Roscoe was changing my lifestyle—from living single to living like a family man. Living quarters which were perfectly suitable for me before the war would no longer do. I had a wife and baby daughter to consider. Even though Katharine was raised in a small Kansas town with a population of less than a thousand, West Texas was still a big shock for her. She'd never seen people living in houses situated smack-dab in the middle of a cotton field. She'd never seen workers who lived in their cars, migrating from one farm to the next during the harvest season. West Texas is a wonderful place with the warmest, kindest people you'll find anywhere, but to a stranger, the Big Country can seem harsh and foreboding.

Right away, Katharine discovered something else about Texas. Football is king. On Friday nights, every man, woman and child who lived in Roscoe

Gordon with daughter Pat at Roscoe.
(credit: Wood Family Collection)

attended the football game. The high school football game was the social event of the week.

Residential rental property in Roscoe was extremely scarce. The few houses which were available were simply appalling. After considerable searching, we settled on a three-room apartment above a funeral home which backed up to the Texas and Pacific Railroad track. At night when the train came rumbling through town, the thunderous noise would almost shake you out of bed. The train noise was bad, but the thing that bothered Katharine most was our back door had no lock. My wife was from Kansas where residents locked their houses. She couldn't comprehend why West Texas people seldom locked their doors. Of course, I understood. Growing up in Taylor County, I doubt if my family ever locked a door. Most of our doors didn't even have locks.

It took several months, but Katharine slowly grew to love West Texas the way I do. She and Bonnie Jay, the wife of local banker Clyde Jay, became very close friends. The banker and his wife were affectionately known as Roscoe's Bonnie and Clyde, referring to Bonnie Parker and Clyde Barrow, the gangster couple who terrorized Texas banks back in the thirties.

Since Katharine had a new baby, most days Bonnie came to visit her. Each morning Bonnie would bring a coke. Katharine furnished the ice. They'd split the soft drink and visit while the baby slept. With me away at school most of the day, Bonnie Jay's friendship meant a lot to my wife.

◆　◆　◆

KATHARINE AND I were constantly frustrated with our housing situation. Our living quarters were so bad I almost switched schools in the spring of 1946. One Saturday evening I interviewed with Snyder's school board. After the interview the Snyder trustees offered me their head coaching job. I didn't accept immediately, mainly because I had promised Ted Edwards I would stay another year at Roscoe if I could find a decent place to live. I asked the Snyder board to give me until the next Tuesday to decide.

The following Monday, Jackie Nemir, my first-string quarterback, approached me and told me his grandmother owned an apartment which had recently come vacant. Katharine and I went to look that evening. The place was very nice, a thousand percent better than the rat trap where we resided. On Tuesday morning I called the school board president at Snyder and declined their offer. Katharine and I both loved Roscoe, and I wanted to keep my promise. Knowing several outstanding football players would be returning next season also greatly influenced my decision.

◆　◆　◆

DURING THE SUMMER I went back to college to work on my master's degree. That's how I met Murray Evans, an assistant football coach at Hardin-Simmons. Murray told me about a young man—a GI fresh out of the service, who the Cowboy coaches planned to start at quarterback the next fall. He claimed the player had the potential to be the best football coach ever produced at Hardin-Simmons. The young man's name was Morris Southall.

Wood family gathering at Abilene in 1946.
Top: Troy, Gordon, Dick, Garland. Bottom: Lucille, Marie, Deloria, Alvina.
(credit: Wood Family Collection)

◆　◆　◆

THE SUCCESS of my 1945 football team triggered an interest among male students at Roscoe High. That second season, my football squad consisted of thirty-three players, almost double the number of the prior year. We began the season with high expectations, and for a time, our optimism was justified.

Our first game was against Hamlin. Roscoe walloped the Pied Pipers 26–7. Then we played Ballinger. We should have played the Bearcats on our home field, but because a huge crowd was expected, the contest was moved to Sweetwater's Mustang Bowl. Giving up our home field advantage was definitely a mistake because Ballinger always fielded a good team. During the thirties and forties Ballinger was the winningest high school in Central Texas. In a hard fought contest that would be our only loss of the season, the Bearcats edged my Plowboys 12–0.

Next, we traveled to Kermit where Alton Green took the opening kickoff and rambled ninety-five yards for a touchdown. Our easy score only served to infuriate the Yellowjackets. We escaped with a 20–14 victory by scoring in the final minutes. District play began the following Friday, and we scored at will. Every ballcarrier on my squad crossed the goal line at least once as Roscoe crushed the Roby Lions 54–6.

My offense was clicking. My defense was coming together. Team confidence was high, maybe too high, the Friday night we played the Colorado City Wolves. It was not an evening to remember.

We missed tackles. We missed blocks. Every time our offense started to roll, a penalty, a fumble, or an interception would halt us dead in our tracks. In spite of all the dumb mistakes, though, Roscoe still had a chance to pull out a win. Late in the fourth quarter, my Plowboys put together a sustained drive to score and tie the game at 13–13. A bobbled snap caused our extra point try to sail wide, and that's how the game ended.

Coach Darrell Royal once said, "A tie is like kissing your sister." But in my opinion, a tie is often much worse than losing. For a coach, tying an opponent you should have beaten handily can be more agonizing than a loss. On numerous occasions my football teams have been eliminated from the playoffs because of a tie, and I can tell you I agonize over those games much more than the ones we lost.

Despite our tie with Colorado City, Roscoe was still in the hunt for the district championship when we met Rotan's Yellowhammers. Since Rotan was also in the running for the district crown, a large crowd was anticipated. So once again we gave up home field advantage and moved the game to Sweetwater, this time with more pleasant results. My Plowboys romped and stomped, topping the Yellowhammers 20–6.

◆　◆　◆

ONE OF THE FEW FRESHMEN on my 1946 Roscoe football squad was Malcomb Hammock. When the season began, Malcomb weighed in at ninety-five pounds, but he was a stout competitor, so I kept him on the varsity squad. One afternoon I ran into his mother at the grocery store. She told me her son was all excited because he had gained some weight. According to Mrs. Hammock, Malcomb was up to a hundred pounds.

"That's terrific, Mrs. Hammock. I'll see his weight gets changed on our game program," I promised.

At the time I fully intended to make the change, but I got busy and forgot about my conversation with Malcomb's mother. I ran into Mrs. Hammock again the following Monday. She told me Malcomb was devastated because our football programs still listed his weight at ninety-five pounds. She said her son cried all weekend.

"Well, I know how to fix that," I declared. "You tell Malcomb to check this week's program real close."

On Friday night our programs listed Malcomb Hammock at a hundred and five pounds.

◆　◆　◆

FOR THE SECOND YEAR in a row, the Merkel Badgers were undefeated in district play when their schedule collided with ours. My Plowboys were also undefeated in district, our only blemish being the disappointing tie with Colorado City. Merkel's coach was Carroll Benson, a longtime friend and an extremely talented football coach.

My game plan was to run the football, ram it down Merkel's throats. After Bobby Lee Emerson took the opening kickoff and ran it back to the thirty-five, that's exactly what we did.

With Harold Duvall and Harold Haynes gouging out huge holes

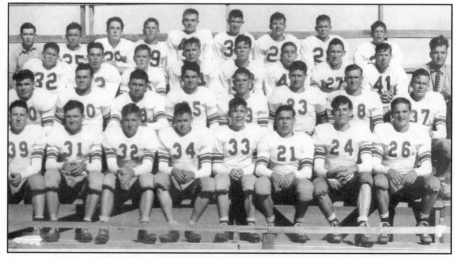

1946 Roscoe Football Squad (Won 6, Lost 1, Tied 2).
(credit: 1947 Roscoe High Yearbook)

in Merkel's defensive line, my fullback and leading ground gainer Alton Green shouldered the lion's share of the ballcarrying chores. Grinding out yardage in chunks of three and four yards, my Plowboys methodically moved the football down to the Badgers' four-yard line. There, Green crashed over right guard. Alton was dragging two purple and gold defenders when he crossed the goal line. We missed on the extra point try. At the half, the score was still 6–0.

Our game against Merkel the previous year had gone down to the wire, and during the second half, that's exactly how this game progressed. Both teams stuck to a ground-gobbling ball-control strategy, pounding mercilessly on one another, unwilling to risk a pass, and hoping the other would make some mistake which would turn the tide.

Late in the third quarter my Plowboys began a drive which came down to fourth and three on Merkel's forty-five. Instead of playing safe, I sent in my punter with instructions to call a fake punt, which we had worked on in practice and which I was absolutely certain would work. The Badgers weren't fooled. Merkel defenders swarmed all over my punter when he tried to run, dropping him for a ten-yard loss. The play revitalized the Badgers and gave them the football on our forty-five. Merkel drove in to score, but we blocked their extra point try.

Neither team was able to score again, and the game ended in another heart-breaking tie. Final score: 6–6.

◆　◆　◆

ON MONDAY after our tie with Merkel, I got wind of a peculiar story. Somehow the Badger coaches had found a copy of our scout notes in the visitors' dressing quarters. That's how they knew about our fake punt play. Man, was I hot. To think one of my own players cost us the ballgame. Realizing I'd have no peace until the allegation was either confirmed or repudiated, I hopped in my car and drove straight to Merkel where I confronted Carroll Benson.

"That's right, Coach Wood. My assistant coach found your scouting report right there on the gym floor next to the visitors' dressing room," Benson told me, verifying what I'd heard.

"Let me see the notes. I wanna know which of my players could be so stupid."

"I'll let you see 'em, Coach Wood, but only under one condition. You have to promise you won't say one word to the boy the notes belong to."

For a few seconds my anger wouldn't let me agree. I wanted to strangle the witless kid who had ruined my football season. I wanted to hurry back to Roscoe and tell everyone what he'd done, scream his name from the rooftops. Then I reconsidered. Benson was right. The game was over, and no matter how loud I yelled, I couldn't change the outcome. What good would it do to punish a boy for something I knew in my heart he didn't do intentionally?

"Alright, Carroll, I'll accept your condition. I promise not to say a word to the boy," I conceded, still a bit reluctant.

The notes Benson handed me had a player's name scribbled across the top of the page. The name was *Malcomb Hammock*.

Later, I learned the whole story. On the afternoon before our Merkel game, Malcomb was on his way home from football practice when he stopped by the school gym. A pickup game of basketball was in progress. When Malcomb was invited to join, he dropped his school books on the floor near the gym locker room which doubled as a visiting team's dressing room. After the basketball game broke up, Malcomb remembered to pick up his books, but he apparently left his scout notes lying on the floor.

I kept my word until many years later. By then, my harsh feelings had long disappeared, and the episode was too good a story not to tell.

After I moved on to coach at Seminole, Malcomb Hammock gained a lot of weight. For Roscoe coaches, Al Milch and Mo Hedrick, Hammock evolved into an awesome football player. Malcomb played two years at Arlington State Junior College then accepted a scholarship from Florida where he was drafted by the pros.

Malcomb played thirteen years of professional football with the Saint Louis Cardinals. He was team captain for ten of those years.

◆　◆　◆

AS THE SEASON wound down, we clobbered Loraine 26–0 then zeroed in on Snyder's Tigers 27–0, hoping someone else could accomplish what we couldn't—beat the Merkel Badgers. As it turned out, the Colorado City tie came back to bite us. Merkel romped through the rest of their schedule to capture the district title and advance to the state playoffs. Even though Roscoe finished the season with a record of six wins, one loss and two ties, when the state playoffs got underway, my players and I were working out for basketball.

◆　◆　◆

DURING THE SUMMER of 1946, Ted Edwards, the school superintendent who hired me straight out of the navy, accepted a similar position at Seminole, Texas. After I arrived at Roscoe, Ted and I worked very close and had become good friends. It was through his influence I was offered the head football coaching position at Seminole High in January of 1947. The job represented better pay and a fantastic opportunity. Seminole's population of thirty-four hundred was almost three times the size of Roscoe. Yet, Seminole was classified 1A, the same as Roscoe High.

Early that spring Katharine, Pat and I moved to Seminole so I could coach spring training. As soon as we were settled, I drove to Abilene, looked up Morris Southall and persuaded him to become my assistant coach. That would be the second best decision I ever made.

CHAPTER SIX

Moving On
(1947–1951)

A NEW COACH often finds himself facing disenchanted players and irate parents who remain emotionally attached to the former coach. Over the years I've learned to understand and respect those feelings. I've never changed jobs without some remorse because of the players, friends and close relationships I left behind. I have never actually been fired, but I've pressed my luck to the limit on numerous occasions. If I had been dismissed, I would have been disappointed if my players and their parents didn't have strong feelings about my departure.

My arrival at Seminole High School was met with bitter animosity. The athletes were on strike in support of the old coach, vowing not to play for me. Realizing the volatile situation needed a prompt diffusing, I invited members of the Letterman's Association to meet with me in the school gymnasium. Here's what I said:

"I'm here to talk with you men at length. If you have any questions, ask them now before you leave this meeting. I understand and appreciate the relationship you had with your previous coach, but I want you men to understand one thing. I had nothing to do with his leaving. What I'd like to accomplish here today is to come to an understanding. Here is my proposition. If you choose to stay and play for me, I'll be honored, but if you decide not to play for me, that'll be fine too. But when we meet in the high school hallway, I don't want you to turn away or lower your head. I want you to stop and speak to me because I'll admire you for supporting your old coach, and I will never hold it against you. If you really don't believe you can play for me, then go ahead and quit now. There'll be no hard feelings on my part."

My forthright approach totally disarmed the young men. When all was said and done, I lost one player. He had a sour attitude from the beginning, mostly because his dad was so close to the departed coach.

When I faced similar situations at Stamford, Victoria and Brownwood, I used the same tactics with similar positive results. I truly believe the best way to solve a problem, especially with young people, is to meet face to face and shoot straight.

◆ ◆ ◆

WHEN KATHARINE, Patricia and I moved to Seminole in the spring of 1947, a new housing development was getting underway on the edge of town. Ex-war veterans, who could come up with the required hundred-dollar down payment to qualify, were subsidized with low interest loans. The houses consisted of two bedrooms, one bath, a combination living/dining area, and a small kitchen—about nine hundred square feet total area. Compared to our dilapidated Roscoe dwellings, these modern GI houses seemed like the Taj Mahal. I immediately applied for a loan. Construction began a few weeks later.

In early August, Morris Southall and I attended coaching school together. He, his wife Lorene, and their young son Terry moved to Seminole a few weeks later. By the time they arrived, our new home was almost complete. A short tour of Seminole rental properties convinced Morris and Lorene the GI houses were a real bargain, so the Southalls cut a similar deal with the homebuilder. The lot the Southalls selected was across the street and only a few doors down from ours.

While they waited for their house to be built, Morris and Lorene took up residence in a tourist court. Their less-than-desirable living quarters consisted of one 12 x 12 room, which was generously called a kitchenette, and a tiny bathroom. Lorene was pregnant, and there was no place for Terry to play. Except for a graveled front parking area, the tourist court building was completely surrounded by sand.

With fall football practice only days away, Morris and I were working fifteen hours a day, much too busy to worry about who was living where. Katharine was the person most disturbed over the Southalls' housing situation. After we moved into our new home,

Katharine began driving to the tourist court each morning to pick up Lorene and Terry and bring them back to our house. For a few weeks that worked fine. Katharine and Lorene enjoyed each other's company. Pat and Terry became great friends.

One evening Katharine informed me she and Lorene had come up with a solution to the Southalls' horrid living situation. The answer was simple. The Southalls would move in with us.

Two families living in a two bedroom, one bath, nine hundred square foot house. I wasn't necessarily in favor, but Katharine assured me she and Lorene had talked it over. They both thought it was a wonderful idea.

We divided the house into sections. Katharine, Pat and I shared one bedroom. The Southalls took the second bedroom. We agreed on a set routine. Katharine would get up first and start breakfast. Morris was second up. When he was finished with the bathroom, I rolled out of bed. By the time I bathed and dressed for school, Katharine had breakfast ready. Lorene was the last one out of bed, but she was generally there to share breakfast with us. After Morris and I departed for school, Lorene washed the breakfast dishes.

Living together in such cramped conditions had all the ingredients to either make or break a friendship. Fortunately, everyone got along fine. From the day they moved in until Morris and Lorene moved into their new house that December, not one unpleasant incident occurred. After the Southalls moved out, Katharine and I actually missed their company. That was the beginning of a warm friendship that's lasted more than fifty years.

◆　◆　◆

EVEN THOUGH Morris and I were raised in West Texas, Seminole's extreme climate still came as a mild surprise. Neither of us was prepared for the raw power of Seminole sand storms—hard driving wind, mixed with sand that would peal the paint right off your car. Many afternoons our football team practiced in brutal weather. Right off, we discovered wind burn is even more painful than sunburn. On really bad days we tied handkerchiefs around our faces so we could breathe. In the evenings when Morris and I came home from practice, our wives would have wet towels stuffed around the bottom of the doors and around the windows to keep the sand out.

The worst sand storms usually preceded a brief thunder-shower. First, the wind would pick up, then the sand would blow in, obliterating the sun and turning the sky a reddish color. When the rain arrived, it didn't rain water. It rained mud balls. When the showers stopped, cars and buildings all across town would be caked with streaks of red mud.

Seminole High played their games in an old stadium across the street from the high school. The playing surface was a disastrous disgrace. Patches of bare ground dotted the field. What little grass remained was thin and looked like it hadn't been fertilized or watered in years. Near mid-field the turf was pitted and scarred by the ravage tilling of football cleats and completely void of grass.

Mostly, the sad condition was caused by football teams, junior high through high school, who practiced there. That's a pet peeve of mine. Why coaches choose to work out on their game field is beyond my comprehension.

Discontented with the playing field situation, Morris and I began to look around for another place to practice. We discovered a nearby vacant lot which we thought would make an ideal workout facility. The open area was less than a block from the high school, close enough to the players' dressing quarters so we could hustle them on and off the field without losing practice time. When we approached Ted Edwards, he liked our idea. His encouragement was all we needed. Morris and I went to work.

For several days we hauled in sand and spread it with a tractor, covering the entire lot with some eight inches of sand. We put out grass seed, and using long rubber hoses, we set up three strategically-located pulsating sprinklers to water the area. We'd barely finished when the wind began to pick up. An hour later a raging sand storm swept through. The wind and the sand blew all afternoon and all that night.

When the wind finally died, Morris and I went to inspect the damage. To our dismay, the sand and seed we had so optimistically placed was long gone. All that was left of our hard labor were three small mounds of sand directly beneath the water sprinklers.

Hoyt Starling, Seminole's mayor, lived right across the street from our proposed practice field. When he noticed Morris and me surveying our windswept ruins, he hiked over to complain. Starling's bathroom fronted the same street as our sand blown lot.

Unwittingly, during the ferocious blow, the mayor had neglected to close his bathroom window. Starling advised us he was forced to scoop out his bathtub that morning before he could bathe. The sand from his tub filled a five-gallon can to the brim.

On another occasion, Coach Southall accompanied our junior high track squad to a track meet in Levelland. After the meet ended and as the boys climbed into the station wagon they traveled in, a sand storm struck. Driving back, blasting gusts of wind rocked their car. Several times the wind shoved their vehicle completely off the pavement. The air was so thick with sand Morris could hardly see the road.

Three miles south of Plains, Texas, sand was piled so high on the highway they had to turn back and find an alternate route. Morris and his frightened youngsters wound up traveling down a narrow unpaved county road which the wind had blown clean, driving forty miles out of their way in order to reach Seminole.

◆　◆　◆

IN AUGUST, two weeks before school started, we loaded our football players onto a school bus and transported them to a boy scout camp overlooking Lake Sweetwater. We used the scouts' parade ground as our practice field. Several converted military barracks filled with army surplus bunk beds served as sleeping quarters, but because of the oven-like heat inside, most of our youngsters preferred to sleep on cots outside under the stars.

Coercing our third coach, Earl Brasfield, into handling the cooking chores, Morris and I limited our talents to coaching football. Fortunately, Earl turned out to be a much better cook than he was a football coach. The meals he prepared were excellent. Team members were served three meals a day. Many of our players ate better at fall camp than they did at home.

Football camp lasted a week. We left Seminole on Sunday afternoon and returned the following Saturday. Our workouts lasted an hour and a half in the morning and an hour and a half in the afternoon. Between practice sessions we kept the boys busy with skull sessions, watching game films and thinking football.

On Thursday, we bussed our squad into Sweetwater to scrimmage their high school team. Sweetwater's football coach was Pat Gerald, a good friend and one of the finest men to ever coach in

West Texas. Because of the unforgiving August heat, our scrimmage sessions were limited to forty-five minutes. We'd rest the kids for half an hour then scrimmage another forty-five minutes.

◆　◆　◆

COMPARED TO MY JOB at Roscoe, coaching at Seminole High was like I'd died and gone to heaven. My job description continued to include head football, basketball, and track coach, but with three assistant coaches assigned to help me and no math classes to teach, coaching three sports was no problem at all.

Seminole High Coaching Staff:
Morris Southall, Gordon Wood, Earl Brasfield.
(credit: 1948 Seminole High Yearbook)

From the very first git-go, Morris Southall coached our quarterbacks and ballcarriers. Morris had a remarkable knack for teaching things I couldn't—like how the quarterback takes the snap from center, how to handoff, how to pitch out, and how to pass accurately. Coach Southall provided strength in areas I was weak. After he took charge of our backfield, a fumble or a pass interception by our offense was an absolute rarity.

With Coach Southall's input, we modified my winged-T attack. Many of our changes were borrowed from Warren Woodson, the innovative football wizard Morris played under at Hardin-Simmons. We altered our backfield set and revised our line blocking assignments to make them more effective. As the football season approached, we waited in anxious anticipation.

◆　◆　◆

BECAUSE OF THE TURMOIL created by the players' strike, no one expected much from Seminole High's football squad that first

Seminole's back field—The Four Horsemen:
James Powell, Bobby Hunter, Val Joe Walker, Ralph Jones.
(credit: 1948 Seminole High Yearbook)

year. Several sportswriters picked Seminole to finish last in our conference, but along with the benefits of three assistant coaches, I inherited an exceptional group of athletes. My football team won the district championship easily, going nine and one, before an old nemesis, Merkel, defeated us in bi-district play 19–12.

◆　◆　◆

POSSIBLY THE MOST satisfying achievement of my days at Seminole was in the spring of 1948, when our track team won the Texas Class A State Meet. That was the first of eight state championships Coach Southall and I would share. Our thin-clad squad consisted of twenty-three boys. Morris worked with the sprinters and the hurdlers. I handled the distance runners and the relay team.

Normally, track meets are all day events held on Saturday, but to run and practice all week, preparing for possibly ten minutes of competition on Saturday, can be incredibly boring for a finely tuned athlete. To stimulate our track squad's competitive juices, we began

Seminole High's 1948 State Champ Track Team.
(credit: 1948 Seminole High Yearbook)

a series of mini-meets with Denver City and Andrews, both of which are within thirty miles of Seminole. Each Wednesday the three track teams would congregate and compete against each other. On Saturdays, we traveled to track meets in Odessa, Lubbock, and Big Spring. Watching how well our speedsters performed, our expectations began to soar as the district meet approached.

Val Joe Walker and James Powell ran the low hurdles for Seminole. Generally, they finished one and three, in that order. Jack Young, a hurdler from Andrews, usually placed second. Even though Powell always finished third, he was a feisty competitor. After every race James would come to me and ask if I had noticed how he was gaining on the two much swifter contestants.

Jack Young also ran the high hurdles for Andrews, and he was outstanding. He finished first in every meet that spring. It was at the district meet the idea of Val Walker running the high hurdles first emerged, and the idea wasn't mine. James Powell was the one who instigated the whole thing.

Walker, Young, and Powell had just run the low hurdles. Young had come in first, mostly because Val Joe got his foot tangled in the seventh and eighth hurdles. This was the first time Jack had outrun Val all spring. As usual, Powell placed third. Several Andrews' fans began to heckle Walker as he, Young, and Powell jogged off the track.

"Hey, Jack! Wouldn't you love to race Val Joe in the high hurdles? Bet he'd trip over every one!"

"Yeah, I sure would! I'd beat him even worse in the high hurdles than I did in the lows!" Young yelled back, allowing his fierce competitive relationship with Walker to seep out.

Val Joe was always a quiet kid. He didn't say a word. He lowered his head and continued on. It was James Powell who picked up on Young's challenge, and then he wouldn't let it rest.

"If I was you, Jack, I wouldn't get too cocky. If Val was to run the high hurdles, he'd beat you like a dirty rug."

In 1948, Texas track rules allowed an athlete who won any event at the district level to enter as many as five events in the next higher meet. The next Monday, Powell went after Val Joe, encouraging him to run the high hurdles. First, James pulled up one hurdle. Then he set up two. Then three. At practice on Wednesday afternoon, Walker ran a full set of high hurdles which Coach Southall timed at 15.2 seconds. When we checked the stopwatch, Morris and I couldn't believe our eyes.

The next morning I stopped Ted Edwards in the school hallway to tell him about Walker's time on the high hurdles. Our superintendent had run track at Howard Payne when he was in college. Ted had a peculiar habit of lowering his head, tucking his chin against his chest, and peering at you over the rim of his eyeglasses when he wanted to make a point.

"No way! That's a physical impossibility," Edwards responded, glaring at me over his eyeglasses. "I've run hurdles all my life, and I never saw anyone run a 15.2."

"You better come down to the track and watch then, Ted, because that's the right time. Morris Southall and I both saw Val Joe do it."

Still not believing my story, Superintendent Edwards came down to the track that same day and timed Val Joe on the high hurdles. This time Walker ran a 15.1.

Two weeks later in the regional meet at Odessa, Val Joe won both the high hurdles and the low hurdles with Jack Young of Andrews coming in second and James Powell third.

Seminole's 440-relay and one-mile-relay teams also finished first. James Powell, Ralph Jones, Charles Baker and Val Joe ran the 440. Powell, Bobby Hunter, Jones and Baker ran the mile relay.

Richard Stanfield, our discus man, was another major factor in our drive for the state finals. In two weeks time, right at the end of the season, Richard's throws improved from 120 feet to 147 feet. Jack McReynolds, our quarter-miler, and Claude Mack, a freshman who ran the mile, also qualified for the state meet.

◆　◆　◆

AT THE STATE TRACK MEET in Austin, Seminole got off to a rough start. Even though he hadn't done well in earlier meets, Val Joe was entered in the broad jump. On his first try he sprained an ankle. He was in obvious pain as I checked him out.

"I'm sorry, Val. I can't let you take your other two jumps. You're too important to our team in the other events. We can't afford for you to get hurt."

"How about letting me jump one more time, Coach Wood? I hit twenty-three feet on my first try. If I can get in one more like that, I oughta have a chance of finishing in the top two or three."

"Okay. One more, but that's it," I pronounced firmly, crossing my fingers and saying a short prayer under my breath.

Val nailed his second leap, soaring 22 ft. 11 in. to place third. Then he won both the high hurdles and the low hurdles. Our 440-relay team finished second. Our mile-relay team finished fifth, and Stanfield took fifth in the discus. Val Joe wound up scoring twenty-seven points to win individual honors.

◆　◆　◆

KATHARINE WAS RAISED a Presbyterian. I was raised a Southern Baptist. My four years at Hardin-Simmons, a Baptist school, further strengthened my Baptist beliefs. In Roscoe, my wife and I resolved our religious differences by attending a Methodist Church, but Katharine was never truly satisfied with the solution, and to be honest, neither was I.

Shortly after we moved to Seminole, Katharine discovered a Presbyterian church directed by Collis McKinney, a dynamic young minister. She immediately connected with the friendly congregation, but to her dismay, I refused to join the church. One Sunday the young pastor approached Katharine. I'm sure he was concerned for my soul, but it was probably my mule-stubborn attitude that prompted our preacher to suggest the two of them coerce me into joining his church.

"Oh, no! I won't take sides against my husband," Katharine proclaimed. "You can proselytize on Gordon Wood all you want, but please don't expect me to get involved. I plan on living with that man for the rest of my life."

In spite of Katharine's reservations, the pastor set out to convert me. In fact, he preached a whole series of sermons especially for my benefit, explaining exactly what Presbyterians believe, the basis for those beliefs, Presbyterian doctrine, etc.

In the end I capitulated and joined the Presbyterian church. Maintaining my stubborn independence, and to show the choice was mine and not my wife's, I saved my trip down the aisle for a Sunday when Katharine was in Kansas visiting her mother. No matter how individualistic I tried to appear, though, I joined mostly to make Katharine happy. In matters of religion and family, women generally get their way.

◆　◆　◆

OUR SOCIAL LIFE revolved around the church and our friends on the school faculty. Watermelon suppers, card games, domino games—Katharine was absolutely shocked to learn how seriously West Texans take their dominos.

Katharine frequently chided me for being so competitive when we played parlor games with friends. One evening, we attended a party where the guests played a spelling game called Anagrams. I challenged a word Katharine had spelled out and lost. I was so upset I grabbed the dictionary from her hand and ripped out the page containing the word. Katharine didn't say a word. She only glared at me, making me feel guilty as hell.

Defiantly justifying my uncivilized behavior, my response to her was, "If I was into losing, I wouldn't be a coach!"

◆　◆　◆

1948 PRODUCED ANOTHER winning football season. My Indian squad won six, lost three, and tied one. Seminole was in contention for the district title until the final three weeks, but late season losses to Monahans, Denver City and Andrews ended our year on a sour note.

F.O. Scroggins, one of my Hardin-Simmons teammates, was the football coach at Monahans in 1948. That was the first year Class A schools were allowed to advance past a regional playoff. Scroggins' Loboes went on to capture the Class A state crown, beating New Braunfels in the finals by a score of 14–0.

◆   ◆   ◆

KATHARINE AND I were happy in Seminole. Better pay, better housing, and with three assistants to help me coach, our lives had improved dramatically. In those three short years our daughter Pat evolved from a baby in diapers to a beautiful young girl who adored her father. Her admiration for me was returned ten fold. My heart swelled as my love for her grew day by day.

But every coach's job depends on the support of his school board. The controversy began during the fall of 1949.

◆   ◆   ◆

SEMINOLE HAD A STRANGE relationship with its bus drivers. The school system owned the bus body. The drivers owned the bus chassis. Each bus driver furnished his own gas and maintained his own bus. I'm not sure why the school system elected to operate this way, but somehow the question of cost efficiency came up. Seminole's school trustees directed Superintendent Edwards to determine the per mile expense of operating Seminole busses and to compare those costs to what Kermit and Andrews paid for similar service.

When Edwards reported back to the school board a few weeks later, his figures revealed Seminole was paying almost twice as much for bussing students as either Andrews or Kermit. When Seminole bus drivers got wind of the superintendent's negative report, they threw a hissing fit, claiming Edwards was after their jobs. The bus drivers began lobbying the school trustees to determine which board members were in favor of changing the bus arrangement and which members were satisfied to leave things alone. When school board elections came up in November, the bus drivers actually went out and picked up voters, providing free transportation for anyone who would vote against the men on the school board who favored revising the school bus system or supported Ted Edwards.

After the election, the bus drivers began a campaign of malicious gossip, accusing Ted of siphoning money from a swimming pool project he had helped the city build. All the finger pointing prompted the school trustees to bring in a man from the University of Houston to audit every school system expense.

Several days after the financial expert arrived, he showed up at my field house, insisting I re-inventory all the equipment under my jurisdiction.

"Whatta you mean you want a recount on every piece of equipment? I just finished with my inventory. Why can't we use that?" I objected, allowing my temper to show.

"No, that won't work. We'll have to recount every piece. That's what I'm being paid to do," the man told me, standing his ground.

"Alright, we'll do it your way. Here, you take the jock straps, and I'll count the shoulder pads. Then we'll decide who gets to count the dirty socks," I said, pitching him a canvass bag filled with worn-out and un-washed athletic supporters.

The man counted about half the bag before he capitulated.

"Oh, crap!" the expert conceded. "This isn't worth it. It's a total waste of time."

"That's what I've been trying to tell you. I've got every sock, jock and jersey numbered and counted. I can tell you exactly how many shoulder pads, hip pads, thigh pads, pants, and shoes the school owns. Every item is listed right there on my inventory sheet. Why can't you use those numbers? What sense does it make to count everything over again?"

At their request, I later appeared before the school board to explain what a waste of time it was to re-inventory my athletic equipment. I was right as rain, but I don't think my testimony made me any points.

◆　◆　◆

COACH SOUTHALL and I worked hard. We were young and ambitious, and excited about our prospects. We not only coached football, we also coached basketball and track—junior high through high school. When the girls' volleyball coach went down with the flu, Coach Southall assumed her duties for several weeks. During the spring we somehow sandwiched in three weeks of football training. Morris and I left for school around 7:30 each morning. We hardly ever arrived home before eight in the evening.

We did an excellent job of coaching that 1949 season, perhaps the best job we'd ever done. But our record of 4–4–2 didn't show it. Our talent pool was thin, and injuries hurt us. Our Indians only won four football games. Meanwhile, friction continued to build, not only between the school trustees and the school superintendent, but because of my relationship with Ted Edwards, hard feelings spilled over into other areas, like the football booster organization.

Despite the varsity's mediocre record, we had plenty of reason to be optimistic. That fall our freshman football squad, which Morris Southall coached, was loaded with talent. His ninth graders finished the season undefeated, beating junior high teams from Midland, Odessa, Lubbock, and all the schools in our district. Our freshman kids were simply awesome. None of their games were closer than fourteen points.

◆　◆　◆

IN THE SPRING of 1950, I.L. Lassiter, the school superintendent at Winters, Texas, contacted me and offered me their head coaching job. I told him I wasn't interested, but he kept after me, and I agreed to come to Winters and talk. I was planning a trip anyway. I intended to enroll at Sul Ross that summer to finish work on my master's degree. On my drive back from Alpine, I went to Winters where the school trustees made me a world of promises and a lucrative job offer impossible to refuse.

When I returned to Seminole, Ted Edwards was in Lubbock working on his doctorate at Texas Tech, so I typed out a letter of resignation, hunted down Doctor Dow, the school board president, and gave him my letter.

Before the day was out, I began to have second thoughts, thinking how stupid I was for leaving with those freshman kids in my football pipeline. Every one of my assistant coaches was convinced Seminole High School would be a championship contender before those players graduated.

Early the next morning I hurried down to Doctor Dow's office to tell him I had changed my mind. Luckily, he hadn't mentioned my resignation to any of the other trustees. He reached in his desk and handed my letter back to me, telling me he was delighted I had decided to stay. After I left the trustee's office, I walked down to talk with the president of the quarterback club. I was certain he'd be happy to hear I was staying. His hostile attitude took me by complete surprise.

"If that's what you want, Coach Wood, I suppose we can put up with your kind of coaching for one more year."

"What? Surely you don't mean what I think you said?"

"You heard me, Coach. I said I reckon we can put up with you for one more year."

His words hit a sore spot, and I lost my temper. I seldom cuss, but to this day I'm not sorry for the way I responded, "You sons-a-bitches here in Seminole are so damn ignorant. You don't know a good football coach when you see one, so I'm telling you straight out. I wouldn't coach in this town with you as president of my quarterback club for any amount of money."

I stormed out, took my letter back to the school board president and slammed it down on his desk. I was mad, real mad, mostly at myself for acting so foolish—resigning, then taking it back, and then resigning again. Katharine, Pat and I loaded our belongings and moved to Winters before the month was out. Morris Southall succeeded me as head football coach at Seminole High School. I was happy about that.

Leaving Seminole was a purely emotional decision. Sure enough, that outstanding group of freshmen players turned out to be an awesome bunch of athletes. Three years later my Stamford Bulldogs would face those same young men in the state playoffs. But life, like football, is a funny game. Occasionally you make a bad turn, head off in the wrong direction, and end up exactly where you wanted to go.

◆　◆　◆

AT WINTERS, I was back in my element, closer to Abilene, closer to my family, but I faced an enormous task. The football program at Winters High School was in shambles. Losing had become a habit. The previous season the Blizzards had not won a single game. Winters competed in a rugged AA district along with Ballinger, Brady, Coleman, and San Angelo Lake View—schools with good coaches and strong football programs.

To my good fortune, I inherited a group of athletes who were anxious to learn and anxious to win. My Ice Warriors took to the modified winged-T offense like ducks to water.

After the unmitigated disaster of the previous season, sportswriters from Fort Worth to Abilene assumed Winters' football team would finish dead last in our district. The second week of September my ballclub took on the Snyder Tigers. The schedule called for the contest to be played in Snyder. Our team bus arrived

Coaching football at Winters High School with assistant coaches
Howard McChestney (left) and Otis Holliday (right).
(credit: Wood Family Collection)

Friday afternoon, in time for my players to eat a light pre-game meal before they suited out. The school had arranged for us to dine at a downtown cafe which was owned by a fellow I'd known at Seminole. The owner recognized me immediately and came to my table to talk while we waited for our food to arrive. I had heard local gamblers were betting Snyder would win by five touchdowns. I asked him if what I'd heard was true.

"Yep, that's right, Coach Wood, but if you're interested, I can find you a better deal than that. I can lay all the money you want and get you forty points. You wanna put down a bet?"

"No, I'd better pass, but if you wanna make some easy money, you bet on Winters tonight. No way Snyder can beat us that bad." My positive attitude wasn't based on coach's emotion. The previous week my team had scrimmaged a good Sweetwater club, and we had held our own.

I don't know whether the restaurant owner took my advice, but that evening Melvin Kurtz, my running back, gained more yardage than the entire Snyder team. Winters trounced Snyder 18–6, and a whole slew of Blizzard fans went home richer than they arrived.

The next week my Cold Wave Warriors chopped down Albany who was favored by two touchdowns. Then we faced my long time nemesis, Merkel, in what had developed into an annual grudge match. Winters scored in the waning minutes to pull out a hard earned 6–0 victory.

A 41–14 loss to Colorado City took some of the wind from our sails, but we bounced back to knock off Roscoe 24–19 and mangle Eastland's Mavericks 35–2. My Blizzards surprised everyone by entering district play with a record of five wins and one loss.

Unfortunately, Melvin Kurtz, the team's co-captain and star running back, broke his leg in the Coleman game. Wayne Badgett, Zane Hensley and Gayland Broadstreet took up some of the slack, but we never quite regained our winning groove. Winters' lone district win came over lowly San Angelo Lake View whom we pasted 45–0.

Our most disappointing loss was to Ballinger. Winters hadn't beaten the Bearcats in thirteen long years. A Ballinger touchdown with less than three minutes to go allowed the Bearcats to eke out a 19–13 win and extend their jinx over Winters to fourteen.

◆　◆　◆

BASKETBALL HAS ALWAYS been important to me. A close, spine-tingling basketball game can cause my heart to pump even faster than a last second drive by a football team. Every football coach should encourage his players to participate in basketball—especially his backs and ends, the skilled positions. Basketball develops quickness and hand-to-eye coordination. These days so many coaches insist their kids concentrate on one sport—football. They have their players spend the off-season beefing up in the weight room. In my opinion, that's poor thinking. You'll never convince me lifting weights develops better athletes than running up and down the court, jumping, jerking, dribbling and learning how to compete.

At Winters, like all my previous stops, my job was not only head football coach but also head basketball coach and head track coach. A major consideration in my accepting the Winters' assignment was their promise to improve and enlarge the high school basketball facility. However, in spite of constant assurances, no improvements had been done when basketball season rolled around, and I saw no indication that any were planned.

Winters High put one heck of a basketball team on the court that year, but hardly anyone noticed because of the poor facilities. The high school gymnasium was a tiny cracker box, absolutely pathetic. Spectator seating was limited to one row of benches down each side of the court. Anyone else who wanted to watch was forced to stand. Our fans were jam-packed inside the gym at every game. We had to lock the doors to keep people out, so we'd have room to play. The situation was a civic disgrace.

Winters' school district extended southward to include oil camps down near Hatchell where several of my best athletes lived. When the basketball season began, the boys' parents were enthusiastic and supportive, but as the season dragged out, parent interest waned. In order to keep my players, I was forced to taxi the kids home after practice and after games. As time went by, this became a real burden, both on me and my 1949 Ford.

When Stamford called, asking me to interview for their head coaching job, I'd had my fill of empty promises and hauling players. I was primed for a change, and Stamford was a choice coaching job. In my mind it was the best job in West Texas. If I'd known what the future held, I probably wouldn't have played so hard to get.

CHAPTER SEVEN

The Beginning
(1951–1955)

WHEN I INFORMED Stamford's school trustees it would take forty-nine hundred dollars a year to persuade me to leave Winters, their mouths dropped open. Stamford's school board enjoyed a well-deserved reputation for being a bunch of tightwads. Carl Cook, the previous Stamford coach, had quit when the trustees refused to raise his salary to thirty-five hundred a year. Of course, Coach Cook had made another grievous mistake. Even though Cook's 1950 football team won seven and lost only three, he had lost to Anson, Stamford's number one and most hated rival.

That evening when I arrived home, I told Katharine not to worry about moving because no school board in Texas would pay anyone that much money to coach football.

Nevertheless, L.W. Johnson, Stamford's school superintendent, called me the next day and invited me back for another interview. During the second meeting, board members briefly quizzed me about my coaching philosophy. Another concern was whether I'd be satisfied with their current assistants as my coaching staff, but the discussion kept revolving back around to dollars. The trustees must've asked me twenty times if I'd consider working for less pay. Each time I said no. I had made up my mind about salary, and I refused to budge.

Eventually the trustees ran out of questions. They asked me to step outside while they talked things over. I was told not to leave until they reached a decision.

The trustees' discussion lasted a long time. As I stood in the school hallway outside the meeting room, I could hear heated argument and raised voices. I'd about decided the whole thing was a waste of time when the door swung open, and Superintendent Johnson called me back to the meeting.

L.W. Stenholm was president of the school board. He was a highly successful cotton farmer who owned much of the best farm land in the area. Stenholm was also the tightest dadgum Swede in Jones County. Without a doubt he'd been the one most opposed to hiring me.

When Stenholm cleared his throat, the room suddenly became silent. Every eye in the room was directed at me, watching my reaction as the president announced the board's decision.

"Coach Wood," Stenholm advised, "every member of this board, except myself, wants to hire you to coach here at Stamford High School, and every man here tonight, except me, is willing to pay you forty-nine hundred a year. Now, I personally don't think there's a coach in America who's worth that much money, but I'm gonna go along with the board's wishes and make it unanimous."

Maybe I should have been happy with the school board's decision, but during my late night drive back to Winters, I kept wondering whether I really was worth the ridiculous salary I'd asked for. Why should Stamford pay me forty-nine hundred dollars for doing work I'd gladly do for free?

1951

WHEN I ASSUMED the reins as head coach at Stamford, the situation was similar to the crisis I'd faced four years earlier at Seminole. About half my players were on strike in support of the former football coach. The circumstances were a little different because only half the players supported the old coach. The others were glad he was gone. Many of the young men resented his coaching style—his demanding, marathon practice sessions, his abusive manner, and the way he treated individual players.

The coach I replaced was Carl Cook. Before he came to Stamford, Carl worked as an assistant coach at Breckenridge where harsh treatment and lengthy workouts were commonly accepted as the price players had to pay to propagate winning football. Coach Cook was a brutal taskmaster—rough on players, tough on his assistants. His football practices resembled an army boot camp. Hour after hour of head-on blocking and tackling were regularly intermixed with long, strenuous sessions of wind sprints. Any player who lagged behind was verbally assaulted with insults to his manhood.

Some players liked Cook's slave-driver coaching style and believed his methods were the right way to produce a winning football team. Others didn't agree. Many players thought Carl was too strict. Many had become totally disillusioned with football.

◆ ◆ ◆

THESE EVENTS occurred in 1951, and many Texas football coaches at that time hardly subscribed to extreme coaching practices similar to those I superseded in Stamford. However, it is my personal observation that Coach Paul "Bear" Bryant, because of the rugged pre-season camp he operated and the cruel coaching methods he sanctioned at Junction in 1954, ruined more coaches and did more damage to Texas football than any coach before or since. Bryant was much too rough on players, but because he was so successful, many young coaches chose to emulate his coaching style.

Over the years at coaching clinics, I've often heard football coaches brag how tough they were on their players, and how so many kids quit the team because of their long, brutal workouts. Here's how I respond to that kind of irrational thinking:

"How many boys did you start with?" I ask.

"About forty-five. We ended up with twenty-six, and every one is a heckava ballplayer."

"How many of those who didn't quit were seniors?"

"Oh, about sixteen."

"Then what are you gonna do next season when all those seniors graduate? Who's gonna play for you next year?"

A coach who intentionally runs off players may field a winning team this season, but he'd better plan on moving a lot. He'll never be successful long term. Long, hard practices and running off future players doesn't solve problems. It creates problems. When a player quits football, it's not the player who failed. It is his coaches. For every player who quits football, somewhere there's a coaching staff who could have kept him on the team and made a football player out of him.

Another point hardly ever considered by high school coaches is—when a player quits you may also lose younger brothers who might play for you later. Kenneth West, who was a senior my first year at Stamford, is a perfect example. If Carl Cook had continued to coach at Stamford, Kenneth would almost certainly have quit football. He was sick of Cook's abusive tactics and had already decided to skip spring training. Kenneth played tackle, and at 195 pounds, he was the biggest member of our football squad. He was a devastating blocker and a stalwart of my 1951 team, but here's my point. Kenneth's younger brothers, Don and Royce, were even better football players. Don was a hard-nosed, fierce competitor. He lettered three years for me at guard. Royce was an even more outstanding lineman—named all-district in 1955 and all-state in 1956.

◆ ◆ ◆

TO DIFFUSE the terse feelings, I reverted to the same tactics I used under similar circumstances at Seminole. I invited all the male athletes to meet me in the school gym. There, I addressed their complaints face to face. I told the boys if they were unhappy about the coaching change to go ahead and quit if that's what they thought was right, but not to hold harsh feeling against me afterward. I assured the young men I was interested in them as individuals. Even if they decided not to play for me, I wanted them to speak to me in the school hallway, to stop and visit with me and tell me how they were doing in school. When the smoke cleared, not a single boy quit football because of the coaching change.

◆ ◆ ◆

COMPARED TO PREVIOUS football programs I'd inherited, Stamford was in fairly good shape. My coaching staff consisted of two fresh-faced assistants—Pete Ragus, a graduate of Abilene Christian College whom I hired, and Frontz Myatt who was working at Stamford High when I arrived. Neither of the assistant coaches understood my winged-T offense, but they were both enthusiastic and willing to do anything I asked—and they did it with a smile.

During spring training, our workouts were short and efficient. Each practice began with a brief skull session. Then we ran the squad through a series of intense drills which combined their skull session lesson with blocking, tackling and ball handling. When the players learned what they needed to know, we sent them to the showers. Both my players and assistant coaches were shocked by the lack of physical contact. I doubt if any of them believed a coach who was so easy on his team could win consistently. Years later, several of those players would tell me they initially thought I was some kind of wimp coach.

One of my football players that first year at Stamford was Kenneth West, my longtime assistant coach at Brownwood. Kenneth has told me many times that playing football for me was fun, whereas he and many of his teammates were absolutely miserable playing for the previous coach.

◆　◆　◆

FOUR OF THE BEST ATHLETES at Stamford High were Max Kelley, Kenneth Lowe, Keith Miles and Dan Smith. We were in the final week of spring practice when I ran into the four boys late one afternoon. They were at the City Drugstore, each enjoying a fountain coke. Anxious to get better acquainted, I ambled over to their table and pulled up a chair.

"How you guys doing?" I inquired.

"Fine, Coach. How about yourself?" Keith Miles answered.

The young men weren't necessarily delighted to have me join their conversation, but I persisted. Max, Ken, Keith and Dan had been part of the group who supported Carl Cook. I figured I stood a better chance of winning their confidence if they got to know me off the football field.

For several minutes we talked about football and school. The conversation was slightly strained as I struggled to find common ground with my new players. Finally, I pushed the right button.

"You fellows like to fish?" I asked.

"Sure do," Max Kelley replied. "You a fisherman, Coach Wood?"

"Yep, but I never use bait. I like to whistle up the fish, then pick out the ones I want to eat."

"Come on, Coach! Nobody can whistle up fish!" Kenneth Lowe argued. Kenneth had hardly spoken a word until we started talking about fishing. Now all of a sudden, I had his full attention.

"I sure can. As a matter of fact, I'm so sure I can do it I'll bet each of you a steak dinner I can whistle up a whole slew of fish."

The boys huddled for a few seconds to talk things over. Then they accepted my bet. They wanted to meet after school the next afternoon for a demonstration.

May Kelley
All District

Kenneth Lowe
All District
All State

Keith Miles
All District
All State
Second Team

Dan Smith
All District

Stamford's catfish whistling skeptics.—
Max Kelley, Ken Lowe, Keith Miles, Dan Smith
(credit: 1953 Stamford High Yearbook)

What my players didn't know was—a few weeks earlier I had met a man named Reginald Baird. Mr. Baird was in the oil business, and by Stamford standards, he was fairly well off. He and his family lived on a farm at the outskirts of town. About a thousand yards behind the Baird residence was a small stock tank which was chock-full of large catfish. Reginald had trained the fish to come to the surface at feeding time. Before he would begin feeding, Reginald would whistle loudly, and huge fins would literally cover the water surface. Some fish would swim to the water's edge and take their food right from the owner's hand.

I was so impressed, I had driven out to watch Baird feed his fish on several occasions. I was excited. Man, did I have a surprise in store for my skeptical players.

Per our agreement, I met the four teenagers in front of the high school the next afternoon. We drove out to the Baird place in two cars. Max Kelley and Dan Smith rode with me. During the trip, Dan Smith kept shaking his head.

"No way, Coach Wood. No way you can catch fish just by whistling."

"I can do it, Dan. You'll see," I bragged. I was supremely confident the fish would come when I whistled, but for insurance, I brought along a half loaf of bread.

When we reached the farm, we parked our cars, skirted around the Baird's two-story house and hiked down to the fish pond. My teenage companions were grinning like a bunch of possums as they stationed themselves on the bank to watch my fish whistling demonstration.

I whistled loudly and waited. I whistled again, but not a single fish surfaced.

"What's the matter, Coach Wood? I thought you said they'd come right to the top," Kenneth Lowe snickered, questioning my fish whistling ability.

"Yeah, Coach. Where are all those fish you promised?" Max Kelley cackled.

"They'll be along. You fellows be patient," I advised, but to be perfectly honest, I was getting worried about the bet. Every time I had accompanied Reginald Baird, the big fish came to the top immediately.

I tried again, using a different whistle tone, but still the fish refused to show. I tried again and again, whistling louder and louder. Finally, I resorted to my backup plan, which was throwing chunks of bread on the water.

"That's not fair, Coach Wood. You're supposed to whistle up the fish. I thought you said you didn't use bait," Dan Smith whooped. Now the boys were in stitches, rolling around on the ground, holding their sides and laughing like crazy.

I was still whistling and pitching bread on the water when the four giggling disbelievers left fifteen minutes later. For the life of me, I couldn't understand why the fish wouldn't come to me like they did for Reginald Baird.

What I didn't understand when I made the bet with my players was there were no secrets in Stamford. Reginald Baird's daughter, Dorothy, was a junior at Stamford High, and at the time, she was dating Kenneth Lowe. So Kenneth knew all about the Baird's catfish pond. After they left the drugstore, the four teenagers borrowed a minnow seine. That night they sneaked onto the Baird's property and seined every fish out of the tank. According to Kenneth Lowe, they didn't leave even a single minnow.

A couple of weeks later, Max, Ken, Keith and Dan, claiming they'd caught a lot of fish at Lake Stamford, invited their friends to a fish fry. They also invited my wife and me. Katharine and I thoroughly enjoyed the fish and the boys' company, and I never suspected a thing. I truly didn't know how badly I'd been had until

Kenneth Lowe told the story at Stamford's football banquet in January the following year.

◆　◆　◆

THE CUSTOM AT STAMFORD was to have high school football players report for fall camp on Monday, two weeks before school started. Players brought cots and bed clothing and slept under the grandstands at the football field. From Monday through Saturday, the players never left the area. Players ate their meals at the school cafeteria. We coaches rousted the boys out of bed at seven o'clock each morning, allowing them ten minutes to wash up before we ran them through a short warm-up workout of calisthenics and agility drills. Then we hustled the team to the school cafeteria for breakfast.

Fall camp consisted of football practice twice a day, once in the morning and again in the afternoon. After the first few days, our players walked around in a daze. Even the slightest movement would cause their sore muscles to shriek with pain.

Two-a-days were tough, on both players and coaches, but in my mind, they served a dual purpose. Two-a-days coagulated our boys, jelled them into a team—whipped soft, flabby babies into lean, muscular young men. Those August workouts also equipped everyone who participated with a kind of mental toughness. Any young male who has survived football two-a-days is better prepared to face the battles he will come up against in real life. Many of my ex-players have told me they look back on those fall camps as some of the most gratifying days of their lives. They say they've reached back to lean on those rigorous days of August football practice when they faced real-life hardships—using it as a point of reference, knowing if they could survive two-a-days, they can survive most anything.

These days, with well-meaning administrators and legislators trying to de-emphasize sports, football coaches are forced to choose between spring training and early fall practice. If a coach works his players too hard, they quit. A coach who runs a program like we did back in the fifties would have players' parents up in arms. He'd be fired before the season began. Maybe that's progress, but I'm not so sure we're turning out better students or better kids.

During the years I coached at Stamford High School, no athlete ever graduated who couldn't read, write legibly, and do arithmetic. Our teachers taught kids to read using phonics. They taught math using multiplication tables. Today, in the name of progress, those old tried-and-true teaching methods are tossed aside. Teachers are forced to teach reading by word recognition instead of sounding out word syllables. Schools teach "new math" which makes absolutely no sense to parents trying to help their children. Many schools don't even teach their students to multiply and divide, under the mistaken assumption they'll always use a calculator. Our schools are turning out computer smart nincompoops, without a lick of common sense and without the mental toughness that made their parents successful.

◆ ◆ ◆

GIVEN THE MOTHER LODE of talent on my 1951 football squad, I should have won my first football state championship. If I had been a better coach, I would have, but I made several crucial coaching mistakes. One mistake involved Kenneth Lowe. Kenneth was an outstanding athlete. He went on to play at SMU where he was a backup for Don Meredith, the most talented quarterback to ever graduate from a Texas high school. Kenneth played running back for me. I should have played him at quarterback which was his natural position. When we began spring training, Kenneth started out as a running back, and I never had the gumption to move him to quarterback. Several years later Ken told me he wanted to play quarterback but was afraid to ask.

Jerry Prewit was another mistake. Jerry was fast as greased lightning and tough as nails, but because he was small, I played him almost exclusively on defense. I was overly concerned about his size, thinking he'd get hurt running the football. At Brownwood, I won two state championships with running backs smaller than Jerry Prewit.

◆ ◆ ◆

SEVEN DAYS BEFORE our season opener, I loaded the team onto a school bus and drove them over to Abilene to scrimmage the Abilene High Eagles. My kids were scared to death. Abilene High School was ten times the size of Stamford.

Abilene's coach was Pete Shotwell. He had two assistants, Shorty Lawson and Bob Grosscose, who were capable coaches and knew what they were doing. His other three assistants were more hindrance than help. Instead of showing the Eagle players what they were doing wrong and helping them, they made fun of the boys.

Their whole attitude really bothered me. Coaches should be there to teach and help players improve. Young men respond best to positive instruction. Ridicule seldom yields results.

When I sent my second line players in to scrimmage, Jerry Prewit went in as a running back. During our pre-season two-a-days, Jerry had developed bad blisters on the heels of both feet, so he was wearing tennis shoes instead of cleats. On the very first play, Jerry spurted through the middle, cut to his right, ran through the diving grasps of two Eagle defenders, and dashed up the sideline for an eighty-yard touchdown. Pete Shotwell was truly impressed.

"Good gosh almighty, a hundred and thirty pounds and wearing tennis shoes. And that little fellow's running all over us," Shotwell exclaimed, shaking his head as if he couldn't believe what he'd just seen.

That afternoon my scrawny Bulldogs wound up kicking the dookie out of the Eagles. I should have been elated over my team's performance, but as our old school bus rattled back up the two-lane blacktop toward Stamford, my mind was troubled. I felt empathy for the Abilene players. Their coaches were so disorganized. Those Abilene coaches weren't teaching football; they were persecuting players for not knowing how to play.

Apparently I wasn't the only one who noticed. Two years later, Abilene High replaced Pete Shotwell with a new coach named Chuck Moser. Moser would lead the Eagles to three consecutive state championships and an unbelievable 49-game winning streak.

◆　◆　◆

ACROSS THE PACIFIC our nation was engaged in another bloody war which began in June of 1950, when North Korean soldiers armed with Soviet weapons crossed the 38th parallel to invade South Korea. In the fall of 1951, however, truce negotiations were underway and peace seemed eminent. Even though our hearts were with the thousands of American boys who continued to fight and die in the deadly battles, the Korean War seemed a million miles away.

Cotton prices were up to thirty-six cents a pound. More Jones County acres were planted in cotton than any year since 1937, and a bountiful harvest was anticipated. For the first time in memory the unpredictable West Texas weather had cooperated to allow maximum production.

Although I can't recall a single Stamford family who owned a television set, many of us knew someone in Abilene or Fort Worth who did, and much of the local coffee shop talk centered around the remarkable phenomenon which let people watch without paying. *Texaco Star Theater* and the *Fireside Theater* seemed to be the favorite programs. Most Stamford residents were content with listening to local radio station KDWT, where they could get the latest farm market news and enjoy weekday afternoon soap operas like *Just Plain Bill* and *Stella Dallas.* On Saturday evenings, every teenager in town tuned in to the *Saturday Night Hit Parade* to find out which song was number one. In September, as my Bulldog football team prepared to face the Haskell Indians and their highly rated new coach, Royce Smith, the nation's number one recording was Patti Page's "Tennessee Waltz."

Movies at the downtown Grand and State Theaters were always a special treat but usually not recent releases. Generally, movies came to Stamford theaters after they had made the rounds in larger cities. Still, the downtown theaters served as the town's social center. Most people who grew up in Stamford watched a picture show at either the Grand or the State on their first real date. Afterward, if a girl was lucky, her date would treat her to a soft drink at the City Pig or maybe a single dip ice cream cone at Tom's Ice Cream Parlor.

For those who couldn't wait for popular movies like *The African Queen,* starring Humphrey Bogart and Katharine Hepburn, or *A Streetcar named Desire,* starring Karl Maden, Vivien Leigh and Marlon Brando, the Majestic Theater in Abilene was a pleasant, forty-mile, after-church Sunday afternoon drive.

Of course on Friday nights, West Texas movie theaters played to an empty house. Every man, woman and child worth knowing were screaming their lungs out at the high school football game.

◆ ◆ ◆

A MAJORITY of our Haskell game was played in a pouring rain, but the downpour had little effect on the end result. After the opening kickoff my Bulldogs stopped the Indians cold. Three plunges into a stout defensive line led by Kenneth West, Charlie Davis and Johnny

Webb netted Haskell four yards. A sickly Indian punt, which Davis almost blocked, was returned to Haskell's thirty by a slippery jackrabbit named Jerry Prewit. On our first play Kenneth Lowe took a handoff from Wash and slashed over right tackle for nine yards. On our second try Max Kelley rambled twenty-one yards to score. Eldon Moritz, my sophomore kicking specialist, punched through the extra point, and the outcome was never in doubt.

Final score: Stamford 19, Haskell 0.

◆　◆　◆

IN THE WEEKS that followed, my Bulldogs continued to improve. We traveled to Ranger to squeeze out a 7–0 win over a class outfit coached by O.C. "Stubby" Warden and which featured all-state halfback Jimmy Comacho. Jerry Prewit scored our only touchdown with Moritz nailing the extra point. Wayne Wash, Max Kelley, Kenneth West and co-captain Paul Phy provided the spark to salvage our narrow victory.

A near capacity home crowd of thirty-five hundred braved an icy north wind to watch us rally to overcome a seven-point deficit and thump Albany 21–7. In a rock-'em, sock-'em scoring drive late in the third quarter, Stamford ballcarriers Kenneth Lowe, Max Kelley, and mighty-mite Jerry Prewit marched seventy yards with Lowe bulling over left guard for the final yard. We scored again after Albany received the kickoff and bogged down. In the fourth stanza Lowe rammed in from the three for our final TD.

◆　◆　◆

AS OUR UPCOMING CLASH with Ballinger drew closer, my Bulldogs were undefeated and getting better every week. Ballinger wasn't in our conference, but the contest had special significance for blue and white boosters. You see, Ballinger held an embarrassing eight-year hex over Stamford. Bulldog fans were more than ready to see that hex end.

By Friday morning excitement was at a fever pitch. In the City Barber Shop, at the Beauty Bar Hair Salon, and at Nat's Cafe, where farmers and merchants gathered for morning coffee, the dominant topic of conversation was whether this was the year Stamford's beloved Bulldogs would break the shackles of their losing streak to

Ballinger. In anticipation of a victory, many local merchants decorated their store windows in school colors.

Every student, grades seven through twelve, and a majority of Stamford's adult population participated in Friday morning's pep rally. The emotional crowd began screaming even before the cheerleaders lined up to lead yells. At the height of the spirited hollering session, as the crowd's fanatical mood reached a crazed frenzy, the ear-piercing noise could be heard all the way downtown. The loud shouting debacle ended with the band playing Stamford's school song. As yell leaders and pep squad members joined hands with members of the football team, you could see the fierce determination in my young men's eyes.

My football squad had the hosses, and they definitely had the desire. Now, the trick was to defeat Ballinger—a feat no Stamford eleven had achieved since World War II.

◆   ◆   ◆

THREE THOUSAND moans of dismay filled Stamford's stadium when Ballinger's shifty halfback Harold Merrifield took the pitchout, swept around right end and darted twenty yards into Stamford's end zone. After Elroy Payne banged the ball through the uprights for the extra point, every trace of confidence had disappeared from the homeside stands. Stamford fans were both troubled and disillusioned. How could their Bulldogs allow Ballinger to score so easily, and on their second possession of the night? Would Stamford's high hopes be dashed yet one more time? And how about this hot shot new coach with his newfangled offense who demanded big wages and promised so much? The coffee shop quarterbacks had warned that the new coach was too easy on his players, and now Ballinger was proving them right. If this coach, who the Abilene sportswriters called "Babe," couldn't beat Ballinger, how would he ever beat Anson?

At that moment, with the possible exception of my wife and daughter, not a person in the grandstands believed Stamford had a chance to win. Bulldog faithful had witnessed the scenario too many times before. Down on the field, I could feel the game slipping away. My hands were clammy, and my stomach was doing flip-flops as I gathered my anxious troops around me.

"Alright, every man in this huddle knows we're a better

ballclub than Ballinger! Now let's go out there and prove it. Wayne, you stick to our game plan. Keep the ball on the ground, and let's run it down their throats. No mistakes now. You linemen, remember your blocking assignments and do your job."

Paul Phy fielded Ballinger's short kickoff, dodged through a charging wave of red and black defenders and ran the ball back to the mid-field stripe. With Lowe and Kelley taking turns running the football, our offense pounded away at the Bearcats. In six tries we moved the ball to Ballinger's twenty-five for a first down.

After Kelley was stopped for no gain, I subbed in co-captain David Bashford with new instructions for our quarterback. Coach Ragus had noticed Ballinger's defensive halfbacks were cheating up, expecting a run. We decided to make them pay.

Hardly anyone noticed when Kenneth Lowe set up at wingback outside our right end. Wash took the snap from center Glen Lewis, faked a handoff to Bashford and nimbly rolled out to his right. By that time Lowe had sprinted past the Bearcats' defensive halfback. Wash chunked a perfect strike as Kenneth set his foot and slanted toward the red flag marking the right corner of the goal line. The partisan crowd went crazy when Lowe gathered in the football and loped untouched into the end zone. Their boisterous applause was premature. Moritz missed on the extra point try, and Stamford was still behind.

Three minutes later Stamford went ahead for good. Taking advantage of a Bearcat fumble, my charged-up Bulldogs drove forty-five yards in seven plays. Wash carried the football on a quarterback keeper for the final yard. Jaw breaking defensive play by Curtis Johnson, Jerry Ulke, Keith Miles and Paul Phy totally shut down the Bearcat offense for the remainder of the game. When Kenneth Lowe lunged across the goal line in the fourth quarter for our final tally, Stamford fans were ready to party.

Final score: Stamford 19, Ballinger 7.

◆　◆　◆

EARLY IN OCTOBER, one of the women teachers at Stamford High School quit quite suddenly. The teacher was newly married and discovered she was pregnant with her first child. Morning sickness and other complications made it impossible for her to continue teaching. Our high school principal, J.R. Dyer, called Katharine and asked if she would be willing to substitute until a replacement could be found for the expectant teacher. The job included seventh-grade language arts and ninth-grade English. Katharine agreed to take the job temporarily.

Katharine's morning classes included a ninth-grade, all-male class. The students in that class included Bob Harrison, who would later be selected an all-state center, and Charles Coody, who would become an all-district quarterback and lead my 1954 golf team to a state championship. As the ninth-grade English class convened, one of the boys challenged Katharine's authority.

"Hey, Teach! I reckon you know we've already run off one teacher!"

"Oh, is that right? I thought she quit because she was pregnant," Katharine rebutted.

The boys were shocked by Katharine's frank language. In 1951, people said a woman was "expecting" or "in a family way." "Pregnant" was considered improper—a social no-no. The boys snickered as Katharine continued, "I want all you boys to know one thing. I'm not very good at discipline, but I know someone who is. I live with him, and I can assure you he is a real expert when it comes to discipline."

Her unexpected declaration ended the snickering and the funmaking. From that day forward she commanded her students' undivided attention. When Harrison and Coody turned in late homework, Katharine rewarded them both with D's.

◆ ◆ ◆

AFTER OUR BALLINGER VICTORY, Abilene sportswriters began to predict Stamford would win District 5–AA. Their articles ignited a heated debate over which was the best 2A team in West Texas, an argument that wouldn't be settled until November 3, when Stamford met Anson.

In October, while New York Giant fans savored third baseman Bobby Thompson's dramatic bases-loaded, ninth-inning home run off Dodger pitcher Ralph Branca to complete the greatest comeback in baseball history, my Bulldogs were busy clobbering football teams out in West Texas. Scoring in every quarter, we romped over Seymour's Panthers 42–0. Next, we lowered the boom on Rotan's Yellowhammers 21–0, and on the last Friday in October, we white-washed Snyder's Tigers 20–0. Seven games into the season and we were undefeated. As our showdown with Anson approached, Stamford's invincible defense had allowed only two touchdowns.

◆　◆　◆

STAMFORD FANS WERE OVERCOME with delirious anticipation when Max Kelley broke through to block a Tiger punt in the first quarter, but their celebration was short-lived. We gave the ball right back on a botched handoff two plays later. Neither side could get anything going offensively, and the quarter ended with the score knotted at 0–0.

In the second quarter Anson drove deep into Stamford's end of the field before our defense stiffened and we held on downs. When we took possession, I subbed in Raymond Maxwell, instructing Wash to run a Statue of Liberty play we'd been working on all week. My trick play ended in disaster when Anson's defensive end knifed through our blockers to steal the football and fall on it at the thirty-three.

Our defense bowed its neck and refused to budge. Savage, tooth-rattling tackles by Kenneth West and Jerry Ulke shoved the Tigers back, and we regained control of the ball on our thirty-five.

With Wayne Wash barking the signals, our offense came to life. Kenneth Lowe slashed over right tackle to the forty-two and a first down. Kelley snaked his way to Anson's forty-three. Then Lowe was off again, barreling to the thirty-one before four weary red and black defenders could drag him down. Kelley rammed over left guard to the twenty-two, then Wash followed a path cleared by center Dan Smith for a first down at the nineteen. Two plays later Lowe steam-rolled a lone tackler at the three to score. Moritz booted the extra point.

Anson came roaring back. Don Watts returned the ensuing kickoff to their forty-eight, and Tiger halfback Willie Goza rambled around left end for a first down at Stamford's thirty-nine. A keeper by Anson quarterback Ken Helms gained five more.

A quick whistle aided Anson's touchdown drive. After Helms hit Kenneth Scott in the letters with a bullet pass on the seventeen, Wayne Wash nailed the red and black receiver with a bruising tackle. The impact caused Scott to lose control and the ball sailed high in the air. A diving Jerry Prewit caught the loose football long before it hit the ground, but the game officials ruled the play dead and gave the pigskin back to Anson on our fourteen-yard line. Goza capped the comeback drive with an end sweep. At halftime the score was 7–6 in favor of Stamford.

As the Stamford school band marched off the playing field, the Tigers charged from their dressing room with fire in their eyes. Anson coach Fagan Mullins had apparently pulled out all the stops in his halftime pep talk. I wish I knew what he said because that's when the tide turned in Anson's favor.

We fumbled the kickoff, and the Tigers pushed us back to the ten-yard line. A short punt gave Anson possession on Stamford's thirty-eight, and they came out passing. Helms hit receiver James Bowen for thirteen, then Scott for fourteen. Two bucks between the tackles and an incomplete pass put Anson on our five. On fourth down Helms rolled out and drilled Eugene Steel in the end zone for the go-ahead points.

On the kickoff we fumbled again, this time turning the ball over on our thirty-eight. An interception by Wayne Wash kept the Tigers from scoring again, but Stamford's offense kept shooting itself in the foot. On several occasions we pounded deep into Anson's end of the field, but each time we got close to the Tigers' goal line, a fumble or a penalty killed our drive.

Final score: Anson 12, Stamford 7.

The loss was a bitter pill for my previously undefeated Bulldogs, but with two conference games left to play, we retained a slim thread of hope some other school could do what we couldn't— beat Anson and allow Stamford to crawfish into the state playoffs. The next Friday we blasted Colorado City 55–6, taking our frustrations out on the hapless Wolves. In our final game my Bulldogs mauled Hamlin 32–6.

◆　◆　◆

WHEN I RESIGNED at Winters, Morris Southall was offered their head coaching job, and he accepted. Morris and I continued to be close friends, keeping in touch, talking by telephone regularly. Back in July, we had shared a room at coaching school, but during football season, we were both up to our eyeballs with gridiron battles.

Perhaps that's why I was so surprised when I scanned the sports page on Saturday morning after our Hamlin game. Anson had defeated Rotan 33–0, eliminating any chance of my Bulldogs participating in the playoffs. But right there on page 6A was the shocker. Winters had upset Ballinger 13–6 to capture the 9–AA title and advance to the playoffs.

Naturally I was happy for Morris, but I felt like an ugly bridesmaid wearing a brand-new formal. My Stamford football club finished nine and one, and I'd be home coaching basketball while everyone else was invited to dance. Marty Robbins recorded a song several years later which expressed my feelings precisely, "My Bulldogs were all dressed up with no place to go."

◆ ◆ ◆

KENNETH WEST was a mainstay on my 1951 football squad, thin at the waist, thick in the shoulders, strong as an ox. He was a good kid with an easy going smile, quick to learn, always good-natured and a pleasure to coach. Kenneth came from an extremely poor family.

The Wests lived in an old run-down house which didn't enjoy the convenience of an indoor toilet. Kenneth's mother was a teacher, but her health was bad, and she couldn't hold down a steady teaching job. Kenneth's father worked for Bryant's Implement Company, Stamford's John Deere dealer, but his low

The West brothers—Kenneth, Don, Royce.
(credit: 1952, 1955, and 1957 Stamford High Yearbooks)

wages were barely sufficient to keep food on their table. During their high school years, Kenneth and each of his two brothers would practice football then dress and hurry downtown to sack groceries or work at the movie theater until closing time.

Kenneth was an outstanding lineman, a devastating blocker

and a head-hunting tackler. After the football season concluded, Kenneth received several scholarship offers. During the spring of 1952, I called him to my office to talk about college.

"I can't go to college, Coach Wood. I need to go to work and help my family."

"Listen here, West. I appreciate your concern for your family, but I want you to consider your own future. You're a bright young man. A college education can open up opportunities you'll never even dream about if you don't go. I want you to take a few days and think hard about what you want out of life. Then I want you to come talk to me again."

It took some talking, but eventually I convinced Kenneth to accept a college scholarship. Even though more lucrative offers were available, he chose Hardin-Simmons University so he could be close to his family. Kenneth's football coach at Hardin-Simmons was Murray Evans, a long time friend.

While he attended Hardin-Simmons, Kenneth held an after school job, working evenings and on weekends. During the summer he worked full time sanding floors for a contractor. Coach Evans was a big help. Knowing the West family's dire situation, he excused Kenneth from spring workouts, except for the three weeks of actual football practice.

Every week during the four years he attended college, Kenneth sent money home to his family.

◆　◆　◆

KATHARINE HAS OFTEN expressed her pity for coaches' wives who live in cities with more than one high school, because they miss out on the community spirit and the cordial relationships a small town offers. Our first few years at Stamford we lived on Cuba Street. For a couple of years we rented. Then when another house came up for sale a few doors away, we purchased a home.

Living on Cuba Street was a happy chapter for our family, especially for Pat and Katharine. Twenty-two kids under ten and almost that many dogs lived within a two-block area. All the children knew each other, and they kept something going all the time. On Cuba Street there was almost no traffic, and no person who lived in the friendly area ever considered fencing their yard. Children were free to roam the neighborhood and play wherever

The Cuba Street Gang—
Six-year-old Pat (the tomboy) with Stamford playmates.
(credit: Wood Family Collection)

they pleased. Mothers were in constant contact, and they established certain strict rules—children were not allowed to go into another family's home to get a drink or to use the bathroom. Every morning at eleven-thirty the children went inside and took a nap until four o'clock. (This may seem harsh, but in those days Polio was prevalent on every parent's mind. Doctors didn't have a clue what caused Polio, and the best advice they could come up with was to rest your kids and keep them inside during the heat of the day.)

In the summer of 1951, the deadly threat of Polio struck particularly close to home when Morris Southall's second son Silas was stricken with the horrid, child-crippling disease. Fortunately, the Southalls had moved to Abilene that summer while Morris worked on his master's degree, so expert medical treatment was readily available. With swift diagnosis and specialized care, Si recovered. Many children weren't so fortunate. When Morris and Lorene carried Si to Abilene's Hendricks Hospital for a spinal tap, a procedure used to detect polio, they were shocked to find a ward full of severely disabled children.

1952

DURING THE SPRING of 1952, O.M. Isbell replaced Pete Ragus as my assistant football coach. Coach Ragus was leaving to accept an assistant coaching job at Miller High School in Corpus Christi. In 1958, Pete would be promoted to head coach, and in 1960, his Corpus Christi football team would win the Class 4A state championship. After the 1960 season, Coach Ragus beat me by one vote for Coach of the Year honors. I voted for Pete.

Coach Isbell was a graduate of North Texas State College. His arrival brought to Stamford an outstanding math teacher and an exceptional coaching talent. Isbell was a quick learner and an astute scout, but his volatile temper and pessimistic personality would eventually force me to limit his game day presence to out-of-town scouting duty. When there were no games to scout, I assigned him to the press box.

As Coach Isbell and I prepared for fall football practice, the nation's number one song was Kay Starr's "Wheel of Fortune," followed closely by Johnny Ray's "Walking my Baby Back Home." Over in Abilene, *High Noon*, starring Gary Cooper and Grace Kelly, was advertised as the must-see movie of the year.

Up-to-date women's wear stressed femininity. Cinched waistlines, molded bodices and wide skirts worn over multiple layers of stiff petticoats were the rage among young women. Hathaway shirt ads, aspiring to stimulate sales of their new shirt colors, urged men to, "Never wear a white shirt before sundown." Of course in Stamford, not many men owned a white dress shirt, much less a tie. Blue jeans rolled up to expose white socks, topped with a solid white tee shirt beneath a Bulldog letter jacket was the standard uniform for Stamford High males.

◆ ◆ ◆

EACH YEAR in mid-August, fall football camp convened at the high school football stadium. A chain link fence topped with three strands of barbed wire surrounded the stadium complex. Enclosed within the fence were our game field and two practice fields. The basketball gym, where our football squad suited out for practice, and the school cafeteria were close by. Stamford High provided two women to cook our meals, but several mothers also volunteered to help with the cooking. The food served was mouth-watering and plentiful. No Bulldog football player ever left our cafeteria hungry.

On Sunday evening, team members were instructed to report with cots and bedclothes. Sunday night the entire football squad slept at the football field. Monday morning we began two-a-days. Every night the stadium gates were locked with the boys inside, and as far as I know, none of our players ever left the confines.

On Wednesday afternoon, Coach Isbell overheard the boys talking about female cheerleaders who were slipping into the stadium after dark to talk to the players. Thinking the girls' nightly visits might pose a problem, he came to me, and we set out to investigate.

A quick inspection of the stadium grounds confirmed the story. On the visitors' side of the stadium we discovered a hole where the girls had tunneled under the fence. That evening we laid a trap for the sneaky yell leaders.

Our cheerleaders that year were Jo Ann Frizell, Tillie Metz, Llada Moore, Nancy Pardue, Charlene Terry, and Barbara Schoonmaker, and I believe every one of the young ladies were in the group that slipped under the fence along about nine o'clock Wednesday night. Coach Isbell and I silently watched the girls negotiate the fence and scurry across the football field. After they reached the homeside bleachers, we turned on the water sprinklers. Fifteen minutes later, after the ground was good and wet, we flipped on the stadium lights. You should have seen the cheerleaders' startled faces as they scattered like barnyard chickens, screaming and yelling to high heaven. Coach Isbell and I were laughing so hard I thought our sides might split. By the time the girls crawled back under the fence, they were thoroughly soaked and covered with mud.

Our boys especially enjoyed the way Coach Isbell and I handled the girl problem. For several months afterward, the cheerleader caper was the talk of high school. Even after all these years, I still laugh every time I think about those girls' desperate expressions and their high-pitched screams as they scrambled back underneath the stadium fence.

◆　◆　◆

BEFORE THE SEASON opened, Houston football guru Mitchell

Williamson picked Stamford as the fifth best AA team in Texas, behind Phillips, Hereford, Wellington and Quanah. I whole-heartedly agreed with his thinking. Even though eleven seniors graduated off my 1951 ballclub, Stamford's stable was still blessed with plenty of hosses. During the long off-season I had made up my mind. This year I intended to be invited to the big dance.

My blue and white Bulldogs kicked off the season by drubbing the Haskell Indians 20–0. In back-to-back home games, we pasted Ranger 19–7 and smothered Albany's Lions 52–13.

When Stamford traveled to Ballinger for our fourth game, the Bearcats were undefeated and ranked fourth among Abilene area AA football teams. Ballinger played a vicious brand of ball-control football. They seldom passed, preferring instead to grind down their opponents with a punishing ground attack and hard-nosed defense.

According to area sportswriters, Stamford was favored to win, but as every coach in West Texas knew, strange things could happen when you played Coach Doug Cox and his wily Bearcats on their home turf.

◆ ◆ ◆

MAX KELLEY plunged across Ballinger's goal line from the three to climax an opening 74-yard drive, but then things took a turn for the worse. Kenneth Lowe, our multi-threat tailback and number one ballcarrier, came limping off the field. A twisted knee would sideline him for the remainder of the game.

Ballinger charged right back. Two quick passes from quarterback Jerry Bell to ends Bobby Bird and Bill Maedgen got their offense rolling, and the Bearcats hammered out sixty-four yards to tie the score at 7–7.

In the second quarter Ballinger's Mike Egan intercepted a Moritz pass and returned it to our twenty. When the Bearcats broke from their huddle, they lined up in a TCU spread formation. Our defense was totally confused. We were still running around trying to figure who covered who when the ball was centered. Bell took the snap and tossed a screen pass to his right end Bobby Bird who followed behind four red and black blockers to dance untouched into our end zone.

With the score 13–6, the situation looked bleak for my Bulldogs. For a majority of the contest Stamford had been on defense with Ballinger's freight train offense methodically chewing us up. I signaled for a time-out and called my exhausted troops to the sideline. I was explaining how important it was to maintain our poise when one of my players chimed in, "Get a smile on your face and keep it there!"

Another player added, "And if you can't smile, just keep saying 'cheese' so those Ballinger clowns will think you're smiling!"

On the very next series my blue and white gladiators stopped Ballinger dead in their tracks, and Stamford wound up winning the game 42–13. From that day forward, Charlie Davis, a Stamford co-captain and the best defensive lineman who ever donned a Bulldog football uniform, became a true believer. Any time an opposing team began wearing us down, Charlie would remind his teammates to keep their poise by saying, "cheese-cheese."

◆　◆　◆

CHARLIE DAVIS was the oldest of three brothers I would coach at Stamford, each an outstanding athlete and each an absolute joy to coach. Ernie would co-captain my 1954 team and be our leading ground gainer. In 1957, Don would start for me at fullback. All three brothers—Charlie, Ernie and Don—would be selected all-state. After they entered college, all three were named little all-American. All three would graduate, and all three would be inducted into McMurry University's Hall of Fame.

Charlie's father was killed in an oil field accident when Charlie

The Davis Brothers—Charlie, Ernie, Don.
(credit: 1953, 1955, and 1958 Stamford High Yearbooks)

was thirteen. His mother worked as a waitress in a downtown cafe, but early in the fall of 1952, she left Stamford to find a better paying job. She didn't necessarily abandon Charlie and his two brothers. She sent them money regularly, and she came home when she could, but the boys were essentially expected to fend for themselves. Charlie, being the oldest, assumed responsibility for looking after the other two. Donald and Ernie idolized their big brother, so they never challenged or disobeyed Charlie's strict rules of behavior.

Spike Dykes, who later became the head football coach at Texas Tech, was a member of the Bearcat squad Stamford beat that evening. Dykes was a sophomore that year and second-string center. Many years later at a coaching clinic in Tucson, he related this story.

Coach Dykes said he was sitting on the Ballinger bench enjoying the game when their starting center came off the field with his nose bleeding and a tooth missing. Doug Cox, the Bearcats' coach, called out, "Spike, get in there and play center!"

Spike said it was fourth down. He jumped from the bench and hurried in to snap the football. When he lined up, there was Charlie Davis directly across the line of scrimmage with a huge, wide smile pasted on his face. Spike confessed he was scared to death. He claimed no football player ever took a worse whipping than he did in that game.

◆　◆　◆

BY LATE OCTOBER the race for president was in full swing. Democrats had nominated former Illinois governor Adlai Stevenson. Republicans were touting General Dwight Eisenhower using the catchy slogan, "I like Ike."

With Kenneth Lowe injured, I shifted Wayne Wash to tailback, promoted Eldon Moritz to starting quarterback, and my football machine never missed a lick. Wash scored three touchdowns and passed for two others as my Bulldogs shellacked Seymour 48–0. For an encore, we crushed Rotan 41–0, and buried Merkel's Badgers 38–7.

◆　◆　◆

YEAR AFTER YEAR, District 5–AA's toughest foe was always Anson. Even though my 1951 Bulldog club won nine games, a 12–7 loss to Anson had canceled our post-season plans. No matter how well Stamford played or how many points we scored, our route to the state playoffs had to include a win over the red and black Tigers. 1952 would be no different. As our annual bout approached, Anson was also unbeaten.

. By game time all my riders were back in the saddle. Kenneth Lowe had spent a whole week in Fort Worth where TCU trainer Elmer Brown worked on his banged-up knee. Brown's therapeutic magic had apparently worked wonders. Kenneth's knee seemed good as new. My pigskin arsenal was locked and loaded.

Our game plan was to run the football and not make mistakes. Anson coach Fagan "Moon" Mullins subscribed to the same theory. From the opening kickoff, the two teams bludgeoned one another. Bloody noses, split lips and black eyes were prevalent on both sides of the line as a kind of trench warfare developed, with neither team able to cross into enemy territory.

Late in the first quarter Kenneth Lowe broke loose and raced twenty-nine yards to score, but after his TD scamper, the bloody stalemate resumed. At halftime Stamford held a slim 7–0 lead.

In the second half our gritty line play and a grinding ground attack began to wear down the Tigers. In desperation, Anson switched to an aerial game. Their change in strategy produced little fruit. Stamford's defensive line, led by Curtis Johnson, Charlie Davis, Edward Eckdahl, James Thompson and Keith Miles, hounded Anson quarterback Kenneth Helms on every pass. Our secondary, which included Larry Simmons, Jody Foster, Buddy Gray and Wayne Wash, covered Tiger receivers like a wet blanket.

Anson's dam finally crumbled late in the third quarter when their punter fumbled a fourth-down snap from center. Stamford assumed possession on the Tigers' twenty-six, and on the first play from scrimmage, Kenneth Lowe sliced through a weary red and black defense for our second touchdown.

The Tiger's wheels fell off completely in the final quarter. Larry Simmons hit paydirt when he waltzed thirty-one yards to cap a 54-yard drive. Minutes later Max Kelley plunged in from the one. Then George Humphrey intercepted a Helms' pass and ran it back twenty-three yards for a touchdown. Our final tally came after Larry Simmons intercepted another Helms pass on Anson's fifteen. Wash skirted around left end to finish off a totally demoralized Tiger team.

The Beginning

Final score: Stamford 41, Anson 0.

◆　◆　◆

A FLU EPIDEMIC fell on West Texas like a ton of bricks the next week, and football games were canceled left and right. On Friday morning, Colorado City's coach called to tell me he didn't have enough players to field a team. Not a single member of my football squad objected when the Wolves forfeited. Even though we had whipped Anson handily on the scoreboard, my kids were pretty beat up.

After a week off to recuperate, we wrapped up the district title, ending a perfect season by spanking Hamlin 49–0.

◆　◆　◆

WHILE MY BULLDOGS were cruising through their schedule, Morris Southall's Blizzards were fighting for their lives. Winters' season had boiled down to the last game. A Friday night clash with Ballinger would determine the 9–AA district champ. The winner would take home all the marbles and advance to the state playoffs. With our bi-district game against Tahoka a week away, Katharine, Pat and I traveled to Ballinger to root for Winters.

No group could have been happier than the Wood family when Coach Southall's ballclub thrashed the Bearcats 40–13 to capture the 9–AA crown for a second straight year. Driving home that night, though, a crazy thought crossed my mind. What if both Morris and I kept on winning, and our teams met in the state playoffs?

◆　◆　◆

ON A COLD THANKSGIVING DAY before a sellout crowd of thirty-eight hundred frostbitten fans, my Stamford football club presented me with an early Christmas present, a gift I'd been hoping for my entire coaching career, a gift I'd longed for since 1940, when I accepted my first head coaching job at Rule, Texas. After twelve years and a hundred and three football games, I finally got what I wanted—a victory in the Texas High School Football Playoffs.

My super-charged Bulldogs wrapped up the package in grand fashion. Five different men, Humphrey, Wash, Moritz, Gray and Kelley, scored as Stamford whomped up on Tahoka thirty-four to zip.

◆   ◆   ◆

WE'D NO SOONER DEFEATED Tahoka than there I was face to face with that same group of freshman players I'd fretted about leaving behind when I quit at Seminole three years earlier. They were all seniors now, and as predicted, they were absolutely awesome. Sportswriters at the Abilene paper picked the Indians to beat us by two touchdowns. Locally, there was a great deal of interest in the game, and a whole lot of gambling.

With neither coach wanting to risk losing on the other's home field, we agreed to play the regional contest at a mutual site, selecting Snyder because it was midway between Seminole and Stamford.

On Saturday morning when our team bus groaned up to the stadium gate, gambling out in the parking lot was in full swing. Indian supporters were giving seven points. Bulldog boosters were every bit as confident, so the betting was hot and heavy. One gambler was out there waving a fist full of dollars. Most everyone on our bus knew the man. He'd grown up in Stamford but had moved to Abilene where he went into the air-conditioning business and made a ton of money. The man was obviously drunk. Even though Seminole was favored to win, the inebriated gambler began betting by taking Stamford and giving seven points. When he ran out of takers at seven points, he started giving fourteen points, then twenty-one points. Finally, he gave twenty-eight points and bet Seminole wouldn't cross the fifty-yard line. Before the man's friends stopped him, he bet one Seminole man that the Indians wouldn't make a first down.

The high rolling gambler never watched a single down of the football game. The Snyder police arrested him when they caught him urinating in the parking lot.

Here's the weird part. That afternoon Stamford beat Seminole 35–0, so the intoxicated gambler won most of his bets. He came close to winning his wager Seminole wouldn't make a first down. Stamford held the Indians to only seven first downs. Seminole only crossed the fifty-yard line once, so he almost won that bet too.

After the game, several of the gambler's friends collected his bets. Turned out, he'd won four hundred and fifty dollars betting on Stamford. That's exactly how much it took to bail him out of jail.

◆   ◆   ◆

The Beginning

IN 1952, THE BEST HIGH SCHOOL football official in Texas was John Hart. Hart worked our quarterfinal game against Childress. The Bobcats were the toughest opponent we'd faced all year. At the half my Bulldogs were clinging to a 14–13 lead, but late in the third quarter, we scored another touchdown. Several minutes later, Charlie Davis intercepted a deflected LaNeal Castleberry pass on the Bobcats' twenty-seven and returned it to their eight. An unnecessary roughness penalty moved the ball down to the one, and Kenneth Lowe slanted off left tackle for the final yard. Moritz's extra point kick pretty much cinched a victory.

After Stamford went ahead by two touchdowns, a lot of extracurricular activity began to take place—kicking, biting, scratching. The Bobcats were taking their frustration out on Bulldog linemen.

Childress players had gathered about their quarterback to call another play when John noticed a Stamford man in the Bobcats' huddle. Hart stuck his head inside to see what was going on.

There was Charlie Davis down on one knee, telling the Childress boys they were beat, and there wasn't a darn thing they could do to change the outcome. He asked the Bobcat players to play clean and finish the game with dignity. When he finished, Charlie left their huddle and hurried back to take his defensive position at the line of scrimmage. The game ended without further incident.

◆ ◆ ◆

OUR SEMIFINAL CONTEST took place on a windswept Saturday afternoon before a full house at Abilene's Fair Park Stadium. It was the largest crowd to ever attend a Stamford football game. With the game about to get underway, I was in a sweat. TCU trainer Elmer Brown had volunteered to drive from Fort Worth to properly tape Kenneth Lowe's knee and work his magic on my star running back. Elmer was a genius at getting injured players ready to play. After Kenneth injured his knee in the Ballinger game, his parents took him to Fort Worth where Elmer worked on the knee every day. A week later, Kenneth was able to play, but he played with a lot of pain.

Ten minutes before game time Elmer Brown still hadn't arrived, and I was getting very nervous.

"I don't know why you're so worried, Gordon. If Brown don't

show, I'll tape Lowe's knee. It ain't that big a deal," Coach Isbell advised, trying to console me.

"You sure you know how, O.M.? I don't want Lowe to hurt his knee again, but we'll be in a heck of a mess if he can't go."

"I can handle it, Coach Wood. Kenneth won't be able to tell whether it was me or Elmer Brown who did the job," Isbell assured, and I made one of the worst decisions of my career. I let my assistant coach tape my all-state running back's knee. Kenneth would tell me later that Isbell just stuck pieces of adhesive tape all around his kneecap. He said his knee would have been better off without any tape at all.

◆　　◆　　◆

LADY LUCK DEALT STAMFORD a bad hand on the very first play of the game. Kenneth Lowe re-injured his knee while running to receive the opening kickoff. Lowe had to be carried from the field.

TCU's trainer arrived shortly after our tailback went down. Car trouble had caused him to get a late start that morning. Working quickly, Elmer shot Lowe's knee full of Novocaine, retaped the bad knee with half a roll of adhesive tape, and pronounced Kenneth fit to play.

In the early going neither team could get rolling, as each school's offense stumbled and stammered against the other's determined defense. When Stamford regained possession of the football with less than three minutes left in the first quarter, I decided to roll the dice. This was a high stakes, winner-take-all game. I realized Kenneth Lowe wouldn't be able to go full speed, but my finely-tuned scoring machine was sputtering. With Brown promising my multi-talented ballcarrier could play without much risk of further damage to his knee, I sent Kenneth back in at tailback.

For a short while my gamble worked. On three running plays, Lowe slashed his way to Terrell's forty-one, but there the Tiger defense stiffened. On fourth and long, I threw caution to the wind and bet the farm. I sent in Jody Foster with orders to go for it. Lowe's roll-out toss to Keith Miles gave my blue and white dogs a first down at Terrell's twenty-nine.

A turnover kept me from raking in my chips. On the next play, Tiger defender Tom Norton leaped in front of Stamford receiver

Howard Vest to intercept Lowe's hurried pass, and our scoring opportunity disappeared.

Stalwart play by Stamford's defensive unit held off Terrell's offensive powerhouse until midway in the second quarter, but then the Tigers' tremendous size advantage began to tell. Led by the power-packed blocking of Wayne Boles and Charlie Greene, Terrell began a clock-eating, 75-yard march toward our goal line. Two minutes remained in the half when Tiger quarterback Rupert Henry sneaked in from the three. When time ran out in the first half, Stamford was still trailing, 7–0.

After Stamford's second half kickoff, the Tigers reeled off a couple of first downs, but when they reached the fifty-yard line, blue and white defenders, Larry Simmons, Curtis Johnson, James Thompson and Dan Smith, simply drew a line and refused to budge.

Max Kelley fielded Terrell's fourth-down punt and ran it back to our thirty. In four running plays, Stamford rammed the football to mid-field where our struggling offense bogged down again. On fourth down, Lowe sailed a high spiraling punt into the waiting arms of James Harris. Harris headed straight up field then cut left to the sideline where three red and white blockers had set up to screen off Stamford's charging defenders. At the forty-five, Harris stiff-armed the last grasping Bulldog tackler and sprinted for our goal line. Tom Norton's extra point kick was wide, but it made no difference. Stamford's luck had run out.

A blocked quick-kick attempt led to another Terrell score. The game ended with the Bulldogs on Terrell's one-foot line, desperately trying to score and salvage some dignity.

Final score: Stamford 0, Terrell 20.

Game statistics in Sunday morning's newspaper would show Stamford's offense outgained Terrell 194 yards to 166. We also racked up fourteen first downs to the Tigers' eleven. Norton's interception of Kenneth Lowe's pass in the first quarter, Harris' 83-yard punt return, and Wade Driver's block of Lowe's quick-kick were the key plays, but the game was also won in the trenches. Inside their twenty, Terrell played as tough a defense as any I've ever seen.

When *Abilene Reporter-News* sportswriter Fred Sanner interviewed my sweat-soaked, battle-weary gladiators in the locker room, our kids were generous in their applause for Terrell's defensive line, especially monster tackle Wade Driver.

"Yeah, I kept trying to block that big number sixty-four all afternoon," guard Woody Crider groaned, "but he was too fast. Seemed like he was always behind me, and I couldn't find him."

"I didn't have any trouble finding him," chimed in Buddy Gray, who played in our backfield. "Every time Moritz handed me the football, there was Driver looking me right in the eye."

The following weekend Terrell ripped Yoakum 61–13 to win the State 2A crown.

1953

BUDDY GRAY was a sophomore when he enrolled at Stamford High. His mother was going through a rough time, so she brought Buddy to Stamford to live with relatives in the Swedish Community south of town. Buddy was extremely bright and smart as a whip, but cocky as he could be.

During the spring of 1953, I noticed Buddy picking on Wayne Wash, another member of the football squad. Soaking wet, Buddy weighed maybe 155 pounds, whereas Wayne weighed around 170. Standing six-foot-two, Wash was not only a superb athlete, he was also a perfect gentleman, courteous to both his teachers and his coaches. Buddy's malicious attitude disturbed me, so I called him in to talk.

"Buddy, I see you're picking on Wayne Wash. You probably think Wayne is afraid of you, but I'm telling you Wayne Wash is not afraid of any kid at Stamford High School. You pay attention to Max Kelley and Keith Miles. They don't mess with Wash because they know better. If you keep picking on Wayne, one of these days he's gonna get fed up and beat the dog outta you."

"You're wrong, Coach Wood. Wayne can't whip me," Buddy bragged, cocksure of himself as always.

"You'd better listen to me, Buddy. Wayne Wash won't only whip you. It won't even be a close contest."

The very next day Wayne jumped over Buddy, knocking the spunky junior to the ground when he went to intercept a pass. That flew all over Buddy. He leaped up and slugged Wayne in the mouth, but Wash didn't fight back. Wayne just pushed Buddy back and looked at him sadly.

"I don't want to fight you, Buddy, but I reckon that's the only way we'll get this settled. After school, let's you and me go out in the country and get it over with."

Stamford's 1953
Tri-Captains
Buddy Gray,
Wayne Wash,
Max Kelley.
(credit: 1954
Stamford High
Yearbook)

That afternoon the two boys took off, inviting Max Kelley along to referee.

Along about dusk, my doorbell rings. It's Buddy Gray, and he's bloody as hell. He looks terrible. When Katharine saw Buddy's blood-splattered, beat-up face, my wife burst into tears and rushed him inside to clean him up.

While Katharine was bawling and wiping at the blood, I asked Buddy what happened. Buddy informed me that he and Wayne had settled their differences, and they wouldn't be fighting anymore. When I asked who won, Buddy's short, undaunted analysis of the fist fight caused me to bust out laughing.

"Well, I reckon Wayne actually won, Coach. But I was doing pretty good until he got in that lucky lick."

Their senior year Buddy and Wayne were captains of my football team along with Max Kelley. From that day forward, Buddy and Wayne were best friends. After he obtained a master's degree from Texas Tech, Buddy continued his education at Texas University where he received a doctor's degree. Buddy wound up at SMU teaching math. Eventually, he became Dean of Academics and was instrumental in helping several gifted Brownwood students obtain scholarships. When he retired in 1988, Buddy was president of SMU's Deadman College.

◆　◆　◆

NO ONE IN STAMFORD had much money, but some were dirt poor. Possibly no family struggled more than Curtis Johnson's family. Even though the Johnsons lived on a fairly good farm, they lived a Spartan life. Curtis' father was extremely suspicious of prosperity. The first time I met Curtis was in the fall of 1951. He was curly headed and good looking, but he was wearing bib overalls and worn-out work boots. Anyone could tell he was an impoverished farm boy.

Curtis was close to tears that morning he came to see me. His dad and uncles had told him Stamford High School had no use for country kids, and we coaches wouldn't allow a poor farm boy like him to play for the Bulldogs.

Since Stamford was essentially an agricultural community, the young man's statement both astounded and disturbed me. Most every Stamford High athlete was connected with farming in one way or another. Here is how I responded:

"Curtis, there's no way I could ever be prejudiced against country kids. I grew up on a farm and lived on one until I finished college. I know all about morning farm chores and the work country boys have to do after school. I can't promise how much you'll get to play, but I will guarantee you this. I want you on my football squad, and you'll get exactly the same chance as every other boy who comes out."

My assurance was all Curtis needed. He left my office smiling, and he showed up for football practice the very next day. Curtis Johnson turned out to be a stalwart lineman and as ferocious a blocker as ever played for Stamford High.

Curtis was close to graduation when he dropped by my office in the spring of 1953. He was wrestling with decisions about his future. No one in his family had ever gone to college, and Curtis wasn't sure whether he should. Of course, finances were a major consideration. The Johnson family had no money for college expenses.

Curtis was a really good kid, so I was anxious to help him resolve his dilemma. I assured him he was a good enough football player, and if he truly wanted to go to college, I could arrange for him to play on scholarship at any number of schools. Curtis left my

Stamford's Curtis Johnson.
(credit: 1953 Stamford High Yearbook)

office telling me he'd think about our conversation and get back to me after he talked with his father.

That evening when Curtis informed his family he was planning to attend college, his hard-edged father threw a hissing fit. In fact, he became so irate Curtis was afraid his dad might hurt him. For more than a week Curtis came to school early and went home after dark. To avoid his father's wrath, Curtis slept in their barn, with his mother slipping food to him.

A couple of weeks later Cutis went to his father again. Mr. Johnson was still dead set against college, but at his wife's insistence, he had reluctantly agreed to listen.

"There's no way you can go to college, Curtis. We can't pay the tuition."

"You won't have to, dad. Coach Wood says if I play football the college will give me free tuition."

"How about a place to live? That'll cost a lot of money."

"I'll live in the athletic dormitory. My room won't cost a thing."

"Who'll feed you? This family's got no extra money for food."

"The college. My scholarship will include all my meals."

"Books. Who'll buy your books?"

"They'll pay for all my books too."

Mr. Johnson still wasn't convinced. He glared at Curtis and shook his head.

"That's exactly what's wrong with this country, son. Here your mom and I are, working night and day, trying to scratch out a living, and you're gonna get everything you need for free, just for playing football. That's exactly what's wrong with this whole dang country. Nobody appreciates hard work anymore. We've got a bunch of crooks running the government, and they hold onto their jobs by handing out freebies." Then Curtis' dad threw up his hands and stomped out of the room.

For a while Curtis yielded, promising his father he would get a job and forget about college. However, in late August before school started, Curtis packed his meager belongings in a grocery sack and hitch-hiked to McMurry College in Abilene. Curtis played football at McMurry for four years, made excellent grades and graduated without any help whatsoever from his family. For many years, because of his decision to attend college, his relationship with his father was strained.

Until so many Texas banking institutions went bust in the mid-eighties, Curtis Johnson worked in the savings and loan industry. These days he resides in Austin where he is an immensely successful stockbroker.

◆　◆　◆

ON JULY 27, 1953, a truce agreement was signed at Panmunjom, and every person in America breathed a sigh of relief. Three bitter years of combat, in which thirty-four thousand brave U.S. soldiers gave their lives, fighting for a cause many people back home never quite understood, finally came to an end.

◆　◆　◆

IN AUGUST, near the end of our fall football camp, we scrimmaged Abilene High School again. The Eagles had a new head coach, imported from McAllen, Texas. The difference in coaching techniques was absolutely amazing. Every time an Abilene player made a mistake an assistant coach was right there pointing it out, explaining what the boy had done wrong, patting him on the back and encouraging the young man to do better. The Eagles didn't look real sharp that afternoon, but I was confident Abilene's football fortunes would improve after the new coach got his message across.

On the bus ride home I felt much better about the Abilene kids. Even though my coaching plate was more than full that fall, I kept up with the Eagles' progress in the newspaper. The Warbirds got off to a rousing start, beating Highland Park in their first game, then tying a good team from Sweetwater. After easing by Breckenridge and stomping all over Borger, the Eagles looked like they might go a long way, but Abilene competed in a bare-knuckles, last-man-left-standing 4A district. Tough losses to Odessa Permian and Pampa eliminated their playoff chances.

The next season Abilene beat Highland Park and Sweetwater before they lost to Breckenridge 35–13. The Eagles wouldn't lose again until 1958, when Sweetwater beat them 19–0 in the second game of the season. The game that truly robbed the wind from their sails, though, was the tie with Highland Park in the 1957 state finals which Highland Park won on penetrations.

Of course, the Abilene football coach whose organized approach impressed me so much was Chuck Moser. He and Chesty Walker were the two finest coaches I ever had the privilege to compete against.

◆　◆　◆

FOOTBALL SEASON in 1953, began much like my previous two at Stamford High. While Maureen Connolly was sailing through the U.S. Championship Tournament, becoming the first woman, and only the second player, to win all four major tennis tournaments, and while the Yankees were winning their fifth consecutive World Series, my Bulldogs were chewing up West Texas football teams.

On September 11, we romped past Haskell 58–0 and followed with a 41–6 massacre of the Quanah Indians. After we drubbed Albany 48–21, my hungry dogs kept on rolling, flattening Ballinger 42–0 and battering Coleman 29–6. Running our string to seven straight, we waltzed by Graham then ruined Rotan's homecoming evening by walloping the Yellowhammers 45–13.

With the District 4–AA lead up for grabs, a field goal by Charles Coody, and touchdowns by Wayne Wash and Eldon Moritz ignited Stamford's 17–0 whitewashing of Colorado City.

Eight straight victories were gratifying, but bitter sweet, because as usual, *they* were out there waiting—the team that always stood between Stamford and the state playoffs—the dreaded Anson Tigers.

◆　◆　◆

FURIOUS DEFENSIVE PLAY by both sides turned what was expected to be a high scoring game into a gut-wrenching defensive thriller. For almost three quarters Anson and Stamford battered one another. Players on both sides of the line grunted and bled, but neither team had been able to mount a serious threat on the other's goal line.

A fourth-down gamble finally turned the tide. On three tries Stamford punched out five yards to move the football to Anson's forty-two. It was the first time we had crossed into Tiger territory since early in the game. Realizing it was now or never, I collared George Humphrey on the sideline. Humphrey was eager to enter the game. He bounced up and down on his toes while I issued instructions for him to relay to our quarterback.

"Number 34, delay pass, Moritz to Wash. You understand?"

"Yes sir, Coach. 34 pass. I got it."

"Alright, get in there. Tell Sosebee and Terry I wanna see some Tigers on their backsides after we make the first down," I dictated, slapping Humphrey on his buttocks to get him going.

Moritz took the snap from center, faked a handoff to fullback Max Kelley, drifted back, and lobbed a pass to tailback Wayne Wash in the left flat. Wash gathered in the football and raced to Anson's twenty-five before Tiger linebacker Franklin Sims slammed him down.

A handoff to Humphrey gave us another first down at the twelve. Carries by Kelley and Wash moved the ball to the four before we ran out of downs. With fourth and two, we settled for a field goal try which Moritz almost missed, sailing the football just inside the left goal post.

Late in the game, utilizing short passes and the demon-like running of all-district fullback Kenneth Helms, Anson reached our twenty-nine, but a swarming defense, led by Dan Hamby, Bobby Bounds, F.A. Sosebee and Wayne Mitchell, halted the drive on fourth down.

Final score: Stamford 3, Anson 0.

In the final game of the regular season, Stamford mowed down Hamlin 20–0, but the victory over Anson virtually cinched a berth in the state playoffs.

◆　◆　◆

AFTER OUR STRONG SHOWING the previous year, expectations were extremely high. I worried my undefeated Bulldogs might be overconfident. Newspapers all across the state were heralding Childress quarterback LaNeal Castleberry as the state's number one field general. Mike Barren, the Bobcats leading ballcarrier, was also being touted for all-state honors. Childress appeared to be much stronger than the team we'd beaten in 1952. As my football team prepared to meet the Bobcats in our Thanksgiving Day bi-district showdown, I hoped my young men would pay close attention to the words of crooner Perry Como's popular tune, "Don't let the Stars Get in Your Eyes."

Coaches often worry too much. My pre-game anxiety was unnecessary. Three minutes deep in the game, lanky, crazy-legged Wayne Wash took the football on a delayed buck and raced seventy-two yards for our first touchdown. Wash's tally prompted a long scoring procession which included Moritz and Max Kelley. Buddy Gray completed the rout by slicing through a downtrodden, soundly-beaten Bobcat defense for two final touchdowns.

In their post game articles, Abilene sportswriters referred to Stamford's defense as a thing of beauty, giving special credit to ends, Bobby Bounds and Wayne Mitchell; tackles, Jimmy Terry and Don Walker; guards, Dan Hamby and Ernie Davis; and linebackers, Kelly Harrison and Bob Harrison for dropping an invincible curtain of iron around Childress' high-scoring offense.

Final score: Stamford 35, Childress 7.

◆　　◆　　◆

AFTER MY BULLDOGS defeated Childress, I began searching for a Phillips' game film. Phillips High School was ranked number one in the state, and I wanted my troops to be prepared for whatever the Blackhawks might try. After numerous phone calls without success, I contacted the football coach at Borger High School who had played Phillips earlier in the season. Borger's coach said he had the game film and agreed to let us watch it. Hastily, I arranged to meet him at his field house later that afternoon.

When my assistant coach, O.M. Isbell, and I arrived, the Borger coach was nowhere around. We located a pay telephone and tried to call him. No answer. We tried to call his assistant coach. No answer. Most likely, Borger's head coach had second thoughts and decided to disappear.

Disheartened, Coach Isbell and I returned to Borger's field house, hoping maybe the coach would show up. That's when we noticed the open ventilation window. The narrow window was about seven feet above ground level, but that was no hill for a couple of desperate football coaches. Coach Isbell hoisted me on his shoulders, and I shimmied through. Once inside, I checked to see if the coast was clear then hurried to the front door to let my assistant in.

We located the Phillips' film, set up Borger's projector, and sat there watching for several hours. We charted every play and every offensive and defensive formation the Blackhawks employed during their game against Borger. When we finished, I chalked a short note on the locker room blackboard informing Borger's coach we had been there and thanking him for allowing us to review his game film. At the bottom of the message, I signed my name.

◆　◆　◆

PHILLIPS WAS AN OIL COMPANY TOWN located about fifty miles northeast of Amarillo. The coach at Phillips High was Harold "Chesty" Walker. We played each other twice. Both times were in the state playoffs.

My undefeated Stamford team met Walker's Blackhawks at Lubbock Jones Stadium on a god-awful, bone-chilling Saturday afternoon in December. At game time a raw north wind was gusting at speeds up to sixty miles an hour. Simultaneously, both a dust storm and a snow storm had hit the Lubbock area. Even before we completed pre-game warmups my kids' helmets were splattered with globs of red mud.

Stamford was leading 7–0, courtesy of an Eldon Moritz quarterback sneak and his kick for the point after. In spite of the bad weather, my Bulldogs were playing great defense and seemed to be in complete control of the game. All that changed on a freak play which occurred in the third quarter.

Phillips' right guard Kenneth Irwin was obviously offside by a country mile when he lunged across the scrimmage line before the ball was snapped. Bulldog defenders were so convinced the game officials would call the play back, they hardly bothered to wave at fullback Larry Lane when he took the handoff and charged down-field. Not one single person screamed or yelled encouragement. Every fan in the stadium had seen Irwin jump offside, but despite the flagrant rule violation, not a flag was thrown. The play stood, and Phillips received a gratis touchdown to tie the score, courtesy of four lax officials.

Mad and upset, Stamford roared back. F.A. Sosebee returned Phillps' kickoff to our forty-seven. Four plays later Buddy Gray followed a clearing block by blue and white guard Lex Kelley and outran three Blackhawks to the right corner of the end zone to put us ahead again 14–7.

In 1953, Stamford was blessed with two excellent punters. Eldon Moritz was our number one kicker. His punts were low and long. Wayne Wash also had a strong leg. Wayne's punts were usually higher and not quite as long, but his booming kicks boasted an extended hang time, allowing Bulldog defenders more time to reach the opposition's return man.

Late in the third quarter a second weird play added to our frustration. Scratching and clawing for every yard, our offense battled its way to the forty-five before it ran out of gas. As our kicking team lined up to punt, Moritz approached Wash and asked if he would handle the next punt. Moritz had twisted a knee during the first half, and although he continued to play, Eldon was essentially operating on one leg.

When Wash kicked, the high flying football hung in the stiff wind and did an abrupt U-turn. Most of our players were downfield and looking back when Phillips' Billy White finally caught up with the ball eleven yards behind the line of scrimmage, fielded it at our thirty-four, and darted down the left sideline for a touchdown.

Phillips sophomore Larry Lane supplied the clincher with nine minutes left in the fourth period when he broke through the middle of our normally impenetrable defense and sped eighty-four yards for the game's final TD.

Final score: Stamford 14, Phillips 20.

◆　◆　◆

NOT ONE OF THE GAME OFFICIALS actually saw Phillips' Billy White field Wayne Wash's wind-blown punt. Every referee was running downfield with his back to the play. The game statistician that crazy afternoon was a Lubbock high school principal who was also a division-one football official. The statistician was right on top of the play. That winter I was speaking at a football banquet and ran into the man. Taking advantage of the rare opportunity, I asked him if Billy White stepped out of bounds after he fielded Wash's punt.

"Step out of bounds," the principal responded. "That kid ran ten yards before he got in bounds."

My bizarre loss to Chesty Walker and his Phillips Blackhawks on that cold, blustering winter day hurt me more than any I'd suffered up until that time.

◆   ◆   ◆

THE NEXT WEEKEND Phillips played Ballinger, a team Stamford had blasted 42–0 in a non-conference bout earlier in the season. Arche Pardue, a good friend and father of two members of my football squad, invited me to accompany him to Wichita Falls to watch the Phillips-Ballinger contest. Arche drove a long, sleek Cadillac, and he had plenty of money. He loved to bet on football games with one exception—Arche would never bet on Stamford, for fear of jinxing us.

During the trip Pardue asked my opinion about which team would win the quarterfinal game. He acted surprised when I replied, "Ballinger has the best team. I'd say they'll win by at least a couple of touchdowns."

"Come on, Coach! Be serious."

"I'm not kidding, Arche. It won't even be close. Ballinger is gonna win big."

"But look at the scores. Stamford beat Ballinger real bad, and we lost to Phillips."

"That don't mean a thing, Arche. I know what I'm talking about, and I'm telling you Ballinger is a much better ballclub."

After we arrived and parked the car, Arche disappeared. There's no telling how much money he bet that day. As I predicted, Ballinger won, and on the way home Arche was real quiet. We were somewhere between Haskell and Stamford when I realized his answers weren't coming out right. I began to suspect my rich friend had bet on Phillips.

"Arche, I hope you didn't do something foolish. You did bet on Ballinger like I said, didn't you?"

"Naw, Coach, I didn't take your advice. I went down there and bet on Phillips. Had to give seven points."

A short time later Arche dropped me off at my house. He started to drive away, then slammed on his brakes, rolled down his car window and threw me his overcoat. I'm sure he'd noticed the out-of-date, threadbare jacket I had on.

"Here, Coach, you take my coat. I lost all my money and my shirt. You might as well have my coat."

Arche drove off before I could object, but I accepted his gift gladly. That was the very best overcoat I ever owned in my entire life.

Ballinger advanced to the state finals before they were defeated by Huntsville 40–6.

◆　◆　◆

IN THE FIFTIES, most high school and college coaches thought weight lifting was bad for football players. If a player lifted weights, he'd get muscle bound and lose his agility.

Something I noticed, though, was several of my best athletes were into lifting weights, and it didn't seem to affect their ability to play. Matter of fact, they played much better with the added muscle. With this in mind, I initiated a weight program for my football players—possibly the only high school weight program in Texas at that time.

Since our athletic budget was limited, we constructed our own weights. One of Stamford's most avid football fans was a fellow named Jimmy Lee. Jimmy worked as a pumper for an oil company, and he could build anything.

For one lifting exercise, Jimmy helped me rig up a four-foot section of steel railroad track. For barbells, we used a steel pipe with five-gallon buckets filled with concrete attached to each end. On rainy or cold days, my football squad lifted weights, in addition to running laps in the school gymnasium.

1954

ANOTHER OF MY FAVORITES at Stamford was a likeable, hardworking young man named Charles Coody. Charles was a gifted athlete, and he participated in several sports—football, basketball and golf. He was as fast as a white-tailed deer and could have run track, but during the spring, Coody spent most of his free time on the Stamford golf course.

Charles was what I classify a sports workaholic. Every afternoon he went to the country club to work on his golf game, practicing his driving and his iron shots. Even as a teenager, Coody could hit a driver farther than most professional golfers. Charles

Stamford's 1954 state golf champs—
Bubba Markham, Charles Coody, Douglas Shamburger, Bobby Calhoun
(credit: 1955 Stamford High Yearbook)

would play eighteen holes, and when he finished, he stayed on the putting green until the grounds keeper turned out the lights.

Coody attacked basketball with the same dogged tenacity. When the weather was too nasty to play golf, Charles came to the school gym to shoot baskets. Many a night I chased him out with him begging me to let him, "take one more shot."

In the spring of 1954, I coached my second team to a state championship. This time it was in golf, not football. Actually, the young men on my golf team didn't require much coaching. My job was more like their tour guide and social director. I pretty much just went along for the ride—but, oh, what a remarkable ride. At the state meet in Austin, my golf squad posted a team total of 641, breaking the previous state record by two strokes and besting the second place AA school by thirty strokes. With Charles Coody leading the way, every member of Stamford's golfing party had their best outing of the season. Coody shot a 156. Bobby Calhoun shot a 160, Bubba Markham a 161, and Douglas Shamburger a 164.

Here's the strange part of this story. My first state crown was in track. My second was in golf. I wouldn't win a state championship in football until two years later.

◆　◆　◆

OUR DAUGHTER PATRICIA was eight and going on nine in the

summer of 1954. Although cotton prices had dropped back to thirty-two cents a pound, Stamford was enjoying a kind of post war prosperity. With cheap labor disappearing, more and more Jones County cotton farmers were investing in mechanical pickers to harvest their crops. Probably half the families in Stamford had purchased a television set, and in the frozen food sections of local grocery stores, a new product popped up—Swanson's TV dinners, the perfect meal for a coach who was never home on time for supper.

After church one Sunday in July, Katharine and I lingered to visit with a local doctor who told us about a home on Wells Street he had recently remodeled. The doctor said he'd be willing to sell if we were interested. Although we were fairly certain the house was beyond our means, Katharine and I went to look.

The doctor's renovated house was a lot nicer than our Cuba Street residence and much larger. Katharine particularly liked the spacious living room and den which were both fully carpeted. Three strategically-located window-mounted swamp coolers kept the temperature inside cool and comfortable.

What clinched the deal, though, was our daughter's approval. A detached garage at the back of the huge lot contained a small apartment with two sets of bunk beds and a half bath which immediately appealed to Pat's fancy. After we moved in, those rear quarters became Pat's private playhouse and the setting for numerous girl slumber parties.

The doctor sold me his house for ten thousand dollars which I financed with a loan from the VA. Our loan payments were less than a hundred dollars a month, but for months afterwards, Katharine and I fretted over the high house payments. Eventually, we realized the house payments wouldn't drive us into bankruptcy, and all three of us grew to love that wonderful house. It was far and away the finest place we had ever lived.

◆ ◆ ◆

BECAUSE OF OUR RECENT SUCCESS, Stamford High's football program was growing in numbers. In 1951, my first year at Stamford, our football squad consisted of forty boys, twenty-one on the varsity and nineteen on the "B" team. By 1954, seventy-six boys participated in football, twenty-six on the varsity, twenty-eight on the "B" squad and twenty-two on our freshman team.

During the off season, Bill Anderson, a graduate of Pepperdine, had been added to my coaching staff. Coach Anderson was hired to "ride herd" on the ninth graders and help with our scouting.

◆　◆　◆

ON AUGUST 31, 1954, Coach Paul "Bear" Bryant, whom Texas A&M lured from Kentucky to turn around a flailing football program, loaded one hundred and eleven naive Aggie football players onto two diesel-fueled busses and hauled them to a desolate, prison-like compound two miles outside Junction, Texas. There, at a hell-hole called the A&M Adjunct, amid the searing end-of-summer Texas heat and hidden from the prying eyes of school officials and newspaper reporters, Bryant forced his players to participate in possibly the most brutal, abusive football camp in history. Not only did he run off three fourths of his team and end the careers of many talented football players, Bryant also did more damage to the Texas coaching profession than any coach either before or since.

While Coach Bryant's thirsty young men practiced without water in one hundred and ten degree temperatures, fall football camp at Stamford was winding down. With twelve returning lettermen, our senior-laden blue and white warriors looked unbeatable.

Our opponents included the usual list of motley ruffians. With quarterback Charles Coody at the helm of a backfield which included stallions like Davis cousins, Ernie and Jody, my Bulldogs mowed through their schedule like a Minneapolis Moline Combine in a Panhandle wheat field. After breezing past Haskell 41–0 in the season opener, the Bulldogs trampled Coleman's Bluecats 48–12 and fought off a last-half rally to top Albany 40–19.

As always, our Ballinger contest was a knock-down, drag-out affair. An interception, which Stamford defensive halfback Ricky Giles returned to the Bearcats' thirty-eight, set up our only score of the first half. In the third quarter Ballinger bounced back, banging out sixty hard earned yards. Bearcat running back Grady Curry capped the Red and Black's scoring drive by bulling his way past Lonnie Bounds and Don West for the TD. Gary Ferguson booted the point after and Ballinger went ahead 7–6.

When Ballinger scored, it marked the first time Stamford had been behind all season. Our stay on the short end of the stick didn't last long.

After Ballinger's kickoff, Coody flipped the football to Jimmy Alexander on an end sweep. Stiff arming one red and black defender and out running two more, Alexander rambled forty-six yards to rack up Stamford's second touchdown. Coody missed on his second extra point try, leaving some doubt about the game's outcome, but Charles fixed that by commandeering a time-killing 73-yard march in the final period. With all-state center Bob Harrison leading the way, Coody called a quarterback keeper and crashed over right guard for the final three yards.

Ballinger manufactured another TD using a pass play from quarterback Maurice Carder to Ronald Maedgen in the final seconds, but their comeback bid arrived too late.

Final score: Stamford 19, Ballinger 14.

◆　◆　◆

EVEN BEFORE the football season was in full swing, sports-writers all across West Texas predicted District 4–AA would boil down to Stamford verses Colorado City, and they were right on target. While my hard-charging Bulldogs plowed through our schedule, defeating Quanah, Graham and Rotan, the Colorado Wolves never lost a step. Both teams were undefeated as our hour of truth came closer.

Prior to our meeting, neither Stamford nor Colorado City had even been seriously challenged. In seven games Colorado City's defense had allowed only thirty-two points.

◆　◆　◆

NO MATTER how good his material, an indecisive coach can cause his team to lose. It was my wishy-washy vacillation that caused Stamford to lose to Colorado City. The Wolves' best player was Hollis Gainey, a gutty, 145-pound streak of lighting who was all elbows and knees.

There's no disputing Colorado City coach Bob Reily had assembled a great football team, but Stamford was even better, absolutely loaded with talented players. No, my Bulldogs lost because I did a horrible job of coaching.

All week long, we worked on our aerial attack. Coach Isbell

and I kept telling our kids that Colorado City had a weak pass defense, and we could throw against them. Since Charles Coody was an excellent passer, we believed everything was in our favor.

Unbeknown to us coaches, things began to work against us even before the game got underway. Bob Harrison forgot to pack one of his cleated shoes, so he borrowed one from a reserve player. Bob wore a size twelve, but the shoe he borrowed was a size ten. Throughout the game our all-state center hobbled around like a cripple. We didn't discover the source of his problem until the following week.

While Coach Isbell ran our players through a set of pre-game drills, I made the mistake of walking down to the opposite end of the field to watch Colorado City warm up. For reasons I can't explain, I became convinced we should run the ball. So instead of sticking to the aerial offense we had practiced on all week, I changed my mind and instructed Coody to keep the ball on the ground.

After three quarters Stamford was down 20–0. My running strategy wasn't working. In desperation, I reverted back to our original game plan. Once Coody started passing, Stamford began to move the football. Beginning on our thirty, Coody hit Mike Wash over the middle for ten yards then connected with end Dallas Christian at the Wolves' forty-six. Faking a pass, Coody tucked the ball and skirted around left end to the forty-one. Ernie Davis snared a lob pass in the right flat and gained eleven before he was slammed to the turf at Colorado's thirty-yard line.

Our sudden offensive spurt surprised the Wolves, but with a twenty-point lead, they could afford to gamble. Abandoning their usual assignments, Colorado City's front line cocked their ears and charged straight for our quarterback on every snap. Grunts, groans, and the pungent smell of sweat permeated the cool night air as Bulldog linemen, Lex Kelley, Wayne Cox, Don West and Ray Gressett, met the bloodthirsty Wolves head on and held them at bay. Mike Wash grabbed another of Coody's bullets at the thirteen then snared one more at the seven. On the next play Jody Davis took Coody's handoff and dashed through a hole wide enough to accommodate a Mack Truck for the TD. Coody's extra point made the score 20–7.

Three minutes later, after Stamford regained possession of the football, tailback Ernie Davis slipped over left tackle and ran for sixty-seven twisting, fighting, breathtaking yards. A final clearing block by his cousin Jody Davis allowed Ernie to reach the end zone.

Stamford kicked off and held the Wolves on downs. Ernie Davis fielded their punt and returned it for another touchdown which would have given us the lead, but the play was called back. One of our players had run into the Colorado punter.

In the final seconds, Coody's passing lit up the stadium. In an amazing exhibition of aerial acrobatics, our golden-armed quarterback completed five straight passes before time ran out with Stamford at Colorado City's five-yard line. Our wild-eyed fans were so worked up they continued to scream long after the game ended.

The final score was 20–14.

If I'd stuck to my original plan, the game wouldn't have even been close. My '54 football team was the best in the state. An ambivalent coach and a couple of bad breaks probably cost Stamford a state championship. When a coach starts second-guessing himself, he should apply for a job selling cars.

◆ ◆ ◆

IN THE WEEKS THAT FOLLOWED, we took our frustrations out on Anson who was undefeated in conference play and tied with Colorado City at the top of District 4–AA. We crushed our Jones County rival 34–0. Then, realizing it was our last game of the season, we buried Hamlin's Pied Pipers 80–13.

Regardless how well we played at the end of the season, it was the loss to Colorado City that cost Stamford a berth in the playoffs. Sick at heart, knowing our team deserved better, we packed up our football uniforms and prepared for basketball season.

I didn't know then, but that game we lost to Colorado City would be the last time my Bulldogs tasted defeat for a long, long time.

◆ ◆ ◆

BOB HARRISON, an all-state center who anchored our Bulldog front line, exemplified the determination and quality of the young people I was privileged to coach at Stamford. While he was a ninth-grade student in Katharine's English class, Bob told my wife he was planning to become a great center like Clyde "Bulldog" Turner. Turner was an all-pro center for the Chicago Bears and my all-American teammate at Hardin-Simmons.

Stamford's 1954 co-captains, Bob Harrison and Ernie Davis.
(credit: 1955 Stamford High Yearbook)

Two summers before his senior year, Bob found himself a job working in a gravel pit in nearby Hamlin, Texas. The work was very strenuous and the temperature extremely hot. Not many grown men could handle pit duty for more than an hour at a time. Bob didn't mind, though. He was using the job to prepare himself for football. Every other hour, four hours a day, Bob was down there in the pit, delighted to do the job other men dreaded.

After work, Harrison drove straight to Stamford High where he climbed ropes, worked out with our homemade weights, and ran wind sprints. After he graduated from high school, Bob went to Oklahoma University where he played for Bud Wilkerson and was selected all-American. Harrison spent nine years in the NFL before he retired.

◆　◆　◆

STAMFORD'S BASKETBALL SQUAD won twenty-six and lost five during the '55 season, running the table to go undefeated in district play and capture a third straight conference championship. My varsity team consisted of ten players—Jimmy Alexander, Lonnie Bounds, Truman Childress, Dallas Christian, Charles

Coody, Doug Kendrick, Bob Harrison, Melvyn Stevenson, Mike Wash and Mack Zimmerman.

Stamford had already clinched district. We were scheduled to meet Childress in a bi-district encounter on Friday night. On Tuesday, my Bulldogs played Anson in our last district game. Mike Wash, a senior, was one of my best players—a good shooter and rail-tough under the boards. Near the end of the Anson game, Mike drove the lane for a lay up. At the top of his leap, an Anson player ran underneath Mike's legs and flipped him backward. Wash tried to recover, but he came down sideways and twisted his ankle. Mike's ankle wasn't broken, but he was hurt too bad to participate in our bi-district battle against Childress. To sub for the injured Wash, I used Lonnie Bounds.

On Friday evening, our gym was jam-packed with two thousand screaming, fanatical fans, and the game went right down to the wire. Stamford scored with only seconds to play to send the game into extra innings.

During the overtime period, the lead changed hands several times. As the tension mounted, the court play became more and more physical. Finally, the referees called a hacking foul on Mack Zimmerman which caused him to foul out. I sent in Bob Harrison to replace Zimmerman. Harrison played center on our football team and threw the discus on my track team. Bob was strong as a mule, a tremendous athlete, but not necessarily a great basketball player.

Less than a minute remained when Charles Coody stole the basketball and drove the length of the court for an easy lay up to put Stamford two points ahead. Everyone was screaming and hollering so loud you could hardly hear yourself think. I was yelling at my team to get back on defense when the game referee came to inform me he had called a foul on Bob Harrison. Getting caught up in the emotional excitement, Bob had knocked down a Bobcat player, sent him skidding across the floor, and then run over him.

Childress made both ends of the subsequent free throws and scored again before time ran out to nail down a 55–51 victory.

◆　◆　◆

IN THE SPRING of 1955, we graduated ten starters and fifteen seniors off our football team. Our one returning starter was Joe Wash, an offensive tackle.

The custom in those days was to have one coach in each district pick the pre-season favorites. Usually the coach whose team won the district title the year before was chosen to make the selections. My assistant coaches and I were attending coaching school in Dallas when the selections were announced. We were absolutely astounded when Colorado City coach Bob Reily picked Stamford to finish first.

Actually, Colorado City should have been picked first, Anson second and Stamford third. When pressed, Coach Reily went even further. He said Stamford was so strong we should go a long way in the playoffs.

A few days later, the *Abilene Reporter-News* came out with a story proclaiming Stamford was the odds-on favorite to win District 4–AA and could possibly contend for the state championship. When our Stamford kids read the story, they began to question us coaches, asking if we really believed they could win state. Of course, we didn't. The players we had coming up that year weren't even in the same class with my '54 team. Nevertheless, when I met with my assistant coaches a couple of days later, I had come up with an answer for our inquisitive young men.

"Every time one of our players asks if we can win state, you tell him, 'You darn right we can—if we work hard and play our best.'"

I can't explain why I told my assistants to say that. But you know what? Both my coaches and players began to believe we could . . . .

CHAPTER EIGHT

The Streak

(1955–1958)

ANOTHER EXAMPLE of the fine young men who played for me at Stamford is Charles Stenholm who presently serves as U.S. Congressman from Texas' 17th Congressional District. Charles' father was L.W. Stenholm, the Stamford school board president who told me no coach in America was worth forty-nine hundred dollars a year.

L.W. Stenholm was a Christian man who strongly believed success is achieved through hard work. He didn't necessarily oppose my sports program, but athletic competition wasn't at the top of his priority list either. Charlie Stenholm was the only player invited to my 1955 fall camp who wasn't at the football stadium every minute. His absence wasn't because of a bad attitude or lack of commitment. During the hours Charles wasn't actually practicing football, his dad had him working on their farm. While his teammates were resting their weary bones, Charles was milking cows, driving a tractor or hoeing cotton.

The Stenholms' strict parental guidance paid enormous dividends because they raised an exceptional son. Charles Stenholm lettered for me in three

Charles Stenholm, all-district football and all-district basketball. (credit: 1957 Stamford High Yearbook)

sports—football, basketball and track. In recognition of his dedication and football skills, Charles was named an all-district end his senior year. He also served as president of the Texas Future Farmers Organization and was a straight A student.

1955

IN FOUR YEARS at Stamford my football teams had lost four games, and yet we'd only been to the playoffs twice. Other coaches could lose two or three games and still go, but not Gordon Wood. Heck, in 1952, Morris Southall's Winters team went to the playoffs with a 6–3–1 record. One thing about Texas coaches, though— we're the dangdest optimists in the world.

Perhaps that's why I took such a shine to Larry Wartes when he applied for a coaching job at Stamford High School. I could tell he had a winning attitude the first time I met him. That was when I interviewed him in my office during the summer of '55.

Larry was a basketball star at Amarillo High School in 1948 when the Golden Sandies won the state championship. One of Wartes' teammates was Boone Pickens who later gained national notoriety as an oil and gas wheeler-dealer. After he finished high school, Larry attended Hardin-Simmons University. He was captain of the Cowboy basketball team his senior year.

During the '54–'55 school year, Wartes coached at Stanton, Texas, but he was looking for something better. After we talked, I was so impressed I insisted he meet with L.W. Johnson, Stamford's school superintendent. Superintendent Johnson was similarly affected by the young coach's credentials and charismatic personality. He gave me his blessing to hire Wartes.

I guided Larry through a grand tour of our athletic facilities and introduced him to John Dyer, the high school principal, and several other important people around town. We wound up at Stamford's municipal pool which I managed during the summer months. We had only been there a few minutes when Superintendent Johnson showed up. I'd been in charge of the city's swimming pool for four years, and this was the first time Johnson had ever dropped by. The superintendent asked Larry what he thought of our town then blurted out the real reason for his visit.

"Young man, don't you think it's time you signed a contract with us?"

Wartes was obviously stunned by our superintendent's blunt approach. Matter of fact, so was I. Nonetheless, Larry remained reluctant to commit. Since it was almost six o'clock, I closed the pool. We bid good-bye to Superintendent Johnson, and I drove Wartes out to the Cowboy Reunion rodeo grounds where his car was parked. Larry and his family were living in Abilene. He'd driven up to Stamford that morning.

"Okay, Coach Wartes. Shoot straight with me. What's keeping you from accepting the job here at Stamford?" I asked before he switched cars.

Turned out, Larry was worried about me. Wartes' coaching duties were to include taking over as head basketball coach. He knew how I loved basketball. I had coached Stamford's basketball teams to three consecutive district titles. Other coaches had warned him I'd be reluctant to let go, that I'd constantly be interfering with his basketball program.

"Look here, Larry. If you're concerned about me sticking my nose where it don't belong, then we only got one problem, and that's salary. If you'll be totally honest with me, I'll be totally honest with you. If we have a difference of opinion, we'll face the issue straight up. Nobody's gonna ask you to change just because we've been doing it some other way."

Wartes' other problem was with salary. He had applied for coaching positions at both Hamlin and Stamford. Hamlin had offered him thirty-eight hundred dollars a year verses thirty-six hundred dollars the Stamford job paid. I addressed his reservations in this manner:

"Larry, if you're into coaching for the money, then you need to get out right now. The least important thing about any coaching job is how much money you're paid. What will make a difference in how happy you are, though, is whether your teams have a chance to win. If you accept the Hamlin job, no team you coach will ever beat Stamford in football, basketball or track."

Wartes left telling me he needed time to think things over. He promised to give me a decision in a couple of days. When he reached Anson, which is about seventeen miles south of Stamford, Larry stopped and called me from a pay telephone. He advised me he had decided to accept our job.

Hiring Coach Wartes was one of the finest decisions I ever

made. Working with him definitely made me a better coach. His wife Joyce taught at Stamford, and she was a terrific teacher. Larry and Joyce were both extremely talented, great with our kids, and devout Christians. They personified my idea of the husband and wife partnership a man needs to succeed as a coach.

◆ ◆ ◆

ALTHOUGH CONGRESS RAISED the minimum wage to a dollar an hour in July of 1955, no coach in Texas made anywhere near that kind of salary during football season. Beginning with fall camp, which convened in mid-August, until late November when conference play ended, sixteen-hour days were the norm. If you wanted to win, that's what the job required. And almost fifty years later, it still does.

When I read that Sam Phillips of Sun Records sold Elvis Presley's recording contract to RCA for thirty-five thousand dollars, I was shocked. How could a fledgling teenage singer like Elvis be worth ten years of a coach's take home pay?

According to the *Abilene Reporter-News*, movies were making a comeback after several years of watching their audiences decline. Sidesplitting comedies like *Mister Roberts*, starring Henry Fonda, James Cagney and Jack Lemmon, and more serious dramas like *East of Eden*, starring James Dean, Julie Harris and Raymond Massey, were the reason.

Number one on the hit parade was "Cherry Pink and Apple Blossom White," but Katharine and I liked Mitch Miller's "Yellow Rose of Texas." Naturally, the boys on my football squad thought no song could match Bill Haley's "Rock Around the Clock," and that's how my fifth season at Stamford began. While Rocky Marciano was training for his September heavyweight bout with Archie Moore at Yankee Stadium, my Bulldogs were rocking and rolling out in West Texas.

We opened the season by scalping Haskell's Indians 21–7 then returned home where we saddled Andrews' Mustangs and rode them hard 19–7. A week later Mike McClellan and Donald Wills took turns stomping on AAA Sweetwater, gaining a total of 280 yards as they crashed through gigantic holes opened up by Joe Wash, Ronald Davis and Royce West. Gathering steam, we kept on rolling, stinging

Stephenville's Yellowjackets 34–0, hooking the Coleman Bluecats 41–6, and streaking past Handley's Greyhounds 41–0.

◆   ◆   ◆

WHEN THE '55 SEASON began, we had already decided Melvyn Stevenson would be our starter at running back. Melvyn was a junior who had lettered and contributed to our success the previous season. He was a tremendous athlete with good speed and sure hands. Another junior named Mike McClellan, who played on the "B" squad in 1954, would most likely be Stevenson's backup.

McClellan also had excellent speed. His sophomore year, Mike won both the 100- and 220-yard dash events in the district meet, but we coaches were suspicious of his football ability. Seemed like every time McClellan touched the football something bad happened. He either missed the designated hole or dropped the ball.

It was during a pre-season scrimmage with Breckenridge we began to suspect McClellan was more than a jet-propelled skinny kid with a pealed head. Late in the second period we subbed Mike in for a series of downs, and he immediately broke for two long

Mike McClellan rambles for a 60-yard touchdown against Burkburnett in a 1955 bi-district game. (credit: 1956 Stamford High Yearbook)

runs. My assistant coaches and I shook our heads in disbelief, but inside we were smiling.

Stamford opened the regular season with Haskell. The Indians had a fine team, and at the half the score was tied. Twice in the first half we were driving for a score, and McClellan fumbled. After he bobbled the second handoff and lost it, my temper thermometer exploded past the boiling point. I sent in another player to replace our feeble-fingered rocket, barely able to control myself as I waited for him at the sideline.

"Son, you're killing us! You've already cost us two touchdowns," I said, grabbing Mike by the shoulder pads and turning him so we were eyeball to eyeball.

"Gosh, Coach Wood, I know it, and I'm sorry. But if you'll leave me in the game, I promise I won't fumble again."

McClellan's terrified expression and his positive response softened my anger.

"Okay, son, I'm gonna hold you to that. I'm gonna send you back in, but if you screw up again, you'll be warming the bench for the rest of the season."

In the second half Mike kept his promise. He didn't fumble again, and he ran for two long gains which set up touchdowns.

It was during the Haskell game we coaches became convinced Mike was something extra special, and we started alternating him regularly with Stevenson at running back. Several games later Stevenson tore up a knee, and McClellan became our full time starter. The rest is history. Mike McClellan was named all-state in both 1955 and 1956. He was the most explosive ballcarrier who ever played for me.

◆　◆　◆

DESPITE MORE THAN a thousand reported UFO sightings, Air Force Secretary Donald Quarles proclaimed in October of 1955, that no flying saucers had ever flown over the United States. His statement was based on an in-depth summary prepared by his department. Nevertheless, West Texans continued to believe in science fiction phenomenon. In Odessa, weird lights and strange objects were observed above the night skies. In Levelland, unidentified flying objects were alleged to have stalled numerous car motors.

Perhaps the Air Force overlooked my high flying Bulldogs

who were sailing through our conference schedule. Rotan was certainly no trouble. We bopped the Yellowhammers 26–6. Colorado City held out for a while, but a sixty-yard punt return by Ricky Giles broke their back. When Anson's Tigers came to visit, we twisted their tails 44–6.

No one paid much attention to the winning streak until we mauled Hamlin 26–6 in our conference final, but after Stamford whipped up on Burkburnett in a Thanksgiving Day bi-district game, the implications began to sink in.

Thirteen in a row. It was the longest winning streak in Stamford history, but with Chesty Walker and his mighty Phillips Blackhawks blocking the way, Bulldog boosters were worried the coffee shop talk about Stamford being jinxed in the playoffs might be right.

◆ ◆ ◆

CHESTY WALKER coached at Phillips for eighteen seasons, 1939 through 1956. During that time his Blackhawks won one hundred and seventy-two games, lost twenty-three, and tied eight. Three times his teams finished the season undefeated, but because no state champion was declared for small schools in many of those years, Walker only claimed one state championship. That was in 1954, the season before our teams clashed for a second time in the playoffs.

Some statisticians discard Chesty's amazing coaching accomplishments, alleging he enjoyed a built-in recruiting system because of his school's connection with Phillips Oil Company. There's some truth to those allegations. Every football player at Phillips High School was in some way financially connected to the giant oil company which headquartered in Bartlesville, Oklahoma. If Chesty's team needed a skilled player, a Phillips' employee suddenly found himself transferred to Texas. Naturally, the employee brought along his teenage son.

No matter how he obtained his players, in my opinion, Chesty Walker was one of the best coaches I ever competed against. Walker was not only an astute coach, he was an exceptionally good man.

After the '56 football season, Chesty left Phillips to become a member of Coach Paul "Bear" Bryant's staff at Texas A&M. Then he joined Coach Jim Owens at the University of Washington and played a major role in the Huskies' 1960 and 1961 Rose Bowl Championships.

◆　◆　◆

THE DEFENDING STATE CHAMPS were working on a streak of their own when our teams met in Childress. Since Phillips lost to Ballinger in the 1953 quarterfinals, they had gone twenty-six games without losing, a 20–20 tie with Dumas being the only blemish to their record. During the '55 season, Walker's Blackhawks piled up 534 points in eleven games, but on that bright, sunny December afternoon, the roughnecks who terrorized the Texas High Plains would come no closer to Stamford's goal line than the 32-yard line, and that would be on a fruitless drive late in the fourth quarter.

All season long we'd been pointing for a showdown with Phillips. The Blackhawks were defending state champs, and I was absolutely certain Stamford's playoff trail would lead to a last-man-standing bout with Chesty Walker. Each Monday I'd have my offense spend half an hour working against a mock Phillips' defense. I had also devised a unique 5–4–2 defense to stop Walker's powerful running attack. I called the unusual defense "The Phillips 5."

◆　◆　◆

FOR MUCH OF THE FIRST QUARTER the two teams felt each other out, playing conservative, both coaches holding their cards close, each hoping the other would make some mistake.

Neither team had made a first down when Phillips' punter Stanley Wilder kicked the ball out of bounds on Stamford's thirty-six. That's where my rabbit-quick Bulldog backfield went into action. On first down Don Wills banged through the stubborn Blackhawk defense to the forty-one. Quarterback Jack Mills sneaked to the forty-nine. Then Wills and Mike McClellan took turns blasting over Phillips' tacklers to gain a first down at the Blackhawks' seventeen.

On first down, Stamford surprised Phillips' defenders by passing. Mills faded back and fired a line drive to end Truman Childress. Childress outjumped a Blackhawk defensive halfback to snag the pass and tumbled into the end zone. Melvyn Stevenson kicked the extra point, and Stamford had all the points we would need for victory.

University of Texas coach Darrell Royal once said, "Luck is

where preparation meets opportunity." Possibly that describes how we scored our second touchdown, but most likely it was simply a "fluke" play.

Late in the second quarter our running game bogged down, so Jackie Mills called a pass. This particular passing play called for Stamford end Dallas Christian to run straight at the Blackhawk defensive halfback and cut across the middle. The pattern was designed to open up Mike McClellan who was trailing behind Christian.

McClellan was wide open, but Mills threw to our other end, and the pass went incomplete. I subbed in Don Martin, with instructions for Mills to call the exact same play again.

Phillips' defensive halfback was a boy named Jolly, and he was darn smart. He saw what we were doing, and he wasn't fooled the second time. Instead of following our end, he stuck with McClellan. Mills, our quarterback, wasn't a strong passer. His throw was at least ten yards short. Jolly was in perfect position to make the interception, but when he charged toward the football, he tipped it up and the ball bounced behind him. McClellan, who was scrambling back fast, grabbed the football, whirled around, and dashed forty-one yards for a touchdown.

Pass interceptions by Donald Wills and Mike McClellan and a fumble recovery by T.C. Rice contributed to Stamford's victory, but it was stouthearted defensive play which clipped the Blackhawks' wings. Our tightwad defense yielded only ninety yards to Phillips' high-octane offense. Blackhawk quarterback Stanley Wilder attempted seven passes, but with Bulldog rushers in his face on every play, he completed only two for a total of five yards.

Abilene reporters were so impressed by Stamford's defensive unit that they named this *Roll of Honor* in Sunday's game report—ends, Truman Childress and Dallas Christian; tackles, Joe Wash, Dale Robinson and Royce West; guards, Milton Hinze, Tommy Schoonmaker, Ronnie Davis and T.C. Rice; center, Arche Pardue; secondary, Donald Wills, Mike McClellan, Ricky Giles and Nickey Jackson.

Final score: Stamford 13, Phillips 0.

Our victory celebration didn't last long. After the game we discovered our next opponent would be Breckenridge, the defending AAA state champions. Breckenridge had been moved back to AA for the '55 season.

Later that afternoon when we couldn't agree on a mutual site,

Stamford High principal John Dyer flipped a coin. Breckenridge coach Emory Bellard was all smiles when Richard Wood, a member of the Breckenridge School Board, called it right. Our road to the championship wouldn't be easy. Breckenridge never lost at home.

◆　◆　◆

FROM 1951 THROUGH 1959, Breckenridge struck the mother lode, winning four state championships outright and sharing a fifth with Cleburne in 1959. The fifties were the glory years for the county seat of Stephens County which boasted a population of sixty-five hundred and a football stadium which seated eight thousand. Oil rich high rollers and wealthy ranchers bankrolled at least a part of the green team's success. In Breckenridge, good jobs were readily available for men whose sons possessed extraordinary football skills.

Occasionally, Breckenridge recruiting got a little out of hand. One story I heard was about a Shackleford County farmer who refused to move to Breckenridge so his muscular son could play football for the Buckaroos. While the farmer and his family were away visiting relatives one weekend, someone jacked up their house and moved it into Breckenridge.

◆　◆　◆

IN 1955, BENNETT WATTS, the Bucks' field general, was without question the best quarterback in Texas. I was sharing a noon meal with the Pardue family a few days prior to our game with Breckenridge when Watts' name was mentioned. Arche Pardue, Sr. was the gambling friend who gave me his overcoat back in 1952.

Arche Pardue, Jr. played center for my ballclub, taking over the starting job when projected starter Douglas Monzingo went down with a knee injury. After the '55 season, Arche, Jr. would be selected all-district.

When Arche, Sr. casually remarked he wished we had Bennett Watts on our team, Arche, Jr.'s hair stood straight up.

"Your wrong, Dad! We don't need Bennett Watts because we've got Jack Mills! Jackie can run circles around a fruitcake like Bennett Watts any day of the week!" Arche, Jr. was so upset he eventually left the table without taking another bite.

Embarrassed by his son's outburst, Arche, Sr. turned to me, grinning sheepishly, "I guess I won't make a mistake like that again."

Stamford's 1955 Co-Captains Jack Mills and Joe Wash.
(credit: 1956 Stamford High Yearbook)

Jackie Mills was more grit than flash, not nearly as talented as Bennett Watts, but that didn't make one iota of difference to Jack's teammates. They believed in Mills the same way they believed in every other man on our football squad. As far as my Bulldog players were concerned, our lowly reserves were better than the best players on other teams.

At Stamford and at Brownwood my players and coaches believed in one another. At both schools I posted a sign above the locker room doorway which read:

> *Players believe in players.*
> *Coaches believe in coaches.*
> *Players believe in coaches.*
> *Coaches believe in players.*

And that's why we won.

◆ ◆ ◆

A STANDING ROOM ONLY CROWD of more than eight thousand fans congregated inside Buckaroo Stadium to watch my blue and white Bulldogs face off against the green-clad warriors of Breckenridge. Green helmets, green jerseys, green pants—no football team in Texas wore more terrifying uniforms than the Buckaroos. Visiting teams often complained about playing Breckenridge at home because of the intimidation. Visiting coaches said when their kids emerged from the locker room, every grandstand spectator would be on their feet screaming and yelling. The crowd noise would almost knock you to your knees. Then they'd look down at the opposite end of the field and see those humongous players in those green uniforms, and their out-of-town boys would go stone cold.

Breckenridge seldom lost on their home turf, even when they went up against schools like Wichita Falls and Abilene—cities ten times the size of Breckenridge.

◆ ◆ ◆

FROM THE OPENING KICKOFF until the final second ticked off the clock, many fans never sat down as two determined football teams bashed heads. Neither team was having much success against the other until a mix-up in the Buckaroo defense gave Stamford the first break. Fleet-footed Mike McClellan took full advantage, slipping through a narrow seam to dash seventy-three yards for an opening quarter TD.

For the remainder of the half, our fired-up Bulldogs controlled the line of scrimmage, outplaying and outmanning the Buckies. At the half, Stamford was clinging to a slim 6–0 lead.

Midway through the third quarter we stretched our lead to 13–0 when Jackie Mills threw a perfect 23-yard strike to Donald Wills. A thirteen-point advantage when you're playing on Buckaroo turf doesn't necessarily mean you're winning, though. Breckenridge proved that by taking our kickoff and pounding the football sixty yards into Stamford's red zone, pulling to within six points with a twenty-yard Bennett Watt toss to wingback Jerry Payne.

After banging away at each other for almost four quarters, one play finally decided the winner. Using head-knocking, ball-control football, Breckenridge had methodically rammed the ball down to Stamford's seven-yard line. When Watts tried to score on a keeper play, Bulldog defensive end Don Martin cut him off and grabbed the football out of Watts' hands just as Mike McClellan delivered a jarring tackle. The Buckie quarterback was so rattled by McClellan's hard blow that he came to our Stamford bench when he ran off the playing field. I met the groggy Buckaroo signal caller at the sideline, turned him around and headed him back in the direction of the Breckenridge bench.

Final score: Stamford 13, Breckenridge 6.

◆　◆　◆

THE FOLLOWING SATURDAY we traveled to Arlington to meet New London in the state semifinals. After beating Breckenridge on their home field, our players and coaches figured we were the best football team in the world. Boy, were we in for a surprise.

Back in 1937, an explosion at the New London school killed three hundred students and teachers. It was one of the worst disasters in Texas history. In 1955, though, New London's mind was on football. Their football team was undefeated, and holy mackerel, their players were simply awesome. The Wildcats were coached by John Ramseur whom I would later hire to coach with me in Victoria.

At halftime our cupboard was bare. Stamford was trailing 12–0. It was the first time all season we'd been behind in a game. While my stunned gridiron gladiators headed to our locker room, New London fans were so sure they would win they were already celebrating.

Inside our dressing room, while the clatter of nervous cleats echoed off the concrete walls, I surveyed the grim faces of my young men, trying to think of what I might say to prod them to play better. Facing the same situation, another coach might have chewed his team up one side and down the other, but I'd come a long way with these kids. Every man on my squad wanted to win just as much as I did. Griping them out wasn't what they needed. What they needed was to know I still believed in them. My halftime speech was short. Here's what I said:

"Okay, listen up! We're getting beat because we're making too many mistakes." I paused to let that thought sink in before I continued, "Coach Isbell and I are gonna point out the mistakes you're making and explain how to correct them. Then I want you to go out there the second half and play like the champions I know you are."

And that's what they did. Donald Wills got us started on the long road back. After Dallas Christian returned the second half kickoff to our forty-three, Wills carried the ball three consecutive times, scampering thirty-three yards to score on his third try. Two series later, after setting up the play with a long incomplete pass, Mike McClellan took the handoff from Mills on a delayed draw up the middle for sixty-two yards and our second touchdown.

After our defense stopped a fourth quarter New London drive at Stamford's forty-eight, we began a game-clinching, time-consuming touchdown drive. Our 170-pound pile driver fullback Donald Wills personally guaranteed victory by ripping off the last 14 yards with a bruising run over left tackle. At the ten-yard line, Wills collided with a Wildcat linebacker, bounced off, and staggered into the end zone.

Ricky Giles averaged forty-five yards on four kicks. His long punts and the stouthearted defensive play of Truman Childress, Royce West and Don Martin were the keys to shutting down New London's steam roller offense.

Final score: Stamford 20, New London 12.

Minutes after he scored his dramatic touchdown, we discovered Donald Wills had broken his collarbone when he banged into the New London linebacker. My Bulldogs were headed for the AA finals, but without our magnum load fullback, the road to the championship had now become an even more challenging test for Stamford's pigskin soldiers.

◆ ◆ ◆

WHEN AN ASSISTANT COACH at nearby Ennis heard Hillsboro coach P.T. Galiga might shift his three-year, 185-pound all-district guard Merlin Priddy to the backfield, the coach wiped his brow and exhaled loudly, "So they finally figured it out. We've been shaking in our boots for three years wondering when they'd get around to it. I suppose that decides who'll win this district."

Priddy started out slow, but by season's end, he was a ball of fire. In four playoff games, Merlin gained 710 rushing yards. After Hillsboro beat Weslaco to advance to the state finals, Weslaco fullback Billy Russell could only shake his head in humble amazement.

"Priddy killed us. I tried to tackle him on a kickoff return, and he almost knocked my head off."

When Stamford principal John Dyer correctly called the coin toss, we elected to decide the state championship at Fair Park Stadium in Abilene. Since Christmas fell on a Sunday and neither team wanted to play on Christmas Eve, we made the unusual decision to play the game on Monday, December 26. Merlin Priddy and the soaring Hillsboro Eagles were next on our list.

◆　◆　◆

HALF AN HOUR before the biggest game in Stamford history, Fair Park Stadium was packed to capacity. Abilene coach Chuck Moser and Phillips coach Chesty Walker were standing near the visitors' dressing room when Hillsboro coach Pug Galiga emerged and stepped over to say hello. After they shook hands, Coach Moser asked Galiga what he thought of Stamford's offense.

"I don't think they'll give us much trouble. We've beat teams a lot better than Stamford," Galiga replied.

"What about Mike McClellan? How do you plan to stop him?" Moser asked.

"Oh, McClellan's got a little speed, but he's not nearly as good as the papers say he is. We've played a bunch of teams with backs better than him."

After Pug walked away, Chesty turned to Moser and chuckled, "You know what, Chuck. That man is in for a rude awakening."

◆　◆　◆

INJURIES USUALLY play an important role in every championship run. Injuries are something a coach can't control—the kind of thing that drive coaches nuts and turn our hair white at an early age. So when Joe Wash, our all-state tackle, went down with a knee injury early in the second quarter, my heart sank.

My concern was short-lived, because when assistant coach Larry Wartes, student trainer Raymond Olson and I dashed onto the field to check on our gargantuan lineman, a huge smile was scrawled across Joe's face.

"We got it won, don't we, Coach Wood?" Wash grinned and

nodded toward the scoreboard which displayed the surprising score: Stamford 20, Hillsboro 0.

Joe was right. Three first quarter fumbles had tarred the Warbirds' feathers. One of the fumbles had been recovered by Wash, the other two by T.C. Rice. Wash had to be helped from the field, but his injury wasn't serious. Before the game ended, Joe was begging me to send him back in.

Eleven thousand spectators watched Stamford score twice more in the second half while Hillsboro continued to sputter and cough up the football. In the final analysis, though, it was Stamford's defense which chilled the Eagles and warmed the hearts of blue and white faithful. Mike McClellan, the game's leading ground gainer, would finish with 107 yards in fifteen attempts. With Melvyn Stevenson and Don Campbell filling in for an injured Don Wills, our offense never missed a lick. Ends, Truman Childress and Don Martin; tackles, Dale Robinson and Royce West; guards, Tommy Schoonmaker and Ronald Davis; center, Arche Pardue; and defensive backs, Ricky Giles and Nickey Jackson all did yeoman duty in shutting down the Eagles' attack. Stamford's defense

Gordon and Katharine with game ball after Stamford captured 1955 state championship.
(credit: Abilene Reporter News)

limited Hillsboro fullback Merlin Priddy to fifty-three yards on seventeen carries.

Final score: Stamford 34, Hillsboro 7.

Less than an hour after my Bulldogs captured the first state football crown in Stamford history, a huge sign appeared alongside State Highway 277, a mile south of Stamford. The sign read:

STAMFORD
HOME OF THE STATE AA FOOTBALL CHAMPIONS
1955

◆ ◆ ◆

IN JANUARY, the Texas Sportswriters Association honored me by selecting me as "High School Football Coach of the Year." More than four hundred people attended the achievement dinner in Dallas where I accepted my award along with G.E. Hastings of Avoca, "High School Basketball Coach of the Year," Tommy Duncan of Paris, "High School Baseball Coach of the Year," and Beverly Rockhold, "High School Track Coach of the Year." Blackie Sherrod, who was then a sportswriter for the *Fort Worth Star-Telegram*, presented the awards. Every recipient was expected to say something when he accepted his award. Some of the coaches were long-winded, but my acceptance speech was rather short. After Blackie handed me my award, I leaned forward to speak into the podium microphone and said:

"From now on, I reckon I'll appreciate you sportswriters a whole lot more."

I've never cared much for long speeches or long sermons.

◆ ◆ ◆

IN 1956, JONES COUNTY found itself gripped in the jaws of the worst drought since 1917. Cotton stalks withered and died in the sun-scorched fields. Farm ponds turned into dried-up mud puddles. Cattle sold at the lowest prices since the Great Depression. Fort Phantom Lake, Abilene's major source of drinking water and which is located in the southeast corner of Jones County, shrunk so low a man could wade across without getting his shirt wet. On Sundays, every church prayer included a humble request for rain.

For all of 1956, only 1.76 inches of rain fell on Wink, Texas.

That record still stands as the least annual rainfall ever recorded at any Texas rain station. Before the severe drought ended in the spring of 1957, more than two hundred and forty Texas counties were declared national disaster areas.

The first week in April a choking sand storm smothered Stamford and all of West Texas, blocking out the sun and causing street lights to flick on in the middle of the day. With people seeking refuge by staying home, business in downtown Stamford came to a standstill. In Odessa and Midland, high winds accompanied the suffocating squall. When the brutal, breathtaking blow finally let up, broken glass from shattered windows littered the two cities' business district sidewalks.

During the long, blistering hot summer, one dust storm after another rumbled through West Texas. Even our annual August football camp was briefly suspended by gusting winds, but with the nucleus of a state championship team returning and seventeen straight wins under our belt, team spirit remained at an all time high. Our line was big and tough. Our backs were lightning quick. My dogs were ready to rumble—Stamford style.

1956

FOR FIVE CONSECUTIVE years, Stamford opened the football season by whipping up on the Haskell Indians, but shortly after the '55 season ended, the Texas Interscholastic League slapped Haskell with a one-year suspension. Substituting Quanah's Indians for Haskell's Indians yielded similar results—a 46–12 Bulldog victory. Ballinger and Andrews fared no better. Stamford's win-streak had reached twenty when we journeyed to Sweetwater to face Coach Elwood Turner and his AAA Mustangs.

◆　◆　◆

AFTER THE OPENING KICKOFF, Stamford moved the football sixty-five yards down to Sweetwater's ten where a determined red and white defense stiffened and stopped us cold. Then the Mustangs retaliated with a long drive of their own. A fumble at Stamford's twenty-six killed Sweetwater's scoring opportunity.

Early in the second quarter a pair of keepers by Bulldog quarterback Nickey Jackson and a six-yard gain by Mike McClellan provided the springboard for Stamford's only score. On first and ten, Jackson backpedaled and launched a long bomb to six-foot-four Dallas Christian. Christian was wrestled to the ground by Mustang defender John Bryant at the thirteen. Three plunges by Kenneth Ivy at the interior of Sweetwater's defensive line pushed the ball to the Mustang ten. On fourth down McClelland circled wide around left end and outran a lonely red and white halfback to the corner of the end zone. Christian's extra point kick was straight and true. At the half, Stamford led 7–0.

Sweetwater opened the second half by taking the kickoff and marching sixty-one yards to score in nine plays. Their drive was climaxed by a six-yard off-tackle slant by Mustang halfback Donnie McNeal. McNeal banged across Stamford's goal line with three blue and white tacklers hanging on to his jersey. On the point-after try, hard charging Bulldog linemen, Dale Robinson and Royce West, shoved Sweetwater blockers into place kicker Jimmy Feagan's line of fire, causing his extra point shot to ricochet back into the Mustang ball holder.

When the final second ticked off the scoreboard clock, Sweetwater had outgained Stamford 222 yards to 183. They also led in first downs fourteen to twelve, but Stamford was still clinging to a 7–6 lead.

Sweetwater would get their revenge a year later, and their heart-breaking vindication would set in motion a chain of events which changed my life.

◆　◆　◆

STAMFORD'S VICTORY STRING continued as the Bulldogs skinned Coleman's Bluecats 40–6 and rode the windswept coat tails of jet-propelled Mike McClellan, who rushed for 173 yards on nineteen carries, to win a 19–7 slugfest with Brownwood. A week later Nickey Jackson fielded Anson's opening kickoff and lateraled to McClellan, who streaked eighty yards past surprised Tiger defenders for a TD. Before the game ended, five different Bulldog ballcarriers stomped across the Red and Black's sacred stripe as Stamford crushed Anson 40–0.

In late October, after Yankee hurler Don Larsen pitched the first ever perfect game in a World Series to beat the Dodgers 2–0, a hot new song was climbing the charts. The singer was a brash teenager with sideburns and long, greasy hair who had performed at a high school assembly in Midland only a year earlier. The song was "Heartbreak Hotel," and the young man was Elvis Presley. I thought Elvis was some kind of hillbilly beatnik who needed a haircut, but Katharine and Pat thought he was cute.

While Elvis was trying to subdue his quivering pelvis so he could appear on Ed Sullivan's Sunday evening television show, my Bulldogs were also on tour, getting in a few hot licks and breaking hearts all across West Texas.

Midway through the third quarter of our Nacona game, I was so embarrassed by the scoreboard numbers I sent my starters to the showers. My benevolence didn't help much, because our Bulldog reserves managed to score twice more before the game ended.

Final score: Stamford 60, Nacona 12.

Realizing I was coaching a monster I couldn't control, the next week I collared my starters and went to my bench early.

Final score: Stamford 26, Hamlin 6.

◆　◆　◆

AN INTERSCHOLASTIC LEAGUE realignment after the '55 football season moved Colorado City up to District 3–AAA to join Sweetwater and Lamesa and brought Seymour's Panthers into the District 4–AA fold. Colorado City always fielded competitive, tough-to-beat football teams, but replacing the Wolves with Seymour wasn't necessarily good news for Stamford or for other 4–AA old timers. In 1955, Seymour and Burkburnett shared the 3–AA title. Burkburnett gained the playoffs only by the toss of a coin. With twenty-four letterman and eight regulars returning, Texas sportswriters picked Seymour to be nipping at Stamford's heels all the way to the 4–AA finish line.

As things turned out, the Panthers were easy pickings for my revved-up Bulldogs. Stamford cashed in on four Seymour fumbles for four touchdowns.

Final score: Stamford 47, Seymour 0.

Stamford's twenty-seventh consecutive victory surpassed the streak of twenty-six straight by Phillips, a string which had ended with the Blackhawks' loss to Stamford in the '55 playoffs. That same weekend another high school located forty miles south of Stamford crushed San Angelo 20–0 to log their thirty-third consecutive win.

The Streak

◆　◆　◆

AFTER THREE PLAYOFF visits in two years, Bulldog fans didn't need a road map to find Childress. They knew the way by heart. On two consecutive weekends, three thousand Stamford citizens endured the 135-mile, two-lane voyage to support their beloved Bulldogs, and they weren't disappointed.

The first weekend, we humbled Perryton's Rangers. After a two-week layoff, our guys looked a little rusty. A 29-yard pass to towering end Dallas Christian netted our only touchdown of the first half and at intermission we were leading by a meager six points.

Midway through the third, Perryton mounted a serious threat. Driving from their own twenty down to Stamford's thirty-three, the Rangers appeared to be on their way to knot the score. If Perryton had stuck to their running game, they might have, but instead they elected to get tricky.

Ranger quarterback Del Ray Munts took the snap, faked a pitchout, then whirled and fired a jump pass to his right end. Problem was, the red and white right end was lying on his backside. Mike McClellan was there instead. McClellan gathered in the wobbly pass and headed left. When he reached the sideline, he flipped on his after-burners, leaving would-be tacklers grabbing at thin air. Eighty yards downfield our fleet-footed sprinter sailed into the end zone, and Perryton's spirit was broken.

Final score: Stamford 27, Perryton 0.

The following Friday we returned to Childress to face Canyon's Eagles. In the first half our defense limited Canyon to ten yards total offense and no first downs. Leading 34–0 at the midway point, I cleared our bench, saving our starters for more crucial battle duty. Darryl Schoonmaker, our second-string quarterback, logged more minutes than Nickey Jackson, our starter. Every man on my football squad saw plenty of action. Larry Denson, a running back we moved up from the "B" team and who wasn't expected to play, scored our final touchdown.

Final score: Stamford 48, Canyon 12.

On a foggy December Friday night at San Angelo's Bobcat Stadium, Stamford got off to a slow start against Crane. After struggling early in the game, our offense finally cranked up and came to life on its third possession. Starting from their own twenty-two, my

Bulldogs began to roll. McClellan ripped off eleven yards. Ivy added seven. Jackson hit Dallas Christian with an aerial bullet for twenty more. Stamford's 78-yard scoring drive culminated when Jackson lobbed a 12-yard jump pass to Christian in the end zone.

From that point the game was no contest. A rigid defense, led by T.C. Rice, Royce West and Donald Davis, held the Golden Cranes to nineteen yards on the ground and a total of four first downs while Stamford backs Ken Ivy, Larry Ivy, Mike McClellan, and Stanley Hill ran wild.

Final score: Stamford 39, Crane 6.

◆ ◆ ◆

IN 1957 AND 1958, Terrell's Tigers reeled off a winning streak of twenty-seven games. That string might have been several games longer had they not encountered a crew of not-to-be-denied Bulldogs at Dallas Dal-Hi Stadium in mid-December of 1956.

Coach Leon Vineyard's offense relied mostly on a 185-pound keg of dynamite named Bill Flowers. Flowers had scored nine touchdowns in Terrell's three playoff contests. The Tigers' stingy defense, bulwarked by 160-pound center Bill Marshall, had allowed only thirty-one points since they lost to Ennis in the fifth game of the season.

Gang-tackles and fierce head butting governed game action for most of the first stanza with Dale Robinson, T.C. Rice and Royce West usually being the last men to climb from underneath the pile.

A Tiger fumble set up our first display of real fire power. Gaining possession at Terrell's twenty-seven, Ivy and McClellan took turns pounding the ball to the five. From there McClellan squirted off right tackle for the TD. Duane Lindsey booted the point after.

Following our kickoff, Terrell attempted to run end sweeps, but that strategy died a quick death. Time after time, Stamford defensive ends Charlie Stenholm and Dallas Christian brushed away waves of red and white blockers so linebackers Larry Ivy and Donald Davis could make the tackle.

After McClellan returned a Terrell punt to Stamford's forty-five, our Bulldog offense shifted into high gear. Fullback Stanley Hill slashed over left tackle for eighteen. McClellan danced around right end for nineteen. Jackson rifled a strike to Stenholm in the left

Stamford's 1956 tri-captains, Dallas Christian, Mike McClellan, Dale Robinson. (credit: 1957 Stamford High Yearbook)

flat for three then hit Christian over the middle for seven. Hill banged down to the two to gain the first down, but there an embarrassed Tiger defense stiffened. On fourth down with 4:10 left in the half, McClellan dived over right tackle for our second TD.

Stamford scored again after Larry Ivy recovered a fumbled pass reception by Terrell end, John Keller. At the intermission, the score was 20–0, and Terrell was beat. Most of the second half, we played second-stringers.

Final score: Stamford 39, Terrell 7.

In the locker room after the game, Mike McClellan, who won both the 100- and 220-yard sprints at the 2A state meet in 1955, was asked by *Star-Telegram* reporter John Morrison why he hadn't been able to shake loose for one of his patented long gainers. McClellan had gained 159 yards on nineteen carries and scored three touchdowns, so it wasn't the smartest question asked that day. Nevertheless, Mike answered like a true gentleman, praising his blockers when he politely shouldered Morrison's inquiry.

"I should have, because the blocking was there. It's always there—I just seemed to be cutting the wrong way all afternoon."

McClellan's response was typical of every player I coached at Stamford—confident, no brag, just fact, and always supportive of his teammates.

◆　◆　◆

AT THE HELM of Brady's aerial-minded offense was a 130-pound quarterback named Tony Sanders. Tony spent two years as the team manager before Coach Chuck York suited him up and handed him the job of directing his black and gold Bulldogs to the playoffs. Brady's big gun, however, was Fletcher Fields, a 200-pound triple-threat fullback who could run, pass and punt. Prior to our championship game, Fields had passed for 435 yards and carried the mail for 783 yards.

When heavy rain began pouring from a dark Tuesday night sky, Stamford residents were happy, but confused. Happy, because the moisture was the answer to their prayers. Confused, because they worried the weather might hamper their Bulldogs' chances of repeating as AA State Champions—a feat no other AA school had accomplished.

Which team would reign as 1956 State AA Champions would be decided at Abilene's Fair Park Field. The stadium seated ninety-four hundred. Despite the threat of rain, a sellout crowd was expected. Although Christmas was only a week away, many Stamford business establishments announced they would be closed on game day.

When tickets went on sale Tuesday afternoon, Stamford fans gobbled up twelve hundred in the first two hours. Another three hundred were sold by four o'clock Wednesday afternoon. The scene was set for a classic West Texas showdown, and every football fan in the Big Country waited anxiously for the curtain to open.

◆　◆　◆

BY GAME TIME the weather had cleared. The sun was out for the first time all week. The temperature had climbed into the mid-forties, but a howling north wind forced the seven thousand football-crazed fans who packed the stadium to stay bundled up. Brady won the mid-field coin toss and elected to receive.

In the early going, Brady used an unorthodox passing

formation, but it didn't fool our defense one bit. From our scouting reports, we knew that Sanders, their pint-sized quarterback, never did the passing. Sanders would line up behind center in a "T" set. Then Brady's center would snap the ball between the quarterback's legs directly to Fletcher Fields. Actually, this gave us a tremendous advantage because we had discovered Brady's center always ducked his head to look back on passing plays.

Brady's weird formation may not have fooled us, but Fields' accurate passes sure gave us fits. We quickly learned that a dry ball and a slippery field can greatly enhance an aerial oriented attack. With our pass defenders slipping and sliding on every play, Brady drew first blood, slicing sixty-three yards through Stamford's proud defense to score after the opening kickoff. A 33-yard strike from Fletcher Fields to halfback John Bradshaw climaxed the painful operation.

Kenneth Ivy took Brady's kickoff and ran it back to the thirty-six, but our offense couldn't get untracked. Twelve minutes deep into the game, Stamford hadn't made a first down.

It was late in the first period when the wind provided a needed jump start for our sputtering offense. Fletcher Fields' punt sailed high, got caught in a wind gust and fell dead at Brady's twenty-two. Five plays later McClellan scooted over from the seven. Duane Lindsey missed the extra point by a hair, leaving the score tied at 6–6.

Several minutes later Arche Pardue recovered a Brady fumble on Stamford's thirty-five to set up our second touchdown. Kenneth Ivy and McClellan shared the load, methodically chopping through a swarming Brady defense to the twenty-four. A Statue of Liberty play furnished the razzle-dazzle trickery needed for the go-ahead score. Nickey Jackson faded back as if to pass, faked a handoff to Ivy, then shoved the ball behind his back to Stanley Hill who shot around left end and scampered in for the TD.

As time clicked off the scoreboard clock, the two teams traded mistakes. McClellan intercepted a Fields pass and returned it to Stamford's twenty-nine. Two plays later Brady's Edlin Hahn stole a Nickey Jackson toss at the fifty. Time ran out shortly after Charles Stenholm recovered a Joe Cole fumble at Stamford's eighteen.

◆   ◆   ◆

CONTRARY TO WHAT many believe, a coach should never criticize his players at halftime. A coach should encourage his team. During the mid-game break I want my players to wash their faces, clean their shoes, change socks and get comfortable. Then I point out the mistakes we've made on offense and defense and explain how to correct those mistakes.

I'm totally sold on the idea that the first series of plays in the third quarter decides the game's outcome. Consequently, my teams usually came out showing something different, maybe three or four plays with some little wrinkle we hadn't used before. During the Brady game intermission, I revised our offensive game plan to better utilize fullback Kenneth Ivy. Ivy would respond by carrying the ball seventeen times for 109 yards. He would end up as the game's leading ground gainer.

Before my ballclub took the field, I made one final point. I told my kids I knew they were the best team, but if Brady played real good and we played real bad, Brady would beat us. I reminded my players that they only had twenty-four minutes left in this game, but they had a lifetime to remember who won the state championship.

That halftime conference seemed to revitalize my Bulldog squad. They charged back onto the playing field with fierce determination. Confirming their resolve, they took the second half kickoff and ground out fifty-one hard earned, bone-crunching yards. A pitchout from Jackson to McClellan netted the final fifteen.

With Stanford enjoying a thirteen-point lead, Brady threw away their rushing playbook and went to an all-passing game. The strategy almost worked. Fields completed four long passes before his aerial show stalled out at Stamford's twelve-yard line.

After Stamford punted, Brady's stubborn bunch showed they weren't beat yet. They marched right back to the pay window. A Fletcher rocket to Dorman Riddles closed the gap to seven. Fields nailed the extra point and narrowed Stamford's lead to six.

Brutal line play accentuated our game-clinching touchdown drive. Heavy breathing and angry groans echoed across the muddy playing field as Royce West, Dale Robinson and Arche Pardue carved out big holes for McClellan, Hill and Ivy. After an offside penalty moved Brady back to their five, McClellan raced wide to the right corner for the game's final touchdown.

Final score: Stamford 26, Brady 13.

After the game, delirious Stamford well-wishers jammed the

concourse outside our locker room. Inside, back slaps, bear hugs and wide toothy grins dominated the dressing area. Then for a few minutes the locker room fell silent as Mike McClellan gathered his teammates close, wiped back his tears of joy and stumbled through a short prayer of thanksgiving. After Mike's amen, war hoops filled the air as exuberant Bulldogs let out their pent-up emotions.

Stamford High principal James Simpson was the first man to receive a victory baptism. Coaches Isbell, Wartes, Anderson and I followed close behind. I didn't mind the fully-dressed shower or the ride home in wet clothes. No man in Texas was happier than Gordon Wood that day.

◆　◆　◆

BY THE TIME we reached Stamford, a jubilant victory celebration was well underway. Stamford streets were filled with merchants and residents who couldn't come to the game. They had huddled around their radios back home, cheering loudly on every exciting play.

Chief of Police Jack Tidwell met the team's chartered bus at the city limits sign, and with red light flashing, his patrol car headed a parade through downtown. Following close behind were two long school buses loaded with band members and the pep squad. An extended caravan of honking private cars brought up the rear.

Even after the long parade circled the square several times, the party mood continued. When the school busses stopped at the high school to unload, pep squad members filed out, formed a line and led a snake dance back toward downtown. All along the way people grabbed on to join in the fun, and by the time the snake dance finally dispersed, the string of joyous rumba dancers wrapped all the way around the square.

At the National Guard Armory, loads of homemade cakes, pies, cookies, sandwiches, soft drinks and plenty of cold milk were waiting, and a juke box was blaring. Earlier in the week, Mrs. Bill McClellan and Mrs. Arche Pardue sort of spearheaded a movement which began as an idea and ended with every football and band mom participating. More than a thousand smiling faces crowded into the armory, laughing, slapping backs and swapping football stories. My hand must've been squeezed and shook several thousand times that evening.

After the armory party broke up, most of the football squad and their dates went to Arche Pardue's house where they sat around and relived the thrills, unwilling to let the exciting day come to an end.

◆ ◆ ◆

THE NEXT MORNING I was still in bed, basking in an afterglow of the previous day's events and rummaging through Saturday morning's paper, when a reporter from Fort Worth called. Katharine answered the telephone.

"It's Herb Owens with the *Star-Telegram*. He wants to know how it feels to win back-to-back state championships," Katharine advised, covering the mouthpiece with her hand.

"Tell him it feels good," I answered smugly. "Real good."

◆ ◆ ◆

IN 1957, TEXAS, like a majority of the nation, was enjoying a burst of prosperity unlike any in history. But prosperity didn't come without worry. Two things troubled people most—a nuclear war with Russia and the sorry state of our rock-and-roll teenage generation. A story in the *Fort Worth Star-Telegram*, reporting that a government-funded study had determined an all-out Soviet attack would only take out one fourth of the U.S. population, did little to ease our anxiety.

Every evening, television warned us our children were "going to the devil." On weekdays you could actually see it happening—on a popular afternoon TV show called *American Bandstand* where teenagers gyrated wildly in barbaric displays called the Mashed Potato and Locomotion. The afternoon program was hosted by Dick Clark, a former disk jockey. Clark didn't seem at all alarmed by the girls' skin-tight skirts, the strange color combinations, like pink and charcoal, or the boys' long, greased hair combed back in "duck-tails." Movies like *Blackboard Jungle,* starring Glen Ford and Sidney Poitier, and *Rebel Without a Cause,* starring James Dean and Natalie Wood, promulgated a feeling of helplessness among parents.

Those of us who taught and coached at Stamford High School were never bothered by the negative outlook, because we held a different perspective. If the kids in our classrooms and on our playing field were the least bit representative, we knew our country's future would be in good hands.

Our faith in our Stamford youngsters was fortified at the

annual January football banquet hosted by the Bulldog Pep Squad. Corsaged party dresses, button-down shirts with narrow ties, freshly-buzzed flattops, and scrubbed cheeks were the order of the day. Bright, alert young faces crowded into the school cafeteria to enjoy a scrumptious meal of turkey and dressing topped off with cherry pie. Then our young people listened attentively while guest speaker Mike Brumbelow, athletic director at Texas Western College in El Paso, paid tribute to Stamford's gallant state champions. Brumbelow compared football to the game of life, explaining that each requires courage and stamina; both are based upon competition; both have a set of rules; and both require discipline and teamwork to succeed.

Following the meal, Kenneth Ivy and Carolyn Boedeker were named football king and queen by Toast Mistress and Pep Squad President Peggy Harvick. After numerous other awards and thank-yous, the banquet closed with everyone joining hands to sing the school song and recite the Lord's Prayer.

◆　◆　◆

A GOOD EXAMPLE of the kind of young people Stamford graduated is Anne Hudson. Anne was an honor student and a pep squad officer. After she finished high school, she continued her studies at the University of Colorado, spent a year at Harvard, then obtained her law degree from Catholic University in Washington, D.C. After college she joined Bruce Babbitt's staff as an assistant attorney for the Secretary of the Interior. A few years ago Congressman Stenholm was having problems funding the construction of Lake Ivie, a water project near San Angelo which was vitally important to West Texans. Charles' project was held up in committee red tape. He was told funding approval would take maybe two years. Frustrated with the turtle-slow system, Stenholm took his problem to Anne, and in less than a month the project was back on track. Construction on Lake Ivie was completed in 1990. The huge reservoir provides much needed water for Midland, Odessa, San Angelo and many West Texas cities.

◆　◆　◆

IN MARCH, Bulldog football players and coaches were treated to a second banquet sponsored by the Quarterback Club and the

Chamber of Commerce. This party was held at the National Guard Armory. Our guest speaker was Oklahoma University coach Bud Wilkerson.

Coach Wilkerson totally mesmerized the audience. He kept everyone in stitches and on the edge of their seats as he laced his winning football philosophy amongst anecdotes derived from his coaching experiences while guiding the Sooners to three national championships. Near the end of Wilkerson's speech, master of ceremonies Bill Teague of Abilene stole the show when he raced up with an urgent telegram for Coach Wilkerson. Supposedly, the telegram was from Southwest Conference coaches Paul "Bear" Bryant, Abe Martin and Darrell Royal. The telegram read like this:

"Regarding your recruiting of Texas football players—STOP!"

◆　◆　◆

SPRING BROUGHT AN END to the decade-long drought which choked all of Texas. Of course in Texas, one excess is usually followed by another. When the sky finally opened up, the bottom dropped out. Torrential April and May rains virtually wiped out the Jones County cotton crop. Massive flooding occurred throughout the region bounded by the Pecos River on the west and the Sabine River and Longview on the east. Lake Texoma, near Denison, crested to burst over its spillway for the first time in history, washing our roads and wreaking havoc all the way to Shreveport. Normal rainfall for Stamford is twenty-three inches. By year's end a record thirty-five inches would fall, most of which arrived along with wind-driven thunder and lightning storms.

◆　◆　◆

ALTHOUGH I TURNED the track team over to Coach Isbell in 1955, so I could concentrate on football, spring sports were still very important to me. At Stamford, three fourths of our track squad also participated in football. Speed was a key ingredient to the Bulldogs' success on the football field.

In those days Texas Interscholastic rules wouldn't allow a high school athlete to sign a letter of intent until April 15. It was a silly rule because it created a lot of unnecessary turmoil. For years I'd watched as college recruiters wooed, badgered and propositioned my senior track stars from early January until mid-April. Recruiters were a real problem for Val Joe Walker at Seminole during the spring of 1948, but for Stamford's Bob Harrison in 1955, college recruiters made life miserable for Bob and his family. One scout would take him to lunch. A second scout would pick Bob up after school and drive him home. A third took him to supper. A fourth met him after supper and stayed with him until late at night. All the high-pressured distraction affected Bob's track performance. His second-semester grades were also negatively affected.

Harrison's tremendous strength made him an important member of our track squad. His senior year, Bob placed fourth in the shot put during the regional meet, but he was capable of doing much better. I truly believe recruiting pressure kept him from being one of the best shot put and discus men in the state.

Knowing Mike McClellan would face even more intense recruiting, I proposed a rule change to the Interscholastic League which would permit athletes to sign their letter of intent in January. My proposal came too late to help Mike, but perhaps it did cool some of the frenzied recruiting.

Coach Isbell's track squad captured the state crown that spring, compiling a total of forty-four points. Mike McClellan finished first in the broad jump, second in the 220-yard dash, and won the 100-yard dash. Our relay team, which included Donald Davis, Robert Hardin, Charlie Helmer and McClellan, also won first place.

During the spring of '57, Mike McClellan and Glynn Gregory of Abilene were the two most sought-after athletes in Texas. Mike eventually decided on Baylor University, mostly because of his mother's strong religious influence. Unfortunately, Baylor football was at a low ebb. McClellan's freshman year, the Bears didn't win a single ballgame. Mike was never actually unhappy at Waco, but he never quite connected either. A late night hazing incident in the athletic dorm, which ended in a fist fight between Mike and several upperclass football players, finally convinced him to leave.

At mid-term Mike transferred to Oklahoma University where he played with Stamford teammate Bob Harrison and shared playing time with all-state scat back Jimmy Carpenter from Abilene. Lining up alongside Carpenter and McClellan was another great West Texas halfback—Jakie Sandefer from Breckenridge.

1957

IN DETROIT, Ford Motor Company introduced a brand-new car—the Edsel, but in West Texas, nobody got too excited. A reliable Ford pickup remained the transportation of choice. Katharine, Pat and I were perfectly satisfied with our 1949 four-door, battleship-gray Ford sedan.

In New York, Christian Dior introduced the chemise dress, promising women comfort in place of style, but in Abilene, men took one look, renamed it "the sack dress," and instructed their wives to send it back. West Texas men preferred their women show off their curves.

In Wichita Falls, sportswriter Randy MacPhearson picked Seymour to finish first in District 4–AA. Now that caused a real flurry in Stamford. What part of New York was this guy from? How could a sportswriter for an important paper like the *Record-News* be so dumb? Wasn't Stamford the reigning AA kingpin? Hadn't the Bulldogs won thirty-two in a row? Heck, why would Randy go and write something ugly like that when everyone in town was counting on a three-peat? All week prior to our opening game with Quanah, morning coffee talk centered around the sportswriter's ignorant prediction.

I read the article and posted it on the dressing room bulletin board for all my coaches and players to see. MacPhearson's prediction was based on pure, simple logic. Seymour coach Marshall Gearhart had six starters and eleven lettermen returning, whereas graduation had riddled Stamford's ranks. Only four lettermen were returning from our 1956 championship squad—fullback, Stanley Hill; halfbacks, Donald Davis and Robert Hardin; and end, Rufino Escobedo.

MacPhearson's analysis actually made good sense, but I figured my Bulldogs would make him eat his words before the season ended.

◆　◆　◆

OUR 1957 SCHEDULE was tougher than usual. Wanting to avoid teams which were usually easy marks, I had revamped our schedule to include schools with stronger football programs—substituting Slaton for Andrews, Brady for Coleman, and with Coach Ray Overton's Indians off probation, Haskell for Nacona. Stamford's lineup of proposed victims also included two rugged AAA outfits, Sweetwater and Brownwood.

Even though we clubbed Quanah 25–6 in our season opener, something was missing. Our defense played well, but our offense never seemed to fire on all cylinders.

A week later Stamford won by taking advantage of a couple of lucky breaks. Midway through the first quarter, Ballinger halfback Jerry Candler backed across the rear end zone stripe on a fourth-down punt to give Stamford an automatic two-point safety. Then after the two teams traded punts for three quarters, Fred Upshaw lost the football when he tried to dive over left guard on a quarterback keeper. Fred recovered his own fumble in the Bearcats' end zone for our lone TD.

Final score: Stamford 8, Ballinger 0.

Victory number thirty-five came at the expense of Slaton's Tigers, but we never looked sharp. Seventy-five yards in penalties and two lost fumbles kept our offense bogged down all evening.

Final score: Stamford 26, Slaton 0.

◆　◆　◆

MY RELATIONSHIP with Sweetwater coach Elwood Turner went all the way back to our college days when he was a star fullback for Abilene Christian College. During the war we both served in the navy, and for a short time, we were both stationed at San Diego. After the war, Elwood took the head coaching post at Albany. He moved to Sweetwater in 1954, when Pat Gerald resigned. Over the years Coach Turner and I had faced each other on numerous occasions. My teams had never lost to one of his.

During the week prior to our Sweetwater contest, a flu epidemic swept through West Texas, and many football games were canceled. At Stamford, six of my starters were out sick, including all three of my tri-captains—Robert Hardin, Andy Swenson, and Jackie Bounds. Thursday morning, L.W. Johnson, my school superintendent, called me to his office to talk about calling off the Sweetwater game. Here's what I told him:

"If we were playing any coach other than Elwood Turner, I'd say call it off. Before Elwood accepted the Sweetwater coaching job, he agreed to play Stamford every year, and he's honored that agreement even though we've beat him every time we've played.

Coach Turner has an excellent team this year, and he deserves a shot at ending our winning streak."

On paper Sweetwater looked awesome, but due to a rugged non-conference schedule, the Mustangs were still looking for their first win that cool, crisp Friday night in September.

A fumble, which Sweetwater end Don Bishop recovered early in the first quarter, set the stage. An old Breckenridge Buckaroo option trick opened the chute. Mustang halfback Glenn Reed got the show started by scampering wide right to place the football at Stamford's forty-six. On the next play quarterback John Bryant faked to his fullback James Parker, kept the ball and cut outside left end. As a wall of hostile blue and white defenders converged on Bryant, he waited until the last possible second and flipped the football out to Eddie Scott who was trailing behind. Scott darted past the host of surprised Bulldogs and romped in for the score.

My Bulldogs bounced right back. Quarterback Fred Upshaw returned the kickoff to Stamford's thirty-nine, then on the first play from scrimmage, he hit end Duane Lindsey with a short jump pass. Lindsey was dragging three red and white tacklers when they pulled him down at Sweetwater's twenty-six. Five plays later Stanley Hill dived across from the two, and for a moment, it seemed my Bulldogs had recaptured the magic which graced their predecessors.

Stamford got the ball again when Sweetwater coughed up a fumble near mid-field, but our offense went dead at the Mustang twenty-five. After that it was see-you-down-the-highway for Sweetwater.

Glenn Reed ripped off forty-three yards. Twice, Reed was hit so hard his feet left the ground, but each time he regained his balance and kept on going. Charlie Helmer finally slammed the powerful Mustang halfback to the ground at Stamford's twenty-nine.

Sweetwater hammered at the middle and gained a first down at our four. Then Reed sliced inside right end for the go-ahead score.

Less than three minutes later, Sweetwater fullback James Parker took a handoff, burst over right tackle, broke several tackles and cruised sixty-one yards to paydirt.

Our defense played well, holding Sweetwater to one other touchdown, but our offense never got rolling. After thirty-five straight wins, Stamford's victory string came to an abrupt halt.

Final score: Stamford 7, Sweetwater 24.

◆　◆　◆

TWO HOURS AFTER OUR LOSS, Stamford assistant coaches Larry Wartes, O.M. Isbell and Bill Anderson convened at my house on Wells Street for our usual Friday night postwar conference. Coach Isbell had been assigned to scout the Brady-Coleman game and was late getting back. Coach Anderson covered the Seymour-Electra game. Bill was full of questions when he barged through the front door.

"I heard on the radio we got our tails kicked. How'd that happen?" Anderson quizzed, nodding his head affirmatively to Katharine who was manning the coffee pot.

"Our kids played their hearts out, but Sweetwater shut us down all night long. It just wasn't our night," Wartes replied. "How about Seymour? Can we beat 'em?"

"They'll be tough. The Panthers are well coached, and they have some outstanding players. They run a belly offense. I got all the dope—personnel, plays, formations, their defense."

"Let's see what you've got," I said, and the discussion about our loss ended.

Thirty minutes and another pot of coffee later, Coach Isbell arrived. Isbell had one question.

"How are the boys taking it?"

"Right now, they're feeling pretty low, but they'll be okay by Monday. Our guys sure wanted to keep the streak going. Right down to the end they thought they could take Sweetwater," I answered. "What did you find out about Brady?"

Stamford coaching staff:
Bill Anderson, Gordon Wood, Larry Wartes, and O. M. Isbell.
(credit: 1957 Stamford High Yearbook)

Isbell spread his scouting sheets out on the dining room table, and we went to work. In many ways all of us were relieved the streak was over, and yet, every coach there felt like crying. But there was no time for tears. A tough game with Brady was only days away.

◆   ◆   ◆

TWELVE-YEAR-OLD PAT was the one who took our loss the hardest. She was only ten when her favorite team last lost a football game. Pat's bedroom walls were covered with banners, pictures and memorabilia, reflecting the glory of past victories and past seasons. Ordinarily, Pat was not an emotional child, but when I tucked her in bed that night, her eyes were filled with huge tears.

◆   ◆   ◆

CHUCK MOSER once confessed his hair began to fall out near the end of Abilene's 49-game win-streak. A winning streak may sound like fun, but it carries a tremendous burden for those charged with keeping it going. Coaches feel it. Players feel it. Maybe my hair didn't fall out, but something inside me clicked during the long winning streak. When it ended, I wasn't the same man. I had a different outlook on what I wanted, and what I expected.

◆   ◆   ◆

ON FRIDAY NIGHT, October 4, Stamford righted itself and got back on the winning track. A 59-yard blast off right tackle on the second play of the second half by Bulldog fullback Donald Davis provided the winning margin, and we squeezed by Brady, the school we had faced in the '56 AA state finals.

Final score: Stamford 13, Brady 7.

Next morning, though, very few people were thinking about football because scientists in the Soviet Union had accomplished the unthinkable. They had beaten the United States in the race for space by sending a steel sphere satellite into orbit. Not since Pearl Harbor had America felt so threatened. The mere idea that the Reds could beat us in anything struck fear into every citizen's heart.

Possibly no other single event in history did more to focus this nation's attention on our need for better education than the unexpected launching of an enormous round ball the Russians called "Sputnik."

The Streak

While Washington politicians blamed the opposing party, formed committees and launched investigations to determine who was at fault, my Stamford coaches and I concentrated on our X and O world. Brownwood, a school three times the size of Stamford, was next on our schedule.

◆　◆　◆

IN 1957, BROWNWOOD'S FOOTBALL program was a civic disgrace. The Lions didn't play good football, and their fan support was pathetic. Our game was played at Brownwood in dilapidated old Lion stadium. On the home side, a concrete grandstand contained 2,250 reserved seats. Students, band members and pep squads of both schools were required to sit in steel framed bleachers on the opposite side of the playing field.

When Stamford requested tickets to pre-sell, Brownwood High School sent us 1,150 reserved tickets, and Stamford sold every one. A majority of the spectators at our Brownwood game that evening drove a hundred and twenty miles to watch their favorite team play.

Brownwood took the opening kickoff and drove to mid-field where a fumble by Lion halfback Fred Carpenter was recovered by Rufino Escobedo. That set up our first touchdown. Charles Helmer circled around left end for twenty-seven yards, then Donald Davis blasted over tackle for twenty-eight yards to put Stamford ahead 6–0.

The Lions were a stubborn bunch. Taking advantage of a 22-yard scamper by Harold Reese and a long pass from quarterback Tommy Butler to Charles Watkins, they marched sixty yards in eight plays to score. Bob Teague booted the extra point, and Brownwood took a 7–6 lead.

In the second quarter, the two teams kept hammering away at each other's goal line. Brownwood scored on a twenty-yard Butler to Plummer pass. Then Stamford fullback Charlie Helmer retaliated, scoring on a 25-yard draw play. Only a few minutes were left in the second stanza when Helmer hit paydirt again. This time Charles went thirty-nine yards using the same draw play. At halftime Stamford led 19–13.

Here is an important footnote to this story. Harold Reese started this game at halfback for Brownwood and played most of the game. Harold Reese is a Negro. He was one of the first black players to integrate high school football in Texas.

◆　　◆　　◆

IN THE OLD BROWNWOOD STADIUM both teams sat on the home side, with the players' benches being situated along the twenty-yard lines at each end of the field. When the ball was on the opposite end of the field, it was difficult to sub a player in between plays. If a coach wanted to substitute, his sub had to be running onto the field before the previous play ended.

Early in the final quarter, Stamford was still leading 19–13, but the Lions had driven down to our four. I sent in Stanley Hill to substitute for Robert Hardin at defensive halfback. When Hardin reached the sideline, I talked to him then instructed him to go back in for Hill the very second the next play was over. After a Brownwood quarterback sneak gained only a yard, Hardin went back in, sending Hill scurrying back to our bench.

My defensive safety, Tom Lovvorn, looked up and saw Hardin lining up in the defensive backfield. Thinking Hardin had come in to replace him, Lovvorn started to run off the field. Tom ran a few yards, realized what had happened, turned around and hurried back to his safety position.

On the next play, Brownwood tried to pass, and Stamford linebacker Bobby Gamblin slipped through to throw the Lions' quarterback for an eighteen-yard loss. The play was called back, and the game officials penalized Stamford five yards, moving the ball down to the one-yard line. (Note: This game was played before the half-the-distance-to-the-goal-line rule change.) Before we Bulldog coaches could register a protest, Brownwood lined up and ran another play.

When the play ended, the referees spotted the ball on the one-foot line. I called time-out and charged out onto the playing field.

"What was that penalty for?" I yelled.

"Too many men on the field. You had twelve men on the field when the ball was snapped," the official responded.

"If we did, they're still out there. Count 'em."

"Don't have to count 'em. Your safety thought you had twelve men on the field."

"Ref, you can't make your calls based on what my players

think. My safety wouldn't know whether we have ten, eleven, or twelve men in the game."

"Well, we can't do anything about it now. I don't know why you're complaining. That was fourth down. Your team has the football."

"Oh, sure. We've got the ball on the one-inch line. If you hadn't called the penalty, we'd have it on the twenty-three."

"I'm sorry, Coach. We can't do anything about it."

I was steaming mad when I stormed back to our bench. I grabbed a surprised oversized sophomore named Wendell Robinson by the collar. Robinson played center. I gritted my teeth and issued these instructions.

"Wendell, you go in there and tell Upshaw to call two quarterback sneaks using wedge blocks. On the third play he's to punt the football outta there. You got that! Two quarterback sneaks, then punt!"

"Yes sir, Coach Wood. I understand. I'll tell Fred exactly what you want." The big sophomore center seemed immensely relieved when I turned loose of his jersey and sent him hightailing toward our huddle.

Robinson was normally a quiet, reserved youngster, but when he repeated my instructions, he included a slight personal alteration. Inside the huddle, Wendell flashed a wry grin and told our quarterback, "Coach says you're to call a wedge block, quarterback sneak and follow me ninety-nine yards for a touchdown."

That's exactly what happened. Fred Upshaw ran into a big pile of players at the center of the line and bounced back. Somehow, he stayed on his feet and broke loose, dodging, changing directions, giving ground, then running back across the field. Fred must have run two hundred yards before he finally crossed Brownwood's goal line.

Ninety-nine yards and two feet, Upshaw's touchdown scamper was the longest run from the line of scrimmage I've ever seen.

◆ ◆ ◆

AS THE WEATHER COOLED and Jones County farmers harvested their sparse, waterlogged cotton fields, my Bulldogs regrouped and embarked on a brand-new winning streak.

Number three on our abbreviated list was Anson. We overpowered the Tigers 27–0. Next up was Haskell. We smacked the

Indians by the same score 27–0. Hamlin gave us some trouble, but eventually the Pied Pipers succumbed 9–0.

Now only one team stood between Stamford and the state playoffs—the undefeated Seymour Panthers. Would Randy MacPhearson's pre-season prediction be validated?

Over in Abilene a new movie, starring Burt Lancaster and Kirk Douglas, was playing to rave reviews. In my mind, the movie, entitled *Gunfight at the O.K. Corral,* described our upcoming 4–AA shootout precisely. At the time I had no idea, but it would be the last game I coached for Stamford High School.

◆ ◆ ◆

SPORTSWRITERS ACROSS TEXAS were split about equally. Half believed Stamford would win. The other half predicted Seymour would come out on top.

When John Morrison with the *Forth Worth Star-Telegram* phoned, I thought he wanted my opinion, but instead, he asked to speak to Katharine. I've never given good telephone interviews, so it's understandable why some writers preferred talking to Katharine.

"That's right, John. Gordon doesn't think we can win. Says they outweigh us by twenty pounds per man. And Seymour's quarterback Billy Ryan, he's the best ball handler in the state."

Katharine paused, listening to Morrison's analysis before she added her own thoughts.

"I certainly hope we beat that bunch. It would sure seem funny around here with football ending so early."

◆ ◆ ◆

ALL SEASON LONG, Coach Marshall Gearhart's Panthers had been pointing for Stamford, and after defensive halfback R.L. McClung intercepted a first quarter Bulldog pass and returned it for a touchdown, Seymour unleashed an awesome arsenal of firepower. With split-T magician Billy Ryan directing the pedal-to-the-metal, ball-control show, twin-terror Panther ballcarriers, Larry Martin and Eddie Sytak, took turns clobbering a staggering Bulldog defense.

The Panther's second tally came on double-reverse, with Ryan flipping the ball out to McClung who was running wide left. Then McClung handed off to Martin going in the opposite direction.

Martin evaded a desperate lunge by Bulldog defensive end Rufino Escobedo, shook off a groping Burt Pardue and trotted in for the TD.

Seymour's defense, bulwarked by linemen Bill Moss and Johnny Rogers, totally shut down Stamford's on-again, off-again ground attack. At the half my Bulldogs had managed only forty-three yards total offense and one first down. It was not a night to remember.

Final score: Stamford 0, Seymour 19.

◆ ◆ ◆

AFTER THE SEASON the Texas High School Coaches Association selected me to coach the North squad in the annual Texas All-Star game to be played in Houston when coaches school convened there in August.

Basketball season was underway, and I was looking forward to helping Larry Wartes coach our boys to a sixth consecutive district title. The last thing on my mind was leaving Stamford when I picked up the Abilene paper in January and read about Keith Harshbarger resigning at Victoria High to take the athletic director's job at Sherman.

"You know, Katharine," I mused to my wife who was sitting across the breakfast table. "I wouldn't be a bit surprised if Andy Tomb calls me today."

◆ ◆ ◆

ANDREW S. TOMB was a doctor I'd befriended when we lived in Seminole. In the interim, between the time I left Seminole and 1958, Doctor Tomb moved to Victoria where he had become very wealthy. Andy was also up to his neck in local politics. The good doctor was president of both the school board and the Chamber of Commerce.

Sure enough, Doctor Tomb called that afternoon to offer me the coaching job at Victoria High School. At first I told him I wasn't interested, but my friend was very persuasive.

"Gordon, our school trustees are meeting with several other coaches a week from Saturday. How about we fly you down here to visit with us? We'll pay your expenses and buy you a meal at the country club. Whatta you say? You and I haven't had a chance to see each other in a long time."

"Alright," I reluctantly agreed, "I'll do that, but you're wasting your money. I'm not leaving Stamford."

At their expense, Victoria's school board flew me from Abilene to Victoria. Doctor Tomb and two other trustees met me at the airport and hustled me straight to the country club. When we arrived, the dining room was crowded with local dignitaries, school board members, and some twenty football coaches they intended to interview.

As we entered the dining room, Doctor Tomb put his arm around my shoulders and turned to his colleagues.

"Okay, here he is, fellows. You folks got your man, and I've got mine."

Several coaches told me later they realized right then and there they were wasting their time. Every man in the room knew, if I wanted the job, it was mine, even before I answered the first question.

Despite the hearty introduction, I still wasn't sure I was a candidate until several hours later when the school trustees offered me ninety-five hundred dollars a year to come to Victoria. That was fifty percent more than I was making at Stamford. Their proposal forced me to take a hard look at my circumstances. I was forty-three. My record at Stamford included eighty football wins against only six losses, five consecutive district basketball championships, seven consecutive district track titles, and one state crown in golf. I'd been producing winning teams for twelve years, ever since the war ended, and all I had to show for my efforts were a seven-year-old car, a mortgaged house and the clothes on my back. I knew if I didn't leave Stamford now I would never leave. I was a fish who needed a bigger pond. I loved my job at Stamford High School, but I knew I couldn't say no to Victoria.

After I left Stamford and my assistant coach Larry Wartes took the reins, Stamford High won two more state championships in 1958 and 1959, so some people think my leaving was a career mistake. I don't agree. A lot of wonderful things happened to me and my family in Victoria. Besides, life doesn't come with a road map. Sometimes a detour down a muddy road is necessary to make you appreciate the path you've been traveling. Sometimes a wrong turn will take you right where you belong.

CHAPTER NINE

Two Years in Another Country

(1958–1960)

DURING THE YEARS I coached at Stamford, Morris Southall was coaching at Winters. Morris and I had remained close friends. Each summer we went to coaching school together, sharing a hotel room. Our families enjoyed the friendship too. Katharine and Lorene had so much in common. Our daughter Pat and the Southalls' oldest boy Terry were great friends. Katharine and I frequently met Lorene and Morris in Abilene where we'd catch a movie or watch a Hardin-Simmons basketball game. Telephone calls between the Wood household and the Southall residence were a regular occurrence.

When the Victoria coaching opportunity came up, the first call I made, after I talked with Katharine, was to Morris Southall to invite him to team up with me in South Texas. I was fairly certain he'd agree. After winning back-to-back district titles his first two seasons at Winters, Morris had suffered through some lean years and an unbelievable streak of bad luck. In 1956, Coach Southall's Blizzards had their conference all but sewed up when Coleman staged an amazing comeback, scoring three touchdowns in the final five minutes to wrest victory from certain defeat and deny Morris his third district crown.

The stress of competing in the same district with Ballinger, Brady and Coleman—schools which produced excellent football teams year after year and which were twice the size of Winters—was eating at my friend. Morris is a terrific coach, knowledgeable, patient, good with kids, but he agonizes over his losses.

When Morris agreed to come with me, I was ecstatic. If he hadn't, Coach Southall might have quit coaching and switched to school administration or teaching, and the two of us would have missed sharing some of the greatest moments two men could possibly experience.

◆　◆　◆

MY SECOND CALL was to John Ramseur, a big dark Dutchman whose coaching skills I greatly admired. Ramseur was head football coach at New London when our teams clashed in the state quarter-finals in 1955. Since that December afternoon in Arlington, John and I had become good friends. We'd worked together on numerous occasions during the two years I served as a director for the Texas High School Coaches Association. I had promised myself many times, if the opportunity ever arose, I'd add John Ramseur to my coaching staff. A few words were all it took to entice John into joining me at Victoria. John's only condition was that he be allowed to teach physics. His request surprised me.

"Physics? John, why on God's green earth would you want to teach physics?" When I was a student at Hardin-Simmons, I flunked physics, along with most of my fellow athletes. I couldn't imagine anyone actually wanting to teach the subject.

"Because it's easier, Coach Wood. Most coaches want to teach physical education or history because they think those are the easy courses, but if you teach P.E., you're physically worn out when the school day's over. If you teach history, you're up half the night grading papers. Teaching physics, I'll have maybe twelve or thirteen kids in my class, everyone of them smart as they can be. Teaching kids who are smart and anxious to learn is nothing but fun."

Coach Ramseur's analysis made good sense, and from that day forward, I tried to hire coaches who could teach more difficult courses. My last year at Brownwood my coaching staff included three coaches who taught math, one who taught English and two who taught science.

Unfortunately, Coach Ramseur and I never realized our goal of coaching together, at least not for a full season. John joined my Victoria coaching staff that spring and traveled with us to Houston in July to coach the North all-star squad. John was our defensive line coach. With the all-star game scheduled for Saturday night, we were working hard to get our team prepared. Our first practice session began early each morning before breakfast. John and I had dressed for practice and were leaving the dressing room when he stumbled into me.

"What in the world is wrong with you, John? You haven't been nipping, have you?" I teased, ribbing him for his spastic behavior.

"No, I'm having trouble with my eyes. I'm not sure what's wrong. Last night I was reading a book, like I do every night before I go to sleep, and I had to quit because I was seeing double."

"Maybe you'd better skip practice this morning, John," I advised, truly concerned because I could see Coach Ramseur was really worried. "Why don't you go back inside and have Eddie Wojecki check you out. You take it easy, and we'll get along without you this morning." Eddie Wojecki was Rice University's trainer, one of the best in the state. Wojecki was the designated trainer for our North all-stars.

After practice, I went to check on my assistant coach. Eddie had looked him over, and what he found wasn't good. Wojecki already had John lined up to check into Texas Medical Center, Houston's world-renowned hospital complex.

That was on Thursday morning. By Saturday, Ramseur's condition had deteriorated to the point where he couldn't speak. He died the following Monday.

◆ ◆ ◆

AFTER KENNETH WEST graduated from Hardin-Simmons, he served two years as a second lieutenant in the U.S. Air Force. Kenneth completed his military obligation in January of 1958. Several days later he dropped by my office at Stamford High School to say hello. When I inquired about his future plans, Kenneth informed me he had an aunt who taught at Baytown. Her school had a temporary vacancy. Kenneth was thinking about moving to Baytown, so he could teach there the second semester.

"Do you have a teaching certificate?" I asked.

"No, I don't, but my aunt tells me they're in a real bind. She's assured me her principal will hire me without one."

"Well, I'm planning to move to Victoria. If you'll go back to school this spring and get yourself a teaching certificate, I'm sure I can find you a coaching job down there."

My proposition was made without the slightest suspicion of what the future held. I was simply trying to help out one of my ex-players who needed a boost. Who would have dreamed my offer would launch an incredible coaching association which would last for more than twenty-five years?

As suggested, Kenneth enrolled at Hardin-Simmons and obtained his teaching certificate. That fall, he moved to Victoria and began his coaching career. His first job was at Victoria's Crain Junior High.

◆　◆　◆

IN THE SPRING OF 1958, a few weeks before hip-swiveler Elvis Presley was inducted into the U.S. Army, Katharine, Pat and I moved to Victoria. For the first few months we rented a house, but near the end of May, I bumped into C.E. Erwin, a fellow I'd known at Seminole. Back in Seminole, Erwin and his brother-in-law had owned an electric service company. C.E. was a hard worker, but his brother-in-law partner wasn't. Eventually their differences caused them to split up, and C.E. relocated to Victoria where he'd done quite well.

Erwin's South Texas success was an amazing story of rags-to-riches. When C.E. arrived in Victoria, he had fifteen dollars in his pocket. Somehow, he convinced the local Sinclair distributor to lease him a big truck stop out on U.S. 59. His gasoline business became an overnight sensation, mainly because C.E. understood people and knew how to push exactly the right buttons. He offered cash discounts to any trucker who would stop and allow him to fill their tanks. Many evenings, eighteen wheelers would be lined up for blocks waiting to "fill up" and get their cash discount.

Shortly after our arrival, Erwin sold his truck stop lease for a small fortune and plunged headfirst into real estate. C.E.'s real estate partner was Albert Dick who owned the three largest grocery stores in town. Because of the new jobs being created by area industrial expansion, Victoria was experiencing an unbelievable population explosion. Real estate was hot, and Erwin and Dick played the game fast and loose, pulling off some of the dangdest money-making land deals you could imagine.

C.E. was not only a wheeler-dealer, he was also a world-class salesman. Three days after I ran into him, I signed a contract agreeing to have him build me a house in a new residential addition he and Albert Dick were developing. Before fall football season kicked off, Katharine, Pat and I were enjoying the luxury of a three-bedroom, two bath, brand-spanking-new home. Dollar for dollar, the deal Erwin made me on that house still ranks as the best buy I ever made.

◆ ◆ ◆

WHEN SCHOOL BEGAN in September of 1958, any high school girl who wasn't wearing a full-skirted "rock n' roll" dress layered with petticoats was plain and simple "out of fashion." Blue suede penny loafers worn with rolled-down white socks were also a must. For guys, though, the uniform remained pretty much the same—blue jeans with the cuffs rolled up, topped with a multicolored plaid shirt. Almost any kind of leather shoe would work.

Gordon Wood—head football coach at Victoria High School.
(credit: Wood Family Collection)

Occasionally at the grocery store, you'd see a grown man walking around in Bermuda shorts, but not Gordon Wood. I never thought a man's hairy legs were all that attractive. Probably the wildest thing I ever owned was a loud plaid sports coat Katharine bought for me. I wore it twice before I donated it to our church rummage sale.

◆ ◆ ◆

IN AN ATTEMPT to eliminate so many tie games, both the NCAA and the Texas Interscholastic League adopted a major rule change for the 1958 football season—allowing an optional two-point conversion after every touchdown. Coaches all across Texas were wrestling with the possible repercussions. If a team went for two and won the game, the football coach would be hailed a genius. If he went for two and lost, he'd probably find a "For Sale" sign planted in his front lawn.

Even though Morris Southall and I inherited a number of good players at Victoria, our pool of football talent was short on one vital

Coaches Southall and Wood reunited in Victoria.
(credit: Wood Family Collection)

ingredient. Our linemen were plenty big, but our backs lacked the game breaking speed which greatly contributed to our past success. Still, we had left good jobs at Stamford and Winters to become two of the highest paid coaches in the state, so expectations were extremely high as our Stingaree football team opened the season against Port Lavaca. To our pleasant surprise, we cracked the Sandcrabs 33–0.

The following week our competition improved dramatically. At intermission Victoria held a slim 7–6 edge over Corpus Christi Carroll. Our offense came alive in the second half with senior tailback Kenneth Jones rolling for 161 yards and scoring twice.

Final Score: Victoria 19, Carroll 6.

Then we ran into Darrell Tully and his Spring Branch Bears.

◆　◆　◆

AT THE COACHES CONVENTION in Houston the previous summer, I had been elected President of the Texas High School Coaches Association. Darrell Tully was selected vice-president.

Tully coached at Spring Branch High School where he had revived a decadent football program, improving from 1–8–1 in 1956 to 6–4 in 1957, after Darrell took over. He had been runner-up behind Abilene's Chuck Moser for Coach-of-the-Year honors in 1957.

Tully was not only an exceptional coach, he was also a captivating storyteller and a fierce domino player. Darrell coached at Spring Branch until 1964, compiling an enviable 63–23–2 record before he checked in his cleats to become full-time athletic director for the Spring Branch School District. He was inducted into the Coaches Hall of Honor in 1968. Darrell retired in 1978. He and I remained close friends until he passed away a few years ago.

◆ ◆ ◆

EVERY FALL, LEG CRAMPS were always a nagging problem. Coach Southall and I were particularly concerned about muscle cramps that first year in Victoria. In South Texas, the stifling humidity hung in the air like predawn mist over a Louisiana swamp, and the searing early fall temperatures easily equaled those in Stamford and Winters. We were determined to avoid the problem, so we insisted our players take salt pills before and after workouts. In addition, we added salt to the players' drinking water. At first, the boys wouldn't drink our saline mixture, but when a football player gets thirsty enough, he'll drink salt water and a whole lot of it.

◆ ◆ ◆

SPRING BRANCH HIGH SCHOOL is located on the western edge of Houston. We arrived on Friday afternoon around five o'clock, three hours before game time. As our team filed off the bus, the air was hot and muggy with not a trace of a breeze. Our dressing quarters were only a few steps from the bus, but perspiration matted my short-sleeved shirt against my skin before I could reach the locker room door.

Our game that humid September evening evolved into a defensive battle with neither team able to score in the first half, but by the middle of the second quarter, half our kids were on the sidelines suffering from severe leg cramps. Morris and I were totally baffled. All the salt we'd forced down our players' gullets hadn't helped one bit.

Late in the third quarter, Tully's Bruins pushed down to

Victoria's one-yard line, first and goal. Three stabs at the right side were stopped short by Stingaree linemen Lawrence McElroy, Wesley Johnson and Joe Hutchins. In desperation, Spring Branch tried a fourth-down pass which Ken Jones intercepted in the end zone for a touchback.

A nine-play, eighty-yard drive followed our magnificent goal line stand, and when Stingaree quarterback Mike Abernathey squirted in from the three, the Bears were finished.

Final score: Victoria 7, Spring Branch 0.

◆　◆　◆

A FEW YEARS LATER, Baylor head coach Grant Teaff, Baylor assistant coach Bill Yung and I conducted a clinic for junior high coaches at a Baptist encampment near Waco. One of our guest speakers was a former trainer for the Dallas Cowboys and the Miami Dolphins. One of the things the trainer stressed was giving players plenty of liquids. He recommended keeping gatorade, or one of several other expensive thirst quenchers, available during practice. After the trainer finished speaking, I cornered him.

"What if a school can't afford those exotic drinks? What can a coach give his players in place of canned drinks?"

"Give 'em ice water, and plenty of it," the trainer told me.

"Ice water? My boys can't get in shape drinking ice water."

"Sure they can. Give your players all the ice water they want and when they want it."

"What about leg cramps? Won't they get leg cramps if they drink too much water?"

"Let me tell you about leg cramps, Coach Wood. More kids get leg cramps from too much salt than too little."

His advice shook me, because so many coaches in those days labored under the ridiculous assumption their players couldn't get in condition if they drank too much water. Because of those stupid beliefs, one or two Texas kids died every year from heat exhaustion.

From that day until I retired, my practice field had ice water available for players. My teams didn't take water breaks. Any time one of my kids got thirsty he knew he had permission to get a drink without any criticism from his coaches.

◆　◆　◆

VICTORIA'S THIRD WIN in a row turned a lot of heads. Football polls all across the state moved the Stingarees into their top ten 4A elevens. That's when the nightmare began. A team that could do nothing wrong suddenly became a team that could do nothing right.

First, Port Arthur whitewashed us 12–0. Next, flexing Victoria High's new-found financial muscle, our football team boarded a chartered, twin-engine silver bird and winged across South Texas to the Mexican border to take on Harlingen. First-class travel accommodations did little to change our luck. Playing on a muddy field, which many a West Texas bullfrog would gratefully call home, we splish-splashed to another loss. My Stingarees were leading 13–6 when the Cardinals scored late in the fourth quarter. Their successful two-point conversion broke our hearts.

Final score: 14–13.

Victoria dropped two more before our badly listing boat righted itself. My Stingarees regrouped to win their last three contests, but the victories came too late. Conference losses to San Antonio Jefferson and San Antonio Alamo Heights essentially eliminated my football team from playoff contention. District 15–AAAA was no different than 4–AA. One loss and you'd be home on Turkey Day. Two losses and you *were* a turkey.

Our season ended with Victoria in a three-way tie with Alamo Heights and San Antonio Harlandale for second place—the exact same slot the Stingarees occupied the previous year before I showed up amidst all the high expectations.

◆ ◆ ◆

MY DECISION TO ACCEPT the Victoria coaching job was greatly influenced by my friendship with Doctor Andrew Tomb. After I moved to Victoria, that friendship flourished. Once or twice a week, we'd get together for lunch, or I would drop by his office for coffee.

Doctor Tomb kept a lot of irons in the fire. In Seminole, he'd been deeply involved with alcoholic rehabilitation. In Victoria, he had become involved in a program to assist unwed mothers. One morning he was telling me about an infant he'd helped put up for adoption. The expectant mother had asked that the child be adopted by Protestant parents. Victoria's population was largely

Catholic, and the doctor was telling me how difficult it was to find a suitable Christian home there.

Katharine and I had been trying to have a second child for several years without success. We'd discussed the possibility of adopting many times. Two years earlier we had come close to adopting a Greek boy, but the boy was eleven, the same age as Patricia. We both felt bringing another child the same age as our daughter into our family would be a mistake.

"You know, Doc, if I knew a baby's background and exactly where he came from, I might be interested in adopting."

My friend and I briefly discussed the options and left it at that. I never suspected anything would come of our casual conversation.

Several weeks later, Katharine, Pat and I were in Austin at the state basketball tournament. It was past midnight when the telephone in our hotel room rang. When I answered, Andy Tomb was on the line.

"I've got that child you want, Coach."

"What? You've got what?"

"The baby you want to adopt. I've made all the arrangements."

I rolled out of bed and carried the telephone into the bathroom. Keeping my voice low so Katharine wouldn't hear I said, "Doctor Tomb, what the heck are you talking about?"

Andrew Tomb was an impetuous man. He seemed perturbed I wasn't ecstatic about his unexpected news.

"Gordon, you told me you wanted a baby. I've found one that's perfect for you."

"Look, Doctor, I haven't even mentioned this to my wife or daughter. We need some time to think this through."

"Alright, you and Katharine talk it over. But I need an answer. When you get back to Victoria, you call me and tell me what you've decided."

"Sure, Doc. Let me talk with my family. We'll let you know something the minute we're back in town."

After I hung up, my mind was an absolute mess. I took a moment to collect my thoughts. Katharine was asleep, so I decided to wait and tell her about Andrew Tomb's baby the next morning. I went back to bed myself, but I didn't sleep a wink all night.

◆　　◆　　◆

KATHARINE AND I desperately wanted another child, but thirteen-year-old Patricia was the family member who ultimately made the decision. Initially, Pat was in favor, but when she found out the baby would be adopted, she changed her mind.

We arrived home from Austin on Wednesday morning. That afternoon I took my teenage daughter for a ride to explain the adoption process, and hopefully, obtain her consent.

"Pat, your mother and I have tried to have another child ever since you were born, but it's not going to happen. The only way for us to have a baby is to adopt one. Our family needs to make a decision about this, but if you have even the slightest doubt, we won't do it."

We drove and talked for a long time with Pat wavering back and forth. One minute she'd say she wanted the baby, the next minute she'd think of some reason we shouldn't. I turned the car around and headed for home, not sure what her decision would be. When I pulled alongside our front curb, Pat jumped out and ran inside to find a book of baby names Katharine had purchased. By the time I walked through the front door, my daughter was flipping through the pages, trying to decide on a name for her new brother or sister.

The next day I called Doctor Tomb, and we started the adoption process. No two children have ever been closer than Pat and her adopted brother.

◆　◆　◆

SUNDAY MORNING the baby was due. Katharine and I were both beside ourselves, bumping into each other, grinning like two happy possums, overwhelmed with nervous excitement. I stayed home, in case the hospital called. Katharine dressed and went on to church. On Sundays she taught a morning, pre-service bible class.

Katharine had no sooner walked out the door than the telephone rang. It was the hospital. The nurse advised me the baby had arrived in good health, and it was a boy.

"That's great," I told the nurse, trying to sound calm, like this was just an ordinary, everyday event. "But I want you to go check one more time and make sure it's a boy baby. I don't want any mix-ups. I want to be absolutely sure when I tell my wife."

My heart was racing like a souped-up drag engine while I dialed the church to tell my wife. She came right home, but when she got there, we realized there really wasn't a darn thing either of us could do to speed up the process. Not knowing what else to do, we hopped in the car and drove back to church. When we reached the church, Katharine wheeled into a parking space close to the front entrance, and we hurried inside to catch the morning service.

After church, we discovered Katharine had left the motor running.

◆ ◆ ◆

INITIALLY, THE HOSPITAL told us we'd have to wait a couple of days before we could come get our baby, but Monday afternoon, they called to say the baby was doing so well we could pick him up.

When you adopt a child, a lot of strange thoughts run through your mind. You ask yourself silly questions like:

"What if I don't like this baby?"

"What if he grows up to be some kind of hoodlum?"

All it takes to resolve those questions is one time holding that child in your arms and cradling him against your chest. After that, your heart is so full of love no force on earth could make you give him up. I'll guarantee there's not an ounce of difference in the way you feel about an adopted child than one you made.

A proud father with new son,
Jim Wood.
(credit: Wood Family Collection)

We named our baby son Jim, and the immeasurable joy he's added to our lives cannot be described in words.

◆ ◆ ◆

I CAN'T EXPLAIN precisely why I decided to leave Victoria. Even now I can't say my reasons make a whole lot of sense. I liked the people, the teachers, my assistant coaches and my players. My family lived in a nice home, and after my first season, I was rewarded with a five-hundred-dollar raise. Katharine was happy and deeply involved with our church. Pat loved her school and had lots of friends.

One of the reasons I left was because of the enormous prosperity. I feared my children might grow up judging people by the size of their car, how expensive their home, or how much money they earned. Another factor was alcohol. At the end of each school year, almost every spring weekend, senior students at Victoria High would throw outlandish graduation parties. Many of these parties cost thousands of dollars, and alcohol was served at many of the parties. Even though my daughter Pat and the Southall's son Terry were several years away from graduation, Victoria's casual attitude about teenage drinking was a great worry for me and Coach Southall.

There were other reasons, like lack of fan support for my football team. I think I was also homesick. Okay! Maybe I didn't miss the droughts, the sandstorms, and the bone dry weather, but I sure did miss West Texas football fans with their unwavering passion for football.

◆ ◆ ◆

BY MID-OCTOBER of 1959, my Stingarees were still in contention for the 15–AAAA conference crown. Our backfield speed had improved, but our main strength was in our line. Most of my linemen could have played for any team in the state.

Victoria's record was three and one the night we played the blue and gold Mules of Alamo Heights. Our game was played in San Antonio. It was a vital contest. Both teams were in a dead-heat with San Antonio Highlands for the district lead.

It was a close game, decided by a late touchdown. Alamo Heights scored their winning TD on a dive play over the center of the line. Saturday morning the *San Antonio Light* ran a picture on the front page of their sports section showing a Mule ballcarrier diving into the end zone—without the ball. In the photograph, the football was lying on the ground, two yards shy of the goal line.

A caption underneath the picture read: *How to score a touchdown without the ball.*

◆ ◆ ◆

AFTER THE LOSS to Alamo Heights, I was upset and discouraged. We had lost a critical game we should have won. When Victoria played in San Antonio, we were forced to use San Antonio game officials, and in my mind, that always put us at a disadvantage. My convictions were reinforced by the picture in the San Antonio newspaper.

Sunday afternoon, my assistant coaches and I were at the high school reviewing scouting reports for our upcoming contest with San Antonio Jefferson and watching films of our game against Alamo Heights. About halfway through the film, the subject of fan support came up, and one of the coaches said he'd heard Victoria High only sold two hundred and twenty-five adult tickets for the Alamo Heights game. The coach said Roy Greenwood, the school's business manager, told him the 125-mile drive was just too far for most people.

I was already in an ugly frame of mind because of the poor officiating we'd had forced on us, so the news flash hit me like a lightning bolt. My head pounded like a bass drum as the projector reeled off more depressing pictures of our Friday night loss.

Finally, I could contain my feelings no longer. I turned to Coach Southall and declared, "I don't know about you, Morris, but I'm gonna start looking for another job."

CHAPTER TEN

Home is Where the Heart Is

(1960)

SEVERAL THINGS actually made my mind up about changing jobs and moving back to West Texas. My mother died in 1956, and my father had moved in with my sister. Dad was eighty-four years old. My mother's death affected his mental state. Frequently, my father would go off on a tangent and become impossible for my sister to handle. She'd call, and I'd jump in the car and head for Abilene to settle him down. We'd talk, and he'd be okay again. After my visit, dad would be fine for three or four weeks, then he'd start ranting again. It's a heck of a long drive from Victoria to Abilene. As time went by, it became longer and longer.

Another factor was my age. In 1959, I turned forty-five. At the time, I expected to retire when I reached sixty-five, a date which was only twenty years in the future.

In 1958, Victoria's electorate had voted against allowing their school teachers to participate in the social security program. (For Texas teachers to enjoy the benefits of social security, it has to be voted in. Consequently, very few school districts allow their teachers to supplement teachers' retirement with social security.) Anyway, without social security, life after sixty-five looked rather bleak. Katharine hadn't worked since we married. If we stayed in Victoria, we'd be forced to spend our retirement years trying to survive on teachers' retirement income alone.

◆　◆　◆

IN JANUARY OF 1960, I interviewed for the head coaching position at San Angelo Central High School. San Angelo was a member of prestigious District 2–AAAA along with Abilene, Big

Spring, Midland and Odessa. In those days, if your team could get past District 2–AAAA, getting to the state finals was pretty much a cinch. With a wide base of passionate football fans, a built-in pipeline of outstanding athletes, and a modern football stadium which seated seventeen thousand, the coaching post at Central High ranked among the ten best high school jobs in Texas.

Because of some ridiculous political squabble, the San Angelo School Board was split right down the middle—three trustees on each side. I had to interview separately with each group. Both groups advised me to play it cool and not let the other side know they were in favor of hiring me, because that would cause the other faction to vote against me. From start to finish, their entire selection process was childlike and absurd, but I wanted the job. I had little choice except to play along.

Emory Bellard, who was coaching at Breckenridge, was the other coach being seriously considered. In my mind I had an edge on Emory. One reason was because my Stamford team had beaten his on their home field in the 1955 state quarterfinals. A second reason was because my good friend G.B. "Blackie" Wadzeck was the superintendent of schools at San Angelo.

A couple of weeks after the San Angelo interview, Darrell Royal called me in Victoria and invited me to ride with him in his airplane to the National Coaches Convention in New York City. I was delighted to accept. Coach Royal was a man I greatly admired, and his friendship meant a lot to me.

At the coaching convention I ran into Gerald Breeding, a San Angelo sporting goods dealer. Breeding informed me San Angelo had hired Emory Bellard. His news hit me like a bombshell. I immediately telephoned the president of the San Angelo School Board. The president was a graduate of Texas University.

"That's right, Coach Wood. We've hired Emory Bellard as our new coach. He's already accepted."

His words chilled my heart. San Angelo was a job I'd coveted for years. I'd been absolutely certain I would be selected.

"But on what basis? Why would you choose him over me?"

"Well, two things. Number one, Darrell Royal recommended Emory."

"Hell, man, I'm here in New York with Coach Royal right now. He invited me to fly up here in his airplane along with his

Texas coaches. Darrell is one of my best friends. He would've recommended me if you'd asked."

"Well, we didn't ask him about you, Coach Wood. Maybe we should have."

"Okay! What's the other reason you hired Bellard?"

"Your salary. Coach Wood, you're making ten thousand dollars a year at Victoria. Coach Bellard is only making seventy-five hundred at Breckenridge. We thought he'd be happier here than you because we can only pay eighty-five hundred."

"What made you think that? I wanted to coach at San Angelo. Salary was never a factor in my decision to seek your job."

I meant what I said. Three weeks later I accepted a coaching job at Brownwood High School for even less money—seventy-five hundred a year. Losing the San Angelo post was a bitter disappointment, and for a time my heart was heavy. In retrospect, San Angelo made an excellent decision. Emory Bellard was an exceptional coach. He did a great job at San Angelo Central, and everywhere he coached.

◆　◆　◆

SOMETIMES OPPORTUNITY doesn't come knocking. Sometimes it just ambles up and takes you by the hand, leaving you little choice except to follow.

Several weeks later, yielding to the insistence of board member Bob Ross, Brownwood's school superintendent J.D. King contacted me to ask if I'd be interested in their coaching vacancy. Brownwood's close proximity to Abilene was a major factor in my decision to follow up on King's inquiry. The next weekend I met with Superintendent King. He promised I could bring along Morris Southall and another coach I wanted to hire. When our meeting concluded, we shook hands to consummate our deal. Neither of us realized the awesome consequences of that cordial gesture.

At Brownwood I replaced Roland "Slim" Warren. Slim had been coaching football at Brownwood High since 1953, and he was a good coach. His 1959 team went eight and two, but Coach Warren had one unforgivable fault. He couldn't beat Breckenridge, and if you couldn't beat Breckenridge, you didn't go nowhere. Brownwood had won one district championship in forty years, and that championship was won during a year Breckenridge was voted out of Brownwood's district.

One of the first friends I made after I moved to Brownwood was local mortician Groner Pitts, who fancies himself the resident expert on Lion football. Groner's analysis pretty much summed up the situation I inherited.

"The Lions," Groner told me, "spend most of their time facing third and long."

◆　◆　◆

A WINTER SNOW STORM slashed across West Texas the day Katharine, Pat, our new son Jim and I moved to Brownwood, causing traffic pileups and shutting down schools from Weatherford to Odessa.

To my family's good fortune, we had purchased a house from my old friend Leonard King whose family operated a music store in Brownwood. Leonard was opening another store in San Angelo and had put his house on the market only a few days before I accepted the Brownwood coaching position. Our arrival coincided perfectly with his leaving.

For three days I toted boxes, rearranged furniture and unwrapped dishes. I was so busy unpacking I neglected to shave. On Monday, February 15, I'd had all the moving this football coach could handle. By eight o'clock that morning I was on duty at Brownwood High—not actually working. Mostly I was snooping around the athletic facilities.

Max Emfinger and Ben Elledge were both second semester sophomores the day we first met. The following fall they would play key roles in Brownwood's drive for the state championship, but at the time, I didn't know one player from the other. My face was covered with a three-day beard the afternoon I approached them on the practice field.

"Hi, fellows. Are you guys football players?" I asked in a feeble attempt to be friendly.

"Yeah, what's it to you, mister!" Emfinger answered indignantly.

"Oh, nothing. I'm just looking around, trying to meet everyone," I mumbled. I should have introduced myself, but to tell the truth, it was my first day, and I was a bit intimidated by the situation.

As I walked away, Emfinger turned to Elledge and asked, "Who was that old guy?"

"Probably the new janitor. But if the principal catches him looking like that, he'll be looking for another job tomorrow," Elledge declared, taking two steps back and flinging the football to Lawrence Elkins who was circling impatiently downfield.

Imagine those young men's surprise the next day when I assembled the football team at the high school auditorium to watch films of my Victoria games. Of course, by then I'd shaved.

◆ ◆ ◆

BROWNWOOD IS LOCATED sixteen miles from the state's geographic center. In the early days, right after Texas gained its independence from Mexico, there was a lot of talk about making Brownwood the state capital, the reasoning being that travel would be equidistant for elected representatives from all areas. Unfortunately, that didn't come to pass, and Texas missed out on a wonderful opportunity. Nowhere else in the world will you find people so friendly, so loyal, or more supportive of one another. If you're from out-of-state, though, you might find Brownwood Fridays a little strange. Because on Fridays, Brown County residents go absolutely nuts—about high school football.

In the spring of 1960, as golfer Arnold Palmer was winning the Masters Tournament in Augusta, the ranks of Lion believers had dwindled to an all time low. We began spring training with only six returning lettermen, and they were the scrawniest bunch of rag-knots Coach Southall and I had ever seen. The biggest member of our team was Ronnie Moore, a tackle who tipped the scales at 178 pounds.

After the maroon and white game, which marked the end of our spring practice, I complained to Katharine, "There may be eleven football players out there, but I sure haven't found 'em yet."

An article which appeared in the *Brownwood Bulletin* confirmed my assessment with this pre-season analysis:

"Team depth: None."

"Defensive line: Very small and inexperienced."

"Offensive backs: Below average."

"Defensive backs: Below average."

"Team size: Very small compared to last year's squad."

"Main strength: This team does not have any strong spots."

"Main weakness: Lack of experience, speed, size, age and strength."

◆　　◆　　◆

EVERY COACH WORTH HIS SALT has to be a good yard man. If a coach wants a nice field to play on in the fall, he has to care for the field during the summer. Few schools budget adequate funds for proper lawn maintenance, so coaches and players are expected to do the lion's share of the work—fertilize the field, cut the grass, water the lawn. At Hardin-Simmons, I was force-fed everything I needed to know about yard maintenance.

When I arrived to coach at Brownwood in the spring of 1960, the high school played their games in an ancient facility off Austin Avenue. The playing field was in terrible condition. Slim Warren's football teams had not only played their games on the old field, they also worked out there.

Hoping to improve the condition of our game field, I started to work the minute school let out. Two local business men, Bill Williams and Stuart Coleman, actually performed most of the hard labor.

The top soil on the stadium field was so poor and so hard it would hardly grow grass, so we hauled in maybe twenty truck loads of sand. Then we plowed up the ground and ran over the field with disks to break up the dirt and mix in the sand. Our budget wouldn't allow for fertilizer, but my co-workers knew a man who operated a poultry farm which housed about ten thousand chickens. The poultry farmer agreed to furnish us with all the chicken manure we wanted. He even agreed to load it for us if we would provide the truck to haul it. Finding a truck was easy. I contacted local contractor Herman Bennett, and he loaned us a truck.

There's no telling how many loads we hauled in, but in two days we had the field completely covered with about three inches of chicken manure. We'd no sooner finished spreading the manure than a summer shower dropped about an inch of rain on us. The rain lasted about thirty minutes. Then the sun came out again, pushing the temperature back past a hundred degrees.

Talk about stink. Our playing field put off a smell that would stagger even the most stout-hearted man. The stench emanated off the field, affecting several blocks around the stadium. Now

Brownwood is real big on football, and in the name of football, Brownwood citizens will suffer just about any indecency, but the smell we forced on the town was too much.

One lady who lived near the stadium came to complain, "Coach Wood, I'm the biggest football fan in Brownwood, but me and every member of my family are sick to our stomachs. Isn't there something you can do?"

Of course there wasn't. All we could do was wait for the manure to dry. The woman had no sooner left than here comes a car loaded with four men from the Brownwood health department. They leaped out of their car and began telling me about all the people who were calling city hall to complain about the smell. Naturally, they blamed me for creating the problem.

I told them there was nothing I could do because we had no way to remove the manure. I promised not to haul in any more, but that didn't seem to satisfy them. The health men left in a huff. As they drove away, I knew they were headed to the school superintendent's office, and I was in big trouble.

Perhaps ten minutes passed before J.D. King, the school superintendent, appeared on the uneven expanse between the high school and the football stadium. He's headed in my direction, walking fast. I could tell he was steaming mad. His hat was bouncing up and down with every step.

"Coach Wood, the health department is all over my back because of you . . ."

"Wait a minute, Mister King," I said, interrupting him before he could finish. "I already know how unhappy those health department folks are. They were out here before they came to see you."

"Well, what did you tell 'em?"

"I told them that J.D. King is my boss, and I'm doing exactly what he instructed me to do."

The superintendent's face turned a beet red. He stammered and started to say something. Then he said, "Aw, to hell with it!" He threw up his hands and stormed off.

J.D. King was one of the finest men I ever worked under. Generally, he had a terrific sense of humor, but that hot, humid summer afternoon, my superintendent was not amused.

◆　◆　◆

IN 1960, TWO THINGS dominated national headlines—the cold war and desegregation. When Negro minister Theodore Roosevelt Thompson was served food at Kress, H.L. Green, and Sanger lunch counters in downtown Dallas, the incident made front page news all across the country. In May, when U-2 pilot Francis Gary Powers was shot down over the Soviet Union, every U.S. citizen held their breath, hoping the embarrassing episode wouldn't escalate into an all-out nuclear war.

With world tensions at an all time high, sports occasionally provided a welcome break. In June, Floyd Patterson became the first boxer in history to regain the heavyweight title by knocking out Ingemar Johannson in five rounds. In August, the Summer Olympics were held in Rome, and because the event was televised, more people watched the games than ever before. To everyone's dismay, the Soviets dominated the competition.

◆　◆　◆

BROWNWOOD TWO-A-DAYS began in mid-August as Democrats and Republicans were wrapping up their national conventions. As expected, the Republicans nominated vice-president Richard Nixon to head their ticket, but the Democrats raised many a Protestant eyebrow by choosing Jack Kennedy, a Catholic, as their presidential candidate.

Our first tipoff as to what lay in store came during a scrimmage with Austin High School. Austin rolled into Brownwood with two bus loads of football players. Our Brownwood boys were so intimidated by Austin's size that they were literally shaking in their cleats when the practice match began. To everyone's surprise, though, Brownwood stopped Austin's offense cold on their first series. We were even more astonished when our offense easily moved the football against Austin's defensive team.

Midway through the scrimmage, an Austin player blindsided Ronnie Moore, hitting him square in the back and knocking him to the ground. Moore jumped up and started slugging at every Austin uniform in sight. Brownwood players on the sideline surged forward, wanting to join in, but I held them back. The fighters on the playing field were in full pads, so nobody was doing much damage to anyone else. The on-field fisticuffs did accomplish something positive, though. Moore's bare-knuckle barrage fired up his

*Ronnie Moore, tri-captain,
all-state—Brownwood's 1960 state
championship team. (credit: Fred Nobs,
Brownwood photographer)*

teammates, and from that point forward, my scrawny Lions kicked the dog out of Austin.

◆ ◆ ◆

OUR FIRST regular game was scheduled against San Angelo Central. The Bobcats were coached by Emory Bellard who, nine months earlier, had outmaneuvered me for the San Angelo post. The Central High squad outweighed my bony Maroons by some twenty pounds per man, and the Bobcats were a heavy favorite. Sportswriters all across Texas picked San Angelo as one of the top teams in the state.

On Thursday, the *San Angelo Standard-Times* quoted Coach Bellard as saying, "We hope to win by a huge margin because that's the only way we can justify the long, hard practices we've put our players through."

Shortly before game time, Morris Southall and I met with Coach Bellard at a restaurant in downtown Brownwood where he and his team were eating a pre-game meal. While we were talking, a San Angelo player eased up and laid a Brownwood newspaper on the table in front of us. In the sports section was a weekly "pick-it" contest wherein Brown County readers tried to predict the correct score of the upcoming high school game.

"Look here, Coach Bellard. One of these men thinks we won't beat Brownwood more than 36–7."

That was the closest score any of the weekly guessers predicted. To his credit, Coach Bellard was truly embarrassed by his player's tactless behavior. As we left the meeting, Coach Southall exhaled through pursed lips and sarcastically offered this comment,

"Heck, Gordon, I reckon we oughta be happy if they don't totally embarrass us like forty-five or fifty to nothing."

◆　◆　◆

FOUR THOUSAND FLABBERGASTED FANS watched as Brownwood's riled-up Lions struck with lightning-like fury. On our second play from scrimmage, Lion quarterback Ben Elledge hit Lawrence Elkins in the right flat. Elkins reeled in the perfectly thrown over-the-shoulder pass and rambled fifty-six yards to score standing up.

Two and a half minutes later, junior halfback Max Emfinger picked off a hurried San Angelo aerial and outran two orange-clad players to the Bobcat goal line.

A short punt set up our third TD. Starting at the Bobcats' thirty-nine, Brownwood halfback John Cadenhead was stopped for a gain of one. Then Elledge gained eight on a quarterback keeper, and Emfinger blasted off tackle for four to give us a first down on the twenty-six. On the next play Emfinger took a quick pitchout from Elledge and rifled a strike to Elkins who was all alone at the end zone flag. Nine minutes into the game, Brownwood held a commanding 22–0 lead.

When the game ended, my maroon club had scored twice more, recovered three fumbles and intercepted six passes, including four by Max Emfinger. San Angelo never knew what hit 'em.

Final score: Brownwood 34, San Angelo 6.

◆　◆　◆

OUR SECOND GAME was against Killeen. Ray Ragland, a 205-pound fullback who carried the football like a westbound freighter, spearheaded the Kangaroos' crunching ground attack. Killeen had dropped a heart-breaker to San Antonio Burbank in their season opener, but the 'Roos were nobody's patsy. They were well coached, and with ten lettermen returning, they were expected to be a playoff contender. Killeen's front line averaged 182 pounds, a 17-pound bulge over Brownwood's skinny grunt soldiers.

Thanks to Max Emfinger's breathtaking return of the opening kickoff for a touchdown and some tough running by bull-necked ballcarriers John Cadenhead and A.D. Carnes, Brownwood winged into halftime with an 18–12 lead. In the second half, the Lions continued to dominate. Then two interceptions and a long punt return by Kangaroo speedster Ray Fielder allowed Killeen to grab a 20–18 advantage.

Late in the game, Brownwood drove sixty yards to Killeen's twenty, but when Carnes' fourth-down try was stopped inches short of a first down, only four minutes remained on the clock. It appeared the 'Roos had the game in the bag. A couple of minutes later, though, Killeen's fullback Ray Ragland was met head on at the line of scrimmage. The mind-jolting impact jarred the ball loose, and Brownwood recovered on the Kangaroos' thirty-six.

In four running plays Brownwood moved the ball to the twenty. We had used our last time-out and were facing fourth and five when Coach Southall called down from the press box. Morris advised that Killeen was overloading on our strong side. Heeding my assistant's suggestion to try a weak side pitchout, I grabbed a reserve player, gave him some hasty instructions for my quarterback, and sent him scurrying toward our huddle out on the field. Fearing time might run out, I was especially emphatic. Cadenhead was to take the ball, get the yardage needed for the first down, and run out of bounds. John followed my orders explicitly. Even though Mike Greer had leveled the defensive halfback and there wasn't a single Kangaroo defender standing between him and the goal line, Cadenhead ran out of bounds at the twelve.

You could hardly hear yourself think as I sent in Jesse Hernandez with the next play. The school band was blaring. Our cheerleaders were excitedly running along the sidelines urging their maroon heroes on. Every spectator in the grandstands was on his feet and yelling like crazy.

We called a three-deep pass, but when Elledge rolled out, all his receivers were covered. Ben tucked the ball under his arm, cut behind Terry Dummer's clearing block and sprinted for the end zone. Forty-four seconds remained on the scoreboard clock when Elledge trotted across the goal line to secure our spine-tingling victory. When the game ended, Brownwood faithful were totally exhausted and so hoarse they could hardly speak.

Final score: Brownwood 26, Killeen 20.

◆　◆　◆

MY FATHER PASSED AWAY the next week. My two assistants,

Morris Southall and Pete Murray, took charge of the football squad while Katharine and I were in Abilene to attend the funeral. Dad's memorial service was mostly a small family gathering. My father had outlived most of his numerous Taylor County friends. We buried him on Wednesday alongside my mother.

My father's death hurt me deeply, but as callous as this may sound, dad's passing was a kind of relief for everyone. He was a good man, a wonderful father, and he'd lived a full life. Every one of us children loved him dearly, but he was no longer the father we'd known. His mind was failing, and he had become a tremendous burden for my sister. Sad as it may seem, death is often a blessing.

◆　◆　◆

THE NEXT WEEKEND Brownwood slipped past Waco University 19–6, but then the unbeaten Temple Wildcats came to town and our win-streak came to a screeching halt. The Wildcats were coached by Jay Fikes. Coach Fikes was a close friend, but we disagreed on a lot of things. Jay's teams played rough—throwing elbows, helmet slapping—that kind of stuff.

Brownwood scored on a 73-yard opening drive and had the ball again after Elkins recovered a bobbled Wildcat handoff on Temple's forty-two. On the next play, Temple's noseguard punched our center, David Smith, in the mouth. When I complained, the game officials slapped us with a fifteen-yard penalty. Consecutive carries for twelve, eighteen and thirteen yards by Emfinger negated the penalty, but when Brownwood reached the three, Temple's burly noseguard smacked our center again. This time David's lip was split so bad we had to remove him from the game. A fumble on the next play wiped out our opportunity to go ahead by two touchdowns.

The Wildcats scored twice in the second quarter and once more in the third. My Lions put up a courageous fight, but once the Wildcat's got us down, their brute strength was too much to overcome.

Final score: Brownwood 22, Temple 26.

◆　◆　◆

JAY FIKES AND I met while we were athletes on scholarship at Hardin-Simmons. Jay's first head coaching job was at Hamlin, Texas. In 1944, he moved to Littlefield where he realized amazing success. His maroon and white Wildcats captured the Class A state title in 1949. The first time a Gordon Wood team played a Jay Fikes team was in 1947, when I was coaching at Seminole.

In 1954, Coach Fikes accepted the head coaching post at Temple High School. Jay was inducted into the Texas High School Coaches Hall of Honor in 1975.

Jay Fikes possessed a unique sense of humor, and he loved to pull jokes on other people. Consequently, his victims were always trying to get even. Amusing stories about Jay's demented behavior are too numerous to tell, but my favorite Jay Fikes story occurred while we were attending coaching school in Dallas. I was in the hotel lobby when I ran into Harold Ratliff, perhaps the most famous Texas sportswriter of all time. Ratliff asked me if I knew a Coach Jay Fikes.

"Yes, he's here in the hotel. I just left his room," I replied.

"I've been trying to get hold of him. I need some information for a story about his Littlefield team," Ratliff informed me.

"Well, you call up to room 404. I'm sure he'll be glad to talk to you."

Ratliff immediately went to a hotel phone and called Fikes' room. When Ratliff introduced himself, Jay assumed it was another coach trying to put something over on him.

"Coach, I'd like to find out about your football schedule for next season," Ratliff inquired. "Maybe you could tell me what you think about your opponents."

"Well, let's see. We open up with Notre Dame. Then we play Army, followed by USC. We oughta be three and 0 by the time we play Texas University."

"Be serious, Coach Fikes. I want to know about your team and your schedule."

"I am being serious. After we whip up on Texas, we're gonna beat . . . ." Jay went on and on, telling Ratliff about all the big time games he was planning to win. Then he hung up.

Ratliff was totally baffled by Coach Fikes' strange demeanor. He was shaking his head when he walked back to tell me about their bizarre telephone conversation.

"That's the craziest fellow I've ever talked to. The man is a total fruitcake," Ratliff told me.

"No. No, Mister Ratliff, Jay's not like that," I said, defending

*Associated Press
sportswriter
Harold Ratliff
presents "Texas
High School
Coaches Award"
to Gordon Wood
during coaches
banquet in
Dallas, 1959.
(credit: Wood
Family Collection)*

my longtime friend. "He probably thinks you're someone trying to
play a joke on him. Why don't you call him again and explain who
you are?"

Ratliff did try again, and again his inquiries were met with
similar zany answers.

Several minutes later Fikes showed up in the hotel lobby. I
grabbed him by the arm and ushered him over to meet Harold
Ratliff. When Jay realized the man he'd been talking to was actually
the Harold Ratliff, he was embarrassed beyond words.

◆　◆　◆

ON OCTOBER 12, Russian premier Nikita Khrushchev scared the
living daylights out of every American by removing his shoe and
using it to pound on a United Nations' podium while he
condemned the free world for resisting communist aggression.

Brownwood's maroon troops were not nearly that intimidating, but after our loss to Temple, my Lions regrouped and began kicking the daylights out of Central Texas football teams.

On October 8, our rugged defense led the way. Brownwood's first touchdown came when Mike Greer, a defensive tackle, grabbed a Stephenville fumble in mid-air and rambled fifteen yards for the TD. Charles Coffey's interception and 38-yard runback set up Brownwood's second tally. A blocked punt accounted for our final score.

Final score: Brownwood 22, Stephenville 0.

Then we really got rolling. Brownwood opened district play with a 25–0 win over Mineral Wells. A.D. Carnes, James Crow, Ronnie Moore, and Doug Young were the defensive superstars the next week when we blanked Vernon's Lions 16–0 in a rain-soaked battle. Graham was the district's pre-season favorite, but an 8–7 loss to Breckenridge put the Blue and Red with their backs to the wall. My Lions finished the job, bulldogging the Steers 24–8.

◆ ◆ ◆

A FEW DAYS AFTER I moved to Brownwood, I went downtown to get my hair cut. When the barber discovered I was the new high school football coach, he began to razz me and tell me how Brownwood kids always choked up when they played Breckenridge.

"Yep, our boys are afraid of those green uniforms. We'll never beat Breckenridge," the man told me.

"Come on! Surely you don't mean *never*?" I argued, trying to control my temper.

The barber kept riding me, perhaps not realizing the maddening effect his words had on me. "Yes, I do. I put my money on Breckenridge every year. You'd be surprised how much money I won last year."

I waited until the barber finished with my hair. Then I let him have it.

"You know, if every football fan in Brownwood is as sorry as you, then Brownwood doesn't deserve to beat Breckenridge!"

I slammed two bucks on the counter to pay for the haircut and stormed out the door, promising I'd never come back—and I never did. When someone starts talking about losing, I've never been much of a diplomat.

When word got around about the barber's defeatist attitude,

his customers began to get their hair cut elsewhere. Eventually, the man closed his shop and left town.

◆　◆　◆

BROWNWOOD WAS RIDING an emotional high during the week prior to our Breckenridge contest. That turned into a real problem. On Saturday night, people began to show up at Weakley-Watson's downtown hardware store where high school football tickets were sold. By Sunday night, there was a long line waiting to buy tickets.

A week earlier Coach Southall had anticipated the problem. Morris suggested we limit the number of tickets one person could purchase, but when I submitted that idea to Superintendent King, he just laughed.

"Coach, if somebody wants all the tickets, they can have 'em. That'll save the school a whole lot of time and trouble."

By eight o'clock Monday morning, the ticket line stretched all the way around the block. Roland Elledge, my quarterback's older brother, was first in line. When the ticket window opened, Elledge told the ticket man he wanted two hundred and sixty-seven tickets.

The next man in line was Bill Williams, the Brownwood businessman who helped me with the previous summer's ill-fated game field project. Bill leaned past Elledge and advised he'd take all the rest. You can imagine what happened then. A riot almost broke out. People who had been waiting in line all night overheard Williams and began to scream bloody murder.

The Weakley-Watson employee in charge of ticket sales got scared and refused to sell tickets to anyone. Instead, he gave every person in line a number and told them to come back at three o'clock that afternoon.

Later that morning, at a quickly called emergency meeting, the school trustees decided no person could purchase more than four tickets.

Because of the demand for tickets, additional bleachers were brought in, and a stadium which normally seated 3,750 fans was enlarged to accommodate 5,250. The stage was set for one of the most important and most exciting football games ever played in Brownwood, Texas.

◆　◆　◆

Home is Where the Heart Is

PRIOR TO THEIR 1960 ENCOUNTER, Brownwood and Breckenridge had squared off on the gridiron thirty-three times. Brownwood had won only one of those games, and that was back in 1940. Twenty years without a victory is a long time, especially in West Texas where football is a life and death matter.

Brownwood started strong. After kicking off to the Buckies, our defense, with Ronnie Moore, Mike Greer and Eddie Daniel doing yeomen's duty, held the green-clads on downs. Then in nine plays, with Emfinger and Carnes ripping for big gains, Brownwood punched out sixty yards to go ahead 6–0.

In the second quarter a fifteen-yard penalty helped sustain a 69-yard Breckenridge scoring drive. Greenie backs Buddy Langford and Floyd Swaim shouldered most of the load, but highly-touted Troy Kennedy gouged out the final yard.

Breckenridge's second score was a gift. A fumble set the Bucks up on the Lions' thirteen. Langford immediately rammed the ball over left tackle for five, and when Swaim met only minimum resistance as he collected the final eight yards, Brownwood fans began to wonder if their high hopes wouldn't be dashed yet another time.

Some last minute maroon heroics eliminated all those negative thoughts. With only a minute and twenty seconds left in the second quarter and with the ball on Breckenridge's twenty-nine, Lion quarterback Ben Elledge backpedaled and fired a pass to Lawrence Elkins who loped in for the TD, cutting the Buckies' lead to 14–12.

Brownwood dominated play for most of the second half but couldn't seem to make a dent in the stiff greenie defense. One Brownwood drive was stopped at the thirteen. A pass interception killed another. Ferocious defensive play by James Crow, Ronnie Davis, Gerald Pitts and Doug Young kept the Buckaroos under constant pressure and on their end of the field.

An outstanding defensive play in the fourth period finally turned the tide in the home team's favor. Breckenridge had driven down to Brownwood's twenty-six when Larry Elkins knifed through to trip up Buckie fullback Troy Kennedy for no gain on a fourth-down try.

With time running out, Brownwood marched down to the Buckaroo twenty-one. A key play in the drive came on fourth and ten with barely two minutes left on the clock. Like a seasoned pro, Elledge coolly faded back and fired a never-to-be-forgotten bullet to

Elkins at Brownwood's forty-two for a first down. Three plays later Elledge teamed up with ends Eddie Daniel and Elkins for a pass and lateral which moved the ball past mid-field to the Breckenridge forty. Then Elledge hit fullback A.D. Carnes on a screen pass. Carnes almost broke for the TD before he was bulldogged to the ground at the twenty-one.

As my Lion team broke from their huddle, people all over the stadium were frantic, hollering and running around like they'd gone crazy. Half the huge crowd was pulling for Breckenridge. They were screaming at their boys to dig in and hold the line. The other half was for Brownwood. They were yelling even louder. A frenzied hysteria enveloped the stadium as Ben Elledge barked his signals and took the snap from center.

Elledge drifted back, and with the patience of Job, waited for his wingback John Cadenhead to get open. Then he launched his rocket, which John grabbed at the ten. Cadenhead bulled over three green-clad defenders before he crashed into the end zone.

Final score: Brownwood 18, Breckenridge 14.

After the game, ecstatic Brownwood fans mobbed the playing field, hoisted Lion players on their shoulders and carried them to the locker room. Inside the dressing room, the excitement was like an electric current. Coaches Pete Murray and Morris Southall and myself were the first fully-clothed victims to hit the showers, but before our happy players were through, every sportswriter in sight received a victory baptism.

Saturday morning sports headlines in the *Fort Worth Star-Telegram* read: THEY SAID IT COULDN'T BE DONE.

Bill Stovall's story in Sunday's *Brownwood Bulletin* was headlined: YOUNG TEAM RATES LION HALL OF FAME.

In the final regular season game my Lions clobbered Weatherford 28–0, and Brownwood headed for the playoffs—for the first time since 1953.

◆ ◆ ◆

OUR BI-DISTRICT OPPONENT was Snyder. We played the Tigers in Brownwood on a Saturday afternoon. In a game that wasn't nearly as close as the score indicated, A.D. Carnes, John Cadenhead, Charles Coffey and Eddie Daniel provided the spark for our 29–20 victory.

A few minutes after the bi-district game ended, my assistant coaches and I met with Monahans coach Ray Pope. Pope's Loboes had defeated Levelland 32–14 on Thanksgiving Day and were in line to face Brownwood in the quarterfinal round.

All summer long we'd fertilized and watered our home field, trying to get it back in better condition. But despite the attentive care, by mid-season, the stadium field was again in horrible shape. Now in late November, the playing surface was an absolute disaster, with hardly a speck of grass left.

When I proposed we choose a neutral site for our second-round playoff bout, Coach Pope shook his head no.

"Look here, Ray, our home field is in terrible condition. How about we forego a coin toss and agree to play in Abilene?" I suggested.

"No. Home and home," Pope responded stubbornly.

"I know what you're thinking, Coach Pope. You think Brownwood's playing field is so bad I won't play here even if I win the coin flip, but you're wrong. If we flip for home and home, there's a fifty-fifty chance I'll win. And if I do, I can guarantee you, we'll play the game right here in the sand."

Even after my warning, the hard-headed Lobo coach still wouldn't consider playing at a neutral site, insisting we flip for home field advantage. When BHS track coach Gus Snodgrass called the flip and got it right, Pope almost fainted.

The Loboes weren't nearly as stubborn as their coach. At the half Brownwood fans leaned back to enjoy the halftime show, hoping the maroon band would perform as well as their football team. The Lions had raced out to a 30–0 lead. Much of the second half was played with Brownwood second-stringers.

A lot of money changed hands that afternoon. One Monahans gambler, who had watched our Snyder game, was in the parking lot taking Monahans and giving twenty-one points right up until game time. At the half the man paid off his bets and went deer hunting.

Final score: Brownwood 37, Monahans 16.

◆ ◆ ◆

WEATHER WAS EXPECTED to be a big factor when we met Jacksonville in Waco. During the week prior to our game, the Baptist city was doused with more than two inches of rain. At game time, the turf at Baylor Stadium resembled a Louisiana swamp. A heavy cloud cover hovered overhead, keeping the temperature down near freezing. Inclement playing conditions seemed to favor Jacksonville since they were defense oriented.

The Indians' offense relied on a methodical "three yards and a cloud of dust" ground attack which was popular in college ranks at the time. Gary Roundtree, a slick little field general, and Robby Robbins, a powerful, hard-to-bring-down running back, were the keys to their success. Weight-wise, the Indians' front line, which was anchored by future all-American Pete Lammons and center Jimmy Conner, outweighed Brownwood by twelve pounds per man. Jacksonville would be the toughest team we faced all year.

◆　◆　◆

JOHN "PETE" MURRAY WAS AN ASSISTANT at Albany when I persuaded him to join Morris Southall and me in Brownwood. Coach Murray was a good-natured, long, tall drink-of-water—country as he could be, always agreeable and a delight to work with. During the five years he was with us at Brownwood, Pete provided Coach Southall and myself with enough laughs and humorous stories to last us a lifetime. When football season ended, Pete coached our basketball team, and he did a great job there too.

When Brownwood took the field that afternoon, it was misting and freezing cold. People in the stands were bundled up in heavy coats and blankets, anything to keep warm.

Well, Pete shows up in a short-sleeved shirt. But over his shirt, he's wearing a clear plastic raincoat. From up in the stadium seats, the spectators couldn't see the raincoat. They thought Pete was down there on the field in his shirt sleeves.

Brownwood won the game 12–6. It was a hard fought, bone-bruising battle, but after the game, many of the sportswriters were more interested in the crazy coach who stood on the sidelines without a jacket than they were about game details.

Fact is, all three of us Brownwood coaches looked rather comical that afternoon. Seeing we were poorly prepared for the chilly weather, R.H. Cason brought us hats with side flaps that pulled down over our ears. Cason was a Brownwood resident who worked for a feed store located in Comanche. Printed in large

Max Emfinger rips for a nine-yard gain against Jacksonville.
(credit: Fort Worth Star-Telegram*)*

letters on the front of our hats was an advertisement promoting his business which read: MOORMAN FEEDS.

◆　◆　◆

DURING THE WEEK prior to our state championship clambake with Port Lavaca, an electric-like current of anticipation filled the air. According to numerous letters to the editor published in the *Brownwood Bulletin*, the entire town was "bursting with pride." Early in the week, Brownwood's city council officially declared Friday, December 16, 1960, as "Brownwood High School Lions Day." The proclamation, which urged every Brownwood citizen to be on hand at Austin's Memorial Stadium to support the Lions, was signed by Mayor W.C. Carpenter. Almost every car in Brown County had some kind of sign painted on the windows which urged their favorite team to: "Boil the Sandcrabs!"

　　Me, I worried about the weather. I worried about rain. I fretted about field conditions. On Wednesday, when I heard a light mist was falling in Austin, I called the grounds keeper at Memorial

Stadium to make certain they had the field covered. A wet playing surface had inhibited my scoring machine the previous week. I wanted to make sure my Lions wouldn't have to mud wrestle for the state title.

When *Fort Worth Star-Telegram* reporter John Morrison called, he had a few questions for me, then he asked to speak with Katharine.

"Oh, if the weather cooperates, I'm sure we'll win," my wife declared. She was much more confident than me. "Gordon's been talking about the weather all week, and he spends a whole lot of time watching the sky."

◆　◆　◆

BEFORE OUR TWO TEAMS collided at Austin's Memorial Stadium, Port Lavaca was averaging thirty-one points per game, posting a record of twelve wins against only one loss. The previous week they had rolled over defending state co-champion Cleburne by a score of 20–0. Port Lavaca was coached by Bobby Groff whose offensive preference was to run the football. Running backs Pat McGrath and Sid Baker were his big guns. McGrath had run for 857 yards, averaging 5.3 yards per carry. Baker was their top rusher, gaining 950 yards with an average of 6.2 per carry.

On a blustering, cold, windy Friday night, eighty-five hundred shivering fans watched the Sandcrabs jump out to a 6–0 lead. Port Lavaca's scoring drive came after Ron Cervenka returned an Elkins' quick-kick to the maroon twenty-four. In seven plays the Sandcrabs racked up their first tally. Pat McGrath shoved in from the one with ten seconds left in the first quarter.

Drawing first blood gave Port Lavaca a leg up, but their advantage was short-lived. After the kickoff, Brownwood marched seventy-three yards, ignoring a bothersome 15-yard penalty as if it were simply a bump in the road. A 32-yard pass from Elledge to Coffey and a 16-yard smash over tackle by Emfinger accentuated the scoring thrust. Elledge did the honors on a one-yard keeper. Elkins nailed the extra point, and Brownwood led 7–6.

On our next possession a quick lateral to Charles Coffey gained twenty-nine yards to set the Lions up at the black and gold fifteen. Three plays later Elledge passed to Elkins in the left flat, and Lawrence waltzed in for the six-pointer. At the half the score was 13–6.

Brownwood took the second half kickoff and thundered sixty-two yards to take a 19–6 lead. Coffey scored the TD after he snared an Elledge toss and rambled in from the eighteen.

Late in the fourth quarter, I cleared the bench, making sure every man on my maroon squad participated in our state championship victory.

Final score: Brownwood 26, Port Lavaca 6.

In the dressing room after the game, Charles Coffey was possibly the happiest Lion of all. When Charles gathered in that pass from Elledge and scored, it was the first touchdown of his football career.

"You don't have to ask me what my biggest thrill of the season was," Coffey told reporters. "Lawrence Elkins was a step ahead of me and could have caught the ball, but I shouted, 'let it go' and he did."

When asked to rate Port Lavaca against other playoff foes, Mike Greer and A.D. Carnes agreed the Sandcrabs weren't as tough as Jacksonville. "But they were tough enough," Carnes surmised.

Naturally, all us coaches, including Gus Snodgrass, Autry Crawford and Dale Biggs, received another fully-clothed victory shower.

◆　◆　◆

A SPIRITED POST GAME victory celebration delayed the football team's departure from Austin until about two o'clock that night. Our chartered bus didn't arrive back in Brownwood until four o'clock Saturday morning.

That same weekend Pete Murray's basketball team was playing in a tournament at Abilene. While our football team was nailing down a state championship in Austin, Coach Murray's roundballers had also been winning. Brownwood's basketball squad had reached the semifinal bracket and was scheduled to play again on Saturday.

When Murray's basketball boys assembled at the high school gym Saturday morning, there was Lawrence Elkins anxious to play. It's six-thirty, less than two and a half hours after Elkins stepped off the football bus. Coach Murray wasn't expecting Elkins, but Pete had an extra uniform, so he agreed to let Larry tag along. Pete had to borrow a pair of tennis shoes from the P.E. lockers to complete Lawrence's outfit.

That afternoon in the Abilene tournament, Murray's roundballers got in deep trouble. Midway through the second half,

*Lawrence Elkins, tri-captain, high school all-American—
Brownwood's 1960 state championship team.*
(credit: Brownwood Bulletin)

Brownwood was behind by some twelve points. Coach Murray hadn't planned on playing Elkins, but he subbed him in to rest one of his other players. Lawrence wound up scoring fifteen points in that game, and in the finals, he played the entire game. Brownwood won the tournament.

Lawrence Elkins continued his football career at Baylor where he was selected all-American in both his junior and senior years. Elkins was one of the best athletes and fiercest competitors I've ever had the pleasure of coaching.

◆　◆　◆

CHURCH HAS ALWAYS been important to Katharine. She taught her first Sunday school class when she was seventeen. In the seventies she became an ordained Presbyterian elder. Working in the church has been both a joy and a kind of personal release for Katharine. At church she could be Katharine Wood, not Coach Wood's wife. In fact, one of the church ladies once told her, "Gordon Wood may be a legend on the football field, but when he comes to this church, he's just Katharine's husband."

One of my wife's most satisfying accomplishments was helping establish a church latch key program for underprivileged kids who didn't have a place to go after school. The program included after school snacks, game activities, and tutoring sessions to help the children with their homework. The schools especially appreciated this program because the children involved came to class with their homework ready for the next day. A few years after Katharine got involved, the latch key program was added to the list of charities supported by the United Fund.

Another of Katharine's missions was to organize a soup kitchen through Brownwood's Alliance of Churches. Eventually, the alliance worked out an arrangement to convey this "feed the homeless" program to the Salvation Army.

My wife is a natural born social worker and volunteer. She's been deeply involved with the community hospital auxiliary. Much of her time there has been devoted to the Saint Organization where she works on the Committee for Junior Volunteers. This is the committee which recruits young people to serve as candy stripers and perform other services for the hospital.

◆　◆　◆

ONE SUNDAY MORNING in July, Katharine and I were on our way to church, listening to the radio as we drove up Fisk Street. Pat and Jim were in the back seat. Morris Southall, Pete Murray and I had plans to leave for coaching school the next weekend.

The radio commentator was explaining how desperately Brown County needed rain. According to his weather report, the temperature was already eighty degrees. By mid-afternoon he predicted the heat would peak at around a hundred and two.

As I wheeled into the church parking lot, a wind devil suddenly whirled down the street, picking up bits of paper and street trash, and sending the debris sailing into a vacant lot across the street from our church. I braked to a stop, turned off the key, and turned to Katharine.

"It sure feels good to be home, doesn't it?" I said.

CHAPTER ELEVEN

The Super Sixties

(1961–1964)

THE SIXTIES were an era of turmoil. A story in the *Brownwood Bulletin* referred to the period as a time of "Lost Innocence." Seemed like everyone was mad at somebody for some reason or another. Desegregation troubles were responsible for much of the unrest, with some kind of freedom march or sit-in occurring almost daily. The riot-like atmosphere was contagious, because in August, after the state legislature approved the first sales tax in Texas history, angry school teachers stormed Governor Price Daniels' office demanding a pay hike. To my knowledge, that was the first time Texas teachers publicly protested about their ridiculously low wages.

The cold war was also on everyone's mind. The U-2 incident in May of 1960 acted as a catalyst, but after John Kennedy became president, it was one thing after another. In April of 1961, the ill-fated Bay of Pigs invasion of Cuba embarrassed every American citizen. In August, the Russians closed off the border between East and West Berlin and began construction of the infamous Berlin Wall.

Not all the news was bad. On May 5, Alan Shepard became the first American in space when he made a brief suborbital flight in his Mercury capsule. Watching New York Yankees Roger Maris' and Mickey Mantle's neck-and-neck home run race was probably the most fun event of 1961. As my Brownwood aides and I prepared to open our fall football drills, both Maris and Mantle were in striking distance of breaking Babe Ruth's single-season record of sixty home runs.

1961

I'VE OFTEN HEARD middle age sneaks up on you. One day you wake up and realize you're no longer young. That happened to me

Terry (1961–62), Si (1966–67), Shae (1970–71) Southall—
Morris Southall's amazing sons quarterbacked the Lions to prominence.
(credit: 1963, 1968, and 1971 Brownwood High Yearbook)

in 1961. I looked up one morning, and there's a beautiful young woman living in my house. And when I went to the football field, there was a familiar young man on my football squad.

The two young people were, of course, my daughter Patricia and Terry Southall. Good Lord, it seemed like only yesterday those two were in diapers, and we were sharing our Seminole house with Morris and Lorene.

Terry was a high school junior—muscular, good-looking, and like his father, an outstanding athlete with a strong passing arm. Terry was the first of Morris Southall's three sons to play for me, each a gifted athlete, each an excellent quarterback. Normally, any coach would be drooling over a quarterback with Terry's talent, but in 1961, Brownwood already had a fine quarterback. That was Ben Elledge who led his team to the state championship the previous year.

In some coaching circles a similar situation might have created ill feelings, but not in Brownwood. Coach Southall and I resolved our dilemma by making Terry our second-string quarterback and first-string defensive halfback. Terry responded by being named first team all-district and honorable mention all-state at his defensive position.

◆ ◆ ◆

AS AUGUST TWO-A-DAYS got underway in Brownwood, Hurricane Carla, with winds up to a hundred and seventy miles per hour and fifteen-foot tides, was wreaking havoc all along the Texas coast—knocking down power lines, blowing out windows, washing out bridges and causing millions of dollars in damage. More than four hundred thousand Texas and Louisiana residents were forced to leave their homes and flee for their lives, but in Brown County, it wouldn't rain a drop. Every day during the week my football team prepared for our season opener against Dallas Thomas Jefferson, dark storm clouds would roll in, then blow away, refusing to deliver an ounce of moisture to Brown County's thirsty soil.

Brown County was still bone-dry on Friday night when my Lions put a damper on a tough gang from Dallas, barely squeaking by 6–0. Next, we invited Killeen up to our place and drubbed the Kangaroos 21–0.

My Lions had won twelve in a row when we traveled to Waco to take on Coach Joe James and his unbeaten LaVega Pirates. The Blue and Gold turned out to be miserable hosts. After Brownwood drove seventy-three yards to score on our first possession, the Pirates stopped us cold on a two-point conversion try. However, it was a second-string halfback named Jimmy Grams whose rude manners sent us home with our feelings hurt. Grams recovered a Lion fumble in the end zone for LaVega's only score then swiped another pass at the goal line to halt a last minute Brownwood bid for victory.

Final score: Brownwood 6, LaVega 7.

◆　　◆　　◆

ON OCTOBER 1, Roger Maris finally blasted his sixty-first dinger of the season to break the home run record Babe Ruth established way back in 1927. In keeping with the unstable times, statisticians would insist on adding an asterisk to Roger's record because his feat was achieved in a season eight games longer than Ruth's.

In the meantime, my Lions recovered from their Waco setback and were off on a new tear. First, we went to Temple where my

Maroons extracted revenge for their only loss of the previous season and spanked the Wildcats 18–13. In a 39–0 lashing of Stephenville's Yellowjackets, Brownwood piled up two dozen first downs and 469 yards of total offense.

Vernon played us tough for almost a quarter, then Terry Southall, who was filling in for an injured Ben Elledge, began to click. Southall's long bombs to Charles

Max Emfinger, Brownwood's leading ground gainer in 1960 and 1961. (credit: Fred Nobs)

Coffey and John Cadenhead gave us a comfortable 28–0 halftime lead. In the second half I cleared the benches. The final score was almost embarrassing, 42–0.

At Graham, Lion tailback Max Emfinger shook loose for TD jaunts of thirty-six, fifty-seven, four and three yards as Brownwood dehorned the Steers 39–14.

◆　◆　◆

BRECKENRIDGE SPORTED a misleading season history of four wins against three losses as Brownwood prepared to meet Coach Zac Henderson's Buckaroos on their home turf. Despite their blemished record, though, the green machine of Stephens County was undefeated in conference play, and everyone knew our upcoming skirmish would be for all the marbles. The winner would advance to the playoffs. The loser could start concentrating on basketball.

◆　◆　◆

THE *BROWNWOOD BULLETIN* described the scene as a "Mass Exodus" the Friday night we played Breckenridge, and that pretty well summed things up. More than three thousand Brownwood residents were among the eight thousand spectators who crowded into Buckaroo Stadium to watch their favorite teams go-for-the-gold.

With both sides of the line exerting superhuman effort and neither side making a mistake, the contest boiled down to a brutal test of wills. On several occasions Brownwood pushed the ball into greenie territory, but each time Breckenridge's hard-headed defense would rise up to thwart our attack.

Late in the game Breckenridge worked the ball down to Brownwood's thirty-four. Our defense stopped Buckaroo ballcarrier Ronnie Wimberly for no gain, but then the Buckies top gun, Harry Ledbetter, rifled a bullet to Leonard Tolbert for a first down at the Lion fourteen. Three plays later Brownwood senior linebacker David Smith intercepted a Ledbetter pass in the end zone, but the damage was done. Breckenridge had logged the only penetration of the night. The game ended with neither team scoring, but Breckenridge claimed the conference lead, courtesy of their lone penetration inside our twenty.

Final score: Brownwood 0, Breckenridge 0.

In the weeks that followed, my Lions easily defeated Weatherford and Mineral Wells, but our victories were fruitless. Even though we shared the 4–AAA title with Breckenridge and lost only one game by a single point, my football team stayed home when the big show started.

1962

THE EARLY SIXTIES were exasperating times for most Americans. On the one hand, tensions between the United States and Russia kept us biting our nails. On the other hand, racial problems divided our country. Naturally, at the center of the desegregation tug-of-war were our schools.

At the same time federal courts were demanding all schools be opened to black students, a flood of adolescent baby boomers came of school age. The calamity was compounded by a severe lack of qualified teachers. Being a teacher or a school administrator was not much fun in the sixties.

When school began in 1960, Brownwood High School had an enrollment of 1,070 in grades nine through twelve. In 1962, Brownwood's high school population was still stuck near that same number, even though school enrollments statewide had zoomed fifteen percent. Nevertheless, our farsighted school board anticipated the need for better educational facilities and set in motion a building program which included a brand-new high school. Construction of the new high school commenced during the '61–'62 school year, and when classes began in the fall of 1962, our teachers and students were blessed with a magnificent new learning facility.

Like most southern cities, Brownwood experienced some soul-searching debate over desegregation. However, it didn't cause nearly the hassle here it did in other parts of the country. Several black students attended Brownwood High as early as 1956, and by 1965, all our schools were fully integrated.

Brownwood football teams also fared pretty well in the early sixties. In 1962, we opened our season against LaVega, and with Terry Southall running the show, we extracted revenge for our only loss of the previous season by pounding the Pirates 41–0. My Maroons were still undefeated midway through the campaign when they played Breckenridge and escaped unscathed 38–0.

◆　　◆　　◆

DURING THE LAST WEEK of October, the whole world held its breath. After the United States discovered Russia was building bomber and missile bases in Cuba, President Kennedy imposed a blockade around the island and fear of a U.S.–Soviet military confrontation came extremely close to becoming a reality. Thankfully, the explosive situation was peacefully resolved within a month.

In November, only a few days after Democrat John Connally defeated Jack Cox to win his first term as Texas Governor, one of the most amazing events of the twentieth century took place. On Sunday, November 11, people all across the United States gathered to swallow a tiny cube of sugar saturated with Type 1 Sabin polio vaccine. In one fell swoop, the dreaded threat of Polio was virtually eliminated. No matter your race, your color or your religion, that was a day every person can look back on and sigh with relief.

In Brownwood, the vaccine was dispensed at the high school gymnasium. The Wood family and the Southall family were among the first in line.

◆ ◆ ◆

AFTER WRAPPING UP the conference title with easy victories over Graham and Wichita Falls Rider, my Lions took on Brownfield in a bi-district brawl, using Sweetwater's Mustang Bowl as the scene for the battle. A 47-yard punt return by Phillip Fenton gave us our first points, then Fenton stole a Brownfield pass and ran it back sixty-seven yards to set up our second score. Late in the game Doug Young trapped Brownfield quarterback Teddy Howell in the end zone for a safety, and Jeff Smith returned the Cubs' free kick all the way to paydirt.

Final score: Brownwood 38, Brownfield 6.

The next weekend Brownwood collided with Dumas at Jones Stadium in Lubbock. I don't know why, but Gordon Wood-coached teams have never done well there. We raced off to a 10–0 lead, but after an on-side kick attempt backfired, Dumas rallied to stick us good.

Final score: Brownwood 18, Dumas 36.

Dumas would go on to win the Class AAA championship, defeating Pharr 14–3.

1963

OUR DAUGHTER PATRICIA graduated from Brownwood

Pat Wood, BHS Senior Year (credit: Fred Nobs)

High in June of 1963, and much of our summer was spent getting her prepared for college. New dresses, new shoes, new everything—I discovered all the hidden expenses of a college education for the female gender. Pat had decided on Trinity University, a Presbyterian college located in San Antonio. San Antonio is almost a hundred and ninety miles from Brownwood, and during Pat's freshman year, Wood family automobiles logged thousands of miles traveling those two-lane roads to South Texas.

Attending a private school was so expensive, more costly than Katharine and I ever imagined. In fact, our daughter's college expenses that first year almost bankrupted the family budget. The following spring, when I picked Pat up to bring her back to Brownwood for the summer, I advised my daughter she would either have to transfer to a state school or come back to Brownwood and attend Howard Payne. Given a similar mandate, some girls might have thrown a walleyed fit, but Pat's always been level headed. That's one of the many reasons I love her so much. Pat thought about what I said for a moment. Here's how she responded: "Dad, if you'll let me go back to Trinity for one more year, I'll transfer and never mention it again."

I agreed, and after she finished her second year at Trinity, Pat transferred to Texas University in Austin.

Morris Southall's oldest son also graduated from Brownwood High in 1963. Terry accepted a football scholarship from Baylor University. In the next four years, he would light up Southwest Conference scoreboards and break almost every Baylor passing record.

◆ ◆ ◆

BY PREVIOUS STANDARDS, 1963 would be considered a mediocre year, but we had some great kids—like all-district performers Danny Cochran, Bob Simmons and James Harris. Harris could run a 10-flat 100 and played tailback on offense. James was one of the first Negro kids to really contribute to our football program. Our co-captains were Jeff Smith and Bob Pinto. Smith was post oak tough and lightning fast. Playing at a guard position, Pinto was named our most valuable player. Another valuable player was Richard Carpenter, a devastating blocker with jackhammers for legs.

A 12–6 loss to Stephenville in our first conference game put us with our backs to the wall right off the bat. Then Wichita Falls Rider nailed us with a 33–0 shellacking. Graham was ranked second in the state when we rallied to beat them on their home field 14–13, but it was too little, too late.

Our season ended on Friday, November 22, with a 14–6 victory over Vernon, but Brownwood and Vernon only walked through the game. There was little to cheer about that evening. Earlier in the day, an assassin's bullet had killed our president.

◆ ◆ ◆

AFTER PRESIDENT KENNEDY was shot and Lyndon Johnson took over, seems like everything started to go wrong. Before anyone could find out why Lee Harvey Oswald shot the president, a Dallas night club operator named Jack Ruby gunned down Oswald, right outside police headquarters.

U.S. soldiers had been stationed in Vietnam for several years, sent there as advisors to South Vietnam troops, but in early 1964, the Vietnam situation began to heat up. In March, Defense Secretary Robert McNamara announced that U.S. forces would remain in Vietnam until a Communist takeover was no longer a threat. In August, after North Vietnam fired on a U.S. destroyer in the Gulf of Tonkin, Congress authorized President Johnson to take all necessary steps to prevent further aggression against U.S. forces. The Gulf of Tonkin Resolution launched an escalation of U.S. involvement which, in turn, set off protests and violent demonstrations that tore this county apart.

A movie entitled *Dr. Strangelove: or; How I Learned to Stop Worrying and Love the Bomb,* starring Peter Sellers and George C. Scott, just about scared the pants off everyone who saw it.

Our music was changing too. It was bad enough a German made car, the Volkswagen Beetle, was outselling most American built automobiles, but then four long-haired hippies flew over from England and immediately replaced our music with loud noise. The group, quite appropriately, called themselves the "Beetles," and when they sang, you couldn't make out half the words.

1964

THINGS WERE SURE A MESS as our 1964 football season got underway, and my Lions got themselves in hot water right out of the box. After clubbing Stephenville 34–0, we lost to Cleburne in our second game of the season. Cleburne wasn't in our conference, so maybe I should have shrugged off the loss. But I couldn't. Over the years, one undeniable fact had been pounded into my thick skull over and over again. If my football team lost twice, Gordon Wood would be staying home on Turkey Day.

◆　◆　◆

BILL STOVALL was the best sports reporter I have been privileged to know. He knew the rules. His game reports were accurate, and his analyses on the money. Stovall also kept track of Brownwood players after they graduated from high school. When I picked up the *Brownwood Bulletin* in mid-September, the newspaper contained a story Bill had written about ex-Brownwood players in the Southwest Conference.

Lawrence Elkins, Max Emfinger and Terry Southall were at Baylor. Elkins was considered a sure-fire all-American receiver. Max and Terry were only sophomores, but they were both making strong bids for starting positions.

Ben Elledge and Doug Young were at Texas Tech. Ben had shared starting time at quarterback with James Ellis the previous season. Even though Doug was the smallest guard on the Red Raiders' roster, Coach J.T. King was giving him strong consideration for a starting berth.

Ronnie Moore, a captain on Brownwood's 1960 championship team, had started for Texas A&M the previous year. Stovall predicted Ronnie would be a shoo-in for all-conference.

Stories like that make an old coach's heart swell with pride. Bill's article reminded me I had a dozen other ex-Brownwood players on scholarship at various colleges, and the loss to Cleburne didn't seem nearly so important.

◆　◆　◆

REFOCUSING ON THEIR MISSION, my Lions hitched their belts, hunched their shoulders and came out fighting. First, they clobbered San Angelo Lake View 62–8, then blitzed 4A Abilene Cooper with a first half touchdown-barrage and sent them to the canvass 27–2. After Brownwood blanked Breckenridge 21–0, I began to think my worries were unfounded. That's when we ran head on into Wichita Falls Hirschi.

◆　◆　◆

COACH JESS STILES' Huskies were undefeated in district play the night our two teams duked it out in Wichita Falls. It was a slugfest destined to decide the 4–AAA champ. Two early breaks keyed Wichita's victory. An interception by Hirschi defensive back David Brasier set up the Huskies first TD, and late in the second quarter, Wichita center Kenny Reynold broke through to block a botched punt attempt. Reynold's defensive gem led to another easy Huskie score.

Brownwood tailback James Harris was the star of our comeback try, sprinting for forty-seven yards in the third period to knot the score at 14–14, but a Lion win wasn't in the cards. With Jimmy Thomason, my ace quarterback, sidelined with a knee injury, our offense struggled. Coming into the contest, my Lions were averaging better than a hundred yards in the air. Our passing game never got untracked. In six attempts Brownwood completed one pass, for a minus four yards.

Midway through the fourth, Hirschi mounted a 63-yard drive which proved to be the difference. Huskie end Sidney McDonald provided the big play when he scooped up a wobbly pass at Brownwood's twenty. Two plays later Wichita scored.

James Harris took the ensuing kickoff and ran it back eighty-six yards to pull Brownwood within two points, but a swarming Huskie defense stopped us short on our two-point attempt.

Final score: Brownwood 20, Hirschi 22.

An ugly 0–0 tie with Graham seven days later essentially removed Brownwood from district contention, and our season ended with seven wins, two losses and a tie—my worst record since I moved to Brownwood. With only six returning starters, the future looked pretty dreary. Lion football teams had enjoyed a fantastic ride during my first years at Brownwood, but now the Lions hadn't made it to the playoffs for two consecutive years. Maybe Gordon Wood's luck had run out.

CHAPTER TWELVE

Getting a Second Wind

(1965)

RE-HIRING KENNETH WEST was my second best career decision. Kenneth played for me at Stamford and worked as a junior high coach for me at Victoria. Kenneth would probably have followed Coach Southall and me to Brownwood, but in the spring of 1960, Kenneth accepted an assistant's post at Brady as a line coach for K.Y. Owens. In 1961, Kenneth moved to Coleman where he worked under Bill Yung, who later became head football coach at the University of Texas at El Paso. Even though we weren't working together, Katharine and I continued our close relationship with Kenneth and his wife Shirley. Their son, Gordon Glen, is named after me.

It was a timely stroke of luck when the West family dropped by to visit in the summer of 1965. Kenneth had come to Brownwood to see Doctor Ward Locklear, an ear specialist. A few weeks earlier while Kenneth was at National Guard camp, an artillery blast had damaged his ear drum.

Maybe it was coincidence. I'd rather call it fate. In any case it had only been a couple of days since Brownwood assistant coach Gus Snodgrass informed me he had decided to accept the high school's vice-principal job, so I was looking for someone to replace him. Since Kenneth had a fairly good coaching position at Coleman, I wasn't sure he'd be interested, but I offered the job to him anyway. To my pleasant surprise, he accepted.

When Pete Murray left the following spring to coach at Texas A&I, Coach West took his place as an assistant football coach, and Kenneth fit in like an old shoe. Adding Kenneth West to my coaching staff was simply a matter of the right man coming along at the right time, but it was still one of the smartest decisions I ever made. In many ways, Coach West is as responsible for Brownwood's football success as Coach Southall and myself.

◆　◆　◆

DURING THE SUMMER of 1965, I was invited to appear as a guest lecturer at the Ohio High School Coaching Clinic held in Canton, Ohio. It was there I met Pete Elliot, the head football coach at Illinois University, and learned about his "Illinois Defense." Coach Elliot was a dynamic speaker, but what impressed me was an innovative defensive scheme he advocated. Elliot's "Illinois Defense" allowed smaller teams like those I coached at Brownwood to compensate for size with overloading, blitzing, aggressive pursuit, and gang-tackling.

I was totally infatuated by the awesome potential of Coach Elliot's defense, and during my trip back to Texas, I decided to make it Brownwood's primary defense for the upcoming football season. The "Illinois Defense" represented a radical change in my thinking, but even a winning coach must be willing to change when he finds something better. The defensive strategies I learned in Canton that summer would help Brownwood win six more state championships.

That fall we switched to the "Illinois Defense" and received immediate dividends. My Lions were six games into the season before an opponent scored on us. (A more complete explanation of the "Illinois Defense" is included in my *Game Plan to Winning Football* which was published in 1992.)

◆　◆　◆

DURING SPRING TRAINING and August two-a-days we coaches constantly talked to our players, telling them they were much better than they thought. Over the doorway to our dressing room, we had a sign I borrowed from my good friend Pat Gerald who coached at Sweetwater. The sign read: *Speed, spirit, skill, and poise.*

We told our kids poise is like a duck flying off a farm pond. On the top he looks real smooth, but underneath he's paddling like the devil. It's the same in football. Keep a smile on your face, but underneath you should be giving your very best every second of every play.

At the beginning of every season we asked our players to set goals in this order:

1. *We want to win our first game—at Brownwood our first game was always tough.*
2. *After we win that first game, we want to win district.*
3. *After we win district, we want to win state.*

My coaches and I emphasized eliminating mistakes, like fumbles and missed blocks. Each spring Coach Southall took our quarterbacks and centers and worked with them separately for two weeks, teaching the quarterbacks how to take the snap from center, the proper footwork, and how to handoff. They would also work on passing techniques. No coach in the country could teach a boy how to play the quarterback position better than Morris Southall. During the years we coached at Brownwood, a fumble or an interception was an absolute rarity.

We also stressed eliminating penalties, especially offside and motion penalties, and we let our players know we had zero tolerance for unsportsmanlike conduct. We wanted our kids to play like demons, but no matter how dire the circumstances, they were to always act like gentlemen and keep a smile on their face.

Over the doorway to our weight room, we posted another sign which read: *The desire to win is useless without the desire to prepare.* Brownwood High never graduated a player who couldn't quote those words verbatim.

We spent a lot of time working on speciality teams—kicking and receiving. No football team can win consistently without a good defense, and no team can play good defense without a good kicking game. In a close contest, the team with the best kicking game will usually win. Not one in ten coaches spends enough time working on their kicking game.

During one four-year period in the late sixties, Brownwood lost several games on blocked punts, so we started working on bad snaps. We wanted our punter to know exactly how to react in those situations. Coach Southall had predesignated signals with our center. One time he'd have the center snap the football over the punter's head. Another signal would have the center snap it to the right, or left, or roll it on the ground. Time was devoted to this drill during every practice session because it taught our punters how to run to the football and get rid of it before the defense could reach him. A kicker quickly learns whether he has time to retrieve and punt the football, or whether he's to grab it and throw it away.

In every practice we also worked on other phases of our kicking game—punting, quick kicks, on-side kicks, extra points, field goals, punt returns, kick offs and kick returns. From 1971 through 1985, Brownwood never had a punt blocked. We seldom had an opponent return a kickoff past their thirty or a punt returned for more than ten yards.

My football teams have always operated from a winged-T formation. Of course, we made a lot of changes after Morris Southall joined me at Seminole. This is not the normal winged-T many other coaches use. The offense we used at Brownwood was the Warren Woodson winged-T, an offensive formation Morris Southall learned at Hardin-Simmons when he played for Coach Woodson.

The beauty of Woodson's winged-T is it's simple to teach, and a team can flip-flop the formation and run twice as many plays without materially changing the blocking assignments. (I explained this concept to Texas University coach Darrell Royal in 1960 while we were flying to an NCAA Coaching Convention in New York City. He liked the idea so much he installed it in his offense. Coach Royal has often said my flip-flop formation helped his team win the 1963 National Championship.)

The Woodson winged-T also utilizes angle blocks. Very seldom did one of our blockers go head to head with a player on the opposing team. Many times I've been asked how I could win with such small, scrawny players. Blocking was the key, and we spent a lot of time teaching our kids how to block. Many coaches teach pushing and shoving, without actually showing their players how to block effectively.

Coach Chesty Walker, who I greatly admired, once said, "If you don't line up beat, play hard, and don't make mistakes, you have a good chance of winning," and he was dead right. A team that lines up with confidence, fires off the ball on every snap, blocks effectively and doesn't make mistakes is mighty hard to beat.

Winning is a state of mind. It is achieved by a combination of all the little things a coach teaches his team—like having your players set goals and making them believe they can attain those goals if they work hard—like having coaches who believe in each other and having players believing in other players. Players must also believe in their coaches and believe they're treated fairly. If a coach plays favorites, the players see it right away, and that coach will never command the respect he needs to make his kids believe they can win.

◆　◆　◆

SHORTLY BEFORE we began our mid-August, two-a-day workouts, a race riot broke out in the Watts area of Los Angeles. A week later when L.A. police finally regained control, thirty-five people were dead and more than a thousand injured. The city of angels had suffered almost two hundred and fifty million dollars in property damage. I sure was glad I lived in Brownwood where rain was the major concern.

Our 1965 squad included thirteen lettermen, but only six had registered significant playing time the previous season. Our lone returning offensive starter was center Mike McInnis. Nonetheless, my assistant coaches and I were cautiously optimistic. When we penciled in a possible starting lineup, our offensive line weighed in at an average of 184 pounds per man. Even at Victoria where we thought the players were enormous, Morris and I never fielded a front line that size. Always the comic, Pete Murray suggested we put our linemen on a strict diet. Said if we showed up with so many big players, people would accuse us of recruiting.

Brownwood opened the season by rolling over Stephenville 33–0. The Yellowjackets weren't nearly as competitive as expected. We still weren't sure what we had, even after we edged Cleburne 13–0 and slipped by Dallas Sunset 14–0.

Our unscored-on defense looked great and was the major reason for our success. It was our exasperating, on-again, off-again offensive play that troubled us coaches. Occasionally, we would see a flash of brilliance which would raise our hopes. Then our offense would sputter and revert to its familiar model-T performance. After every game my coaches and I agonized over the game films, astounded that we could make so many offensive mistakes and still win. We were still trying to iron out our offensive deficiencies when Brownwood journeyed to Abilene to face the Cooper High Cougars.

◆　◆　◆

OUR DEFENSE STOPPED Cooper's highly-touted offensive machine cold in its tracks, but what warmed my heart was our offensive show. My Lions scored almost every way possible. First, we took the opening kickoff and marched down to Abilene's twenty-two, with Jimmy Piper, Leroy Deanda, and Wayne Fenton taking turns pounding up the middle. When our drive bogged down, I subbed in Billy Branum, and he nailed a three-point field goal.

After we kicked off, our defense pushed the Cougars back to their four. A nine-yard punt by Cooper's Mitch Miller put our souped-up offense in business at the thirteen. On the first play from scrimmage, Lion quarterback David Henley passed to Kirk Wall, and Kirk made a mad dash for the end zone. Branum converted on the extra point try.

Early in the second quarter Henley unloaded a long bomb to Wall, and Brownwood struck again. Kirk gathered in the football at Cooper's forty-two and outran the blue and red secondary to the goal line. Another long drive, which featured some fancy footwork by Piper and Deanda and some pin-point passing by Henley, set up a second Branum field goal. Minutes later Roy Spence swiped a Jack Mildren pass at the Cougars' thirty-nine. This led to another TD, and Brownwood jogged to the halftime dressing room boasting a comfortable 27–0 margin.

The game ended with Brownwood crushing Cooper 34–0 and posting one of the most impressive victories in Lion history. As usual, our defense was absolutely superb, with Billy Bly, Walter Croft, Jerry Jones and Roy Spence supplying Oscar winning performances.

My football team seemed to have discovered how good they were during the Cooper game because that's when they began to pick up steam. In our conference lid-lifter the Lions ripped Coleman 41–0.

During my first years at Brownwood, the key to a successful season was beating Breckenridge, but the Green Machine had come on hard times. Playing on their home field, we mopped up on the Buckies 39–18. Still, you don't go to Breckenridge and leave without paying some kind of homage. The Buckaroos rudely ended our unscored-on string at five.

Seven days later the Lions honed in on Wichita Falls Hirschi and collared the Huskies 28–7. After we nipped Graham 7–0 and chewed up Burkburnett's Bulldogs 27–0, only Vernon stood in our way.

◆　◆　◆

VERNON PLAYED US TOUGH. With less than four minutes left in the game, the score was deadlocked at 0–0. A short fourteen-yard punt gave Brownwood possession at our own forty-four, and that's where the poise we'd been preaching about paid off. With quarterback Billy Branum barking the signals, and with linemen Pat Humphries, Joe Shaw, Robert Porter, and Roger Richey opening up gigantic holes, Deanda and Piper bulldozed their way to Vernon's three-yard line. It took three stabs at Vernon's stubborn defense, but on the third try, Deanda gouged out the final yard.

Brownwood tacked on an insurance TD after Vernon received the kickoff and failed to complete a pass on four straight attempts. We took over on downs, and sophomore fullback James Hamlett rammed the ball in with thirty-five seconds remaining.

By defeating Vernon, my Lions stretched their winning streak to thirteen. They had escaped from District 4–AAA without a loss. No school in the conference had done that since Brownwood did it in 1962.

◆　◆　◆

EVERY HEAD COACH'S LIFE is filled with problems he can't control—problems with parents, teachers, school administrators, school boards. But one thing a head coach should be able to control is his coaching staff. Before the 1965 school year began, I hired a junior high coach named Bud Wright. Bud was a graduate of Howard Payne and a competent football coach, but he was the most hard-headed human being who ever worked for me.

Early in the season Coach Wright's junior high squad played Cleburne and lost something like 40–6. Generally, Brownwood fielded two ninth-grade teams, but that week Bud only had one game scheduled, so he suited out sixty 14-year-olds for the Cleburne contest. Then Bud only played thirteen players. That's right. Sixty boys suited out. Thirteen played, on both offense and defense.

The following Monday I called Bud to my office and asked why he hadn't played more kids. He answered by telling me he was trying to win the game. He said he wanted his best eleven men on the field all the time. That's when I blew my stack.

"Bud," I told him, gritting my teeth and trying to control my temper, "I've talked to you and talked to you about the way you treat your players, and you don't listen. So I'm now giving you an order. You can play different kids on offense and defense, but I want every man on your bench to play one fourth of every game. If I ever hear you've played only thirteen or fourteen boys in a football game again, you'll be looking for another job the very next day."

Their last game of the season, Wright's ninth graders played Cleburne again, at Cleburne. It's close to a hundred and twenty miles from Brownwood to Cleburne, but I drove over to personally watch the game. Brownwood won 14–0.

Here's what happened. When Bud started playing all his kids, their deflated morale went straight up, and they began to get excited about football. If a junior high coach doesn't play his kids, they don't come out next season, and eventually the varsity suffers the consequences.

◆　◆　◆

THE STATE PLAYOFFS are like a brand-new season, and it should be the most fun time of the year. At Brownwood, after we reached the playoffs, we rewarded our young men by cutting back on our workouts, often as much as twenty-five percent. A football squad which has played ten games should be in good condition, so there's nothing to be gained by running your team 'till their tongues hang out. I can't remember ever losing a playoff game because my players weren't in condition. We also didn't scrimmage or take a chance on getting a player hurt in practice. What we concentrated on was getting our kids mentally prepared.

◆　◆　◆

OUR BI-DISTRICT OPPONENT was Lamesa, a team with a puny 6–4 record. How the Tornados made it that far was a mystery to me. No Gordon Wood-coached team had ever made it to the playoffs with even two losses.

Our two teams squared off before nine thousand sun-splashed fans at Abilene's Public Schools Stadium. Lamesa's gold and black twisters didn't cross the mid-field stripe until they mounted a scoring drive in the fourth quarter. By then, the issue had long been decided.

Final score: Brownwood 20, Lamesa 6.

Dumas was somewhat tougher. The Demons thwarted our

playoff bid in 1962, coming from behind to beat Brownwood 36–18 in the quarterfinals. The previous week Dumas had whipped up on a pretty good Odessa Ector crew. Our winning string had reached fourteen when we returned to Abilene for a no-holds-barred quarterfinal battle with the orange and black brawlers from the Texas Panhandle.

From start to finish the game was a defensive war. Brownwood's only touchdown came on the heels of a ferocious Dumas assault on our end zone. Demon running backs Doug Cothren and Steve Burks had pushed the ball down to Brownwood's thirty-two, but thanks to some outstanding defensive work by George Martin and Joe Shaw, our defense squared its jaw and refused to budge. On fourth and one, Jimmy Piper slipped through to spill Demon quarterback Glen Bonner for a three-yard loss.

Piper's timely save revived our sluggish offense. After Brownwood took possession, David Henley engineered a 65-yard drive, and Walter Croft boomed the extra point through the uprights. Dumas scored in the fourth period, but a penalty robbed the Demons of their point after. And that was the difference in the game.

Final score: Brownwood 7, Dumas 6.

An unusual UIL rule aided us in our semifinal victory over Weatherford. Brownwood had beaten Weatherford two years earlier in a District 4–AAA encounter. Since that game was played in Weatherford, the Interscholastic League ruled the Kangaroos had to return the favor by playing at Brownwood. It didn't make much sense, but in the state playoffs you take whatever favors you're offered. Playing on our home turf was definitely an advantage. We were leading 15–0 when a long touchdown run by 'Roos' speedster Larry Wright on a Statue of Liberty play scared the dickens out of us. Brownwood hung on to win 15–6.

◆　◆　◆

PLAYOFFS CAN MAKE A COACH do crazy things. After we beat Weatherford, we discovered Bridge City would be our opponent for the state title. Bridge City had a great running back named Steve Worster. Several coaches told me Worster couldn't be tackled by one man. They said he was so strong it took three players to bring him down.

Desperate as usual, I was searching for a Bridge City game

film. I must've talked to half the coaches in Texas, calling in every favor owed me, but the Bridge City coach had friends too. Not a single coach in Bridge City's district would loan me their game film. Finally, someone told me about a Galveston high school who had played Bridge City early in the season. The school was about to be closed. That being the case, I figured the coach wouldn't feel obligated to Bridge City. I was right. The Galveston coach easily agreed to let me have his film. But then, he began to come up with all sorts of excuses. First, he told me he couldn't find the film. When I called again the next day, he said one of his assistants had the film.

Three days after the coach agreed to loan me his film, I still didn't have possession. I called him again. This time I used a different strategy.

"Have you located that Bridge City game film for me, Coach?" I asked, expecting another lame excuse.

"No, Coach Wood, I've had my assistant George Brown searching high and low, but seems he's misplaced that film somewhere."

"Wait just a minute, Coach. I want you to understand something. I'm not expecting you to do a lot of work for me for nothing. I'm willing to pay for your time. Here's my proposition. The minute I receive your film and have it in my hands, I'm gonna mail you a fifty-dollar bill."

"Fifty dollars? You're willing to pay me fifty dollars for a game film?" The foot-dragging coach's attitude changed dramatically with the prospect of money changing hands.

"Yes sir, that's the deal. It's close to Christmas. I want you to take the money and buy yourself a new pair of boots or buy your wife a new hat. Whatever suits your fancy."

"You know what, Coach Wood? I'm gonna look real hard for that film. I believe I can have it in Brownwood tomorrow morning."

The film arrived by bus the next day, and I mailed the Galveston coach a fifty. Every penny came right out of my pocket, not from Brownwood High School funds.

◆ ◆ ◆

DURING THE WEEK leading up to our championship match, football fever invaded Brownwood, and excitement reached an unprecedented high. Virtually every downtown business decorated their windows in school colors and exhibited some kind of poster urging the Lions to, "Cage the Cardinals." A contest sponsored by the Brownwood High School Coed Boosters offered prizes for the most original and the largest signs. A large supply of huge maroon and white ribbons boasting the names of Lion players and coaches was sold out within hours after they went on sale at the high school. On Wednesday, Mayor W.C. Monroe and members of the city council voted unanimously to proclaim Saturday as "Brownwood Lions Day." Friday afternoon, the *Brownwood Bulletin* got into the act, publishing a twenty-page state championship souvenir edition.

More than five thousand Central Texas fans were expected to make the long trek to Aggieland to cheer their fighting Maroons to victory. An even larger group of Bay City supporters was expected to be on-hand at Texas A&M's Kyle Field for the Saturday afternoon fracas.

◆ ◆ ◆

FOR MANY REASONS, not the least of which being a limited athletic budget, our football team rarely spent the night out of town either before or after a football game. However, the year we played Bridge City, we decided to bus our team to Bryan on Friday afternoon and spend the night in a brand-new Holiday Inn which was owned and operated by Brownwood contractor Herman Bennett.

Early Saturday morning, Bill Jamar, from Brownwood radio station KBWD, called my room to ask about the weather. I was still half asleep, so maybe that's why I told Bill the weather was perfect—clear and sunny, a great day for a football game. Luckily, I'm not hired to predict the weather. After I hung up, I rolled out of bed, walked to the window and looked outside. It was raining like crazy.

By game time, more dark storm clouds rolled in, and rain was pouring down. Puddles of water were standing all over the playing field.

◆ ◆ ◆

BRIDGE CITY WON the coin toss and elected to receive. The red and white team returned our kickoff to the thirty where a half-dozen maroon uniforms hammered the Cardinal ballcarrier.

Standing six-foot tall, weighing 210 pounds, and clocking a

10.5 in the 100-yard dash, Steve Worster was a two-time all-stater and a vicious runner. Worster's statistics were almost unbelievable. Coming into our championship game, he had rushed for 1,293 yards and scored twenty-two touchdowns. On the first play from scrimmage, Worster took the handoff from Redbird quarterback Joe Langston and started around right end. As Worster turned to cut upfield, Lion cornerback Roy Spence, who didn't weigh more than 155 pounds, came flying in to tackle Worster. Spence delivered a crushing blow right at the knees, and the hard impact echoed all across the playing field.

Our cornerback's punishing blow set the tone for Brownwood's game. Worster was indeed a great player and possibly the most difficult ballcarrier to bring down I ever saw, but my Lions were up to the task. Many times maroon-clad players swarmed into Bridge City's backfield to gang-tackle Worster before he reached the line of scrimmage. In twenty-four carries the heralded Worster gained only eighty-seven yards.

A steady drizzle poured down through much of the game, and the temperature never climbed out of the low fifties, but the miserable weather didn't deter Brownwood's faithful. Chilled and thoroughly soaked, Lion yell leaders stood in inch-deep water to lead frenzied Lion fans in cheering their favorite team to victory. A clever halftime Christmas routine presented by the BHS Band and the Lionette drill team was performed in ankle-deep mud.

A first quarter fumble recovery by Brownwood's Mike McInnis at Bridge City's eight set up our first score. On third and six, after making little headway running the ball, we overloaded the right side with receivers, and Henley fired a pass to a wide open Kirk Wall. Branum added the extra point.

On the first play of the fourth period, after Brownwood shoved its way to the Bridge City thirty-one, Henley rolled out and fired a perfect strike to Roger Richey at the fifteen. Richey waltzed in for the clinching TD, and Branum climaxed the scoring by booting the point after.

Our defense was magnificent that afternoon. Linebackers Walter Croft, Wayne Fenton and Jimmy Piper and a front wall, which included Joe Shaw, George Martin, Larry Hall, Richard Jones, Rollin Hunter and Billy Bly, were among the many mud-caked heroes. And with our stingy secondary of Leroy Deanda,

Terry Beck, Mike Ratliff and Roy Spence keeping the Cardinal passing game bottled up, Bridge City only crossed the mid-field stripe three times.

Final score: Brownwood 14, Bridge City 0.

In the dressing room after the game, Lion Quarterback Club president Bud Gray interrupted the wild celebration for a brief announcement, telling us about an event his booster organization intended to sponsor. Gray said an all-sports banquet to honor the new state champions would be held on December 30, in the Brownwood Coliseum.

"We intend to show you guys how much we appreciate you by filling that place with people," Gray promised. And they did.

CHAPTER THIRTEEN

Putting the Pedal to the Metal
(1966–1969)

AFTER WINNING a fourth state crown, I joined some very elite company. Only the late Paul Tyson of Waco and retired Wichita Falls coach Joe Golding had enjoyed the same thrill. However, the applause I personally received was somewhat embarrassing. My team could never have achieved the feat without the dedication and hard work of my assistants Morris Southall, Pete Murray and Kenneth West. And it was our players who were the real heroes, battling back from a rash of mid-season injuries which would have demoralized a lesser group of kids. Former Texas A&M coach Homer Norton said it best, "A coach can only lose football games. It takes a team to win one."

1966

FOR MOST AMERICANS 1966 was a prosperous year. In Brown County, with the weather cooperating for a change, even our farmers had a good year, increasing their annual income from an average of $2,957 to $3,241.

Saving trading stamps, which could be redeemed for a wide variety of prizes, was every family's favorite game, and if you shopped on the right days, you could get double stamps. A fun evening for many Texas families meant gathering around the kitchen table to paste their S&H Green Stamps in blank booklets while they watched *Batman* on TV.

The government programs initiated in the late fifties to encourage higher education were beginning to pay dividends. Since 1957, the number of students enrolled in graduate schools had doubled, and Texas was playing a big role in the technology boom. In March, Gemini 8, with astronauts Neil Armstrong and David Scott aboard, made the first successful space docking. In April, the world's third heart-transplant operation was performed—in Houston. This event was particularly relevant to avid West Texas football fans who could easily wear out one or two hearts in a season.

◆   ◆   ◆

IF I HAVE ANY REGRETS about being a coach, they would concern my son Jim. I missed so many opportunities to share his growing up. So much of my time was devoted to coaching, attending coaching clinics, speaking at football banquets—doing the things I needed to do as a coach.

Some kids might envy Jim because he went with me to a lot of places and met many famous people, but I never had time to throw the ball around, coach him, help him become a better athlete.

One sad thing about coaching is you're often so busy looking after other peoples' children you don't have time to coach your own. When Jim was growing up, it was his mother who played catch with him in our back yard, not me.

Jim was eight the evening he came home sobbing. My wife was in the kitchen. I was in the living room, scanning the newspaper while I waited for Katharine to call us to the dinner table. Jim wasn't angry, and he wasn't hurt, but I could tell something was wrong.

"What in the world is wrong with you, boy?" I said, laying my newspaper aside.

"Lanetta said my parents have to love me because I'm adopted. She said if you don't love me, some people will come and take me away."

Lanetta was a neighbor girl who was a year and a half older than Jim. Sometimes children can be so cruel to each other. In the kitchen I could hear my wife forsake

Jim Wood—age two.
(credit: Wood Family Collection)

her cooking chores and begin to cry. Always the dutiful mother, I knew Katharine wanted to run to Jim, hug him and tell Jim how much we loved him, but to her credit, she allowed me to handle this family crisis.

"Jim, let me tell you something," I said tenderly. My heart was filled with compassion. "When Pat was born, we had to take her because we didn't have any other choice. But your mother and I chose you, and that makes you extra special."

Jim's eyes lit up, apparently delighted with my explanation. When his sister came home from college a few days later, he ran to tell her.

"Hey, Pat, guess what? I'm more special than you. Mom and dad had to take you, but they chose me."

Luckily, Pat was old enough to

Jim Wood—age eleven.
(credit: Wood Family Collection)

understand, so Jim's announcement didn't hurt her feelings. Actually, she was tickled with the situation, and that made me love her even more.

◆　◆　◆

HEARTS WERE HEAVY all across Texas as Brownwood High began two-a-day practices that summer. On August 1, Charles Whitman, a 25-year-old Austin man, barricaded himself atop the "Tower" at the University of Texas and began shooting at persons below. Before Austin police killed him, Whitman shot forty-four people, killing thirteen.

With so much talent returning from our 1965 state championship team, my coaches and I garnered high expectations. Linemen like Billy Bly, Terry Beck, Rollin Hunter, Jerry Jones, Damon Smith, Mike Fuller and Johnny Lopez had us smiling, but it was our backfield, which included Wayne Fenton, James Hamlett, Roy Spence and Kirk Wall, that made us drool. Also in our pool of exceptional talent was Si Southall, the second son of Morris

Southall. Si was every bit as good an athlete as his older brother Terry who would rain touchdown passes on Baylor opponents every Saturday afternoon that season.

Among the athletes we expected to do well was Mike Davidson, but Mike had a weight problem. The previous spring, Davidson weighed in at 240 pounds. I had cautioned him about his weight. I told Mike if he was really dedicated and wanted to play he would have to lose weight. I was even more specific. I told him if he weighed in at 215 or less in August he would be a starter. If he weighed more, he wouldn't play a down all season. Davidson checked in at 246 pounds.

Our first pre-season scrimmage game was against Haltom City. We played at Ranger, and Mike didn't play a down. After the scrimmage I was heading for the team bus when I noticed Mike's mom. She was sitting in her car, and she was sobbing.

"What's wrong, Mrs. Davidson?" I asked. Of course I already knew why she was crying.

"I'm so sad for my son. He wants to play so badly, but you didn't let him play a single down."

I advised Mike's mother to listen carefully to what I had to say. I told her Mike had the ability to play, but he lacked self discipline. He could easily have lost the weight I'd asked him to, if he had watched his diet and worked out all summer. I explained there was no chance for her son to play unless she supported my program and what we were trying to accomplish a hundred percent.

My conversation with Mrs. Davidson changed Mike's attitude and possibly his whole life. Three weeks later, Davidson tipped the scales at 215, and he started at left tackle in our opening game. Years later, Mike became a pilot for American Airlines. Since the summer of 1966, I don't think he's ever weighed more than 220 pounds.

◆　◆　◆

THREE INCHES OF RAIN drenched Lion Stadium on Friday, so Brownwood opened the football season playing on a muddy field and in a light rain. We scored on our second possession, using a pair of passes from Lion quarterback Roy Spence to Wayne Fenton to fuel our drive. The final eleven yards came on a toss from Spence to wingback Kirk Wall. Rollin Hunter's extra point try was wide, but we held on to beat a scrappy Cleburne crew 12–6. Our defensive players were the real heroes, limiting the Yellowjackets to thirty-one yards on the ground and forty-one via the air. Leading our defensive charge were Billy Bly, Jerry Jones, Rollin Hunter, Lane Bowen, Donnie Fowler, David Wallace, Mike Fuller and Terry Beck.

The following Friday, my Lions won their nineteenth in a row. Playing at home before a full house, we surprised Gatesville's secondary with a couple of long bombs from Si Southall to Kirk Wall and Wayne Fenton, then used a grind-it-out offense to stuff the highly regarded Hornets 32–6.

Brownwood's twentieth consecutive victim was Stephenville whom our Maroons mauled 27–0. Then we faced always-tough Abilene Cooper, and our victory string came to an abrupt end. The Cougars trounced us good 26–7.

Employing a blistering ground attack, we opened district play by blasting arch-rival Breckenridge at Lion Stadium 33–12. Wayne Fenton gained a hundred and eighty yards on sixteen carries, and James Hamlett rambled for forty-two yards on ten carries. Our defense was magnificent. Roy Spence picked up nine tackles followed by Fenton and Mike Fuller with seven and Johnny Lopez with six.

◆ ◆ ◆

AFTER ROLLING OVER District 4–AAA opponents, Burkburnett, Wichita Falls Hirschi, Childress and Graham, my Lions were undefeated in district play as our final game approached. After the loss to Abilene, our maroon squad had jelled, and my coaches and I were confident.

Vernon High coach C.R. (Pat) Pattison was confident too, and he had good reason. Pattison's V-Lions were undefeated, and he had all-state quarterback Ed Marsh running his offense. Football fever was running high up near the Red River.

Morris Southall and his wife Lorene grew up in Vernon, so the Southalls had many close friends who lived there. During the week prior to our game, Coach Southall's friends called to tell Morris that Vernon backs Mike McCauley and Ed Spradlin were hurt so bad they were working out in shorts. No way they'd be able to play on Friday. I'm sure those reports were rendered honestly, but they were, oh, so wrong.

What happened was exactly the opposite. Vernon's starting backfield was on the field for the opening kickoff and played the entire game. Meanwhile, James Hamlett, our all-district fullback, broke his leg in the first quarter. Then Wayne Fenton tore up a knee, and Jackie Alley, Hamlett's backup, got hurt. We wound up depending on two second-stringers, David Wallace and Ronnie Fowler, to lead our rushing attack. Brownwood had plenty of excuses for losing, but there's no denying Vernon had a very good team. They were especially outstanding that evening.

Final score: Brownwood 15, Vernon 28.

Vernon and Monahans tied 7–7 in the AAA state quarterfinals, but Monahans advanced, winning on penetrations.

◆ ◆ ◆

PROBABLY THE GREATEST REWARD for being a coach is seeing your players succeed in life after they leave high school. Roy Spence's story is a great example.

In high school Roy was an outstanding student—popular, personable, and a fierce competitor on the football field. After he graduated from Brownwood High, Spence continued his education at the University of Texas. To my chagrin, he immediately joined the group we called "Hippies" back in the sixties. Roy let his hair grow long, but when he came home to visit, he would duck down in his car whenever he saw me. Roy wasn't afraid of me, but he did respect

my strong feelings about long hair.

When Spence and three of his "Hippie" friends graduated from college, they each kicked in a thousand dollars and formed a public relations firm. Roy borrowed his thousand from a Brownwood bank where his father's friend A.C. Henley was president. Henley was convinced the venture would fail and firmly advised Roy against investing his money so foolishly.

Roy Spence, tri-captain, all-district defensive halfback on Brownwood's 1966 team. (credit: 1967 Brownwood High Yearbook)

However, since Spence's father was co-signing the note, Henley agreed to approve the loan.

To make a long story short, Roy and his partners sold their firm to an English company for forty-nine million dollars. Roy now serves as Chief Executive Officer of the new organization, which is one of the most influential public relations firms in Austin. Roy and his wife Mary are close friends with President Bill Clinton, so close that Roy wrote the President's acceptance speeches for both his Democratic party nomination and when Clinton was sworn in as President.

1967

1967 WAS AN EXASPERATING YEAR for the entire nation, and especially for Texas. Early that summer, the Texas Legislature passed a bill allowing cities to tack on an additional one percent to the already outrageously high two percent state sales tax. Then in late August, Hurricane Beulah, with winds of one hundred and thirty-six miles per hour, came ashore at Brownsville, killing thirteen and spawning one hundred and fifteen tornadoes.

The national news was even more depressing. In January, astronauts Virgil Grissom, Edward White and Roger Chafee were killed when a fire developed in their Apollo spacecraft on the launch pad at Cape Kennedy in Florida. During the long, hot summer, more than a hundred instances of racial violence left eighty-three people dead. The worst rioting took place in Detroit and in Newark, New Jersey.

In Vietnam, with more and more U.S. troops being committed, the war situation was getting worse, not better. To those of us who supported our president and our fighting men overseas, the growing number of anti-war demonstrations was particularly distressing. Even though I was a big fan of boxer Muhammad Ali, I can't say I was disappointed when a federal court stripped him of his heavyweight title for evading the draft. Those of us who served in World War II could never sympathize with a man who shirked his patriotic duty.

◆ ◆ ◆

WITH THIRTEEN LETTERMEN returning from a team that went 8–2 the previous year, expectations were high as we launched our mid-August two-a-day drills.

Heading the list of returning veterans were two-year letterman tailback, Wayne Fenton; ends, Griggs DeHay and Damon Smith; tackles, Mike Davidson and Bob Rothe; guards, Joe McCluskey, Robert Smith and Kenny Thomas; center, Mike Fuller; wingback, Lane Bowen; fullbacks, David Wallace and Jack Alley; and quarterback, Si Southall. In past seasons my Brownwood teams had relied on speed and quickness, but our '67 squad was also blessed with brawn and plenty of muscle. Pre-season polls favored Wichita Falls Hirschi to capture the 4–AAA crown. Brownwood was picked to finish second, but in actuality, the district title was strictly up for grabs. Breckenridge and Burkburnett were also expected to field exceptionally strong teams. Because every school was capable of beating every other member, District 4–AAA had the reputation as the toughest district in the state.

In a frustrating mistake-filled game we came very close to losing, our Maroons opened the season in Cleburne against an angry bunch of Yellowjackets. Brownwood rallied in the second half, taking advantage of a Cleburne fumble to score in the final quarter and eke out a 14–7 victory.

During practices the next week my coaches and I concentrated on ironing out problems and eliminating mistakes. Those efforts paid off, and in our second contest, our Lions blanked a solid Gatesville club 35–0.

◆　◆　◆

WHEN BROWNWOOD FANS reminisce about great comebacks, they generally mention the Lions' stirring 1978 semifinal victory over Bay City, but it was the '67 Lions who wrote the book on comebacks. Strange as it may seem, it all began at the Abilene Cooper game during the halftime intermission. Cooper was ranked as the state's number one 4A team. Jack Mildren, whom many consider to be the most talented Texas high school field general of all time, was the Cougar quarterback. Due to a shaky start and a plethora of Lion miscues, the Cougars were leading 42–0. Most teams would have thrown in the towel, but not my Lions.

Some coaches might have chewed their players out for playing so poorly, but all I did was point out the mistakes we were making and explained how to correct them. Then I told my youngsters we couldn't do anything about the first half. What was done was done, but they could prove to their fans they weren't quitters by playing better the second half.

Our guys went out and played the best they had played all year. When the game ended, Brownwood had the ball on Cooper's five-yard line, about to score their third touchdown. The final score was: Cooper 42, Brownwood 14.

After the game, players from both teams met near mid-field to shake hands. One Cooper player sympathetically advised little James (Squirt) Thompson not to give up, telling him Brownwood still had a chance to win their district.

"District? Hell, we're gonna win the state championship," Thompson proclaimed.

Even though Brownwood lost, it was during that game our players and coaches began to realize this was a team of championship caliber.

With an open date the next week, we used our practices to work on blocking, tackling and execution—especially on pass defense and pass rush. Despite their surprising second half comeback, our kids were embarrassed by the loss to Cooper. That week we had some of the sharpest practices of my entire coaching career. I've never seen a group of players more determined to improve.

We needed the great practices because we played host to old nemesis Breckenridge in our first district contest. After Buckie quarterback Lynn Roy Farmer threw a perfect strike to his end Allen Smith for a TD late in the third quarter, Brownwood was on the short end of the 7–0 score. That's when my Lions hitched their britches and went to work.

David Wallace returned the Buck's kickoff to the twenty-three. Then Si Southall took charge. Cooly barking the signals, Si guided the Lions on a fifteen-play drive, using tailbacks Wayne Fenton and Jack Alley to hammer out seventy-seven yards and a touchdown against the stubborn Buckaroo defense.

Instead of going for a tie, we gambled and elected to go for the win. Southall came through by firing a hard-to-catch bullet past a green-clad defender into the waiting arms of end Damon Smith. The two-point conversion gave Brownwood an 8–7 lead. Minutes later, a pass interception by Lane Bowen set up another Lion touchdown drive which sealed our come-from-behind victory. When the game was over, every fan in Lion Stadium was completely exhausted from screaming.

Final score: Brownwood 15, Breckenridge 7.

◆　◆　◆

OUR SECOND DISTRICT GAME was against Burkburnett, another strong contender. The Bulldogs were coached by Bill Froman, one of the best football coaches in the state. Froman's orange and black Bulldogs gave us all we could handle. In the first half, Burk's speedy running back Charles Hicks ran all over our defense, gaining seventy-five yards on thirteen carries. Bulldog quarterback Jeff Beaver riddled our leaky pass defense with ten completions and ninety-nine yards.

Down 7–3 at the intermission, the Lions proved they were a second half club. On our first possession of the third period, David Wallace made Brownwood's comeback his own personal vendetta. First, Wallace returned a Bulldog punt twenty-four yards to Burkburnett's thirty-four, then he lugged the football six times for twenty-five of the thirty-four yards needed to reach paydirt.

Inspired by Wallace's gutsy one man show, maroon defenders Mike Fuller, Kenny Thomas, Glenn Williamson, Joe McCluskey, Harold Ephraim, Ricky Stokes, Bob Rothe, Mike Davidson, and Ricky Foster dug in and held off a ferocious Burkburnett attack on our goal line until late in the fourth quarter. With 2:41 left in the game, Brownwood had possession at the 41-yard line. On a fourth and one situation, I decided to gamble. Instead of playing it safe and punting, I called time-out and instructed my quarterback to go for the first down.

Knowing Burk's defense would be drawn in tight, we called on sure-handed bulldozer tailback Wayne Fenton to get the job done, but an amazing thing happened when Southall handed Wayne the football. Fenton crashed over the right side, found a gaping hole, and fled untouched for fifty-nine yards and the clinching score.

Final score: Brownwood 17, Burkburnett 7.

◆　◆　◆

ALTHOUGH I'M SURE he's not the first to have coined the phrase, Bill Stovall began to regularly refer to the Lions as the "Cardiac Kids" in his daily sports column. But even Bill couldn't have known how appropriate that label would become before the season was finished. Amazing, heart-stopping comeback victories became the order of the day for those never-to-be-forgotten Lions of 1967.

Brownwood was a seven-point underdog the Friday we traveled to Wichita Falls to face Hirschi's Huskies. A tie with cross-town rival Washington had marred the Huskies' unblemished record, but football polls ranked Hirschi no worse than third in the state. Many sportswriters were predicting the Huskies to go all the way. To reach the playoffs, though, Hirschi still had to beat Brownwood. For both teams this was the "Big One."

Hirschi was every bit as good as their press clippings claimed, and they sailed out in front, taking a 14–0 lead to the halftime dressing room. On their first possession of the second half, the Scarlet and Blue tacked on a third touchdown and appeared on their way to a rout. My never-say-die Maroons had a more exciting ending in mind.

Late in the third quarter, a short punt put Brownwood in business at the Hirschi thirty-nine. My Lions made the most of the unexpected gift. Southall tried a quarterback sneak, found some daylight, and charged twenty-six yards to the thirteen. Then on fourth and five, Si flipped a short aerial to Damon Smith for our first tally. Smith added the PAT, and with fifty-four seconds left in the third quarter, the score was 21–7.

Linebacker Harold Ephraim and middle guard Mike Fuller set up the Lions' second TD when Ephraim jarred Huskie quarterback Tony Wilson and Fuller pounced on the loose pigskin at Hirschi's thirty-seven. When David Wallace plowed across the goal line nine plays later, the scoreboard clock showed 8:11 left to play. Our already bleak situation looked even worse when Damon Smith missed on the extra point try.

Trailing 21–13, Brownwood's defensive unit bowed their necks and refused to budge, holding the Huskies in check and forcing them to punt. When the Lions took possession, they knew it was now or never. After a Lane Bowen pass to Wendell Daniel took the ball to the Wichita twenty-seven, the going got double tough. Carries by Jack Alley and David Wallace gained only five yards. A short pass to Wallace gained another three, setting up a crucial fourth and two situation at the nineteen. Southall dialed Wallace, and David got the job done, smashing his way to the eleven for the first down. Two plays later, a penalty moved the ball back to the twelve. Facing third and eleven, Southall arched a beauty to maroon end Griggs DeHay in the end zone, and we had our third score of the evening.

Down 21–19, Brownwood had no choice but to go for two points. With every fan in the stadium on their feet and screaming their lungs out, Southall handled the pressure like an old pro. Calling a pass-run option, Si circled right, found his receivers covered, fell in behind a tooth-rattling block by Alley, and ran over two giant Huskie defenders. The football only crossed the goal line by a few inches, but the Lions were back in the hunt for the district title. Despite a desperate march in the final minutes, the Huskies were unable to score, and the game ended in a 21–21 tie.

◆　◆　◆

OUR TIE WITH HIRSCHI was a giant step forward, but the Lions still weren't out of the woods. Blocking our path to the playoffs was Wichita Falls Washington. The Leopards were in a dead heat with Brownwood for the district lead. Our winner-take-all contest was played before a sell-out homecoming crowd of five thousand, and our Maroons got off to a fine start. At the intermission, Brownwood held a 14–0 lead, but our kids didn't seem to know what to do with their halftime advantage. Washington took the second half kickoff and scored in one hundred and forty-nine seconds.

Not to be outdone, Brownwood stormed back for our third touchdown. The lightning-quick Leopards weren't the least bit impressed. In less than two minutes they scored again to pull within seven points.

Washington got possession of the ball again late in the fourth quarter and were on their way to a tying touchdown when Lion Edward Robinson saved the day by grabbing an interception. With only 1:25 left in the game, we gratefully accepted the football and ran out the clock.

Final score: Brownwood 21, Washington 14.

With the meat of our schedule behind us, my Lions cruised through the next few weeks, beating Childress 59–0, Graham 27–0 and Vernon 51–0. There's no doubt fortune smiled on Brownwood that season because District 4–AAA had several teams who could have done well in the playoffs. Hirschi and Washington were certainly good enough to win the state championship. In fact, with only two ties to mar their record, Hirschi's season ended without a loss.

◆ ◆ ◆

WINNING BI-DISTRICT was no problem. Si Southall was an absolute wizard at calling signals with a broken cadence, and he used his talent to pull Lubbock Dunbar offside numerous times on crucial third downs. Brownwood crushed the Panthers 28–0.

Our quarterfinal game was played at Amarillo in freezing weather and on a frozen field. Dumas had an awesome team, and at halftime the score was knotted 7–7. In the second half we turned our pounding fullback David Wallace loose, and he was magnificent, carrying the ball nineteen times for 135 yards. Midway through the fourth quarter, Wallace followed behind the vicious blocking of guard Robert Smith to crash into the Demons end zone. Damon Smith tacked on the point after and Brownwood pulled out ahead 14–7.

When penalty troubles slowed our push toward the Demon goal line late in the fourth quarter, we sent in the kicking tee, and Damon Smith nailed a 31-yard field goal. Those points proved to be the difference in the game. Dumas took our kickoff and drove sixty-three yards for their second touchdown. Their successful two-point conversion put the score at 17–15 in Brownwood's favor, and that's how the game ended.

◆ ◆ ◆

DAVID WALLACE is a good example of the many exceptional young men who played for me at Brownwood. David had a great attitude and always gave his best. I can't remember ever criticizing him for anything in a game or in practice. He was the epitome of what a football player should be and how one should behave.

David proved he was a fierce competitor and forever earned my respect in the Dumas game. The weather was freezing. The ground was wet. Everyone on the field was absolutely miserable. Brownwood had the football and had marched down to the Demons' twenty. On fourth down our quarterback handed the ball to Wallace, and he was stopped short of the first down. Coach Southall was up in the press box. He called down to the bench to tell me, "Wallace wasn't running hard that last time."

After the change of possession, David came to the sideline. I

David Wallace, Most Valuable Player, Brownwood's 1967 state championship team. (credit: Fred Nobs)

collared him and told him what Coach Southall said.

"That's right, Coach Wood. I wasn't running hard, but it will never happen again," Wallace replied—and it didn't. From that point in the game, David was a one-man bulldozer. He had an outstanding day.

◆　◆　◆

OUR SEMIFINAL MATCH pitted us against Coach James Cameron and his blue and gold McKinney Lions. The game was played at TCU's Amon Carter Stadium on a Saturday afternoon before a crowd of eight thousand. Cameron was not only a superb football coach, he was also very innovative. My coaches and I were truly scared to death he might pull out some new wrinkle we hadn't seen before.

Early in the game it appeared our fears were justified. On their first possession, McKinney drove deep into our territory, and Carl White booted a 24-yard field goal. Cameron's Lions appeared to be headed for another score when McKinney quarterback Philip Wood hit Mac Cameron with a 43-yard pass on the Brownwood twenty. Three plays later McKinney was camped on the eight and threatening to add to their lead. That's when sophomore defensive halfback Jimmy Carmichael gave Brownwood folks a preview of things to come. He intercepted a Wood pass and ran it out to the forty-six.

Carmichael's interception was exactly the right medicine for what ailed Brownwood's anemic offense. Driving fifty-four yards in eleven plays, our fired-up Maroons shoved in for a touchdown and never looked back. We scored again with three minutes left in the third quarter. Southall did the honors with a one-yard plunge.

When Damon Smith sailed his extra point try between the uprights, Brownwood fans knew they would be returning to their favorite haunt—the state finals.

Final score: Brownwood 14, McKinney 3.

Victory is at hand as Lions make title run in 1967.
(credit: 1968 Brownwood High Yearbook)

◆ ◆ ◆

MY FIRST SEASON at Stamford I learned a hard lesson about big games. My Bulldog club had won seven straight games. We appeared to be a shoo-in to capture the district title, with only Anson's Tigers blocking our path. Traditionally, the Anson contest was Stamford's biggest game of the season, and our boosters were anxious to show their support for the boys. I let people talk me into one of the dumbest coaching mistakes I ever made.

On the Monday morning prior to our Anson game, the school held a pep rally before classes began. Our band was there, our cheerleaders, all the high school students and many of the towns-people. Midway through the rally, both the high school principal and the school superintendent got up, and with great emotion, told my players how everyone was expecting them to play well and bring glory to their school.

On Tuesday night, Stamford held another pep rally with more inspirational speeches—one by city manager Lee Walker. Before he took the city manager's job, Walker had been the football coach at Stamford High.

On Thursday night, Stamford held a third pep rally, this time with a big bonfire. My boys were sky high when they left. Several of my players told me later they didn't sleep a wink that night.

You know what happened. We lost the game. My kids were so keyed up they couldn't hit the floor with their helmets. We turned the ball over nine times on fumbles. The great lesson I learned about big games? Players need to be kept down, not pumped up.

◆ ◆ ◆

WHICH SCHOOL WOULD REIGN as state champions was decided at Austin's Memorial Stadium on a cold, damp, gray Saturday afternoon—a week before Christmas. Brownwood's opponent was unbeaten El Campo, but the Ricebirds were ill pre-pared to face a team with the character and determination of my '67 Lions. Our rock-ribbed defense made a shambles of El Campo's much talked about offensive machine, limiting the pride of the Gulf Coast to seven first downs and 161 total yards.

Our offense was nothing less than magnificent. With David

Si Southall leads David Wallace on a power sweep against El Campo.
(credit: Brownwood Bulletin)

Wallace and Si Southall leading a balanced running and passing attack, the Lions hammered out 354 total yards.

Southall's deadeye 23-yard punt, which rolled out of bounds at the Ricebirds' ten, helped set up our first TD. There, our defense held El Campo to six yards on three tries. Then Wallace hauled in red and white punter Wayne Zaskoda's booming kick and legged it out to the El Campo nineteen. Three plays later, Damon Smith, running a down and out pattern, speared a perfect over-the-shoulder shot from Southall and outran a Ricebird defender to the goal line.

With Wallace, Fenton, and Bowen taking turns rambling inside our tackles, power football and savage blocking by our front line allowed Brownwood to dominate the game for the entire first half. Second quarter touchdowns by Wallace and Fenton and a Damon Smith field goal gave Brownwood a 23–0 lead. As the half ended, the outcome was essentially on ice.

Final score: Brownwood 36, El Campo 12.

My fifth state championship still ranks as one of my most satisfying because our team was a team without standout stars. One coach in our district was quoted as saying it was the weakest team Brownwood ever sent to the playoffs. Fullback David Wallace was

Brownwood's leading ground gainer. He was quick, but not exceptionally fast. David weighed only 160 pounds. Si Southall was a fine passer and an outstanding punter, but he had no great receivers. Si just threw to whoever was open, and they caught it.

Our offensive line was larger than normal, but it was the dedication of guys like Doug Streckert, Robert Smith, Mike Fuller, Bob Rothe and Kenny Thomas, who worked hard and learned to block like blue blazes, that brought us success. On defense, Joe McCluskey, Ricky Stokes, Edward Robinson and Glenn Williamson would have a good game one week. The next week Ricky Foster, Mike Davidson, Jimmy Carmichael, Harold Ephraim and Lane Bowen would be our heroes. The big thing was that none of our players ever had a bad game. To a man, every kid gave his best effort on every play of every game. That's the reason no one performer dominated our show. Brownwood's 1967 state champions were without a doubt—a *team* of champions.

To the showers—locker room bedlam following Brownwood's 36–12 victory over El Campo in the 1967 AAA state final. (credit: Brownwood Bulletin)

◆　◆　◆

I'M NOT EXACTLY SURE when the routine began, but sometime in the mid-sixties Morris Southall and I began stopping for a cup of coffee at the Palace Drug Store after we finished our afternoon radio show at KBWD. The drug store was co-owned by Bob Dunn and Roger Sweeney. Roger handled the public address system for Lion home games, so the place was a hotbed for Brownwood football long before Morris and I began dropping by. Well-known Brownwood citizens like Chief of Police Jack Pike, florist James Hallum, Sheriff Otis Shaw, Dr. Allan Spence, H.O. Casey, George Burns, Marion Baugh and Dr. Fred Spencer were regular afternoon patrons. Before long, more and more people began to meet us there to talk football and inquire about the team. Most afternoons the group also included Groner Pitts, Calvin Fryar, Frank Smith and Attorney Henry Evans, who were members of the widely acclaimed Brownwood Mafia.

Our fifteen minute radio show was the brain child of Brownwood Public Accountant John Arthur Thomason. After our Lions won the state championship in 1960, Thomason went to the radio station and sold them on the idea of my doing a regular radio program. He proposed the station sell advertising for the show and give all the proceeds to me. Thomason even wrote the UIL and obtained their approval to make sure everything was legal. The compensation I received didn't amount to a whole lot, roughly three hundred dollars a month, and I split the money right down the middle with my assistant coaches who did the show with me.

During football season, Coach Southall and I worked the show together. On Thursdays, we would schedule an area guest coach who had a big game coming up. Fridays, we attempted to predict winners. Usually Roger Sweeney and one other person would join us in trying to pick the winners of that weekend's football games. Because of his horrible record, we tagged Roger with the nickname "poor-picker Sweeney."

When basketball season got underway, I invited Don Martin, our basketball coach, to join me. During track season Coach West and I did the program. Morris would come back and work with me the last month of the school year. All of us Brownwood coaches were operating on a string back then, so the extra income was truly appreciated.

1968

1968 WAS ANOTHER troubling year. President Johnson kept making promises about a Great Society, but a lot of people were resorting to violence to settle their differences. On April 4, civil rights leader Martin Luther King was murdered in Memphis, Tennessee. His death set off a series of race riots all across the country. On June 5, only a few hours after he won California's Democratic primary, Robert F. Kennedy was gunned down by assassin Sirhan Sirhan. In August, we watched on television as demonstrators battled police outside Convention Hall in Chicago. Inside the Hall, Hubert Humphrey was busy nailing down the Democratic presidential nomination.

In Asia, the situation was in a steep decline. On January 23, North Korean patrol boats seized U.S. naval ship *Pueblo* which was on an intelligence gathering mission off the Korean coast. North Korea held the *Pueblo's* crew in captivity until the end of December. On January 30, North Vietnam launched a major Tet offensive, attacking numerous cities in South Vietnam. For six hours the U.S. embassy in Saigon was held by the Viet Cong. The U.S. position in Vietnam became so precarious that President Johnson announced to a national television audience that he was halting the bombing of North Vietnam. Then Johnson stunned his critics by declaring he would not run for re-election, saying he wanted to concentrate his efforts on securing a reasonable peace in Vietnam.

◆　◆　◆

OUR '68 FOOTBALL CAMPAIGN kicked off on a sour note too. Abilene Cooper was usually our toughest non-conference game. Even without Jack Mildren, who had graduated and gone to play for Chuck Fairbanks at Oklahoma, the '68 Cougars were outstanding. Mildren had been replaced by Andy Duvall, and Duvall was no slouch at slick ballhandling. Using a crunching ground game, Cooper hogged the football all evening, grinding out 25 first downs and rushing for 261 yards.

Final score: Brownwood 0, Cooper 13.

This was the first time a Brownwood football team had been shut out since a 0–0 tie with Graham eliminated the Lions from district contention in 1964.

Our one-game drought ended the next Friday, and if there was any doubt about Brownwood making another run at the state championship, my Lions proved the naysayers wrong. Fort Worth Trimble wasn't necessarily a great football team, but my explosive maroon troops totally decimated Tech's Bulldogs with long bombs, scintillating runs and rugged defense. When the smoke cleared, the scoreboard told a wild and wooly tale: Brownwood 49, Trimble Tech 6.

◆　◆　◆

BECAUSE BROWNWOOD WON the '67 state championship, I had a hard time finding schools willing to play us the next season. I must've called forty coaches trying to find a game to fill out my nonconference schedule. Finally, I contacted Joe Golding, the athletic director for Wichita Falls schools, and he set me up with a game against Wichita Falls Washington, an all black school. Washington was a member of our 4–AAA District, but after the 1967 season, the UIL had divided the district into two zones. Washington was in the North Zone. Brownwood was in the South Zone. We would play each other only if Washington won their zone and Brownwood won the South Zone. That seemed improbable at the time.

Brownwood and Washington had faced each other on the gridiron on only one previous occasion, but, oh, what a sizzling duel that had been. In 1967, Jimmy Carmichael stopped a last-minute Washington drive by intercepting a pass deep in Lion territory to preserve a narrow 21–14 Brownwood victory. That game was close and exciting. Our '68 clash was nothing less than unforgettable.

◆　◆　◆

WASHINGTON SCORED FIRST, when Leopard flanker back Ervin Garnett got a step on our Lion secondary. Garnett was a yard deep in our end zone when he hauled down a perfectly thrown pass from Felley Donaldson.

Brownwood evened the score in the second quarter after Doug Streckert recovered Donaldson's fumble at the Leopard thirty-six, and the first half ended in a 7–7 standoff.

In the third period, our offense shook out the cobwebs and began to roll. Using a time-consuming, 13-play, 92-yard drive, Carmichael sneaked in from the one for the touchdown. On the extra point try, Leopards Marvin McCarty and Kenneth Jordan rushed in to block Billy Bishop's kick. Our failure to convert would come back to haunt us.

With Brownwood's defense dominating, it appeared the Lions had the game on ice. Few maroon boosters even bothered to cheer when James Thompson gathered in a Washington punt at the Brownwood thirty, retreated to his twenty and fled eighty yards for another score. Thompson's tally gave Brownwood a 19–7 advantage, and even though we failed to convert on the extra point, it didn't appear to matter. With only 9:59 left in the game, the Lions seemed in complete control.

Washington's slick little field general Felley Donaldson didn't necessarily agree. Donaldson was the most dangerous quarterback any of my football teams ever faced. He was quick as a cat and an accurate passer. After he took the snap from center, Felley would drop back fifteen yards. Then he'd run around, dodging our tacklers until he found an open receiver. After the first quarter, our big linemen were totally exhausted from chasing Donaldson. We were forced to send in second-string defenders so our starters could get a second wind. Felley absolutely scared me to death every time he touched the football.

With Donaldson directing the show, Wichita cranked up and roared fifty-six yards to put the Leopards back in the game at 19–13. Lion supporters got a bit nervous when Washington got the ball back and almost scored again, but their fears were calmed when the maroon defense held at the two-yard line and regained possession with less than three minutes left. Brownwood appeared to be home free when Carmichael and Bowen clicked for a first down at the sixteen, but the next three running plays netted only seven yards.

Only six seconds remained on the scoreboard clock when Lane Bowen punted to the Washington forty-seven. Once again, the game seemed in the bag, but once again Felley Donaldson had other ideas.

With only a few seconds left, Washington only had time to run one or two plays. I sent in a tall end to enhance our pass defense with these specific instructions, "Whatever you do, don't try to tackle their quarterback! Keep your shoulders square with the line of scrimmage and keep your hands up! Stay between him and his receivers, and don't try to tackle him!"

My oversized defender completely disregarded my instructions. He crashed through and dived at Donaldson, who nimbly stepped aside. The big end was still sprawled out on the ground when Donaldson launched a 55-yard scoring strike to Ricky Green who had worked clear at the goal line. Then, after we called time-out to let him think it over, Green calmly capped the comeback by splitting the uprights for the game-winning extra point.

Final Score: Brownwood 19, Washington 20.

◆ ◆ ◆

AFTER DROPPING TWO of our first three, Jimmy Carmichael began to blossom into a quarterbacking wizard. With Ricky Foster, Al Chitwood and Doug Streckert gouging out big holes, our ball-carriers, Jack Alley, Billy Bishop and Gary Barron, began to steamroll opposition defenses. Sure-handed receivers Lane Bowen, Perry Young and Jan Brown grabbed every catchable pass. Our defense, bulwarked by Mike Humphries, Danny Mathews, Joe Ynostrosa and Rick Stokes, bowed their necks and made the opposition pay dearly for every yard gained.

Playing at home, our Lions clubbed Lake Worth 40–0. Then we returned to Shotwell Stadium where Brownwood outscored the Abilene High Eagles in a wild one. In a see-saw battle that saw the lead change hands four times in the last hectic eight minutes, our Maroons outlasted the Eagles 31–28.

In conference play, our reserves logged plenty of playing time as the Lions breezed through their South Zone schedule, whipping up on Stephenville 49–7, Breckenridge 52–7, Weatherford 42–7 and Mineral Wells 33–12.

When we looked up, there was Wichita Falls Washington and Felley Donaldson standing in our way. The Leopards had sailed through the North Zone undefeated, to set up a second do-or-die duel. At game time, the two teams were ranked second and third in Class AAA.

◆ ◆ ◆

ON A SUN-SPLASHED AFTERNOON at Midwestern Stadium in Wichita Falls, my frustrated maroon defenders chased an elusive Felley Donaldson for two full quarters. By halftime, our tongues were hanging out, and Brownwood was trailing 7–0. Then, tired of playing the chase and run game, our defense slammed the door shut. After giving up 246 yards in the first half, our Lions hitched their britches and held the Leopards in check while Brownwood's offense got rolling.

Big plays were the key. After Gary Barron and James Thompson barreled forty-one yards to put the Lions in business at the Leopard twenty-four, Carmichael threw a third-down rope to Jan Brown at the twelve. Three plays later Carmichael rode a clearing block by Al Chitwood and slipped in for our first tally of the day.

When Carmichael scored, Brownwood was trailing in penetrations and every other statistical department. A 7–7 tie was out of the question. We had to go for two. Our hearts fell when Carmichael's hurried throw was batted down.

After the kickoff, Perry Young zipped in front of a Leopard receiver to intercept a Donaldson pass. Perry darted sixty-three yards before he was dragged down at the Washington seventeen. A botched handoff, which the Leopards recovered at the fifteen, killed our chances of going ahead.

As the fourth period got underway, a stiff breeze, which seemed to change our luck, rippled through Midwestern Stadium. During the third quarter, Brownwood had faced the wind, but as the quarter ended and we took possession on our own twenty, the breeze was to our backs, acting like a wind in our sails.

In thirteen plays, coming through three times on clutch third-down situations, Thompson, Barron and gutty little Kenny Ephraim pounded out tough yardage against the rock solid Leopard defense. On third and eight with the ball on Washington's twenty-nine, it was air time, and Carmichael dialed his favorite target, Lane Bowen. Bowen made a circus-like catch over the outstretched arms of defender Ervin Garnett and fell into the end zone. Unbelievably, Brownwood scored again before the game ended to escape with a 19–7 victory that was much closer than the final score indicated.

◆　◆　◆

JIMMY KEELING IS ONE of the most dedicated and intense football coaches I have ever known. When I moved to Brownwood in 1960, Jimmy was coaching at Class A Dublin High School. Dublin is located some fifty miles east of Brownwood. After our team made the playoffs that fall, Jimmy came here every day to observe our practices, to watch how we prepared for playoff competition. After he left Dublin, Jimmy coached at a small panhandle school not far from Lubbock. Eventually, he landed the head football post at Lubbock Estacado, a brand-new high school.

Estacado's first football season was played with freshmen and sophomores, so they didn't compete in a regular conference. Jimmy's Matadors played an abbreviated schedule against junior varsity clubs. His second year, Estacado joined District 3–AAA. Playing with no seniors on his squad, Keeling's club romped and stomped. In their first full season of competition, the Mats carved out a perfect 10–0 season record, winning their district and the right to meet Brownwood in the bi-district round of the state playoffs.

Shortly after we beat Washington, my coaches and I met with Coach Keeling to decide on the game site. Jimmy agreed to play on a mutual field, even consented to my suggestion that we play at Shotwell Stadium in Abilene. But he insisted we play on Thursday, Thanksgiving Day. I wanted to play on Saturday, and when we couldn't agree, we flipped a coin. Keeling won.

Some games you lose even before you play. This was one of those games. Monday, Tuesday and Wednesday, it sleeted and snowed. Weather conditions were so bad we couldn't practice outside. This worked to Estacado's advantage because the Mats had enjoyed a week off while we were settling North-South Zone affairs in our district. During their off-week, Estacado worked on offensive and defensive schemes, preparing for either Washington or Brownwood.

Late Wednesday night, Jimmy Keeling, realizing field conditions at Shotwell Stadium were going to be horrible, rousted a Lubbock sporting goods dealer. Together they searched the man's store for mud cleats. Keeling bought every pair in stock.

Before our bi-district game, Abilene ground keepers rolled all the snow off the playing field, and there was a lot. Unfortunately, they didn't remove the thin layer of sleet underneath, and the sun came out shortly before game time. As Keeling suspected, our Thanksgiving Day game was played on a slick, muddy field. Because the Matadors were so young and inexperienced, many sportswriters, and even our Brownwood fans, expected the game to be a blowout, and it was. My players slipped and slid while Keeling's Matadors enjoyed good footing. Estacado crushed Brownwood to register their eleventh win in a row. The final score was 49–0, the most lop-sided defeat ever laid on a Gordon Wood-coached team.

The Matadors were no fluke. They went on to capture the state crown, beating Refugio 14–0 in the championship game.

◆　◆　◆

WHEN I AGREED to move to Brownwood in 1960, one of the major enticements was the school board's promise to build a new football stadium. Plans were underway to construct a new high school, and the school trustees were flush with funds from a recent bond election. They were confident they would have enough money left over to replace old Lion Stadium, which was an embarrassment to the community. Unfortunately, the extra money the trustees counted on slowly evaporated in unexpected construction costs. When all the bills were paid, only a few thousand dollars remained in the kitty. That money disappeared when an opportunity came along to build a vocational building at the high school with matching government funds.

From 1960 through 1968, Brownwood's loyal football fans endured the inconvenience of sorry parking accommodations, walking long distances, and the indecencies of sitting on splintery wooden seats. Because of our success, sportswriters from all over Texas came to watch and report our games. Our press box was so outdated, and often so crowded, many reporters elected to stand on the sidelines. Our football field ranked among the worst in Texas. Even though we coaches worked hard every summer to improve the playing field, by mid-season, it was always in sad condition.

Another move to build a new stadium began in 1967. This effort culminated with a bond election held in December of 1968. A sweetheart deal had been struck with Brownwood football boosters, wherein the boosters agreed to donate half the money needed to construct a stadium with six thousand seats. School board calculations indicated the new stadium would cost the average Brownwood taxpayer two dollars per year. What a bargain! Who could possibly vote against such a great deal—for the community, for the school, and for the football team which had won three state championships in eight years. My coaches and I garnered high hopes.

The stadium bond election was soundly defeated—one month

after Richard Milhous Nixon was elected President of the United States.

◆　◆　◆

ALL OF MY BROWNWOOD COACHES knew they had my complete confidence—to teach football and to discipline our kids, but I had one rule. No one could remove a player from the football program except me. My coaches understood why—because I was the one who had to face irate parents and justify the reason.

Another reason I instituted the rule was because many times I found the situation would look different the next day after everyone cooled down. A coach can do some mighty stupid things during the heat of battle.

Once during practice, one of my linemen kept screwing up. I pulled him aside several times to explain what I wanted, then he would go right back and mess up again. Frustrated, I screamed at him, "Hey, Aaron! If you can't do better than that, you oughta quit football!"

I don't know why I said what I did. Aaron Bird was a good kid, and I liked him. I didn't want him to quit the team. The boy looked at me, crestfallen. His eyes filled with tears. He pulled off his headgear and started walking off the field, shamed by my harsh criticism.

I turned to Coach Southall and told him to send someone in to replace Bird. Then I ran to catch up with my player. I grabbed Aaron by the arm and apologized, "I made a mistake, son. I shouldn't have said what I did. And you made a mistake, because you're not doing a good job."

The boy seemed surprised I would admit I made a mistake. You could see his face brighten as I continued, "If you quit this team, you'll make a loser out of me, and I don't intend for that to happen. Now, you get your butt back out there and try harder, and I'll promise to use better judgement."

A grin came over Aaron's face. He didn't want to quit, but I had embarrassed him and forced him into a situation where he had no other choice. A coach must realize the power he has over his players and temper it with good sense.

◆　◆　◆

COACHES ALSO HAVE an amazing power to persuade. A coach can change the direction a kid is headed—sometimes even more

Perry Young, Most Valuable Offensive Player—Brownwood's 1969 state championship team. (credit: Fred Nobs)

than the youngster's parents. A coach often takes the place of parents, particularly in matters of discipline. Sometimes, the only person pulling for a kid is his coach. He can be the one person standing between them and big trouble.

Perry Young played on my varsity squad in the fall of 1968. His two older brothers, Doug and Robert, had been Lion football players while they attended high school. Doug and Robert were both excellent athletes, and so was Perry, but Perry was hanging out with a bad crowd and doing poorly in school. I called him to my office a number of times and stayed after him, but I couldn't get him straightened out. I punished him severely on numerous occasions, warning him about causing trouble and getting involved with people who did drugs.

Finally, I'd had all I could take. I was mad at Perry. The basketball coach was mad at Perry. Perry's teachers told me he was impossible in class. I called the boy to my office and told him I couldn't put up with his attitude any longer. Then I ushered him to the principal's office, changed his schedule and removed him from the athletic program. The next afternoon, Perry's big brother Doug called me.

"Coach Wood, I want to talk to you about Perry."

"Hey, wait a minute! I've done everything I can for that kid!" I said, my voice revealing my strong feelings about the boy. No way Perry's brother was going to talk me into taking him back. Then, I must have talked for fifteen minutes about the things I'd done trying to convince Perry to straighten up.

"That's right, Coach Wood. I think you've been more than

fair. But what you don't know is our mother and father are in the midst of a nasty divorce, and Perry is caught in the middle. He doesn't know where he belongs. Some nights he stays with his friends. Lately, he's been sleeping in vacant houses. He doesn't know from one day to the next where he'll spend the night. If you coaches won't help him, who will?"

Knowing Perry's situation changed everything. It also put the pressure on me. The way Doug put it, I had no choice. What good is a coach if he's not there when one of his kids needs help? The next morning I got Perry out of class to talk with him. I told him I wanted to help, but I insisted he complete a rigorous workout program to prove to me he seriously wanted to change his ways.

"Perry, if you'll follow through with me on this, you can be as good an athlete as ever graduated from Brownwood High School. If you don't, you're gonna wind up in jail. It's just that simple."

Probably no other person in school could have persuaded Perry to accept the harsh program of exercise and study I set up, but he took my advice and agreed to everything I suggested. That next fall Perry played an important role in his football team's drive to win the district championship. In the state championship game, he caught nine passes for three touchdowns and 204 yards. After the '69 season Perry was selected our outstanding offensive player. He was also named all-district, all-state and all-American.

Perry now teaches at Brownwood High where he is one of the best volleyball and girl's fast-pitch softball coaches in the state.

1969

1969 MARKED THE BEGINNING of my tenth year at Brownwood High. For me, those years simply whizzed by, but in Central Texas, change often comes slowly. Many Brownwood citizens still referred to Morris Southall and myself as the *new football coaches.*

With a new president in the White House and peace negotiations to settle the mess in Vietnam underway, the country was starting to recover from the mental anguish of the mid-sixties. In July, Apollo 11 was launched, and before it returned safely to earth, millions of people would watch U.S. astronauts Neil Armstrong and Edwin Aldrin walk on the moon.

The music we listened to also made us feel good. Popular songs like "Raindrops Keep Falling on my Head" by B.J. Thomas,

"My Way" by Frank Sinatra, and "Okie from Muskogee" by Merle Haggard always made me smile. Of course, when Johnny Cash sang "A Boy Named Sue," I simply cracked up.

The move to *lighten-up* spilled over into the clothes we wore. Hot Pants made their first appearance in 1969, and even though they were originally intended to be worn beneath a mini-skirt, many women chose to wear them without the skirt. Those *hot pants* sure turned a lot of men's heads in Brown County.

Adding to the feel-good atmosphere were the amazing New York Mets. In 1968, the Mets finished in the National League cellar. They were the laughing stock of organized baseball. In 1969, Casey Stengel and his odd collection of misfits captured the National League pennant. Then they beat up on the Baltimore Orioles, winning the World Series in five games.

◆　◆　◆

AT BROWNWOOD HIGH, we football coaches were feeling pretty good too. Our gang of returning lettermen included starting quarterback Jimmy Carmichael and two 10-flat sprinters, James Thompson and Jan Brown. Our offensive line, which included Tommy George, Odel Crawford, Ricky Stokes, Ricky Campbell, Ricky Evans, Bob Wolford, and Perry Young weighed in at an average of almost 200 pounds.

Defensively, we looked awesome. Playing linebackers, Stokes and John Isom were the ringleaders, and they had a strong supporting cast. Lawrence Thomas and Garry Moore were rock solid at the end positions. Bill Weller, Bert Molina, Ronald Nichols, Gene Day and Tommy Roderick were expected to log a lot of time rotating in the interior line slots.

We lifted the lid on our '69 crusade by traveling to Abilene to play on the familiar turf of Shotwell Stadium. Eleven thousand football fans watched as Cooper's Cougars played party poopers for the fourth year in a row. Abilene Cooper was ranked as one of the best Class 4A teams in the state, and they made believers of the Lions, battering my banged-up Maroons 42–22.

The following week Brownwood played host to Woodrow Wilson. The Lions hadn't lost on their home field since 1963. Brownwood hadn't lost a home opener since 1957. That made no difference to the number one ranked Wildcats. They handed us our second lopsided defeat, 28–6.

My team played poorly in the Woodrow Wilson game. Every time we got the ball, a fumble, a penalty or some dumb mistake would put us in a hole. Everyone who knows me well knows how I hate to lose. After the game, I was still stewing over my team's sorry performance when a local sportswriter asked what I thought about my team's execution. I told him I was in favor of it.

Not many top ten polls included Brownwood after we concluded our non-conference schedule by dropping a close game to Coach David McWilliams' Abilene High Eagles 21–7. McWilliams was a graduate of Cleburne High School where he was an all-state linebacker. Years later, David became head football coach at Texas University. Under his direction, the Longhorns captured a Southwest Conference championship, then lost to Miami in the 1991 Cotton Bowl game.

With such an unimpressive pre-season record, who would have suspected our whole season would turn around in a rock-'em, sock-'em affair at Stephenville? That's where my nitty-gritty Lions reached down and found that little something extra that makes champions. A come-from-behind fourth quarter touchdown and rugged defensive play put my Maroons on track for the 4–AAA South Zone throne room.

Final score: Lions 13, Jackets 8.

After our close shave at Stephenville, my improving Lions mowed through our district like a brush-hog behind a John Deere tractor, downing longtime rivals Breckenridge 62–7, Weatherford 43–7, and Mineral Wells 39–7.

That set up a noggin-knocking showdown with North Zone champion Wichita Falls Hirschi. Normally Coach Glen Johnson's Huskies gave us all we could handle, but my Lions were in a murderous frame of mind that Friday evening. Using a crunching ground assault, we struck early then turned the game over to a hungry pack of reserves.

Final Score: Brownwood 35, Hirschi 0.

◆ ◆ ◆

AFTER THE HIRSCHI MASSACRE, we discovered defending state champ Lubbock Estacado had beaten Snyder 38–3. Except for one player, who became ineligible because of age, the Matadors were the exact same team that whipped Brownwood badly in the '68 playoffs. A coin flip on Saturday afternoon set up a rematch with my old friend Jimmy Keeling at Shotwell Stadium in Abilene.

Brownwood came out swinging, taking the opening kickoff and smashing eighty yards to paydirt. Carmichael's passes provided the big plays as he hit three third-down tosses without a miss. Perry Young caught one. Tommy George hauled in the other two. With the ball at the Matador ten, we were facing our fourth third-down situation when Young worked clear in the right side of the end zone, and Carmichael air mailed him a perfect strike.

The Mats needed only three plays to tie things up. After two running plays gained six yards, slippery-hipped Estacado quarterback Kenneth Wallace rolled around right end, cut back to the middle and was off to the races—outrunning three Lion defenders sixty-two yards to the goal line. With both teams botching opportunities to score, the first half ended in a 7–7 deadlock.

Early in the third quarter, Estacado put together an eleven-play drive that reached Brownwood's nineteen before it fizzled. A field goal attempt by Lubbock kicker Larry Miller was blocked by Tommy Roderick, and Lion Lawrence Thomas recovered the ball at the twenty-five.

Brownwood handed the ball right back when the Mats' Robert Boykin fell on a Carmichael fumble at the Lion twenty-two. Five plays later, Wallace curled over left tackle and sailed in for the second Estacado TD. The games turning point and the key to our victory occurred on the point after attempt. Miller's kick went wide right, and from that point forward, the defending champs were in deep trouble.

Carmichael cranked up and put on an amazing aerial exhibition. A juggling catch by Ephraim, a breathtaking grab by Jan Brown and a one-handed spear by Young had the crowd on its feet. A penalty flag and two hard stabs at the middle of the Estacado line by James Thompson moved the ball to the two. On his third straight carry, Thompson slashed over left tackle for the touchdown. Rodney Folsom split the uprights, and Brownwood went ahead 14–13.

That's where our hard-hitting defense took over. With Ricky Stokes, John Isom and Tammy Hollingshead leading the charge, our Maroons stopped the Mats' offense cold on every possession. Brownwood scored again in the fourth, this time in workmanlike fashion. Again it was Carmichael who figured in the big plays. Jimmy picked up twenty-nine yards when he changed his mind on a passing play. Then he hit Young at the Estacado eight. From there Thompson banged it in.

After Thompson scored, we called time-out to check the statistics and decide on strategy. We elected to go for two, and Carmichael drilled one through an end zone crowd to Perry Young. With little more than five minutes left, Estacado was just about done, but my Lions weren't satisfied. Sophomore running back Rodney Folsom drove the final nail in the Mats' coffin when he sprinted twenty yards to the Lubbock eight then rammed over left guard for our final tally.

Final score: Brownwood 29, Estacado 13.

◆   ◆   ◆

ON DECEMBER 7, half the population of Brownwood traveled to Big Spring to watch the Lions slug it out with Monahans. Monahans was a two touchdown favorite, but my Maroons were on a roll. Our surging Lion warriors coolly shoved aside a revved-up Lobo outfit like an unwanted stepchild. They didn't use any dipsy-doodle tricks. Jimmy Carmichael, the Rifleman, didn't throw one touchdown pass. With James Thompson, Kenny Ephraim, Rodney Folsom and Gary Barron taking turns carrying the football, Brownwood rushed for two hundred yards. On defense, Jan Brown, Tommy George and Perry Young shut down the air lanes. Gene Day, Ron Nichols, Garry Moore and Bert Molina were the stars on our defensive line.

Final score: Brownwood 28, Monahans 13.

◆   ◆   ◆

ON TUESDAY, the *Dallas Morning News* used a whole page of their sports section to praise Bonham's Purple Warriors. In the story, Bonham's coach declared that no team in America could play them with an eight-man front. We posted several of these articles in our locker room and made sure our players read them. Then, in a mid-week pre-practice meeting, I asked my players if they thought we should change our defense. My team almost rioted.

Bonham had an outstanding passing quarterback in Bob Jenkins, but on that sunny December afternoon in Fort Worth, Jenkins' strong arm wasn't nearly enough. Two of Jenkins' first four passes fell incomplete, and Perry Young intercepted another. Defensively, Gene Day, Ronald Nichols, Tommy Roderick, Garry Moore and Lawrence Thomas kept the heat on Jenkins, and at halftime, the Warrior QB had thrown only three complete passes for fifty-seven yards.

Meanwhile, Brownwood's ace of the airways, Jimmy Carmichael, came out with both barrels blazing. First, Carmichael hit favorite receiver Perry Young for two touchdowns, then Jimmy sneaked in for our third score. Brownwood was ahead 21–0 before a Jenkins to Anderson connection put Warrior points on the scoreboard.

Late in the game we made a first down at Bonham's fourteen. Leading by a comfortable margin of 21–12, we benched our hosses and let the reserves run out the clock.

◆   ◆   ◆

WHILE SIZE IS IMPORTANT in football, at Brownwood we discovered a small kid could get the job done. My coaches and I often judged a boy more by effort than by size. A high school coach who overlooks desire and selects his players strictly by size will frequently find his team on the short end of the score.

In 1969, we lost three games out of our first five. Then we almost lost to Stephenville, scoring in the last few seconds to pull out a 13–8 win over a team we should have beaten handily. While reviewing the Stephenville game film, I discovered our fullback wasn't doing a good job. Saturday afternoon, I called the boy in and told him I was moving him to second-string. That didn't set well with the young man or his dad. As a junior the previous year, the boy had been a starter on defense. The end result of our conversation was the boy quit the team.

Compounding my already uneasy feelings, Coach Southall informed me Monday morning that our backup fullback was injured and probably out for the season.

"Alright, which of our scout team players runs opponents' plays the hardest?" I asked. Many times we evaluated a boy by his enthusiasm for playing, no matter where he's put.

"That would be Kenny Ephraim. He runs the hardest."

"Kenny Ephraim! But Kenny Ephraim's five-foot-four-inches tall and weighs a hundred and forty pounds! We can't play him at fullback!"

"That's not what you asked, Coach Wood," Morris grinned. "You asked who ran opponents' plays the hardest."

I wasn't happy about my choices, but we were in a desperate situation. That afternoon I called Kenny to my office to talk with him.

"Kenny, we're gonna play you at fullback until we can find someone else."

"Don't worry, Coach. I won't let you down," Kenny responded confidently.

"You don't understand, Kenny. You're too little to play fullback. We're only going to play you there until we can find somebody else who can do the job."

Kenny was anxious to play. He was even more emphatic when he repeated himself, "Coach, I told you! I won't let you down!"

We never found anyone else. Kenny made sure of that. The next game we beat Breckenridge 62–7.

Kenny Ephraim tips the scales at 146 while Brownwood's 142-pound tailback James (Squirt) Thompson and Lion punter Jerry Sims double check Coach Wood's measurements. (credit: Brownwood Bulletin)

Then we won eight consecutive games to land in the state finals against the previously undefeated West Columbia Roughnecks.

West Columbia had two humongous defensive ends. Charlie Johnson, who weighed 225 pounds, played on one side. Johnson went on to play thirteen years in the pros. Their other defensive end was another huge boy named Green. Green weighed 170 pounds.

Our offensive schemes called for our fullback to block the defensive end on power sweeps and sprint out passes. A few days before the championship game, I asked Coach Southall whether Ephraim could handle the blocking assignments.

"Kenny is our fullback. Our plays call for the fullback to block their ends. There's nothing in our playbook that says what size our fullback has to be," Morris answered coldly, and that settled the question.

Kenny never actually cut down either Johnson or Green, but all afternoon he jarred them with vicious blocks, keeping them at bay. On one occasion, Charlie Johnson became so frustrated he picked Ephraim up and pitched him high in the air. On that play, Jimmy Carmichael scrambled past Johnson and fired a sixty-yard

James Thompson picks up first down in 1969 championship game.
(credit: AP Wire Photo)

strike to Perry Young who steamed to the Roughneck eight before being tackled. The Lions beat West Columbia 34–16 to capture Brownwood's fourth state title since 1960.

Our other running back was James (Squirt) Thompson who weighed 142 pounds. Ephraim and Thompson spearheaded our '69 ground attack, each man rushing for more than six hundred yards. Little kids can play if you give them a chance.

◆　◆　◆

ANOTHER PLAYER who had an outstanding game that day was senior linebacker Ricky Stokes. Ricky was a quiet, unassuming young man, but hard working, quick-to-learn and totally dedicated to our football program. When he was a sophomore, Ricky told me nothing in his life was more important than being a Brownwood Lion.

Stokes was named all-district his junior year, and in 1969, he was selected first team all-state. As the season progressed, he began receiving a lot of attention from major colleges. Every day Ricky's mailbox was stuffed with college recruiting letters. All the attention from college coaches changed our linebacker's modest personality. Coach Southall and Coach West believed Stokes' swelled head was affecting his play, so we cooked up a plan.

During our Saturday morning bus trip to Waco's Baylor Stadium, Coach Southall ambled up the aisle and plopped down in the seat beside Stokes. Brownwood coaches almost never sat with players, so Morris' familiar gesture took Rick by surprise. A long, sad frown decorated Coach Southall's face as he glanced at Rick then leaned forward and slowly shook his head back and forth.

Ricky Stokes,
Most Valuable Defensive Player—
Brownwood's 1969 championship game.
(credit: Fred Nobs)

"What's wrong, Coach?" Stokes asked.

"I'm worried about you, Ricky. I've been talking to the coaches at Oklahoma. They say your stock has gone way down these last couple of games. They may not be able to offer you a scholarship after all."

"But, Coach Southall, I've been playing pretty good—got six tackles last game."

"I know, Ricky. You're playing great, but I suppose you're gonna have to do better. There'll be a lot of college scouts in the stands today. Maybe, if you have a real good game, you can change their minds about you." Then Coach Southall patted Rick's shoulder and returned to his seat at the front of the bus.

That afternoon in our championship game, Stokes recorded a season high sixteen tackles. On several occasions he met bigger and stronger West Columbia ballcarriers head on at the line of scrimmage and drove them backward.

After the football season, Stokes accepted a scholarship from Oklahoma University. His freshman year, Ricky's Oklahoma coaches told him he was the best-coached football player they had ever seen.

◆　◆　◆

JIMMY CARMICHAEL completed fourteen of twenty passes against West Columbia, including his last ten in a row. During his three years as Brownwood's quarterback, Carmichael passed for

3,585 yards and 48 touchdowns. After the season, Jimmy was named all-state and all-American and was voted the most outstanding high school player in Texas by the Amarillo Chamber of Commerce.

Dave Campbell's *Texas Football* magazine selected Jimmy Carmichael as the most outstanding quarterback of the sixties.

Jimmy Carmichael—
selected Best High School Football
Player in Texas after 1969 season.
(credit: Fred Nobs)

CHAPTER FOURTEEN

The Fabulous Seventies

(1970–1971)

THE BROWNWOOD MAFIA is a unique, and sometimes mysterious, group of business and professional men whose main excuse
for existence is to promote Brownwood and the West-Central Texas
area. Most of the men were at one time members of the Junior
Chamber of Commerce (Jaycees). In the sixties and seventies, they
were the backbone of our community. It was through their efforts
that Brownwood began attracting new industry, growing while
other Central and West Texas cities were losing population.

Belonging to the Mafia was sometimes expensive. Promoting
a city costs money, and Mafia members often traveled extensively.
If an out-of-town function affected Brownwood, generally one or
two Mafia members were there. Mafia constituents were frequently
observed mingling with elected officials in Austin.

While no one Mafia comrade was more important than any
other, Groner Pitts, a Brownwood undertaker, was the unofficial boss.
Pitts is a native of Cleburne, Texas. He hitch-hiked to Brownwood in
the forties to attend Howard Payne College and never left. After he
graduated from Howard Payne, Groner joined the staff at Davis-
Morris Funeral Home and eventually became a partner.

Stuart Coleman, a local car dealer and rancher, generally acted
as Pitts' lieutenant, but many others were involved. C.C. Woodson,
who headed a southwest publishing empire, was the senior member.
Charles Stewart, a Howard Payne professor; State Representative
Lynn Nabers; District Attorney George Day; Brown County
Democratic Chairman and attorney, Henry Evans; Insurance man,
Putter Jarvis; and Builder, Herman Bennett were among the ring-
leaders.

"Brownwood Mafia" Kingpin Groner Pitts and Gordon.
(credit: Wood Family Collection)

Charles Trigg, Jack Pilon, B.C. Drinkard, George Crews, Frank Smith, Craig Woodson, and Roger Sweeney also held membership certificates, but there were many others who freely gave of their time and energy to promote Brownwood. Heck, even Gordon Wood was a Mafia member.

Although this energetic group accomplished wonders in bringing jobs and prosperity to Brownwood, it was their zany antics which brought notoriety. Groner Pitts was usually the catalyst. Once, the group promoted *Fort Worth Star-Telegram* columnist George Dolan for governor with bumper stickers which read: "Support a Sure Loser." Billboard advertisements with comical announcements of a birthday were also a favorite joke. The Mafia was big on supporting local charities, and the members were usually extremely generous. If a member happened to miss an opportunity to contribute, Pitts made sure no one was left out. Groner has been known to pledge as much as one hundred dollars for a fellow Mafia member.

C.C. Woodson once said, "Every town needs a Groner Pitts." Then, in retrospect, he added, "But in all likelihood, no town could survive two of his kind."

1970

AS TWO-A-DAY PRACTICES got underway in August of 1970, Brownwood's most famous resident was in hot water down at the Brown County courthouse. Mrs. Juanita Phillips, better known in Dallas as Colony Club stripper Candy Barr, was charged with possession of marijuana.

Candy visited with *Bulletin* reporter Harriette Graves shortly after initial deliberations were concluded in Judge Joe Dibrell's courtroom. Candy was dressed in a yellow pullover blouse and a skin-tight brown skirt. Her beautiful blonde hair was gathered in a pile at the back of her head. Her eyes misted slightly as she talked.

"I wish they'd live and let me live," Candy lamented. "I don't really know what the purpose of all this was in the first place. I never have and never will enjoy being exploited. But through my trials and errors, I have found the tolerance and patience to face a situation like this. I've come a long way, baby."

The next day Judge Dibrell threw out all the evidence. The following Monday, he dismissed the case for lack of evidence, confirming what every man in Texas already knew. A pretty girl like Juanita didn't have to smoke pot to have a good time.

◆　◆　◆

AFTER LOSING TWENTY SENIORS from our '69 state championship team, 1970 was supposed to be a rebuilding year. Someone forgot to tell our returning players. After dropping our opener to Brownwood's annual tormentor, Abilene Cooper, my young Lions went on a tear.

Our starting lineup had suffered a couple of bad breaks during pre-season. Shae Southall, the third of Morris Southall's amazing sons, fractured a rib in our scrimmage with Gainesville. Rodney Folsom broke his arm in the same game.

Both Shae and Rodney were still hurting when we traveled to Temple to face the 4A Wildcats, but they didn't act hurt. Folsom carried the ball nine times for fifty yards. Southall completed three of six passes for thirty-six yards. Shae's first completion was to end Hardy Barnes for Brownwood's initial TD. As usual, though, superb defensive play was the key to our victory and accolades were numerous, beginning with tackles Gene Day and Garry Moore.

Linebackers John Isom and Brian Pinto were both magnificent, as was safety Tammy Hollingshead.

Final score: Brownwood 14, Temple 6.

We journeyed back to Abilene the following Friday to face the Abilene High Eagles and complete the third leg of a "murderers row" pre-season schedule. Early season media chatter had predicted Brownwood would be lucky to win one of our first three games. We did much better. Playing flawless football in the first half, my Maroons rolled to a 22–0 lead. Then we hung on for dear life to escape with a 22–20 win.

A sideline parley with all-state Brownwood linebacker John Isom. (credit: Brownwood Bulletin)

With team play improving every week, easy victories became the order of the season. Hosting an excellent South Grand Prairie squad in a non-conference battle, Brownwood blitzed the surprised Warriors with three touchdowns in the first seven minutes. Again, our defense was outstanding. Brian Pinto had eleven tackles. Gene Day and Donald Knight each had eight. Ronald Nichols and John Isom logged seven. Garry Moore recorded five.

Final score: Brownwood 28, South Grand Prairie 7.

Brownwood had never played on synthetic turf until we traveled to Wichita Falls to meet Hirschi High. Our maroon gang liked it just fine. They mopped up on the Huskies 37–0.

Steam rolling through their district schedule, the Lions flattened Graham 42–0, Weatherford 28–0, Vernon 53–7 and Stephenville 55–7.

When Brownwood met Burkburnett in our final conference game, the Orange and Black only had one loss in district play and still had a shot at the title. My high-octane Lions closed the curtain on the Bulldogs' season with an eye-popping defensive performance. When the game ended, Brownwood had captured its fourth straight District 4–AAA championship.

◆ ◆ ◆

PETE MURRAY was the head basketball coach at Brownwood High from 1960 through 1965. That meant he automatically also became an assistant football coach. Pete was a smart coach—dedicated, hard-working, and an absolute delight to be around. He provided me and Morris Southall with thousands of laughs and some of our best stories.

After Brownwood won the state championship in 1965, Pete accepted a coaching position at Texas A&I College in Kingsville. He moved to Lubbock to become the head football coach at Estacado High School when Jimmy Keeling vacated that position. Coach Murray inherited some outstanding football talent, and he made the most of it. Pete's Matadors ran the table to win District 3–AAA for a third consecutive year. And for the third year in a row, the Mats would meet Brownwood in the bi-district round of the state playoffs. Estacado was working on a string of four straight shutouts.

When we couldn't agree on a mutual site, we flipped a coin, and Brownwood won, choosing to play at old Lion Stadium. I could tell Pete was disappointed, but he smiled and made the best of it. He said he had one request. He asked that we play with a Wilson ball when his team was on offense.

Early the next week Coach Murray called me to make sure I remembered our agreement about the Wilson football. This was Pete's first trip to the state playoffs as a head coach, and even over the telephone, I could tell he was nervous. That was all the fodder Coach Southall and I needed to pull off one of our all time best pranks. Morris and I searched through our entire supply of footballs to find just the right ball.

A few minutes before game time, I ambled across the playing field to the Estacado bench. Behind my back I was holding a Wilson football. When I got close, I called to Coach Murray, "Hey, Pete! This is the only Wilson ball we could come up with!" Then I pitched him the football. It was a beat-up old thing with the cover pealing off and the seams busting out. The look on Pete's face was worth a million dollars. Over on our side of the field Morris Southall was about to bust a gut laughing.

Murray was stunned. He stood there with a forlorn expression on his face. I let him stew for a minute or so before I told him I had already given a new Wilson ball to the referees.

Pete eventually saw the humor. After the game he paid me a flattering complement.

"Can you imagine my surprise?" Pete told a reporter. "Here I am in the playoffs for the first time, nervous as all get-out, and he's playing jokes and laughing up a storm. He's been here so many times before. He knows he's gonna swamp you before the afternoon's over."

And we did. My Lions clobbered Murray's Matadors 35–12.

◆　◆　◆

MONAHANS WAS ANOTHER DRAGON that usually had to be slain on our trip to the state finals. In 1970, the Loboes were monstrous. Monahans halfback Billy Phipps was billed as the state's finest, and he didn't disappoint. Phipps rushed for 182 yards, including one 70-yard touchdown jaunt which allowed the Loboes to take a 10–0 halftime lead to the dressing room.

Brownwood kicked off to open the second half. We gained possession of the football after Lobo punter Dub Huckabee kicked us into a deep hole at our seventeen.

Three plays later it was a brand-new ballgame. Facing third and one at the twenty-six, Southall sent Gary Barron charging around right end on a power sweep. Barron broke through a pack of Lobo tacklers, turned on the after-burners and zoomed seventy-four yards for Brownwood's icebreaker. Folsom booted the PAT, making the score 10–7.

Trading interceptions, the two teams didn't do much except bludgeon one another until the Loboes punched down to Brownwood's twenty-two late in the third quarter. Great defensive work by Bill Duncan, Moore, Knight and Day forced the Loboes to try a 39-yard field goal. Huckabee's kick into the wind was wide, but Brownwood was charged with roughing the kicker, giving the Loboes new life at the eleven. Again, with Nichols and Knight furnishing the fuel, the maroon defense rose to the occasion, limiting the Loboes to three yards gained on three tries and forcing another Monahans' field goal attempt. Huckabee hooked that kick to the left.

From there, it was all Lions. Our Maroons cut loose with a long drive, culminated by a clutch 22-yard Rodney Folsom three-pointer. On Folsom's field goal try, the football hit the left goal post and bounced through to tie the score at 10–10.

The Loboes mounted a furious comeback drive in the final minutes, moving the ball to mid-field before Kirk Newton made the defensive play of the day by stopping Phipps for no gain on third and four. On fourth down, Monahans went for six, but Lobo quarterback Valenzuela overthrew his long bomb, and his receiver Jerry Foster couldn't catch up. With 2:21 left, the Lions took possession and ran out the clock. Brownwood advanced on penetrations, 5–3.

◆　◆　◆

PLANO'S ROSTER was overloaded with talent, and they had a fine coach in John Clark. Coach Clark was inducted into the Texas High School Coaches Hall of Honor in 1979. When the Wildcats needed a miracle, quarterback Glenn Hansen, split end William "Nippy" Jones, tight end Roger McEntyre and halfback Pat Thomas usually provided the necessary magic.

Shae Southall, sore ribs and all, guided the Lions to a 21–0 first quarter lead. Using fleet-footed fullback Gary Barron to run for one touchdown, Shae also rifled touchdown passes to wingback Steve Cutbirth and tailback Rodney Folsom.

At that point Hansen shucked his ground game and came out firing. By halftime he had pitched the Wildcats back into the thick of battle. Brownwood was clinging to a shaky 21–14 lead.

Both teams scored again in the third, and going into the final period, the score was 28–21. Every person in the stadium was expecting an exciting finish, and that's exactly what they got. Brownwood marched forty-four yards to Plano's twenty-one where our fake field goal play went awry, and Plano took possession.

Hansen promptly hit Nippy Jones for a first down at mid-field, but Jones fumbled, and John Isom fell on the football. From there, our fired-up Maroons scored in three plays. On third down, Folsom grabbed a swing pass from Southall and scooted down the sidelines for forty-five yards and a TD.

In the final minutes of play, Wildcat hopes for a comeback

were dashed by three Lion interceptions, two by Jerry Cross and one by Tammy Hollingshead.

Final score: Brownwood 35, Plano 21.

◆ ◆ ◆

DURING THE PLAYOFFS, high school coaches can get a little crazy—driving around the state to scout other teams, running up enormous telephone bills talking to other coaches, staying up late studying game films, and always eating on the run. Katharine has often said she could put sawdust on the table during the playoff season, and I'd never know the difference.

A story Katharine tells to prove her point occurred on the Sunday morning after we beat Plano. Leaving our wives to fend for themselves, my assistant coaches and I boarded a plane and flew to Austin to scout the Ennis-Cuero semifinal game. That made for a very long day. We didn't arrive back in Brownwood until around 1:00 A.M.

About eight o'clock Sunday morning, I rolled out of bed and staggered bleary-eyed into Katharine's kitchen, hoping a cup of coffee would perk me up. Katharine asked if I wanted oatmeal or eggs for breakfast.

Without thinking, I groggily replied, "I thought I had already eaten breakfast?"

◆ ◆ ◆

IN A PRE-GAME INTERVIEW, Cureo coach Buster Gilbreth didn't seem worried about being an eighteen-point underdog.

"We didn't come this far to not give our best effort," Gilbreth stated confidently. "We know about Brownwood's tradition, but we've got some guys who can go too."

Folks along the Gulf Coast were calling the Gobblers the Mets of Texas football. Cuero won its District 14–AAA zone by the flip of a coin then nudged favored Kerrville 7–6 to gain a berth in the playoffs. En route to the finals, Cuero had registered three straight upset wins.

Naturally, Brownwood boosters were expecting the clock to strike midnight when Cuero's Cinderella Gobblers met a rowdy bunch of maroon-clad Lions at mammoth Memorial Stadium in Austin. With mouths agape, our surprised fans watched the Gobblers battle the heavily favored Lions to a first half scoreless standoff.

Cuero received the second half kickoff, and Brownwood got its first real break when the Gobblers were forced to punt from their twenty-eight. Steve Cutbirth made the fair catch near midfield and was tackled by an overzealous green and white defender. The resulting penalty moved the ball to Cuero's thirty-two, where my maroon squad put together their longest drive of the day. Rodney Folsom picked up a first down with a ten-yard dash to the twenty. Then on fourth and a long yard at the eleven, we elected to forego the field goal. Gary Barron picked up the first down with only inches to spare.

Like his two brothers, Shae Southall was an expert at altering his cadence count. Southall's wizardry paid huge dividends when the Gobblers jumped offside before the next snap, giving Brownwood a first and goal at the four. Three plays later Shae wedged in behind guard Joe Behrens and center Steve Goodwin for the game's first touchdown.

Coaches Wood, West, and Southall celebrate Brownwood's 1970
state championship along with avid Lion fans Glen West (9) and Jim Wood (11).
(credit: Brownwood Bulletin)

Our defense put the game on ice early in the fourth quarter after Jerry Cross spiraled a punt fifty-five yards into the wind to put Cuero at their own thirteen. When the Gobblers tried to pass their way out of the hole, Cross cut in front of the intended receiver, snared the football, and with a full head of steam, rambled all the way to the eight before being dragged down.

After another long count drew the Gobblers offside again, Folsom spun off left tackle for the score. When Folsom banged in his umpteenth successive extra point, Brownwood held an insurmountable lead. Cuero never made another first down.

Final score: Brownwood 14, Cuero 0.

After the game our locker room was the usual scene of pandemonium, and as usual, Coaches Southall, West, Martin, Blackburn and myself received our victory baptism, clothes and all. I was soaking wet when one of the writers covering the game asked me if I had learned the secret to winning championship games.

"No, but I have learned to carry a change of clothes in my car," I told him.

1971

AFTER THE SEASON many awards came our way. Every key player on our championship squad received some sort of all-something. As head coach, I also received a lot of applause. However, the most gratifying was an event cooked up by the Brownwood Mafia. They called it "Gordon Wood Day."

Some say the day to honor me was Lt. Governor Ben Barnes' idea, but I've always suspected Groner Pitts was the real brains behind the deal. I'm particularly glad he and his co-conspirators Herman Bennett, Stuart Coleman and Putter Jarvis had the good sense to include Morris Southall and my other assistant coaches Kenneth West, Don Martin and Royce Blackburn on Brownwood's honor roll. My assistants deserve just as much credit as me for Brownwood High's gridiron success.

May 14, 1971—that's a date forever etched in my mind, because it was the most fun day of my life. The *Brownwood Bulletin* devoted a full eight page section to proclaim my accomplishments. The section was filled with articles about me and my assistant coaches, plus hundreds of advertisements from "Friends of the Coach."

On the back page was an official looking document which

declared Gordon Wood to be an official member of the Ancient and Protective Order of the Brownwood Mafiosi. At the lower left-hand corner was a caption which read: "Hey Jughead! This is your day!"

That evening, a banquet was held at the Brownwood Coliseum. Dinner tickets sold for five dollars apiece. With so many friends and ex-players coming from all across the state to join the festivities, the event was a complete sellout. Those in charge had to open up the coliseum balcony to accommodate the large crowd.

Former president Lyndon Johnson was the principal speaker. During his final years in office, the ex-president had suffered through some rough times which drained his energy and enthusiasm. After he left the White House, Johnson rarely made a public appearance. President Johnson and Ben Barnes flew to Brownwood in Darrell Royal's private plane, and according to Coach Royal, Lyndon griped all the way, saying he wished he hadn't let Ben Barnes badger him into coming. Johnson's sour mood changed the instant he walked into the Coliseum. The President's appearance triggered a rousing round of applause as every person in the place stood and cheered.

Rev. Jerry Boles from Stamford handled the invocation, and Don Newbury, who later became President of Howard Payne,

Gordon Wood Day in Brownwood. Katharine, Gordon, and President Lyndon Johnson wave to crowd while University of Texas coach Darrell Royal applauds. (credit: Brownwood Bulletin)

acted as Master of Ceremonies. Don introduced President Johnson, and when Lyndon came to the podium, he was beaming from ear to ear.

"Thanks for letting me come back and re-charge my batteries by looking at a crowd of liberty-loving, God-fearing Americans," Johnson declared.

On their way home, Johnson told Darrell Royal he had forgotten what it was like to be around real Americans. Darrell said Lyndon was a totally different man on the trip back to Austin.

The ex-president was followed by a number of impressive dignitaries, as Lt. Governor Ben Barnes, State Senator J.P. Word, State Rep. Lynn Nabers, Brownwood Mayor W.T. Harlow and University of Texas football coach Darrell Royal joined in to sing my praises. It was truly overwhelming. When the time came for me to say a few words, I thanked my players, my coaching staff, BHS students, teachers, choir, band, drill team, administration and everybody else I could think of.

I told the audience, "This is unreal. It's ridiculous to have something like this for a country boy like me." Then I turned to look at my assistant coaches and told them, "There's not a coach on my staff I would trade for any other coach in Texas."

It was an emotional moment. I almost cried. Morris Southall was also close to tears when Ben Barnes presented him with a gold football trophy a few minutes later. 1971 was a great year for Morris. That was the year he served as President of the Texas High School Coaches Association, being the only assistant coach ever elected to that post.

More than sixteen hundred people came to share the evening with Katharine and me. Jimmy Piper, an all-state fullback on Brownwood's 1965 championship team, did the honors of introducing my former Brownwood players, but there were many others from Rule, Roscoe, Seminole, Winters, Stamford, and Victoria.

There were a number of notable quotes that evening. As usual, my wife had one of the best. One of the items on the program was to show a film featuring each of my five state championship teams at Brownwood.

"There's no use in that," Katharine advised. "They can just show the film on the 1960 team or the 1970 team. No one can tell the difference. Only the players change."

My other favorite quote was offered by Brownwood's resident comedian Groner Pitts. Groner always seems to have exactly the right words for every occasion. When asked his opinion of the festivities, Pitts replied, "Shoot! Every day since he came here has been Gordon Wood Day! This one just happens to be official!"

◆　◆　◆

ALTHOUGH OUR HEARTS supported the U.S. soldiers fighting in Vietnam, by 1971, almost every American realized the war was a lost cause. We used sports and entertainment to divert our attention from the ugly mess our government had created in Southeast Asia.

In Brownwood, most everyone cheered when Joe Frazier won a unanimous decision over Muhammad Ali to retain his heavyweight boxing title. Most folks in Central Texas considered Ali to be an unpatriotic draft dodger. Naturally, we were sad when the Baltimore Colts beat the Dallas Cowboys in Super Bowl V. My biggest thrill, though, was watching the Masters Golf Tournament on television. That was the year my ex-Stamford quarterback, Charles Coody, won the Masters.

◆　◆　◆

WE KICKED OFF the '71 football season by returning to Abilene's Shotwell Stadium to take our annual licking from Cooper High. The Cougars had won in each of our last five meetings. They extended their winning string to six, pasting Brownwood 20–7. That loss ended a thirteen-game Lion win-streak.

With several players hurt, our team took advantage of a scheduled open date to recover and prepare for an encounter with Abilene High. With the Eagles coming to our place, we expected to make a better showing. We didn't. Five fumbles and two interceptions did us in, and the Lions lost their second in a row, 20–13.

◆　◆　◆

THERE ARE ONLY two choices when you're down. You can stay down, or you can climb off the floor and keep fighting. My Lions chose to pick themselves off the floor and bounce back. South Grand Prairie was their first victim. With quarterback Shae Southall displaying perhaps the sharpest performance of his career, our offense carved out 367 yards. Lion defenders acted like they were protecting the Alamo, as they outclassed and outfought the Warriors 33–0.

Pre-season polls predicted Wichita Falls Hirschi to finish near the bottom of District 4–AAA, and they were struggling. The Huskies hadn't won a game when they came to Brownwood to open district play. They sure didn't play like losers.

It was our kicking game that finally gave us a leg up late in the third quarter. Shae Southall sailed a boomer over the Huskie safeties, and the ball died on Hirschi's seven. There, our defense went to work. Linebackers Brian Pinto and Gary Smith jarred Huskie ballcarriers with tooth rattling tackles, forcing the Scarlet

Rodney Folsom blasts for long gainer against Wichita Falls Hirschi.
(*credit:* Brownwood Bulletin)

and Blue to punt from inside their end zone.

After Steve Cutbirth signaled for a fair catch at the forty-one, Brownwood scored in four plays. A Southall rocket to maroon-clad end Tim Reid capped the short drive, and Folsom's reliable toe provided the margin of victory. When the last second ticked off the clock, Brownwood was still ahead 7–6.

◆ ◆ ◆

AFTER THE 1970 SEASON, the Texas Interscholastic League realigned a number of AAA and AA districts. As if our district wasn't already tough enough, the UIL elevated Iowa Park from AA to

Brian Pinto, captain and all-state linebacker—Brownwood's 1971 team. (credit: Fred Nobs)

AAA and inserted the Hawks into District 4–AAA. The Hawks were AA state champs in 1969 and shared the state title with Refugio in '70 via a 7–7 tie. Even though they were the new kids on the block, Iowa Park was unbeaten in thirty-four straight games the evening the high flying Green and White came to play at old Lion Stadium.

In pre-game interviews, both Iowa Park coach Tommy Watkins and I predicted ball control would determine the game's outcome, and we were right on the money. On Brownwood's second possession, our Maroons moved the football seventy yards before stalling out, and Rodney Folsom nailed a field goal for three points. The Hawks scored with ten seconds remaining in the first half, using a four-yard pass from Greg Frazier to wingback Jerry Burkhart. Brownwood went to the dressing room on the short end of a 7–3 game.

In the second half my Lions hogged the football, running thirty-seven plays to Iowa Park's thirteen. Offensive end Tim Reid pulled us closer by racking up two points on a freak play. With help from a penalty, Brownwood had hammered down to Iowa Park's thirty-seven. On first and ten, Southall tried a pass, but Shae's aim was off line. James Frazier was standing near the goal line when he leaped to intercept. The green and white defender hit the ground running, but he didn't get far. Reid tackled him in the end zone. The referees ruled a safety.

Ray Thompson returned Iowa Park's free kick sixty-three yards for an apparent touchdown, but the officials ruled Ray stepped out of bounds at the forty-seven. This set the stage for Brownwood's victory charge. Folsom carried twice for a first down at the Hawk forty. Three plays later, facing fourth and five, we went for broke. Southall's pass to Cutbirth fell incomplete, but Hawk defender Kenny Franks was flagged for tripping, and Brownwood got new life.

It was Southall who came up with the big play after Iowa Park stiffened. Rolling right on fourth down, Shae scrambled to the nine for another first down. When three hard blasts against a determined green and white defense netted only five yards, we called on Folsom again. Despite a severe kicking angle, Rodney drilled a pressure-packed 21-yarder, and Brownwood went ahead 8–7.

A few minutes later, an interception by maroon defender Bruce Smith put the brakes on a valiant Iowa Park comeback attempt. After a hard-charging Lion slapped Hawk quarterback Gregg Frazier's arm on a would-be long bomb, Smith grabbed the wounded dove toss and lumbered down to the Hawk thirty-three. With less than three minutes remaining, we used up as much time as possible before Richard Riggins took a pitchout from Southall and raced in for our only TD of the game.

Final score: Brownwood 15, Iowa Park 7.

◆　◆　◆

THE IOWA PARK WIN was a big boost for team confidence. Our kids realized they were better than they had been playing. In the next few weeks they got better and better. Blowing through our district like a West Texas tornado, my ever improving Lions blasted Graham, Weatherford, Vernon, Stephenville, and Burkburnett.

After we nailed down our fifth straight district title, Pete Murray and his Estacado crew were back again to meet us in bi-district. The Matadors played tough, but again, Rodney Folsom's amazing toe saved the day.

Final score: Brownwood 7, Estacado 6.

While Pete Murray was coaching at Brownwood, he and the three Southall boys became very close. After Coach Murray left, he maintained that relationship. To Terry, Si and Shae, Pete was like a big brother. Two years before our 1971 bi-district clash with Estacado, Shae Southall borrowed one of Pete's shotguns. For one reason or another, Shae had never returned the gun.

Even though Brownwood didn't score a lot of points, Shae had an outstanding day against Murray's Matadors. I don't think Shae made a mistake all afternoon. When the ballgame was over and Brownwood had won, Pete ran onto the playing field. He grabbed Shae by the arm and whirled him around so the two were nose to nose.

"You bring my shotgun home!" Pete bellowed, like he was real mad at Shae for playing so well. Of course, Murray was only joking. That was Pete's way of letting Shae know he was proud of the way he had performed. Even when his team lost, Pete Murray never lost his sense of humor.

◆　◆　◆

ANDREWS WAS OUR QUARTERFINAL OPPONENT. The Mustangs were coached by old friend Jimmy Keeling. In 1968, when Keeling was coaching at Lubbock Estacado, his Matadors won the state championship after thoroughly stomping Brownwood in bi-district play. My Lions met Keeling's Mustangs at San Angelo on a cold, damp December afternoon.

Despite the dreary weather, our maroon machine came out blazing. Lion ballcarriers Ray Thompson, Rodney Folsom, Gary George and Richard Riggins chewed up an amazing 326 yards, and Brownwood steamrolled to a 38-0 lopsided victory.

◆　◆　◆

ON SATURDAY AFTERNOON, following our Friday win over Andrews, my coaches and I flew to Tyler in Herman Bennett's airplane to watch the Plano-Jacksonville quarterfinal game. After Plano slipped past Jacksonville 18–17, I approached the Jacksonville coach to ask if my assistants and I might fly to Jacksonville on Sunday afternoon and review his game film.

"Hell no!" the coach replied angrily. "You take that film with you, Coach Wood. You get it developed and keep it for as long as you like. After the way Plano cheated us on the exchange of films, I hope they never win another game."

At the time I didn't understand the man's animosity, because Plano coach John Clark was one of the most highly respected coaches in Texas. I also knew Coach Clark to be a fine Christian man. I couldn't imagine him doing anything to get the Jacksonville coach so riled up. Anyway, I accepted the offer gratefully, and we took the film home with us.

Sunday afternoon, we met with Plano school officials and agreed to play our semifinal skirmish at Amon Carter Field in Fort Worth. After the meeting concluded, John Clark flagged me down. He wanted to talk.

"Coach Wood, I'm not saying you've done something wrong, but you have a great advantage over us," Clark told me.

"I don't understand what you're talking about, John," I replied.

"The Jacksonville film. I know you have the film of our game against Jacksonville. That gives you a great advantage over us," Clark advised.

"You're right, John. I have the game film, but I'm not interested in taking unfair advantage. How about we swap three films? If you want our Andrews' film, you can have it. After I show it to my quarterback club Monday night, I'll put it and two other films on the nine o'clock bus. You'll have all three films by Tuesday morning."

Coach Clark accepted my offer, and we shook hands. Monday night, I put our game films on the bus like I promised.

I began to understand Jacksonville's animosity when we received the agreed upon game films from Plano. All three films were in black and white, nowhere near the quality of the color films I sent them. To make matters worse, one film was strictly offense. Another was strictly defense. The way the films were edited, it was impossible to follow the game continuity.

On Thursday, I received some scout notes which were mailed to me anonymously. The notes showed Plano's all-state halfback, Pat Thomas, playing quarterback on several Wildcat scoring drives. Thinking we had overlooked this in our review of Plano's game films, I blew my stack. Coach West calmed me down, saying he would go back through the films, which he did, but not one of the films showed Thomas playing a single down at quarterback.

◆ ◆ ◆

OUR SEMIFINAL MATCH with Plano was essentially a replay of the previous year's semifinal bout. Many of the key players on both teams had participated in the 1970 playoff game.

Brownwood's problems cropped up on the Lions' first possession, when we failed to convert on a fourth and two play at the Wildcat's forty-two. That early misfire seemed to suck the wind from our sails. Our kids went flat, and they floundered around for the rest of the half. Plano wasn't sharp either, but on the last play of the second quarter, a mix-up on our pass coverage allowed the Wildcats to score and grab a 7–0 halftime lead.

Midway through the third period, our maroon offense finally decided to get in the game. Mixing the brutal running of Ray Thompson and Gary George with some timely passes to Steve Cutbirth and Rodney Folsom, Southall moved the Lions down to Plano's one-yard line. Two ferocious cracks at a stubborn Wildcat defense was all it took. Ray Thompson did the honors. With Plano leading in every statistic, we went for two. Shae rolled out, tossed a perfect strike to Thompson, and Brownwood went ahead 8–7.

After Brownwood took the lead, our Lion defenders scratched, clawed and fought their hearts out. It looked like the one point lead might be all we would need when our defense stopped a Plano drive at the eighteen and Pat Thomas missed a thirty-yard field goal try. Brownwood took possession of the football with only three minutes left, but once again our offense was unable to get the job done. After running only eighty-four seconds off the clock, we handed the ball back to the Wildcats, kicking the ball out of bounds at Plano's forty-three.

When Plano took possession, Pat Thomas came in as the Wildcat quarterback, and we Brownwood coaches went berserk. Our defense had not prepared to defend against Plano's Veer offense with a fabulous athlete like Thomas directing their attack. Thinking the Wildcats intended to run the football, we scrambled around trying to get our kids into a defense to stop the quarterback option. Thomas surprised us by coming out passing. He completed two of three aerials and moved the football about halfway to our goal line before Plano's regular quarterback, Jeff Brumbraugh, came back into the game. Brumbraugh enjoyed a reputation as a great runner, but in the final seconds he proved he could also pass. Jeff lobbed a short pass to Van Davis at the seventeen, then sent Rucker Lewis charging through the middle for nine yards to the Lion eight with twenty-five seconds remaining. After Plano called time-out, Pat Thomas redeemed his earlier miss and drilled a decisive three-pointer through the uprights.

Final score: Brownwood 8, Plano 10.

Following the game, our locker room was unusually subdued. Brownwood coaches and players alike were both shocked and downhearted by our last second loss. While my players were showering, I walked over to the Plano dressing quarters and congratulated their coaches for a great game, telling them we would be at the state finals to support them.

It wasn't until I boarded the team bus for Brownwood that I began to think about what the Jacksonville coach told me about Plano's cheating on the exchange of films. I realized the mysterious scout notes described the exact scenario Plano used in their last drive, with Pat Thomas throwing the football.

That next week, I telephoned the coaches of the two schools who competed against Plano in the game films John Clark had sent me. They each mailed me copies of their color films, and like I suspected, the downs with Pat Thomas playing quarterback had been cut out of the Plano films. In one of their films, Thomas directed his Wildcat team on two long touchdown drives which won the game. The other coach's film also showed Thomas playing quarterback and taking his team for a touchdown. All this important footage had been carefully edited out of the films Plano furnished me.

After Plano nipped Gregory-Portland 21–20 to win the AAA state title, I called Coach Clark to congratulate him. We visited for a while, then I confronted him, "John, your state championship is real tainted, isn't it?"

"I don't know what you're talking about," Clark responded, playing dumb.

"Well, I know and you know, John. If you hadn't sent me those black and white films which had all the downs with Pat Thomas playing quarterback cut out, your team would never have beaten Brownwood. Coach Clark, I have never cut a play out of a film, and I would never allow any coach on my staff to do it. What you did was steal a state championship from my team."

After I accused him of cheating, Coach Clark got kind of quiet. Then he said, "I wasn't the one who cut 'em out."

"Hey, John, you're the man responsible, and I know full well you knew those plays were cut out before you sent the films to me."

"Well, they weren't cut out just for your game," Clark objected lamely.

"You know something, Coach? I don't care why they were cut out. What you did was dishonest. It's called cheating. For the rest of your life, every time I see you, I will know, and you will know, that you cheated my kids out of a state championship."

Clark tried to apologize before I hung up, but I was so mad and upset I didn't listen. Later, I reconciled the matter in my mind, realizing that John Clark was a good man and a fine coach. He just made a terrible mistake.

CHAPTER FIFTEEN

How to Build a Football Stadium Without Money

IN DECEMBER OF 1968, Brownwood voters vetoed a proposal which would have allowed the school district to issue bonds to build a new football stadium. Despite the negative vote, many Brownwood citizens were still determined to build a new stadium. Initially, this group was spearheaded by Calvin Fryar, William Streckert, Bill Jamar, David Krischke, Groner Pitts, Kenneth Day, Herman Bennett and Dr. Guy Newman. After several informal meetings they came up with a unique idea.

The men went to the school board and asked the trustees to figure how much it would cost for Brownwood High School to stay in old Lion Stadium for the next ten years. Several weeks later the school board responded, telling the football boosters it would cost approximately ten thousand dollars a year, which amounted to one hundred thousand dollars over the ten-year period. That was even more than the citizens' group had expected, so they asked the board if they would be willing to pay ten thousand a year to use a new stadium, if the boosters could get one built. The trustees said they would.

Next, the group approached Jack Pilon who was president of Brownwood's First National Bank. Buoyed by their success with the school board, the group asked Pilon to loan them a hundred thousand dollars with no interest for ten years, telling him they would pay the money back at the rate of ten thousand dollars a year. Unbelievably, Pilon agreed to their terms. Now the boosters had a guaranteed one hundred thousand of working money.

With their enthusiasm overflowing, the men went to Howard

Payne and asked the University to pledge fifty thousand dollars to use the new stadium. When Howard Payne agreed, the group went back to Jack Pilon and obtained the same deal for another fifty thousand. Heck, they were halfway home, and they were just getting started.

A request to Brown County yielded another victory. The county commissioners agreed to furnish fifty thousand dollars of dirtwork free of charge. The City of Brownwood also agreed to provide fifty thousand dollars of construction services without charge.

The city owned about ninety acres of land formerly known as Camp Bowie, where eighty thousand soldiers received their basic training during World War II. The property was located on Milam Drive directly behind the city swimming pool and senior citizens center. This was an ideal location for the new stadium. The city fathers agreed to lease the property to the stadium group for one dollar a year for ninety-nine years.

◆　◆　◆

THE NEXT ORDER OF BUSINESS was to go to the football fans. The stadium committee decided the best way to do this was to sell seat options for one hundred dollars per seat. An article announcing their intentions appeared in the *Brownwood Bulletin* a few days later. J.R. Beadel was the first person to respond. Beadel was a long time Brownwood merchant and civic minded individual who supported Brownwood projects with both his pocketbook and personal involvement. He called Calvin Fryar and asked Calvin to come to his place of business.

When Fryar arrived, he was immediately ushered in to see Mr. Beadel. After they shook hands, Beadel told Calvin, "I don't know if we really need a new football stadium, but if we're gonna build one, let's get after it. You can put me down for a hundred seat options."

Beadel's purchase got the seat option concept off to a running start, and before long, more than sixty-five thousand dollars had been raised that way.

Roy Simmons had volunteered to head the fund raising effort, and he came up with another fantastic idea. His proposal was to sell advertising which would be displayed on the back of the sideline benches. Permanent bench advertising went for ten thousand dollars. Nine spaces were available, and they were gobbled up in a matter of days. Advertising purchasers included: The Herman Bennett Company, P.F. & E. Oil Company, Southern Savings and Loan, Citizens National Bank, Texas Bank, J.R. Beadel, C.C. Woodson, First National Bank, and the Brownwood Bulletin.

With the bench advertising money, another ninety thousand dollars was added to the pot.

◆　◆　◆

WITH ALMOST FOUR HUNDRED THOUSAND DOLLARS pledged to pay for construction, the group hired San Antonio architect Harvey Smith to prepare plans for the stadium. Brownwood I.S.D. had several building projects in progress at the time. Smith had previously been selected to provide architectural plans for those projects. A bid date was set for June 21, 1971. Several large contractors took out plans, so stadium boosters were extremely hopeful of getting a bid within their limited budget. The bids were opened by Roy Simmons at the Brownwood Chamber of Commerce offices.

In the sixties and seventies, Herman Bennett was one of the busiest and most successful contractors in all of Texas. He and his partner Ben Barnes were developing property and building Holiday Inns all across the country. Herman developed the Brownwood subdivision where Morris Southall and I live today. Bennett's construction company built both our houses and the house Dr. Guy Newman lived in while he was president of Howard Payne University. I've never heard anyone say they got a bad shake dealing with Herman Bennett.

I was in the Bennett Company's construction office the afternoon before the stadium bids were opened. Herman was running around trying to get the bid bond and all the documents ready to submit. When it came time to fill in the numbers, he went to talk to his chief estimator one last time.

"Have you figured our bid so we'll exactly break even?" Bennett asked.

"No, I haven't. You're not gonna break even at this price. You're gonna lose money," the estimator replied grimly.

"Well, we're still too high. Let's knock off fifty thousand dollars," Herman said.

The estimator shook his head and declared, "I'm not gonna do it, Herman. If you want to go broke, you'll have to do it without my help."

Herman grabbed the bid sheet, walked over to his secretary and instructed her to take another fifty thousand dollars off his bid.

As it turned out, Bennett Company's bid was almost one hundred and fifty thousand less than the next lowest bid. After the bids were opened, I overheard a representative of Abilene's Rose Construction Company complaining to Herman Bennett, "You know, Herman, I don't think we bid on the same set of plans." Herman just laughed.

Despite his low ball price, Herman's bid was still about fifty thousand more than the stadium committee thought they could spend. So Herman took the plans back to his office, looked them over again, and cut another fifty grand off his bid.

A lot of Brownwood people talk about how much time and money they gave to get the new football stadium built, but no other person even came close to Herman Bennett's contribution. Several years ago a banquet was held to honor my good friend. A number of speakers paraded to the podium to voice their praises. One man told this story, which personifies Herman's honesty.

"He's the kind of man you can give a dollar to hold, and when you come back ten years later, Herman Bennett will hand you back the same dollar bill."

◆　◆　◆

BENNETT CONSTRUCTION COMPANY had men working on the project even before the ink was dry on the contracts, and during the initial phase, the work progressed nicely. Then things began to bog down. Plans for the stadium called for a huge earthen berm to be constructed before the concrete seats were poured. The county commissioners had agreed to haul in the dirt required, but their trucks were small, and they could only work on weekends. Work slowed to a snail's pace, and I was getting real impatient.

After school one afternoon I dropped in to talk with H.C. Lewis who owned a local trucking company. I asked if there was any way his company could haul the dirt we needed. Mr. Lewis said sure. He'd be glad to help. It was my understanding that his men would do the work after hours and on weekends and at no charge.

In a few days, Lewis Trucking had ten or twelve vehicles

Gordon, Herman Bennett, and James Cameron examine plans for new stadium.
(credit: Wood Family Collection)

hauling dirt and buzzing around the job, and in short order, the berm work was finished. I had pulled off quite a coup. To tell the truth, I was rather proud of myself—maybe even a bit smug.

My self-satisfied demeanor changed to embarrassment when a bill for almost five thousand dollars arrived in Calvin Fryar's mailbox. I got the work done. I decided to let Calvin handle the monetary negotiations.

"I don't understand about your bill. We never agreed to pay this amount," Calvin told the trucking company's business manager over the telephone.

"Well, Gordon came out here and told us he was in a bind. We sent our trucks to help out."

"I hate to tell you this, but that was free gratis. We don't have money to pay you."

"That's not the way we understood the deal. We need to get paid for our work," the business manager objected.

"Well, that's the way it's gonna be. We appreciate the donation," Fryar declared firmly and hung up.

Calvin eventually worked out a deal which reimbursed the

trucking company for their drivers' wages, but looking back, I realize I should have been more specific in my agreement with H.C. Lewis, because this misunderstanding could have evolved into an unpleasant incident. When all was said and done, though, there were no hard feelings, and after the stadium was completed, my Lions continued their winning ways. A winning football team makes a lot of things easier to swallow.

◆ ◆ ◆

CONSTRUCTION WAS WELL UNDERWAY when Groner Pitts approached me about adding a first class all-weather track to the facility. According to Groner, Howard Payne University had an offer to buy the land which housed their existing track and a small baseball field. Pitts proposed the college take the money from the property sale and use it to build a new track. When he suggested we name the track after legendary Howard Payne track coach Cap Shelton, I jumped at the idea.

Cap Shelton was one of the finest men to ever coach in Texas. When he and his wife died, they left their entire estate to Howard Payne University.

The land sale netted close to seventy thousand dollars which is about what a first-rate track should cost. By that time, though, our stadium group had become experts at bargain basement shopping. When the track was finished, several thousand dollars of college money remained unspent.

◆ ◆ ◆

THE FOOTBALL STADIUM shown on the architectural plans wasn't nearly the stadium we actually built. For instance, the original plans called for wooden seats, which I despise. After the construction work began, I saw Herman Bennett almost every day, and I kept pestering him about the wooden seats.

"Good Lord, Herman! In ten years we'll have splinters in our butts, and we'll be replacing the wood or covering the seats with plastic like we did at Lion Stadium," I grumbled, offering another daily grievance.

Finally, I talked my contractor friend into flying his private plane to Bryan, Texas, to talk to an old boy who manufactured aluminum seats. When we got down there, Herman began to poor mouth the man, telling him we were from Brownwood and how we were short on funds and how everyone in town was donating their time and hard earned money to get a new stadium built. Most everyone in Bryan is an Aggie fan, so Herman went on and on about how many Brownwood kids were enrolled at Texas A&M.

Eventually, we got around to the stadium seating, and the man quoted us a price. I thought his number sounded reasonable, but Herman hit the ceiling. He ranted and raved about how poor we were and demanded the Bryan fellow lower his price, which he did. That still didn't satisfy Herman. He told the man he'd have to do better than that.

Finally, the man lowered his price again. This time he told us, "That's my final figure. I've taken out the last dollar, and I'm not going any lower than that."

Herman carefully examined the man's estimate. I could tell he wasn't through.

"You've got three hundred dollars in here for shipping the seats to Brownwood," Herman argued.

"Yes, that's exactly what it will cost us to get them there."

"Well, you can take that out. I'll send my trucks to Bryan and pick up the seats here at your plant." When the man deducted the three hundred dollars, Herman signed the papers, and we headed back for Brownwood.

Several weeks later Herman called me at the high school. He acted like he couldn't recall the deal he had made for transporting the aluminum seats.

"Coach, I can't remember exactly how we agreed to get those seats to Brownwood."

"Well, I do," I said, suspecting my friend had a good reason for his convenient loss of memory.

"How's that?" Herman asked slyly.

"You were supposed to send your trucks down there and pick that stuff up."

"Well, all my trucks are busy. Is there any way you could find someone else to haul the seats to Brownwood?"

Of course that was the whole purpose of the telephone call. It took some doing, but when I contacted Bob Ross at Ross Porta-plant, he agreed to have one of his truckers swing by Bryan on their way back from Houston, pick up the seats, and haul them to

Brownwood. Naturally, the trucking was provided free of charge. No money changed hands.

The aluminum seats had only been on-site two days when I received a call from the manufacturer in Bryan. He said they were in a jam and offered to buy the seats back from us at a twenty-five percent profit.

I told him, "No Way!" I had the aluminum seats I wanted. I wasn't about to take a chance on losing them.

◆　◆　◆

THE HOME OFFICE of Brownwood's television cable company is in the Dallas-Fort Worth area. When Calvin Fryar, Morris Southall, Bill Jamar and Ken Schulze drove to the metroplex to talk with the cable people about stadium lighting, our construction budget realized another major savings.

The football group left Brownwood hoping to get help with the stadium light fixtures, but to their pleasant surprise, the cable company offered to build the poles, put the baskets on top, mount the lights and do all the electrical work. The total savings amounted to approximately seventy thousand dollars. Even though we already had pole foundations in place and other light poles at the job site, our representatives immediately agreed to the deal. We couldn't believe our good fortune. We shipped the light poles we had on hand back to Houston, again at no cost, and received full credit from the company we bought them from. Our stadium lighting, which was installed by the cable company, ranks with the best in the state.

◆　◆　◆

BY JULY OF 1972, the football stadium was almost complete, but during the course of construction, we had added one thing and another—each of which had increased the cost. Early on, some unexpected foundation problems had added another forty thousand. Anyway, we still owed Bennett Construction Company approximately ninety thousand dollars, and our coffers were empty.

Dr. Guy Newman, president emeritus of Howard Payne University, was a devout football fan and a staunch stadium supporter from the very first git-go. Newman's fund raising expertise was one reason Howard Payne fared so well during his tenure. Dr. Newman called me one morning to advise that we would have to hold one more fund raiser. I told him I had asked people for money so many times I was beginning to feel embarrassed. Ignoring my protests, Guy informed me I was expected to attend a meeting in the conference room at the First National Bank on Tuesday, the following week. I later discovered Dr. Newman sent out a letter of invitation to everyone else. His letter stated that the meeting was vitally important, and if the person was in any way interested in the welfare of Brownwood, he should attend. Naturally, everyone who received Newman's letter was curious. Almost everybody invited showed up for the meeting.

When the men arrived at the bank and saw Calvin Fryar, Jack Pilon and myself, they understood right off what was up—this would be another attack on their pocketbook. After everyone was seated, Dr. Newman walked to the back of the room and locked the door.

"Fellows," Newman announced, "we're about finished with the stadium construction, but we need to raise another hundred thousand dollars to pay Herman Bennett what we owe him." Newman let his words sink in for a few seconds, then he turned to Leesy Watson. "Leesy, I wonder if you would lead us in a prayer before we get started?"

"No, I won't," Watson responded. "But I'll pledge another five hundred dollars, so we can get out of here."

It took less than fifteen minutes to accomplish what we had come for. Jack Pilon kept tabs on the men's donations that morning. Before Dr. Newman unlocked the door, we had commitments for ninety-three thousand dollars. That was our final fund raiser, and everyone involved breathed a sigh of relief.

◆　◆　◆

ANOTHER INTERESTING STORY relates to the fence which surrounds the stadium complex. Funds to install the fence were donated by the Beal Foundation which is headquartered in Midland. Mr. Beal also served on the board of directors of Brownwood's First National Bank. The fence wasn't included in the stadium construction contract, so we put this item out for separate bids. A contractor from Houston was anxious to bid on the fence, so he called Calvin Fryar, and they met at the stadium.

"Somebody told me this was a four hundred thousand dollar stadium," the man remarked as they walked the grounds.

"That's about what it cost in real cash," Fryar told him. "We've had a lot of materials and work donated for the construction."

"My goodness gracious," the contractor exclaimed, "I just put a fence around a stadium that cost a half a million, and it's nowhere near the stadium this one is. If this stadium was in the metroplex, it would cost at least a million dollars."

◆　◆　◆

OUR PRESS BOX WAS BUILT with a donation from the Wendell Mayes Family. The Mayes Family owned KBWD, a local radio station which handles BHS game broadcasts. Mr. Mayes, a wonderful individual and one of Brownwood's leading citizens, had passed away a few years earlier. Bill Jamar, Wendell's son-in-law, was deeply involved in building the football stadium.

One day the family called Calvin Fryar, telling him they had talked it over and wanted to make a substantial contribution. They asked Fryar to find out how much it would cost to build the press box, saying that's how much they wanted to donate. Their only requirement was that KBWD, the radio station's call letters, be spelled out on the front of the press box structure.

Our press box cost about twenty-five thousand dollars. Bennett Construction helped design the layout. Herman Bennett made sure it was spacious and up-to-date. Very few high school stadiums in the country have a comparable press facility.

◆　◆　◆

OUR TICKET BOOTHS were built by three Brownwood brick-layers, Raymond Richardson and two brothers, Bert and J.C. Weathers. The men agreed to donate their time if I could find someone to furnish the brick and mortar. That was no problem. Thirty minutes on the telephone and I had commitments from Weakley-Watson Hardware for the mortar and Texas Brick Company for the brick.

We built two ticket booths on each side of the stadium. The booths are about eight feet apart with pay windows on each side for maximum efficiency. With four entrances, we can sell tickets on both sides of each building when we have big crowds, or we can cut down to one or two windows, depending on how many people are buying tickets.

◆　◆　◆

THE FINAL ORDER OF OFFICIAL BUSINESS was to apply for a certificate of incorporation. This would allow the stadium group to operate as a non-profit corporation. The charter application was filed on March 16, 1971. Calvin Fryar, Bill Jamar, Groner Pitts, William Streckert and Kenneth Day signed that application. The official name on the document was Cen-Tex Stadium Corporation. On May 19, 1972, shortly before the stadium was completed, an income tax exemption was granted by the Internal Revenue Service.

◆　◆　◆

BEFORE THE 1972 SEASON OPENER, the stadium corporation asked for bids for operating the concessions. The best bid received was for five thousand dollars which I felt was ridiculously low. I told Calvin Fryar that wasn't nearly what it was worth.

"How about you let us Brownwood coaches match that bid," I asked and Calvin agreed. I went to the bank, and using nothing but my name for collateral, borrowed the five thousand bucks. Halfway through the first football season, we had cleared enough money to pay off my bank loan.

Wayne Rathke, one of my assistant coaches, essentially ran the concessions for two years before we struck a deal with the band boosters to operate the concessions on the visitors' side. We later turned all the concessions over to the band. That deal required band boosters to return thirty percent of their profits to Brownwood High's athletic department.

◆　◆　◆

LANDSCAPING THE STADIUM GROUNDS was left up to us coaches. A high school counselor named Mike Stegemoller used his summers to earn a few extra dollars, doing landscape work, putting in trees and grass in peoples' yards. I told Mike the prettiest stadium I had ever seen was at Graham, Texas, where they had planted cedar trees around their stadium. The trees were about twelve feet tall, and they were absolutely beautiful.

Mike drove over to Graham, found out what kind of trees were growing there, and placed an order for us. As usual, our spec-

After Cen-Tex Stadium was built, Gordon's brother, Garland Wood, became the football facility's self-appointed groundskeeper. Garland's services were provided free of charge.
(credit: Brownwood Bulletin)

ifications required getting a rock-bottom price. The trees were purchased with profits from our stadium concessions.

My coaches and I set out those trees all around our complex. My brother Garland came to live in Brownwood about that time, and he developed an interest in the stadium. For three years Garland took care of the stadium landscaping—mowing the grass, fertilizing, and watering the recently planted trees. He never received a penny for his work. Many times Garland used his own money to purchase tools and equipment. The trees have filled out now, and they make Brownwood's stadium one of the prettiest in Texas.

◆ ◆ ◆

IN THE MID-SEVENTIES a field house was added. That building was constructed adjacent to the stadium and included dressing rooms and shower facilities for both the home and visiting teams. The project was initiated by a generous contribution from long time Brownwood resident Truitt Ellis, and for a time, we had a pact with the Dick Alexander Estate for the balance.

Dick Alexander was a wealthy Brown County rancher. When Dick died, he willed all his property to the indigent children of Brown County. I drove to Lubbock a number of times to talk with George Gilkerson, the attorney who managed Alexander's estate, and Gilkerson agreed to give our stadium group enough money to build the field house. We even shook hands on the arrangement. Late in the game, however, a group representing themselves as the Brown County Boys Club got wind of the deal and interceded, insisting they should receive the donation from Alexander's estate. I met with the group, telling them I had a firm commitment for seventy-five thousand dollars, and if they persisted with their demands, we might both lose the money. I even offered to split the seventy-five thousand with them, but they wouldn't listen, and my prediction came true. Neither of us ended up getting a dime of estate funds.

When the Alexander deal fell apart, Harry Miller, our city manager, came through for us. Harry arranged to get federal grant money through a job training program. After city forces installed the plumbing and foundation, Harry used the federal funds to pay Raymond Richardson to supervise the building construction. Mr. Richardson was the brick layer who built our ticket booths. The grant money was sufficient to also pay the salaries of several young men who worked alongside Richardson as brick layer trainees. As you might have suspected, we arranged to have the brick and all the building materials donated.

◆　◆　◆

ANOTHER FELLOW who contributed to the stadium's post-construction success is Tom Lafferty, a Brownwood electrical contractor. Tom is an avid Lion fan and an expert electrician. Until the day I retired, either Lafferty or his employee, Junior Grider, was right there to help whenever we had an electrical problem. Their sole compensation was two free tickets to all our home games.

◆　◆　◆

BROWNWOOD'S FOOTBALL STADIUM is a wonderful example of what a small community can accomplish when it sets its mind. I've mentioned the names of many who unselfishly contributed their time and money, but there were so many more who participated. I'll not try to list them all for fear of overlooking someone. Suffice it to say that seeing the way Brownwood people built that great facility gives me tremendous pride in my community. When the complex was renamed Gordon Wood Stadium in 1980, I was absolutely overwhelmed. All my other awards and achievements paled in comparison.

CHAPTER SIXTEEN

Happiness is a Brand-New Playpen

(1972–1975)

IN SPITE OF A FEW minor inconveniences—like no dressing rooms for players and a playing surface full of wrinkles, we opened the 1972 football season in brand-spanking-new Cen-Tex Stadium. Wanting to show off our new facility, we invited Abilene Cooper coach Ray Overton and his Cougars down to our place. It was the first time in years Brownwood's lid-lifter wasn't played in Abilene. The game was a sellout, with a record crowd of eight thousand enthusiastic fans filling every seat.

With only six lettermen returning from our '71 squad, we coaches understood our maroon crew would require a complete overhaul. Still, everyone was excited about our prospects. Shae Southall, the last of the great Southall quarterbacks, had graduated and enrolled at nearby Angelo State, but Dean Low, a strong-armed junior, had Morris grinning. Having sophomore tailback Pete Hicks in his backfield to play alongside lettermen Brian Cutbirth, Gary George and Richard Riggins also added to Coach Southall's positive perspective.

With mainstay linemen like Truman Westfall, David James and Dicky Hall; linebackers, Gary Smith and Don Wright; ends, Oscar Lewis, Jay Allison and Isaac Wells; and a secondary which included Donnie Twiford and Robert Crawford, our defense looked extremely strong. Coach West was sky high on his offensive line which included tackles, Jim Combes and Alan Day; guards, Mike Morgan and David Brock; and center, Don Wright.

◆　◆　◆

THE COUGARS SPOILED our party the night Brownwood High christened the fabulous new stadium, but even though the Lions lost, every fan got their money's worth.

Cooper was leading by a slim 14–7 margin early in the fourth quarter when Cougar quarterback Mike Witte bolted sixty yards for a TD. Witte's touchdown jaunt put the Lions in a deep hole. Brownwood's prospects looked even bleaker when our offense took the kickoff and went three and out. Then a fumble recovery by Don Wright brought new hope. Our Maroons took possession and pushed deep into Cooper territory. On third and long, Dean Low hit towering Truman Westfall with a seventeen-yard scoring strike, and Brownwood climbed back into contention at 21–13.

On the ensuing kickoff, the Cougars took the football and rammed to the forty-six. That's where Big Blue put the game on ice. Cooper fullback Phil Huffman broke loose and thundered fifty-four yards for the clincher.

Final score: Brownwood 13, Cooper 27.

The next week we traveled to Sweetwater. Our Lions were nursing a 3–0 fourth quarter lead, seemingly in control of the game, when the underdog Mustangs landed an unexpected haymaker. Sweetwater had the ball on their own five, second down and twelve to go. There, the Mustang's southpaw quarterback Faron McCain rolled to his left, crossed the line of scrimmage and pitched to his halfback Mike Maloney who was trailing behind. Maloney was almost tackled by Lion safetyman Richard Riggins at the twenty, but Mike sidestepped Riggins and outlegged Brownwood's secondary to the end zone.

Final score: Brownwood 3, Sweetwater 7.

There's an interesting footnote to this story. Mike Maloney is the son of Walter Maloney, the phenomenal running back who played for me when I coached at Roscoe back in the forties. If you play the game long enough, ex-players will come back to haunt you.

❖ ❖ ❖

DATING BACK to the previous year's loss to Plano, the Lions were now saddled with a three-game losing streak. Because of our disappointing 0–2 start, a number of sportswriters began to write Brownwood off as a District 4-AAA contender. Wichita Falls Hirschi was undefeated and ranked tenth in the state. Iowa Park and Burkburnett were also overloaded with talent.

My Maroons quickly corrected the obituaries. First, they christened our new stadium with its first Lion victory, beating Cleburne 14–7. Then we journeyed to Wichita Falls where we put twenty-two points on the scoreboard in the game's final eight minutes to wipe out what the Huskies thought was a comfortable 21–7 lead.

After our last-minute come-from-behind win, sportswriter Bill Stovall had this to say about Brownwood's young football squad, "Gordon Wood's kids grew up a little last Friday night, but Lion fans aged even more."

◆ ◆ ◆

WITH A RECORD of 3–1, Iowa Park looked very strong, and they carried a grudge for Brownwood. My Lions had terminated the Hawks' unbeaten streak at thirty-four the previous year. In '72, we played at their place. Coach Grady Graves and his vengeful Hawks were anxiously anticipating our visit.

After neither team was able to raise much smoke in a scoreless first period, Brownwood put the first points on the scoreboard. Using a pass interception, which Keith Madole returned to the Hawks' eighteen, Dean Low guided the Lions to a second quarter touchdown.

Iowa Park roared back. A Lion fumble set up a 27-yard Iowa Park touchdown drive. Then a quick, over-the-middle pass from Hawk quarterback Greg Frazier to end Jerry Burkhart caught us by surprise, and Burkhart rambled sixty-six yards for the Green and White's second score. Brownwood tied the score when Low hit Keith Madole on a 57-yard catch and run, and the half ended in a 14–14 draw.

A nightmarish third period ended the deadlock. My Maroons hadn't scored in the third quarter all year, and they extended that string. Iowa Park racked up one hundred and twenty-five yards on twenty-two plays while Brownwood gained only twelve yards on seven tries. The Hawks scored ten points in the third. Their first three were via a 27-yard chip shot by green and white kicker Wayne Hallford. A power sweep, which Iowa Park speedster Randy Brown ran for fifty-nine yards, accounted for the other seven.

Final score: Brownwood 20, Iowa Park 31.

Our loss to Iowa Park ended Brownwood's 31-game District 4–AAA win-streak. Nonetheless, we garnered high hopes of winning the district and making another playoff run. With both Burkburnett and Wichita Falls Hirschi still in their path, it seemed unlikely the Hawks would escape District 4–AAA undefeated. A three-way tie seemed very possible, and when things boiled down to the toss of a coin, Brownwood was usually lucky.

Believing they still controlled their own destiny, my Lions romped through district colleagues like kids on an unmade bed. We beat up on Weatherford 34–0, downed Vernon 21–0 and mauled Stephenville 35–6.

In the meantime, Iowa Park lost to Burkburnett. Burk also topped pre-season favorite Wichita Falls. With an Iowa Park-Wichita Falls meeting still on tap, our final district game held the key to our season. Two things could happen if we beat Burkburnett. The district could end in a three-way tie, or Brownwood could tie for the district title with Burkburnett. We preferred the latter, because that would give Brownwood an unobstructed road straight to the playoffs.

◆ ◆ ◆

UNFORTUNATELY, BURKBURNETT had a different idea. The greedy Red River heavyweights decided to hog the district title all for themselves, and they did it in a most convincing manner. A rash of Lion injuries and a slick Bulldog quarterback named Sam Hancock slammed the door shut on our post-season travel plans. Coach Bill Froman's orange and black Bulldogs laid a solid whipping on my Lions—the most one-sided conference defeat since I the took the reins in 1960.

With the multi-talented Hancock working his third-down magic a staggering fifteen times, Burkburnett rolled up an astounding 428 rushing yards. The rugged Bulldog field general led all runners with 165 yards on twenty-two carries, pulling off big play after big play to pick up vital first downs.

Final score: Brownwood 0, Burkburnett 32.

The Bulldogs' victory that evening wrote an end to a number of streaks, for Burkburnett and for my Lions. It was Burkburnett's first victory ever over Brownwood. The conference title was Burk's first in District 4–AAA and their first in any league since 1956.

For Brownwood, the disappointing loss brought an end to an unprecedented run of five straight district championships. It was the Lions' first district defeat on home soil since 1963 and the first shutout registered against Brownwood since the opening game of 1968 when we lost to Abilene Cooper 13–0.

1973

MY WIFE has often accused me of being a newspaper hound. Katharine claims I've never passed a newspaper stand that didn't deserve a quarter. She says the reason we never argue is because I've had my face buried in a newspaper for half our married life.

Although I wouldn't label my reading addiction quite so harshly, I can't deny my obsession for the news, especially for sports news. Second to diagraming football plays on paper napkins at the Palace Drug Store, I suppose reading newspapers was my worst habit in 1973. There was certainly no shortage of news.

In January, former Nixon campaign members, James McCord and G. Gordon Liddy, were convicted of breaking into and illegally wiretapping Democratic party headquarters at the Watergate complex in Washington. This was only the tip of the iceberg. By late April, Watergate repercussions led to the resignations of H.R. Haldeman, White House chief of staff; John Ehrlichman, domestic policy assistant; John Dean, presidential counsel; and Richard Kleindienst, attorney general. Televised congressional hearings of the Watergate scandal dominated the headlines until vice-president Spiro Agnew was accused of receiving kickbacks while serving as governor of Maryland.

To me, the choice between Richard Nixon and liberal Democrat George McGovern had been a no-brainer. Like most everyone else in Texas, I voted for Nixon in the 1972 presidential election. But now I wasn't sure I had done the right thing. It seemed the entire Nixon administration was awash with corruption. President Nixon was in deep trouble as our two-a-day drills got underway in mid-August.

Despite our frustrating 6–4 finish the previous year, for a football coach and his staff, hope springs eternal. Our '73 squad was full of promise. Dean Low, our starting quarterback, was back, along with outstanding ballcarriers Gary George, Pete Hicks, Richard Riggins and Scottye Ratliff. Anchoring our defense were aggressive, cat-quick guys like Oscar Lewis, Jay Allison, Jerry Lloyd, Tony Jones, Jeff Combes and Don Wright.

A pre-season scrimmage against fifth ranked Wharton raised our hopes even higher. Playing at Austin's Memorial Stadium, our defense held the Gulf Coast Tigers to seventy-five yards total offense while our offense carved out one hundred and fifty-five yards.

◆　◆　◆

ABILENE COOPER was working on a string of six straight victories over Brownwood when the two teams met to open the football season. My '73 Lions wrote a happy ending to that story. Striking with lightning-like fury, we grabbed a 14–0 first quarter lead then tacked on another touchdown in the second stanza. Richard Riggins got the Lions rolling with a 34-yard bolt down the sidelines and closed out the scoring by returning an intercepted pass sixty yards with 2:09 left in the fourth. Sandwiched in between Riggins' blasts were a one-yard TD sneak by Dean Low and a 23-yard scoring toss to wingback James Williams.

Defensive heroes were a dime a dozen. Our linebacking crew, which included Gary George and Don Wright, was nothing less than sensational. Super-quick defensive linemen Joe Clifton, Tony Jones, Jerry Lloyd, Jay Allison, Oscar Lewis and Mike Dillard also played a big role in manhandling the heralded Cooper attack and registering a rare Cougar shutout.

Final score: Brownwood 28, Cooper 0.

The Lions returned home to meet Sweetwater the following Friday. A horrible 7–3 loss to the Mustangs had set the stage for our disappointing '72 season. My maroon gang erased all those bad memories by pounding Sweetwater 40–0 before a crowd of six thousand stunned fans.

Playing at Cleburne in our third non-conference contest, my aroused Lions duplicated the Sweetwater score, swamping the Yellowjackets 40–0 in their own backyard.

Brownwood's defense was unscored on. Our offense had racked up one hundred and eight points. My Lions were ranked second in football polls all across the state when Wichita Falls Hirschi journeyed to Brownwood to open 4–AAA district play. The Huskies hadn't beaten Brownwood since 1964. Eight years of frustration came to a head that night at Cen-Tex Stadium.

◆　◆　◆

EVEN THOUGH OUR NEW STADIUM opened in 1972, the grounds were still a little rough around the edges when the '73 season began. During the summer months my coaches and I eliminated most of the playing surface wrinkles by filling the dimples with sand, but despite constant watering and heavy fertilizing, the grass hadn't taken full root. In a number of spots there was hardly any grass.

On the Saturday afternoon prior to our Hirschi encounter, Howard Payne played a game on the Cen-Tex field. As soon as their game was finished, my assistants and I went to work. We set out sprinklers and flooded the field with water—all night Saturday, all day Sunday and Monday. Thinking we should give the field plenty of time to dry for our Friday night game, we stopped watering Tuesday afternoon.

Wednesday night, it rained four inches. The rain continued off and on through Thursday. By game time Friday night, rainwater was three inches deep on some parts of the playing surface. A light rain fell throughout the Hirschi game.

Wichita had a fine ballclub, but not nearly as good as Brownwood. Both teams were undefeated. It was a foregone conclusion the winner would represent the district in the playoffs. Since the game was so important, the UIL bussed in a special crew to referee the game. The hand-picked officials were supposed to be rule smart and totally unbiased.

Before the game, the referees warned coaches from both teams about players' mouthpieces. UIL president Bailey Marshall had charged the officiating crew to pay special attention to mouthpieces. Later, President Marshall told me he hadn't intended the officials call a penalty on every infraction. Nevertheless, before the game began, the head official told us firmly, "If we catch one of your players with his mouthpiece not in his mouth, you'll see a penalty flag!"

The mouthpieces Brownwood used that year were attached to the helmet chin straps, very visible when they weren't in a player's mouth. Too visible, we discovered after the game got underway. Hirschi players had mouthpieces which fit entirely inside their mouth. This made it impossible to tell whether they were wearing a mouthpiece or not.

By the end of the first quarter our Maroons had been penalized three times for mouthpiece infractions, all on one player—Jess Galbreath, who had asthma and kept spitting his mouthpiece out. Then in the second quarter, Lion running back Gary George broke loose. As George powered down to the Huskie twenty-four, his mouthpiece popped out. The officials called the play back and penalized us back to the forty-four. The penalty killed our momentum. Three plays later, the Lions were forced to punt.

Brownwood obviously had the superior team, but the wet field and four overzealous officials combined to shut down our offense. Mouthpiece penalties stopped us on five different occasions. When the first half ended, the score was tied at 7–7. We Brownwood coaches were so frustrated we couldn't see straight.

During the halftime intermission, I cautioned our players about mouthpieces. That helped cut down on second half penalties, but our early momentum had disappeared. The score was still stuck at 7–7 when the fourth quarter began.

Richard Riggins was the fastest player on our team. Riggins was a 9.6 sprinter, and man could he fly. Midway through the fourth period, Riggins took a pitchout from Dean Low and skirted around right end. As Richard turned the corner and headed upfield, a Hirschi linebacker jarred him with a vicious tackle. The collision caused the ball to squirt loose, but it bounced right back into Riggins' hands. Richard grabbed the ball and fell to the ground. Not another soul touched the football, but one of the officials came running up and signaled Hirschi had recovered the fumble.

When Riggins stood up, he had the football in his hands. Exasperated by the sorry officiating, like we all were, he pitched the ball in the air, maybe six feet high. The officials stuck Brownwood with a fifteen-yard penalty for unsportsmanlike conduct. The penalty moved the ball back to our forty-five.

"That's the damndest call I've ever seen!" I yelled, angrily chastising an official as he ran by our bench. My heated observation cost my team another fifteen yards. Now, Wichita Falls had the football on our thirty-yard line.

Hirschi ran three plays and lost fifteen yards. Facing fourth and twenty-five, they had to kick. On the punt, Brownwood's receiver Pete Hicks touched the football at the two and bobbled it into the end zone. Pete ran back, grabbed the ball, and tried to run it out, but the Huskies tackled him in the end zone. The officials called a safety and awarded Hirschi two points. Their call was all wrong. The ball's momentum had obviously carried it into the end zone, not our punt receiver. The situation was a perfect example of a touchback, which is clearly defined in the rule book.

After the safety call, I was totally frustrated. In all my

coaching career, I don't think I've ever seen worse officiating. I signaled for a time-out, called my entire team to the sideline, and told my players to stay in a huddle at the edge of the field. My intent was to force the officials to get together and talk about their call. Surely the men knew the rules well enough to make a proper decision if I forced their hand.

Royce Blackburn, who was on the sideline with me, convinced me we could score and still win the game. He said the only thing I would accomplish by taking our team off the field was to get us another penalty. At the time his advice made sense, so despite my harsh feelings, I relented and allowed my team to play out the game. Without a doubt, that was the worst coaching mistake I ever made.

When the game ended, Hirschi was ahead on the scoreboard 9–7, but to this day, I won't say Brownwood lost that football game.

◆　◆　◆

ON THE THURSDAY following our bitter loss to Wichita Falls, I received the following letter:

Dear Coach Wood:

In reconstructing in my own mind the series of events on the safety I ruled in the Brownwood-Hirschi game, your receiver should have had either possession or imparted new impetus by kicking or batting the ball prior to its going into the end zone for a safety ruling. He neither had possession nor batted or kicked the ball into the end zone, therefore the initial impetus was still from the punt and the correct ruling should have been a touchback.

I know that my error is small consolation in your 9–7 loss. Please accept my deepest apology, and extend it to the fine young men of your team.

Respectfully,
Donald L. Stovall
Dallas Chapter, SFOA

◆　◆　◆

SHRUGGING OFF THE AFTERMATH of poor officiating, my Lions righted themselves and went on about their business. The team's goal was to win a district championship, and to a man, our kids played like champions. Playing in a steady downpour and on a slippery field, Brownwood squeezed out a late TD to beat blood rival Iowa Park 6–0. A thirty-yard scamper by speedster Richard Riggins capped our scoring drive.

Consecutive victories over Graham, Weatherford, Vernon, and Stephenville set up another season's end showdown with Burkburnett. Burk's 7–6 win over Hirschi had put the district title up for grabs. On the last night of the season, Brownwood, Iowa Park and Wichita Falls each had one district loss. An Iowa Park victory over Hirschi and a Lion victory over Burkburnett would have Brownwood sharing the crown with the Hawks. However, by virtue of Brownwood's muddy 6–0 triumph over Iowa Park, the Lions would advance to the state playoffs.

◆　◆　◆

BROWNWOOD THUNDERED to a 14–0 lead in the first quarter, taking the opening kickoff and tearing through the heart of Burk's defense. Our scoring drive spanned eleven plays and sixty-nine yards, with Riggins reeling off the last twenty-nine. After the kickoff, Burkburnett pieced together a modest drive, but then our defense got downright mean. The Bulldogs ran out of downs and punted.

Any hopes for an orange and white comeback were dashed on Brownwood's next possession. Using a halfback pass from Pete Hicks to wingback James Williams and a booming run by Gary George, our revved-up bunch of Maroons moved the ball to Burk's eight. Two plays later Dean Low speared Mike Dillard for the score, and it was all over but the shouting.

Problem was, there was very little to shout about. A few minutes after the game, we learned Hirschi had slipped by Iowa Park 21–20. Our agony was compounded when we heard the Hawks had gambled and lost on a two-point conversion with three minutes left in the game. A Hirschi-Iowa Park tie would have given Brownwood a clear-cut title. Instead, we shared the district crown with Wichita Falls.

While our guys checked in their equipment and began working out for basketball and track, Hirschi represented District 4–AAA in the state playoffs. The Huskies didn't get far. Unbeaten Lamesa drubbed Wichita Falls 31–14 in bi-district play.

Brownwood's 1973 football team, which ended the season with a tainted record of 9–1, may have been the best I ever coached, but we'll never know for sure. Those talented young men were denied their place in the sun by a bungling bunch of game officials. Even though Brownwood didn't participate in the state playoffs, two Lion players, Gary George and Don Wright, were named first team all-state. Jay Allison was selected to the all-state second team.

1974

ATTITUDES WERE MELLOWING in 1974. Whereas political protest dominated national headlines in the sixties, those movements lost steam in the early seventies. Texans began to focus on lifestyle. Long standing dress codes relaxed, and people began to dress more casually. For men, the starched white shirt fell out of fashion. Rose, purple and green became acceptable shirt colors. When Morris Southall, Kenneth West and I attended coaching school that summer, many of our fellow coaches wore synthetic shirts with bright patterns beneath a double-knit suit.

American designer Anne Klein expressed the change in fashion attitudes best when she said, "The first rule of fashion is not being dressed to the teeth."

Mustaches and long hair also became popular with men, and while I maintained my strict rule about no facial hair for football players, I did relax my position on long hair. Yielding to the times, I even let my hair grow out a little. I also grew some very dapper sideburns which extended down below my ears.

◆　◆　◆

DURING THE SPRING and summer of 1974, President Nixon, Congress, and Special Prosecutor Leon Jaworski constantly wrestled over Watergate questions. Most of the debate was about taped conversations which took place in the President's oval office prior to and after the Watergate burglary. At first, Nixon would only agree to release a summary of the tapes, claiming executive privilege. That didn't satisfy Nixon's critics. Eventually, the whole mess wound up in the Supreme Court, and in late July, the judges ruled the White House was wrong in withholding the tapes.

A few days later, President Nixon turned the tapes over to Special Prosecutor Jaworski, and Nixon was finished as president. The tapes revealed the president knew about the Watergate break-in and had ordered a cover up on June 23, 1972. On August 8,

Richard Nixon announced his resignation. The next day Gerald Ford became president. Nixon had been involved in politics most of his adult life. After he became the only president in history to resign from office, he suffered severe mental anguish. Distraught and embarrassed, he totally withdrew from public view.

◆　◆　◆

IN BROWNWOOD, Lion fans were also suffering from mental anguish. Two consecutive years with no post-season games had maroon boosters hurting. They needed a football fix real bad. After the Lions dropped their opening game to Abilene Cooper 14–0, the pain became even more acute. Brownwood's coffee shop quarterbacks were wondering if their favorite team hadn't been jinxed by the opening of the new football stadium.

Brownwood's '74 backfield included Sammy Harrell at quarterback, Scottye Ratliff at fullback, Pete Hicks and Frank Bunnell at tailback, and Ricky Holmes at wingback. Harrell was a nifty passer. This allowed us to utilize the exceptional receiving skills of ends Brad Bowen, Johnny Skeen and Kyle Peters.

Our front line included big hosses like tackles, Jess Galbreath and Larry Carlisle; guards, Harold Barnes and Terry George; and center, Jeff Lemmons. On defense, guards, Jerry Lloyd and Tony Jones; ends, Colt Carlisle and Guion Hobbs; linebacker, Rodney Roby; and safety, Rick Baron were generally near the bottom of the pile.

After losing to Cooper, our Maroons quelled any notions they may have lost their Midas touch. They reeled off nine straight victories to reach the state playoffs for the first time since 1971. In district play our kids scored one hundred and ninety-eight points while allowing only thirty-three.

◆　◆　◆

SNYDER WAS OUR BI-DISTRICT OPPONENT. The black and gold Tigers also brought along a 9–1 record, which included a close 19–12 loss to Midland Lee. Lee had barely nosed out Lion tormentor Abilene Cooper in the 5–AAAA race.

We played Snyder on familiar stomping grounds—Abilene's Shotwell Stadium. The winner was heavily favored to advance all the way to the state finals. After one quarter the score was 7–0. After two quarters, 28–0. After three, 35–0. Then I sent in some frisky reserves who applied the coup de grace by tacking on another touchdown. Our grave digging defense made a total mess of Snyder's vaunted offense, forcing six turnovers. Brownwood's opportunist offense turned five of Snyder's miscues into touchdowns. Our sixth TD came after an explosive 48-yard punt return by Ricky Holmes.

Final score: Brownwood 42, Snyder 0.

Long time adversary Monahans was our quarterfinal foe. My Lions hardly broke a sweat in stretching their win-streak to eleven, crushing the Loboes 35–0.

Our quarterfinal victory set up a shootout against Gainesville. The Leopards were in the playoffs for the first time since 1961. With a record of 9–2–1, they seemed out of place in the heady atmosphere of the state semifinal round. Even with a record of 9–1, my '73 squad couldn't escape the confines of District 4–AAA. Before the kickoff at Baylor Stadium in Waco, Brownwood's top-ranked Maroons were three touchdown favorites.

◆ ◆ ◆

MORE THAN EIGHT THOUSAND boisterous fans watched two determined football teams butt heads and fritter away scoring opportunities for two full quarters. Neither team had scored when the fireworks began. Here's how the nail-biting second half went.

Ray Overstreet, the Leopards gazelle-fast running back, took the second half kickoff and ran it back eighty-nine yards for a would-be TD. When an illegal blocking penalty rubbed out Overstreet's fine return, the Red and White cranked up their offense and scored anyhow, registering three important first downs along the way. Sophomore end Kevin Harris got credit for the touchdown when he pounced on quarterback Jim Price's end zone fumble. Doug Carr's kick split the uprights to give Gainesville a 7–0 lead.

Stunned by the first score they had allowed in the playoffs, my Lions took the kickoff and tore off sixty-five yards in thirteen plays. Getting Sammy Harrell's call to carry the ball four straight times, Lion Scottye Ratliff equalized the touchdowns with a one-yard scoring stab. After a brief chat with the statistician, we decided to go for two. Harrell's pass fell incomplete, and Brownwood was still behind by a point.

After our kickoff, Gainesville methodically shoved their way to Brownwood's thirty where a fumble recovery by Colt Carlisle stopped the Leopard's drive.

Not to be outdone, our Maroons pushed the ball back in the opposite direction. With the ball near mid-field, Harrell worked the option perfectly. He faked a pitch to his tailback then tucked the football under his arm and raced fifty-six yards for the go-ahead score. Once again we went for two and failed, but the Lions were now on top 12–7.

Gainesville wasted no time in reclaiming the lead. Facing fourth and fifteen at his own fourty-four, Leopard quarterback Jim Price stunned Brownwood's punt receiving team by lining up in scrimmage formation and humming a 56-yard touchdown strike to Overstreet who had slipped out of the backfield. Carr booted the point-after, and the Leopards regained the upper hand 14–12.

On the kickoff return our ballcarrier was slammed to the ground at the fourteen. As Brownwood lined up to try for a come-from-behind win, only 5:34 remained on the scoreboard clock. For us Brownwood coaches, it was old hat. Our Lion teams had snatched victory from the jaws of defeat many times. For our '74 squad, this was a brand-new experience. Only once in twelve games had they been behind. The Lions lost that game.

Warming to the difficult task at hand, our maroon troops proved their mettle as they rammed against a tiring red and white defense. Like a seasoned veteran, Sammy Harrell calmly directed the drive, mixing his plays as he let Pete Hicks, Scottye Ratliff and Frank Bunnell shoulder the load on crucial downs. With 1:35 remaining, Brownwood pushed across the go-ahead points. Our third try for two bonus points finally worked, and the score was 20–14. I still have nightmares about that last minute and a half.

Gainesville fielded our kickoff, ran it back to the forty and came out firing. In five plays the Red and White moved down to the Lion twenty-one, but Brownwood boosters weren't worried. In fact, every fan in the stadium knew Gainesville was beat. The Leopards had run out of time. Only one second remained when quarterback Jim Price took the snap and lofted a "Hail Mary" pass in the direction of Ray Overstreet. Unbelievably, Overstreet caught the football and ran into our end zone.

People were screaming. The entire stadium was in a state of

pandemonium as Leopard kicking specialist Doug Carr took his position for the extra point attempt. When Carr's kick sailed wide, every fan in the stadium and even the players on the field were trying to grasp what had happened, but I knew. Our trip to the state finals had been canceled.

Brownwood's battle with Gainesville ended in a 20–20 tie. Penetrations were also tied at 5–5, but Gainesville held an 18–16 edge in first downs, so the Leopards advanced.

Cuero beat Gainesville 19–7 in the state final game.

◆　◆　◆

THERE ARE MANY REASONS young people should participate in high school sports. First and foremost, being part of the team gives kids a sense of belonging. Almost every disgruntled teenager feels like he's an outsider, excluded from the mainstream of school activities. The two young men who went on the killing spree at Colorado's Columbine High School in 1999 are prime examples. They felt left out, and their fierce resentment fueled their wrathful act of retaliation. In my mind, most of our major school problems—drugs, weapons, dropouts, poor learning skills—are spawned by the college-like atmosphere at large high schools where so many kids get lost in the shuffle and where opportunities to participate in a sport, or the band, or the drill team, or even the high school choir are limited to a select few.

Athletics teaches young folks to focus on their goals. Sports teaches that success is achieved through hard work and discipline. Players learn to take steps to achieve their goals. They also learn not to take false steps. I know many adults who work hard and stay busy, but they never get anywhere because they waste so much energy on unimportant projects. Naturally, I believe playing football is the best way to learn how to succeed, but basketball, baseball, soccer—almost every sport, teaches participants to focus on goals. If a young person doesn't participate in a sport, I have no idea where he or she would learn these essential lessons.

Finally, whether you're a great athlete or a mediocre player, being a member of a team provides a basis for friendships that last a lifetime. Men who have experienced the agony of twice-a-day mid-August football practice, or run the bleachers in the basketball gym 'till their legs were numb, or shagged fly balls 'till they couldn't raise their arms above their head will share a common bond forever. Ten years after you graduate, it makes no difference whether you even played in every game. What really matters is you were part of the *team*.

1975

FOR ME, THE '75 FOOTBALL SEASON is especially memorable. Brownwood sure had some great players that year. Our duo quarterbacks Greg Hobbs and Laro Clark were equally superb. All of our running backs, Alan Daniell, Carey Reese, Rory Cunningham, Danny Gamble and Wesley Thomas, were lightning-bolt quick and capable of scoring on every play.

Anchoring our offensive line at center was Jeff Mathers, with Harold Barnes and Terry George at guards, Doug Reid and Eddie Gill at tackles, and Jerry Don Gleaton and Brad Bowen at the end positions. In a pre-season scrimmage against Wharton, our defense made mincemeat of the Tigers' offense. Gritty guys like James Isom, Ray Vess, Kyle Krueger, Chris Franks and Rick Baron did most of the mincing.

Yes, Brownwood had some great players, but what made that year so special for me was a 140-pound junior end named Jim Wood. I had watched proudly as each of Morris Southall's sons took their turn at the helm. Now, it was Jim's turn to shine. Okay, so maybe my son wasn't as athletic as the Southall boys, but Jim sure thought he was good. And when his number was called, he got the job done.

◆　◆　◆

IN KEEPING WITH AN EVENT that had become a Brownwood tradition, we opened our regular season by traveling to Abilene to endure our annual thrashing in Shotwell Stadium at the hands of Cooper's Cougars. Midway through the third quarter, Coach Ray Overton's Big Blue was sitting on a comfortable 21–6 lead. That's when maroon linebacker Chris Franks intercepted a pass at the Cougar seventeen. Three plays later Rory Cunningham hurdled into the end zone.

Brownwood got the ball again in the top of the fourth. This time our Lions needed eight plays to score, capping their eighty-yard drive with a Laro Clark to Jerry Don Gleaton aerial connection. Gleaton grabbed the football at the twenty, stiff-armed a Cooper defender and raced in for the TD. On the two-point conversion, Clark speared Brad Bowen, and suddenly the Cougars' huge lead had been trimmed to a single point—21–20.

With eleven minutes left, the Cougars proved they were as good as their press clippings claimed. Displaying the poise of a battle-seasoned professional, Cougar quarterback Kelley Gill guided his team to the clinching score. He used only six plays to cover the needed sixty-one yards. On third and twelve, Gill rifled a perfect strike to his end Rusty Hamrick who romped in untouched.

Final score: Brownwood 20, Cooper 28.

Brownwood was a 28-point favorite the next week when the Lions played host to Kerrville Tivy. With hot-handed junior quarterbacks Gregg Hobbs and Laro Clark lighting the fire, Brownwood scorched the Antlers 34–0. Brownwood fullback Carey Reese had a big night, gaining eighty-one yards on thirteen carries. Right behind was Rory Cunningham, rushing for fifty-seven yards. Dwayne Hogg had fifty-three, and Danny Gamble ran for forty-six. Jerry Gleaton and Reese each hauled in two passes, but as far as I was concerned, the most satisfying statistic of the evening was a pair of receptions registered by a young fellow named Jim Wood. Jim's first catch was a four-yard touchdown toss from Gregg Hobbs.

Gaining confidence with every game, our Maroons roared through their schedule like a runaway freight train. In game number three, Brownwood starters spent most of the night on the bench as we overwhelmed Cleburne 41–0. Fort Worth Southwest was the Lions' fourth victim. We whitewashed the Raiders 14–0.

◆　◆　◆

BY 1975, DISTRICT 4–AAA had been whittled down to seven schools—Burkburnett, Graham, Iowa Park, Stephenville, Vernon, Weatherford, and Brownwood. We opened district play against Iowa Park. The Hawks were never easy, and our maroon-clads were forced to overcome some early mistakes. When the smoke cleared, though, the Lions had registered their fourth consecutive win.

With that critical game under our belt, we breezed through our conference, and with only one game remaining, we were 5–0 in district play. Without Breckenridge and the Wichita Falls schools, the road to the playoffs seemed much easier.

At least it did until we ran into Coach Leo Brittain's ornery bunch of Steers. Graham fans had been dreaming of a trip to the playoffs since 1963, the last year a blue and red team laid claim to a district title. Like Brownwood, the Steers were undefeated in district. Our winner-take-all head-knocker took place at Cen-Tex Stadium.

◆ ◆ ◆

A VETERAN FOOTBALL OBSERVER might say the nail-biting showdown between Brownwood and Graham was an opportunity for both teams to prove their character. For the sixty-five hundred fans who attended that evening, the hard fought contest was a marathon bar room brawl intermixed with the excitement of a nauseating roller coaster ride. For Brownwood coaches and players, it was our worst nightmare come true.

For three and a half quarters, Graham dominated the game. Late in the first quarter, the Steers broke the ice with a 65-yard scoring drive. Rusty Spring, Graham's leading rusher, did the honors with a 14-yard scamper. In the second quarter, a couple of pass interference penalties set up two more Graham touchdowns, and at the half, Brownwood was in a deep, deep hole.

Our Maroons continued to flounder until late in the third quarter when Spring raced eighty-four yards to the Brownwood two-yard line. With 2:59 left in the third, the Red and Blue pushed across their fourth TD, and incredibly, Brownwood's heavily favored Lions were losing 28–0.

At Brownwood High we coaches talked to our players every day about poise, about character, about keeping a smile on their face, about giving their best on every down and never quitting until the game is over, no matter what the score. What happened after Graham kicked off made every second we coaches spent talking to our kids worthwhile.

With Laro Clark and Greg Hobbs taking turns at quarterback, Brownwood shoved the ball sixty-two yards down to the Steers' thirteen. Hobbs finished off the six-play drive by flipping the football to Jerry Don Gleaton for the TD. A two-point pitch to Alan Daniell made the score 28–8.

Several plays later, Lion Thomas Cooper recovered a fumble at Graham's forty-two, and a maroon surge was in full bloom. A 31-yard, end-over-end touchdown pass from southpaw Gleaton to end

Brad Bowen capped a six-play drive. Bryan Allen booted the extra point, and with 8:06 to play, it was 28–15.

After the kickoff, Graham and Brownwood traded turnovers. Then the Lions regained possession and went on a sixty-yard scoring mission which was aided by a pass interference call at the five. Allen missed on his first extra point attempt, but split the uprights when an offside penalty allowed a second shot.

On the second play after the kickoff, Graham's James Coleman coughed up the football, and Lion Wesley Thomas was there to recover. Now the maroon offense was humming. Danny Gamble raced twenty-four yards to the twenty. Rory Cunningham hammered out eighteen to the two, and Hobbs sneaked in for the score. When Allen kicked the Lions into a 29–28 lead, Brownwood fans went bonkers.

Down at the Brownwood bench, we coaches went a little crazy too. Our Lions had scratched, fought and clawed their way back from certain defeat, proving they had grit and plenty of character.

Unfortunately, the Steers also had character. With every person keeping an uneasy eye on the clock, Graham moved the football from their own thirty-seven to the Lion ten. Three times Brownwood appeared to have the blue and red club stopped, but each time Brian Williams, Graham's blue-ribbon quarterback, reached into his bag of tricks and pulled out a miracle. Twice, the Steers converted fourth and long situations into first downs.

Rusty Spring hadn't kicked a field goal all season, but Rusty was Graham's do-it-all guy. With thirteen seconds left, Spring thumped through a 27-yarder to give the Steers their first district title in twelve years.

Final score: Brownwood 29, Graham 31.

Even though our hopes, our dreams, and the 4–AAA district crown left on the bus for Graham that night, I still get goose bumps remembering how our Brownwood kids never gave up in that game.

The Steers' streak of good luck was short-lived. A week later, in their bi-district game played at Sweetwater, Lubbock Estacado recorded a safety on a first quarter blocked punt and held on to eliminate Graham 2–0.

CHAPTER SEVENTEEN

Pushing to the Limits

(1976–1978)

BROWNWOOD HIGH'S SUCCESS on the football field was directly linked to our off-season philosophy. I honestly believe winning teams are developed from December through July—not August through November.

My assistant coaches and I encouraged all our football players to participate in another sport. Naturally, we wanted our players' energies focused exclusively on football during football season, but when the season was over, we encouraged our kids to shift their attention to a second sport. A boy who played basketball wouldn't even see a football coach until after basketball season was over. Track team members were required to remain in the off-season training program until their first track meet. Then they could cut their off-season workouts in half until the district meet. After the district meet, our thinclads were released from all off-season workouts until they were eliminated from advancing in state competition.

We commenced each off-season workout with a five-minute "listening" period. During the listening period, our coaches took turns talking about leadership, motivation and team goals. Players were expected to look straight at the speaker, concentrate on what he said, and not be distracted. Our listening sessions set the tone for each workout and helped the boys get focused. Following the listening period, the team went through a short series of warm-up calisthenics.

The primary purpose of our off-season program was to increase agility, speed, and strength, so depending on what we coaches hoped to accomplish that day, we then switched to outside strength and agility exercises, or mat drills, or weight-lifting. (A detailed description of Brownwood's off-season workout plan is described in my book, *Gordon Wood's Game Plan to Winning Football.*)

◆ ◆ ◆

WHEN I CAME to Brownwood High in 1960, there was no weight lifting program, and even my biggest players would be considered small by today's standards. However, one player among the scrawny group I inherited was exceptionally strong. That was Doug Young who weighed about 175 pounds.

Doug and a dozen of his teammates had volunteered to help me and my assistants, Morris Southall and Pete Murray, at the rodeo grounds one afternoon. We were setting up folding chairs in the stands in anticipation of an upcoming rodeo sponsored by the high school's Future Farmers of America chapter. We were almost finished when a salesman, who had come all the way from Tennessee, drove up. In the back of the man's pickup was an expensive, stainless steel, weight-lifting machine he wanted to show us coaches.

The salesman unloaded his weight machine and began to assemble the different parts for a demonstration. Even before the man finished loading on the weights, Doug Young began shaking his head negatively.

"That thing won't work," Doug advised.

"Sure it will. This represents the very latest in muscle building technology," the salesman responded, defending his product.

"No sir, it won't hold enough weights to do us any good," Doug argued.

Agitated by Doug's skeptical attitude, the man challenged our strongman to try out his contraption. To prove his point, the salesman loaded the machine with all the weights it would hold.

Doug stretched a little, did a few push-ups, and slipped into

Doug Young—all-state guard in 1962 and Brownwood's strongest player ever. (credit: Texas Tech Archives)

position to do a bench press. Always the showman, he breathed in deeply a couple of times and snorted loudly. Then Doug pushed the weights up with ease.

Doug's teammates cheered loudly and fell into laughing hysterics. The salesman was so embarrassed he loaded the machine into the bed of his pickup and drove off without another word.

In 1962, Doug was named all-state as an offensive guard and as a linebacker. After he graduated from high school, Young played football at Texas Tech, and he was outstanding. Doug got really involved in weight-lifting and won three straight world titles as a power-lifter.

With the help of some generous donations, Brownwood High eventually built an excellent weight-lifting facility. But even with all the up-to-date muscle building equipment, there has never been another Brownwood High player as strong as Doug Young.

1976

BY 1976, FOREIGN CAR MAKERS were making significant inroads into the U.S. automobile market. General Motors, Ford and Chrysler had generally ignored the booming sales of the Volkswagen Beetle in the sixties, but during the seventies, the Japanese came on strong. A gas shortage during the Nixon Years and constant recalls of American manufactured vehicles whetted public appetite for better made, less expensive automobiles. Car buyers also demanded more miles per gallon.

The Japanese proved they could deliver, and in 1976, Nissan became the leading foreign car manufacturer. Somehow, the enemy who bombed Pearl Harbor and killed thousands of American fighting men had become our country's chief competitor and importer, sucking money from our economy and taking jobs from men who put their lives on the line serving their country in World War II.

On April 21, the last gas-guzzling Cadillac Eldorado convertible rolled off the assembly line. Production was halted because of declining sales. The average base sticker price of a '76 model GM car was six thousand dollars.

Despite our economic troubles, the nation celebrated its two-hundredth anniversary of independence on July 4, with festivals and political events all around the country. After suffering through

Vietnam and Watergate, every U.S. citizen needed a confidence boost. The anniversary celebrations sure helped.

In late July, the Democrats nominated former Georgia governor Jimmy Carter for president. Walter Mondale was selected as Carter's running mate. Our mid-August two-a-day practices were just getting started when incumbent president Gerald Ford narrowly edged out Ronald Reagan for the Republican nomination.

A few days before our '76 lid-lifter, Brownwood school superintendent Howard Murchison, Jr. presented B.I.S.D. trustees with what he described as a "bare bones" budget of $4,426,693.

"It's not the kind of budget that this board, this administration, or this community would like to see," the superintendent told the school board.

Translated into English, that meant another year without a pay raise for Brownwood teachers. Murchison's budget proposal was approved without objection.

◆　◆　◆

AS USUAL, Brownwood kicked off the football season against Abilene Cooper, and as usual, the contest was a bone-crushing demolition derby, featuring a pair of gutsy, hard-hat defenses.

Turning a myriad of Lion first half boo-boos into scoreboard fodder, Cooper was sailing along with a fourteen-point fourth quarter lead when gimp-legged Doug Hurt brought the Lions back to life. Hurt was recovering from a knee injury. When I sent Doug into the game, my intentions were to let him play a few downs and take him out. Doug had a better plan. He ripped off forty-two yards the first time he touched the football. That led to a one-yard sneak by Greg Hobbs and Brownwood's first score of the evening.

On our next possession, junior fullback Dwayne Hogg, taking a cue from his running mate, raced twenty-three yards for Brownwood's second touchdown in less than three minutes. Suddenly, a boring game had become a foot-stomping thriller. Sixty-five hundred fans were on their feet cheering and screaming when we rolled the dice, electing to go for two instead of settling for an almost certain tie.

Our two-point try never actually materialized. Two hundred-pound Cougar Tim Orr nailed Lion quarterback Greg Hobbs before he could complete the handoff, and our big bet came up snake eyes. After the bonus point attempt failed, Brownwood fans rewarded their never-say-die Maroons with a standing ovation. That softened our disappointment, but a Lion loss never goes down easy.

Final score: Brownwood 13, Cooper 14.

Brownwood's leading receiver that evening was a sticky-fingered senior named Jim Wood. Midway through the third quarter, Jim ended up at the bottom of a huge pileup after he hauled in his fourth pass. When he trotted back to the huddle, Jim seemed to be favoring his right hand.

"Nice catch, son. You okay?" I asked when Jim came to the bench.

"Yes sir. I hurt my hand a little, but I'm fine," Jim replied.

Jim gathered in his fifth catch of the night a few minutes later and played the rest of the game without revealing how badly he was hurt. Before the game ended, his hand had swollen to twice its normal size. X-rays taken the next day revealed Jim's right hand was broken.

Brownwood's '76 offensive line included Jim Wood, Thomas Cooper, Mike Permenter, Jeff Mathers, Dennis Richardson, Jimmy Patterson, and Rick Baron. (credit: BHS 1977 Year Book)

◆　◆　◆

OUR '76 SQUAD was loaded with talent. Both Greg Hobbs and Laro Clark had started at quarterback the previous season. Newcomer Nathan Allen also looked promising until a broken arm ended his season, but with speedy guys like Doug Hurt, Dwayne Hogg, Doug Hager, Danny Gamble, Jimmy Baker, Bruce Autrey, and Jimmy McQueen, our stable of ballcarriers was jam-packed.

Rounding out our backfield crew was placement kicker Martin Perry. In past seasons, field goals had been a rarity, but Perry's strong leg added an extra dimension to the BHS attack.

Brownwood's offensive line included center, Jeff Mathers; guards, Mike Permenter and Dennis Richardson; tackles, Thomas Cooper and Jimmy Patterson; and ends, Jim Wood and Rick Baron. In the Cooper game these folks proved they could butt heads with the best.

Our stellar defensive troops included Ray Vess, Jimmy Baker, Craig Agnew, Doug Reid, Bryan Allen, Chris Franks, Kyle Krueger, Craig Teal, Eddie Gill, and Paul Turner, and strong defense played a key role when Brownwood blasted Austin Travis High 23–0 in our second game of the season.

In our third game, a 65-yard scoring bolt by Waco sophomore halfback Mike Lively prevented our defense from pitching a second successive perfect game. Even so, our hairy-chested defenders were spectacular as the Panthers of Waco Midway became Brownwood's second victim—33–7.

The Lions took a week off to lick their wounds then jumped head-first into the District 4–AAA melee. An aggressive defensive unit was responsible for our first conference win.

Via a pass interception, Burkburnett had driven down to the maroon thirty-four. That's where blue chip linemen Kyle Krueger and Eddie Gill took charge. On fourth and eight, Krueger and Gill literally assaulted the Bulldog backfield to throw quarterback Jose Thomas for an eighteen-yard loss. A half-dozen plays after Brownwood took possession, Lion fullback Doug Hager dived in from the one. Bryan Allen tacked on the PAT, and Brownwood escaped with a 7–0 win.

In the weeks that followed, my mule-stubborn Maroons barreled through the conference like a California-bound sixteen-wheeler on Interstate 20. First, they flattened Weatherford 42–0. Then Mineral Wells 42–14, Iowa Park 51–8, and Vernon 25–0. When Brownwood beat Graham 35–0 and Weatherford upset Stephenville on the next to the last weekend of the regular season, the Lions had the District 4–AAA title wrapped up.

Midway through the season, *Brownwood Bulletin* sportswriter Bill Stovall nicknamed my awesome defense "Gordon's Gorillas." In our final district game, which was played in a stiff wind and with snow falling, my Gorillas earned their keep, holding off a fiery band of Yellowjackets until our offense could get rolling.

The game's outcome was still in doubt until Brownwood scored three rapid-fire touchdowns in the final three minutes to secure a win.

Final score: Brownwood 35, Stephenville 6.

◆　◆　◆

AS BROWNWOOD PREPARED to meet San Angelo Lake View's blue and white Chiefs in bi-district play, Gordon's Gorillas had allowed the sum total of forty-nine points. At the Lion Quarterback Club meeting on Monday, one of the members asked if the weather might be a factor in our upcoming encounter with Lake View.

"Rain, sleet, snow, wind, cold or heat, these kids have been there before. They'll play well whatever the weather. That tells you something about their character," I told the man.

At San Angelo, my Lions proved they had character. In a hard fought battle played before thirteen thousand wild-eyed, screaming

Coaches West and Wood discuss strategy with defensive guard Craig Teal while Jim Wood listens intently in the background.
(*credit:* Brownwood Bulletin)

fans, my gritty Maroons wrapped an iron curtain around Lake View's potent attack, allowing the Chiefs only five offensive snaps in the final quarter. With the score deadlocked at 7–7, Lion quarterback Greg Hobbs combined the brutal running of Doug Hurt with two timely passes to Jimmy Baker and guided Brownwood down to the Lake View ten. On fourth and one, Hurt took a pitchout, swung in behind a block by fullback Doug Hager and wheeled in for the winning TD.

Final score: Brownwood 14, Lake View 7.

After his team's heart-breaking loss, Lake View coach Clovis Hale paid my ballclub a huge complement. "Brownwood is a great team, the best team we've played in the four years I've been here," Hale told a reporter.

◆　◆　◆

FROM THE DAY HE ARRIVED in Brownwood until the day the school board bought out his contract in 1981, Brownwood school superintendent Howard Murchison was a constant source of irritation.

Since I accepted my first coaching job at Spur High School back in 1938, I had gone out of my way to get along with my school superintendents. Whenever my superintendent had a request or a suggestion, I always gave his interest top priority. I took great pride in the friendly relationships I shared with my superintendents during my forty years as a football coach.

Maybe Howard Murchison took my cooperative attitude as a sign of weakness, but from the moment he assumed command, Murchison seemed determined to brow beat me into resigning.

Our first real confrontation occurred one afternoon at the school administration building. Murchison had called all of Brownwood's school principals and myself to meet with him. When we arrived, the superintendent passed out sheets of paper which had each man's name typed at the top of the page.

"I want you people to write down the annual salary you think each school administrator should make," Murchison advised us.

Every man in the room was stunned by the superintendent's request. I spoke up to protest, "Mister Murchison, this isn't our job. Setting salaries is your job, and the school board's job."

"Well, I want y'all to do it anyway. I want your input," the superintendent said firmly, and for a few moments we men stared at the sheet of paper with our name at the top. I don't think a person in the room actually wrote down a proposed number, for himself or for anyone else.

Undaunted, Superintendent Murchison walked to the front of the room where a blackboard was covered with a bed sheet. As Murchison threw back the sheet, he told us, "I've done a little thinking on the matter. I want you to consider these numbers as a trial run."

Written on the board were the names of all the men in the room, with a proposed salary adjacent to each name. The numbers represented a huge pay raise for every one of the administrators, including the superintendent. The salary shown alongside my name was $16,000. This was less than I was making. Murchison's list had Coach Southall's salary higher than mine.

I studied the chart for a few seconds before I spoke up again, "Mister Murchison, when did you change your mind?"

"Whatta you mean? I haven't changed my mind."

"Yes, you have. The night you were voted in as superintendent, you and I sat right out there in that front office while the school board discussed your qualifications. You asked me what my salary was. When I told you I was making sixteen thousand eight hundred a year, you said, 'Oh, my God, that's ridiculous. You oughta be making at least twenty thousand a year.' Mister Murchison, my football team has only lost one game so far this year. Am I not doing a good job? What is it you want done?" I inquired, doing my best not to show how angry I was.

"I didn't change my mind. I haven't changed my mind." Murchison was flabbergasted. He stammered and stuttered, but he never did answer my question.

For maybe ten more minutes, I watched while Murchison tried to justify his numbers. Finally, I'd had enough. I could no longer restrain my feelings.

"I want to tell you fellows something," I said, rising from my seat. "This meeting is a total waste of time. I've got work to do. I have a game to play Friday night."

I left the meeting and drove to the football field. I'd only been there a short time when Al Milch, the assistant high school principal, came to get me. Murchison had told his administrative group he couldn't sell the school board on his wage proposals unless Coach Wood was in favor. Honoring the superintendent's wishes, I went back to the meeting, but my presence accomplished nothing. All I heard was more of the same rhetoric. Every man there was relieved when, mercifully, the meeting finally adjourned.

As I left the meeting, I was walking alongside Bill Maness, Al Milch and R.E. "Slim" Warren, the high school principal. "You know, fellows," Slim observed. "We might as well face it. We've got a lemon for a superintendent."

"That may be," I responded, defending Murchison, "but I don't care how sour he is. We've got to work and work and work to make a superintendent out of him."

And that was my true attitude that day. Murchison was my boss, and I truly wanted to be in his corner. I would later come to realize the whole purpose of the salary meeting was to diminish my relationship with other school administrators. That's why Murchison set my salary low while he proposed giving every other man a raise. Fortunately, most of the men saw through the scheme.

That next spring Brownwood school trustees met to approve salaries for the upcoming year. During the board meeting, my coaching contract was extended for another year. When the contract document reached my desk, I simply signed it and handed it back to the superintendent's secretary. Over the years I had become complacent to the routine. I had quit reading my employment contract before I signed it. I simply assumed I'd been treated fairly.

A few days later, I ran into *Brownwood Bulletin* sportswriter Bill Stovall. Stovall told me Murchison had refused to divulge the terms of my new contract. When Bill telephoned the superintendent's office to ask about my salary, Murchison had rebuffed his inquiry, telling Stovall he had to get permission from me before he could release any information.

"That's not right," I told Bill. "Murchison has no choice in the matter. I'm paid with taxpayers' money, and my salary is public information." I didn't think much about our conversation until I bumped into Grady Chastain a couple of days later. Chastain served as vice-president on Brownwood's school board.

"Grady, what did the board do about my salary when they approved my contract the other night?" I asked.

"Coach Wood, every man on the school board wanted to raise your salary and your assistants' salaries, but Superintendent Murchison wouldn't let us do it. He said you were hired to win games, and you shouldn't get a raise in salary just because you were doing your job."

Normally, I don't get upset over money. I've always claimed the last thing a coach should worry about is money, but Chastain's news flew all over me. My assistant coaches' wages were among the lowest in our district, and despite the fact my football teams had won or tied for the district championship seven times in nine years, my salary was only about average for head coaches in District 4–AAA.

That same afternoon I was visiting with Dusty Moore at the high school auto mechanics shop building when Howard Murchison drove up. My harsh feelings were still simmering, so I got up to leave, wanting to avoid a conversation with the superintendent while I was in such a foul mood. I didn't move fast enough. Murchison caught up with me as I was about to drive off.

"Bill Stovall called me the other day," Murchison said. "He asked about your salary. I wouldn't tell him until I got permission from you."

"Mister Murchison, you don't have a choice. By law, you have to tell him."

"Well, I'm not gonna tell him unless you give me permission," Murchison repeated steadfastly.

"How much is my salary on the new contract?" I asked, already knowing the answer.

"Oh, it's exactly the same as before. Same contract. Same everything."

"Well, if you're not ashamed of how poorly I'm paid, I guess I'm not. You have my permission to tell anyone who asks how much I make," I said, pausing to get my anger under control. "There's something else I want to tell you, Mister Murchison, and I want you to remember it. I don't have an ounce of respect for you as a superintendent, as an administrator, or as a man. You're about the sorriest, no-good, SOB I've ever known. If anyone ever tells you I've said something bad about you, you can believe them, because it will be the truth."

I shoved my car into gear and drove off, leaving Murchison standing there with his mouth open.

◆ ◆ ◆

ON WEDNESDAY MORNING following our Lake View game, Howard Murchison summoned me to his office. When I arrived, he jumped right in the middle of me.

"Coach, you overspent your food budget last weekend. You'll have to make up the money."

Although I understood immediately what he was talking about, Murchison's accusation took me completely by surprise. A long standing custom for our football team was to treat players and coaches to a post game meal at Lowake whenever we played in San Angelo. Lowake is a tiny town (population forty) located about thirty miles east of San Angelo. The Lowake Steak House is nationally know for its great steaks, but what our players and coaches loved most were their chicken fried steaks. While the meals our boys had eaten at Lowake on Friday evening cost more than our athletic budget allowed, the total overspent amounted to less than a dollar per team member.

"Mister Murchison, we've played a lot of games in San Angelo—playoff games, regular season games. Our teams have always stopped to eat a chicken fried steak at Lowake's."

"Well, you've overspent the amount you had budgeted. You'll have to make that up," Murchison repeated, like he was totally unsympathetic to my argument.

"Okay. I'll agree we exceeded our food budget, but we had an extra large crowd at the football game. Brownwood High took in ten thousand dollars more than we expected. Why can't we pay the extra meal cost with the surplus from the gate receipts?"

"No, that doesn't make any difference," Murchison replied sternly. "Gate receipts go into a different pocket. You have to live within your travel budget!"

I was tired of arguing with the man. I knew this conversation wasn't really about budget. He was using the issue to get back at me.

"Alright, I'll make up the difference, but it'll probably cost you in the long run," I told the stubborn superintendent. Then I got up and walked out without speaking another word.

A few days later Murchison called me to his office again. When I arrived, he was steaming mad.

"Coach, I hear you're going around town soliciting donations to pay for that extra meal money you owe," Murchison accused me angrily.

"That's a damn lie," I responded. I seldom curse, but I was perturbed with the man before I got there. Now I was really hot.

"Well, I know what I know, and I have it on great authority," Murchison persisted.

"That makes it real simple then. You get that great authority and bring him here. He can sit over there, and I'll sit right here. We'll come to a conclusion about your information in a hurry."

The superintendent called Don Clements, the school board president. Clements was a local attorney. At Murchison's request, Clements dropped everything and came to the superintendent's office where Murchison repeated everything he'd told me.

"Howard," Clements testified, "I didn't tell you that. What I said was, 'Coach Wood could do that. If he wanted to, he could come to town, and in thirty minutes, he could raise every dollar you say he owes.'"

Essentially, that was the end of the argument. Murchison thanked the board president and dismissed him. He didn't apologize to me, but he never mentioned the meal money issue again.

◆ ◆ ◆

PERRYTON HALFBACK BRAD BECK had rushed for more than two thousand yards before his red and white Rangers clashed with Brownwood's Maroons in Vernon on a cold, windy November afternoon. The six-foot, 195-pound junior was the son of Perryton coach Don Beck, and Brad was even better than his press clippings claimed.

Beck didn't exactly run foot loose and fancy free through our defense. Brownwood defenders Danny Gamble, Bruce Autrey, Chris Franks, Doug Reid, Craig Teal, Ray Vess and Bryan Allen delivered a number of bone-bruising tackles which Brad would nurse for weeks to come. Still, Beck did gain one hundred and seventy four yards on twenty-nine carries, and it was Beck's six-yard TD scamper in the first quarter and a 45-yard scoring explosion in the fourth that wrecked Lion hopes for another trip to the state final.

Final score: Brownwood 0, Perryton 13.

In early December my close friend Darrell Royal announced

his resignation as football coach at the University of Texas. In twenty years as head coach, Coach Royal led the Longhorns to eleven outright or shared Southwest Conference titles. Royal's resignation surprised many people. He was the winningest football coach in SWC history. Darrell was only fifty-two, but apparently his job was no longer fun. The Longhorns' season had been blighted by injuries and recruiting controversies. Texas limped in with a 5–5–1 record, the worst showing by a burnt-orange football team since Coach Royal became their head coach.

One person close to the Texas coaching legend observed, "Darrell Royal would coach forever if it wasn't for recruiting."

That's the best reason I can think of for a coach to stay at the high school level. No recruiting. No pampering of star players. Every coach plays with the kids that come through his pipeline.

1977

IN 1977, my coaching staff included six outstanding coaches—Morris Southall, Kenneth West, Don Martin, Steve Boothe, Bob Agnew and Fred Strickland. Except for Morris, Don and myself, all the other coaches held additional titles. Steve was also head basketball coach. Kenneth was head track coach. Bob and Fred coached the junior varsity football team. But regardless of other duties, we functioned as a team during football season—totally focused on our goal of winning another state championship.

No head coach can be successful without a good staff—and every member must be unconditionally loyal to the head coach. Bud Wilkerson once told this hypothetical story to illustrate an important point about coaching relationships.

"Why did Bud call that passing play on the forty-yard line?" the barber asked one of Wilkerson's assistant coaches.

"I don't know," the assistant replied.

Wilkerson proclaimed he would consider that coach to be disloyal, saying he would immediately fire the assistant.

A coaching staff is like a family. To be successful, every member must do his job efficiently with every man pulling in the same direction. At Brownwood, we had a saying: Coaches must believe in coaches. Players must believe in players. Coaches must believe in players. And players must believe in coaches.

While all of these ingredients are essential to a winning

program, coaches believing in their fellow coaches is especially vital. If one coach on the staff resents or dislikes another coach, every player will know. This makes it impossible for either of the coaches to be effective. Disharmony within a coaching staff creates a "no-win" situation for both the team and the head coach.

Perhaps the most important trait of a good assistant is a sense of direction. I once hired a coach to work with our eighth-grade team. Even though he did a decent job of coaching, his kids struggled. As their final game approached, the eighth graders were destined to end the season with a losing record. Their last game was scheduled for Saturday night.

Thursday afternoon, I went to watch the junior high workouts. The eighth graders weren't suited out. They were just standing around, doing nothing. Dumbfounded, I asked the boys why they weren't working out, preparing for their Saturday game. The boys told me they hadn't seen their coach, and they hadn't suited out since their last game, which had been played Monday night. Apparently, their coach had more important matters to attend to.

About 9:30 that evening I located the eighth-grade coach. When he told me he had been out looking for a deer lease, I couldn't believe my ears.

"Yep, those kids are so bad there's no use in working out," the coach declared.

"If your players are that bad, you should be working twice as hard with them," I shouted angrily and stormed off. I didn't bother to explain the obvious. In two years those eighth graders would come down my varsity pipeline. In four years they would be seniors—the older players, who would be expected to provide leadership for Brownwood's football squad. Any coach worth keeping should have understood that.

The coach was not invited back the following year. Even though he had a keen football mind, the coach wasn't focused. He wasn't lazy. He simply had no sense of direction. He didn't know where he was going or how to get there. Eventually, he landed another coaching job, but he was never successful. For the next twenty years he moved from one coaching job to another.

◆　◆　◆

DURING THE SPRING OF '77, I was invited to coach the Texas all-star squad in the fortieth annual Oil Bowl. To be invited was a great honor because the Oil Bowl pitted the best Texas high school footballers against the best from Oklahoma. Texas and Oklahoma enjoy a rich tradition of neighborly rivalry, so the contest provided both states an opportunity to showcase their best athletes. However, the game had a much more important purpose. The Oil Bowl Classic was sponsored by Maskat Temple Shrine and the Oklahoma Coaches Association. Each year the game raised thousands of dollars to benefit crippled children in North Texas and Oklahoma. The game's motto was: "Strong legs run—so weak legs may walk."

My assistant coaches were Donnell Crosslin of Wichita Falls High School and Jim Thomason, the head coach at Gainesville High School. Crosslin's long and illustrious career at Wichita Falls was highlighted by a state championship in 1969 and a return trip to the finals in '71, where his unbeaten Coyotes lost to San Antonio Lee.

For Coach Thomason and myself, the Oil Bowl assignment was a reunion of sorts. Thomason's Gainesville teams made it to the state finals in '74 and '76. In the 1974 semifinal game, Thomason's Leopards eliminated Brownwood by way of a 20–20 tie, barely squeaking past us with an 18–16 edge in first downs.

Our Texas roster included Odessa High quarterback Darrell Shepard. Darrell was the most sought-after high school player in the nation that year. Donnie Love from Garland was another blue chipper, a freight train fullback and a rugged linebacker. Both Shepard and Love were headed for Houston University along with Eric Herring of Houston Yates and David Taveirne of Austin Lanier, who were also members of our squad.

Another big gun was David Overstreet. At Big Sandy, David had broken enough records to place him third on the all time Texas rushing list. Overstreet and three other members of our squad— Tim McCollum of Gainesville, Basil Banks of Galveston Ball, and Rick Cross of Rockwall would attend Oklahoma University.

Our star-studded backfield also included Danny Alexander from Archer City, David Darr from San Antonio Churchill, Tim Orr from Abilene Cooper and Butch Murdock from DeSoto. Brownwood High was also well represented. Lion quarterback Gregg Hobbs and defensive tackle Doug Reid had earned a spot on the Texas roster. Hobbs had a scholarship from West Texas State. Reid was on his way to Baylor.

The Oil Bowl contest was played in early August at Wichita Falls on the artificial turf of Memorial Stadium before thirteen thousand fans. Before the '77 game, Texas held a 24–6–1 edge. This prompted a critical comment from outspoken Oklahoma University football coach Barry Switzer.

"To equalize the Oil Bowl game," Switzer mused, "Oklahoma would need about a thousand more high schools to draw from."

Coach Switzer was absolutely right. Texas did enjoy a tremendous advantage. I've never coached a better group of athletes than that '77 Texas squad. On Saturday night, August 6, our Texas all-stars bowled over the Sooners 34–8.

◆ ◆ ◆

1977! WHAT A YEAR! CB radios were the hot item. With almost twenty-five million CBs in use, most every motorist had a CB handle. The movie *Saturday Night Fever*, starring John Travolta, changed the way people danced and the way they dressed. After topping the *New York Times* bestseller list for twenty consecutive weeks, Alex Haley's novel *Roots* was made into a TV movie, and the mini-series completely dominated TV ratings.

◆ ◆ ◆

WITH SO MUCH CHANGE in the air, my Maroons decided to make some changes of their own. Battling perennial 4A powerhouse Abilene Cooper hammer and tong, Brownwood opened the season with a 15–6 victory over the Cougars. In the second half, 232-pound Eddie Gill came close to being a one man wrecking crew as a determined Lion defense held Big Blue to one first down and a minus two yards total offense. Dwayne Hogg, Craig Teal, Dan Newton and Larry Jones also contributed to Brownwood's stout defensive effort, terrorizing Cooper's backfield and applying some bruising licks which Cougar ballcarriers would remember for weeks.

In September, while Chris Evert was nailing down her third straight U.S. Open women's tennis championship and while the New York Yankees were defeating the Los Angeles Dodgers to capture the '77 World Series, my Lions were girding up for their own championship run. In non-conference play, Brownwood put a

35–10 whammy on Austin Travis then carved up Waco's Midway Panthers 28–0.

We opened district play by traveling to Burkburnett, and as usual, the game was a knock-down, drag-out brawl. Brownwood barely slipped past the feisty Bulldogs 24–12.

In October, our Maroons methodically marched through district opponents, downing Weatherford 48–14, Mineral Wells 41–0, Iowa Park 49–0, Vernon 21–8, and Graham 41–14. In early November, a few days after President Carter signed a bill to raise the minimum wage to $2.30 an hour, Brownwood clinched the District 4–AAA championship with a 38–7 win over Stephenville.

◆　◆　◆

AFTER HIS LAKE VIEW CHIEFS lost to Brownwood in the '76 bi-district match, a disappointed Clovis Hale promised his team would be back. Coach Hale made good on that promise. With sure-handed, do-it-all quarterback Gary Speck at the helm and with thousand-yard rusher John Maberry running the football, the unde-feated Chiefs had run rampant through super-tough District 3–AAA. Our bi-district battle of unbeatens took place on a chilly Friday night at Cen-Tex Stadium, and the fiery encounter left seventy-five hundred football fans smoldering. When the smoke cleared, Brownwood had prevailed 56–20.

◆　◆　◆

BRAD BECK and his Perryton Rangers had derailed our '76 playoff run. The '77 Rangers were off on another rampage, rolling through their schedule undefeated.

In their bi-district joust with Andrews, Perryton flattened the previously unbeaten Mustangs 24–6. Our quarterfinal showdown was played in Lubbock, and for most of the first half, the Big Red team outplayed our Maroons. Perryton used a stunting defensive set, and Ranger defenders poured into our backfield on every play, frustrating our offense and cutting off our quarterback sweep which Nathan Allen usually worked to perfection.

Late in the second quarter with the score deadlocked at 7–7, Brownwood got a big break. After being on the receiving end of a vicious, jarring tackle, Brad Beck limped off the field with a knee injury. Beck was a fabulous back who ran like Earl Campbell. His exit seemed to pump new vitality into my Lions.

During the halftime recess, we rearranged our blocking schemes, and our offense immediately picked up. We scored on our first possession of the second half, and then it was like a calvary charge. In the fourth quarter our Maroons racked up another twenty-two points to turn a tight, tense struggle into a mini-rout.

Final score: Brownwood 35, Perryton 7.

After the Perryton game, we discovered Boswell-Saginaw had beaten Atlanta in their quarterfinal conflict. The next morning, which was a Saturday, Coach Southall, Slim Warren, Howard Murchison and I drove to Waco to meet with Boswell officials. Morris and I were especially excited because Neal Wilson, Boswell's football coach, and Bill Anderson, their high school principal, were our longtime friends. We expected to have an amicable meeting because they had been in the playoffs many times.

During the trip to Waco, I made the mistake of telling Howard Murchison how Boswell-Saginaw was growing by leaps and bounds, and how their stadium was much too small to handle a semifinal playoff crowd. I explained how that gave Brownwood an edge if we insisted on a home and home coin flip. Even if we lost, Boswell would want to play on a better field, probably somewhere in Fort Worth. If we won, we would enjoy the advantage of playing in Brownwood.

◆　◆　◆

COACHES AND SCHOOL OFFICIALS are usually in a good humor when they meet to make playoff decisions. They've just won a big game, and they're feeling pretty good about their season. Agreements are generally made without a lot of discussion. The UIL provides a standard form which defines a specific order for settling every playoff game decision. For instance, the form indicates the type of football to be used, where game officials will come from, stadium expenses for the visiting team. All these items are to be decided and written down on the UIL form before you decide on the game site. UIL rules say if the schools can't agree on a neutral site, either party can ask for a coin flip—home and home.

We met with the Boswell officials at the Elite Cafe which is located on the traffic circle at Waco. Everyone had a UIL form, and we were about to get started when Howard Murchison exerted his authority.

"Since I have more experience in playoff games than anyone else in this room, I will run the meeting," Murchison pronounced. Our superintendent's pompous behavior was not only embarrassing, it changed the whole mood of the meeting.

Yielding to Howard's dominating manner, Bill Anderson spoke up, "You seem to be a great authority, Mister Murchison, and a lot more knowledgeable than the rest of us. So why don't you go ahead?"

I could tell from the ice cold tone of Anderson's voice that trouble lay ahead. Everyone took a seat, but you could feel a chill settle over the room.

We had hardly swallowed that pill when Murchison informed us he had a different form he wanted to use, saying his form was more comprehensive and much better than the one provided by the UIL. Then, Howard proceeded to talk and talk about this and that, like he knew all there was to know about everything and had helped make the rules.

Eventually, in spite of our superintendent's bad manners, we got down to business. We easily reached agreement on every item until we got around to picking the game site. That's when Murchison proved beyond a shadow of a doubt that he was a total nincompoop.

"That football stadium you people play in can't possibly handle the crowd expected for this game, and you don't have adequate parking. So we are going to insist on flipping for home site," Murchison declared, completely disregarding the rules of playoff etiquette. Then he made matters worse by letting the cat out of the bag regarding our home field strategy. "You'll have to select another stadium, one that's big enough to handle a state semifinal game. What stadium do you folks choose for your home field?"

Boswell superintendent Glen Reeves took a minute to consider his reply. Then he stood up very slowly and responded in a very loud voice, "Mister Murchison, our football stadium is probably the sorriest 3A stadium in the State of Texas. And you're right. We have very little parking space. But that's where we're gonna play if we win the coin flip. Now let's get on with the flipping."

As you might guess, Brownwood lost the coin toss. Boswell

coach Neal Wilson called tails, and tails it was. Murchison's face turned beet red when Bill Anderson chimed in, "Yeah, we've just got one street leading into our stadium. When we fill that stadium up, you can't get in, and you can't get out."

That's the way things were when the meeting adjourned. I was so mad at Murchison I couldn't see straight. During the drive back to Brownwood, Murchison fretted over the consequences. He kept telling us over and over, "We've made a terrible mistake. We can't do it. We can't play in that place. We'll never get all our fans in there."

"You lost the flip, Howard," I reminded our agonized superintendent. "We have to play where they tell us to play. They can't make us go further than Boswell, but if they want to play in their stadium, that's where we have to play."

Shortly after we got back to Brownwood, Boswell superintendent Glen Reeves called me. This is what Reeves told me:

"Coach Wood, our fans would lynch us if we insisted on playing a semifinal playoff game in our tiny stadium. We're gonna play the game at Farrington Field in Fort Worth. You can tell Coach Southall and Slim Warren about the change in plans, but you are not to tell that good-for-nothing, little chicken shit superintendent of yours. We don't want him to know about the site change until he reads about it in Monday morning's *Star-Telegram*."

Neither Morris nor Slim nor I ever mentioned the change of location to the school superintendent. We made him read about it in the newspaper. That may sound cruel and disloyal, but Howard Murchison never interfered with Brownwood High playoff decisions again.

◆ ◆ ◆

BOSWELL-SAGINAW owned a season record of 12–0–1 before they met Brownwood in the semifinals. The Pioneers' success depended on a ground-gobbling wishbone attack. When my coaches and I reviewed Boswell's game films, we discovered their offense was very basic, utilizing less than ten different running plays and only a few passes. Brownwood had always played extremely well against wishbone offenses. The only wishbone team we ever lost to was David McWilliams' Abilene High Eagles. Every day that next week, we devoted a lot of practice time to our wishbone defense. Our diligence paid off. Gordon's Gorillas kept Boswell's wishbone in check early while our offense racked up points.

Final score: Brownwood 42, Boswell-Saginaw 20.

After we won the game, the walkway outside our dressing room was packed with well-wishers and reporters. As we shouldered our way through, several Brownwood players were asked to express their feelings about reaching the state finals. Lion defender Dan Newton had perhaps the best quote.

"We're just a bunch of guys who got together at the first of the year. No one thought we could do anything," Dan explained, "but we're a bunch of scrappers who get the job done."

In the dressing room I couldn't help but smile when I told my players, "There's just one more river to cross." What I didn't know at the time was how wide and deep that river would be. To get across, we would have to face Donnie Little and the Dickinson Gators. The blue and white Gators had only lost one game, winning twelve straight after dropping their season opener to Huntsville 36–35. Dickinson was ranked second in the state—right behind Brownwood.

◆　◆　◆

THE YEAR before Teddy Gray moved in at Dickinson High, the Gators had a 0–10 record. During his first year as head coach, Gray guided the Gators to a complete turnaround and a 10–0 mark, before New Braunfels sidelined them in the first round of the playoffs. This was Teddy's second year at Dickinson, and his team was packed with talent. In addition to Donnie Little, the Gators enjoyed the services of running back Jeff LaFleur who had rushed for 1,616 yards and 216 points.

Little and LaFleur ramrodded a potent offense which included all-district linemen Marty Harclerode, Bill Cary, Victor Baker, Mike Mackey, Jeff Wyatt and Dean Lansford. On defense, all-state linebacker Tim Gray and big guys like Joe Gregory, Ed Gottlob, Tyrone Briscoe, Paul Warren, William Taylor, David Gilbreath and Ronald Hall led the charge.

At least a dozen college coaches were crowded inside the press box to watch the opening kickoff at Austin's Memorial Stadium that December afternoon. Most of the coaches had come to see Dickinson quarterback Donnie Little, and he didn't disappoint. After Brownwood fumbled on their first play from scrimmage, the six-foot-two, 190-pound blue chipper piloted his team on a 55-yard drive. LaFleur slammed for the final three yards and the ice breaker. That was the first of three opening quarter scores by LaFleur. Jeff later added TD runs of nineteen and thirty-seven yards. His third touchdown came after Brownwood's second fumble of the first period.

Brownwood cut the margin to 21–8 with a 74-yard drive midway through the second quarter and appeared to be gathering momentum. But with 2:54 remaining in the half, Donnie Little took off on the first of two 76-yard dashes which killed our chances. The score at halftime was 27–8.

In the third quarter, Little continued to explode over the right side, chewing up yardage and making first downs. Donnie's second 76-yard touchdown run increased Dickinson's lead to 33–8. An eight-yard Little blast made it 40–8 early in the fourth, and it appeared the Gators could name their own score.

That's when Brownwood's never-say-die Lions showed their class. In the final minutes BHS quarterback Nathan Allen steered his Maroons to three touchdowns, using a pass to Jimmy Baker and a one-yard stab by Dwayne Hogg for the first two scores, and a one-yard quarterback sneak for the third. Allen had Brownwood threatening the Dickinson goal line, about to score again, when the game ended.

Final score: Brownwood 28, Dickinson 40.

Dickinson quarterback Donnie Little gained volumes of praise after the game. His 254 yards rushing on 19 carries established an all time state championship record, breaking the mark set by Bridge City's Steve Worster against McKinney in 1966. When all his '77 statistics were totaled, Little accounted for 1,613 yards rushing, 1,581 yards passing and 135 yards returning punts. His name was listed number one on every blue chip poll. Donnie chose to attend the University of Texas.

Immediately following the game, our team captains Eddie Gill, Doug Hurt and Craig Teal requested a few moments alone with their teammates. As I waited in the hallway outside the dressing room along with my assistant coaches and several members of the press corps, who wanted to interview our young folks, the words of Lake View coach Clovis Hale kept echoing through my mind. After his Chiefs lost to Brownwood in 1976, Hale had defiantly proclaimed, "We'll be back!"

◆　◆　◆

WHEN MY SON JIM DEPARTED for Texas Tech back in August, I was smack in the middle of two-a-day football workouts. The next three months were jam-packed with daily practice, coaching, game film reviews, scouting, and weekend football wars. Although I realized Jim was away at school, I was so busy I didn't have time to dwell on the significance of his leaving, but after the season ended, the full impact sank in on me.

Our daughter Pat was thirty-three and living in San Antonio. After teaching at Corpus Christi for a couple of years, she had lost her enthusiasm for the classroom. Pat was now working for the State Welfare Department and seemed happier than she'd ever been.

His first semester, Jim played for the Red Raiders as a "walk-on," but after the football season, he decided to switch schools. Even though his grades at Texas Tech were excellent, Jim transferred to McMurry University in Abilene at mid-term. Abilene was a lot closer than Lubbock, but Jim was busy with school work, working out for football and learning to become a coach like his father. Jim came home as often as he could, but things just weren't the same as when he was living with us full time.

I suppose Katharine and I always knew the day would come when our children would leave, but to tell the truth, this was scary. Our nest was empty. For the first time in thirty-three years, my wife and I

A natural-born volunteer, Katharine mans the serving line at a feed-the-homeless soup kitchen. (credit: Wood Family Collection)

were living in a house without children. Would living alone, without the day to day responsibility of raising children, affect our marital relationship? What would we do with our new-found freedom?

My solution was to bury myself deeper in my work. Katharine used her extra time to get more involved in church activities and volunteer work. Nevertheless, even though both Pat and Jim frequently came to visit on weekends and holidays, their daily absence left a huge void in our lives.

1978

WHEN I MOVED to Brownwood in 1960, I had every intention of retiring at age 65. In fact, the school's retirement program was a major consideration in my accepting the Brownwood post. However, when I turned 64 in April of 1978, retirement was the furthest thing from my mind. I loved my coaching situation. I truly liked every man on my coaching staff. I enjoyed my relationships with Brownwood High teachers and administrators. Watching the kids I coached mature into responsible adults brought me enormous pleasure. I was happy. I was busy. I still had many goals I wanted to achieve. Every morning I crawled out of bed anxious to get to work.

That's why I was absolutely floored when I received a memorandum listing me as one of eleven Brownwood teachers who were subject to Brownwood's mandatory retirement policy. According to the official looking document, all eleven teachers would be retiring when we reached age 65. As usual, my perpetual tormentor, Howard Murchison, initiated the push to force me to retire.

Insulted by the impersonal tone of Murchison's ultimatum, I made a personal appearance at the very next school board meeting. I advised our trustees that mandatory retirement rules were coming under increased legal attack, and schools which refused to change were losing in court. I requested that they extend Brownwood's mandatory retirement age to seventy.

After a lengthy discussion, Grady Chastain offered a motion proposing the retirement age be changed to seventy. Chastain's motion died for lack of a second.

My birth date is April 26, 1914, meaning I would turn sixty-five in April of 1979. My coaching contract was renewed for another year by the school trustees that same night, but I knew I hadn't heard the last of mandatory retirement. Howard Murchison had a bead on me, and he wasn't about to let the issue die.

◆　◆　◆

WHILE THE SOUTHALL SONS received the most recognition, we constantly had a coach's son in our Brownwood lineup. For much of the sixties and early seventies, either Terry or Si or Shae was directing our offense. In 1974, Jake Harrell's son Sammy was our quarterback. (Sam is now the football coach at Ennis High School. His football team won the 2000 Division II, Class 4A state championship.) In 1975 and 1976, my son Jim was hauling in crucial passes. In 1976, Fred Gamble's son Danny was our tailback and team captain.

Bob Agnew's son Bobby played for us in 1974, and in 1978, Bob's son Craig captained our '78 state champion team. (Craig is now the football coach at Bartlett High. Bartlett won the Class A state championship in 1999.) Don Martin's son Bret played for us in 1979. Wayne Rathke's son Marvin played quarterback and defensive back for Brownwood's 1981 state championship team.

In the spring of 1978, it was Kenneth West's turn to contribute, and his son Glen was outstanding. Like his father, Glen played a line position which is so essential to a football team's success but which is seldom awarded sufficient applause.

Some people think coaches' sons enjoy a favored status, with a spot on the football squad secured and playing time guaranteed. That's not necessarily true. Because of who they are, coaches' sons live under a microscope. They're expected to be better than good, and quite often, their dad is their biggest critic.

During practice one afternoon, Kenneth was working with the defensive line. Glen was playing linebacker. Brownwood line-backers decide the defensive set before each play by calling one side strong, depending on how the offense lines up. Glen was doing a poor job. He set the defense wrong then messed up again on the next play. Coach West was obviously frustrated with his son's performance. Kenneth grabbed Glen's arm.

"Get over here and call it right this time!" Kenneth chastised angrily. As he shoved Glen to the proper side of the line, Kenneth applied a swift, bent knee to his son's buttocks. Both Coach Southall and I immediately bristled. At Brownwood High, touching

Bo Shero, Kirk Chastain, Glen West, and Mike Thomas were selected all-state in 1979. (credit: 1980 BHS Year Book)

a player in anger was strictly forbidden.

Morris turned to me and whispered, "Whatta you gonna do about that?"

I didn't answer for a few seconds. In fourteen years as my assistant coach, I'd never seen Kenneth West exercise anything other than patience and compassion with his players until that very moment. It was the father in him, his over-whelming desire to see his son excel, which prompted the unprece-dented hard kick to the butt. "I guess he can kick his own son if he wants to," I told Morris, and we both grinned, amused by the situ-ation but at the same time understanding the strong emotion a coach experiences when his own son is on the team.

Knowing our assistant coach was already embarrassed by his rash conduct, neither Morris nor I ever mentioned the incident to Kenneth, and it never happened again. Glen did make his father proud, though. Glen was a junior that year, and after the season, he was selected all-district as a linebacker. In 1979, his senior year, Glen was picked for all-state honors.

Naturally, I always figured Gordon Glen West would turn out to be extraordinary. Wasn't he named after me? Like his father, Glen West chose to become a football coach. Glen is now the head coach at Brenham High School, and in my opinion, he is the top young football coach in the State of Texas.

◆ ◆ ◆

TROPICAL STORM AMELIA moved ashore in early August of 1978, forcing people all along the Gulf Coast to board up their windows, batten down their hatches and curse the annual hurricane season which disrupted their lives and destroyed their property. The vicious storm affected weather conditions all across Texas. In Brownwood, the storm's passage was like manna from heaven, bringing cool temperatures and almost four inches of rain which filled Lake Brownwood almost to overflowing.

As our Lions prepared for their season opener against Abilene Cooper, Fort Worth millionaire Cullen Davis was back in the Tarrant County jail. Two years earlier Davis had been incarcerated in the same facility, accused of being the "man in black" who murdered two people and wounded his estranged wife Priscilla during a shooting spree at the six-million-dollar Davis mansion. Now, the Fort Worth industrialist was charged with trying to hire a hit man to assassinate the presiding judge in his bitter four-year-old divorce case. Davis would employ flamboyant Houston attorney Richard "Racehorse" Haynes to defend him again, and because of the money involved and the bizarre circumstances, the on-going Cullen Davis episode would captivate the nation for many months.

Regardless of other distractions, though, every fall, as the temperature drops and school begins, a familiar epidemic races across the State of Texas. The fever particularly affects small towns which garner a deep sense of hometown pride. It's called high school football, and it can grab an entire community and wring it giddy. In 1978, Brownwood was one of those towns.

◆　◆　◆

FROM BORDER TO BORDER, in every Texas football poll, Brownwood was rated number one in Class AAA the evening the Lions battled Coach Ray Overton's Cougars at Cen-Tex Stadium in front of seventy-five hundred frenzied fans. Cooper was ranked tenth in Class 4A. The Cougars had installed a jazzy new offense which was perfectly suited to their multi-talented quarterback Tracy Thomas. Thomas was quick of hand, strong of arm and fleet of foot.

The contest was expected to be a repeat of the previous year's defensive struggle. Instead, things got a bit offensive, and my undersized Lions quickly learned that trying to outscore Cooper's Cougars was comparable to challenging Betty Crocker to a bake-off. Cooper finished the game with 501 yards total offense.

Final score: Brownwood 22, Cooper 38.

(Note: This game was later forfeited by Abilene Cooper.)

Playing at DeSoto the following Friday, we allowed the Eagles to build a 21–7 lead before getting down to business. A deflected pass, which Lion tight end Kevin Taylor turned into a thirty-yard gain, keyed our turnaround. twelve plays and seventy-five yards later, Glen Coles followed a clearing block by tackle Shawn Hollingsworth and barreled into the end zone. Two minutes later, after our defense held DeSoto to a three and out, Coles gathered in the Eagles' punt on the dead run, tight-roped the sidelines and raced fifty-four yards for a touchdown.

In the second half, Brownwood scored twenty-one more unanswered points.

Final score: Brownwood 42, DeSoto 21.

Our maroon squad geared up for conference play by blitzing Round Rock 48–21, scoring an impressive win over a band of vengeful Warriors from San Angelo Lake View 34–9, then racing past Bowie's Jackrabbits 25–7.

◆　◆　◆

IN THE SPRING of 1978, the UIL moved Brownwood into District 11–AAA and divided the district into two zones. Brownwood was assigned to the North Zone along with Crowley, Stephenville, Cleburne, Everman and Granbury. On paper it seemed improbable any team could navigate the North Zone without a loss, but before the season, my players got together and dedicated themselves to winning a state championship. Winning district was the first step toward that goal, and this group of Lions didn't know the meaning of the word "quit." They simply would not be denied.

The Lions' first victim was Cleburne 31–14, then they clobbered Everman 28–6, Granbury 52–3, and Crowley 35–0.

Three days after Dallas oilman Bill Clements edged out Democrat John Hill to become the first Republican governor of Texas in more than a century, Brownwood wrapped up the North Zone title with a 35–0 victory over Stephenville.

◆　◆　◆

MARLIN WAS THE SOUTH ZONE CHAMP. With sure-handed quarterback Lamar Simpson calling the shots and slippery tailback Leon Tubbs running the football, the Bulldogs were explosive and lightning quick. The stubborn purple and gold dogs played us tough for most of the first quarter, then our maroon gang got rolling.

Utilizing the aerial darts of quarterback Scott Lancaster, which featured a spectacular 39-yard diving catch by Derwin Williams in the midst of a tangle of Bulldog defenders, Brownwood raced out to a 14–0 lead. When the Lions took the second half kickoff and breezed sixty-eight yards to go up 21–0, it appeared a mini-runaway was afoot.

Marlin quarterback Lamar Simpson had another ending in mind. First, he spearheaded a 67-yard drive which halfback Curtis Shaw capped with a 15-yard scamper. Next, Simpson moved the Bulldogs fifty-six yards, scoring on a nine-yard pass to Kenneth Jones to pull the Bulldogs within seven points.

With 2:06 left, the Bulldogs were leading in penetrations. Marlin was driving for the potential tying touchdown when Lion tackle Bill Wedeman broke through to trap Simpson for a loss on fourth down. Wedeman's sack allowed Brownwood to regain possession, and on our second play from scrimmage, Glen Coles burst through the left side and hotfooted thirty-nine yards to the Marlin two. Scott Lancaster settled matters by sneaking the ball across the goal line, and every Brownwood booster in the stadium collapsed to their seat, limp from yelling.

Final score: Brownwood 28, Marlin 14.

Playing at Baylor Stadium in Waco the next weekend, sixth-ranked Belton came prepared to roll the dice in our bi-district joust, but it was Brownwood who made the sevens. Our turbo-charged offense hammered out time-consuming touchdown drives on three of our first four possessions then relied on a tightwad maroon defense to hang on for a 20–0 victory.

Brownwood faced Crosby in the quarterfinal round. The game was played in front of twelve thousand fans at Memorial Stadium in Austin. In studying Crosby's game films we noticed a flaw in the Cougars' punting scheme. My coaches and I became convinced we could block Crosby's punts should the right situation develop, but our Lions jumped out to a 21–7 lead, and for a while, it seemed we wouldn't have much use for our discovery. Late in the fourth quarter, however, Crosby scored to close within seven points, forcing Brownwood to pull out all the stops. When our defense held the Cougars on downs with six minutes left in the game, we signaled to defensive end Kirk Chastain to go for broke. On the punt, Chastain crashed through to take Crosby kicker Tiger Blomstrom's punt full on his chest. Maroon linebacker Jeff Walker, who was right behind Chastain, scooped up the bouncing football and returned it to Crosby's fifteen. Four plays later Glen Coles slammed across from the three for the clincher.

Final score: Brownwood 28, Crosby 14.

◆　　◆　　◆

IN 1978, BROWNWOOD'S STARTING BACKFIELD included quarterback Scott Lancaster at 144 pounds, tailback Glen Coles at 155 pounds, fullback Chris Mayo at 130 pounds and wingback Derwin Williams at 155 pounds—an average of less than 147 pounds per man. Lancaster, Coles and Williams were seniors. Lancaster was one of our team captains. After the season all three would be selected to either the first or second all-state team.

Chris Mayo was also a senior, and at 130 pounds, he was the smallest fullback to ever play in a AAA championship game. Yet, Chris was the leading rusher in our title game against Gainesville. Mayo's father was Harold Mayo, a football coach at Howard Payne University. Possibly, his family background accounted for Mayo's great attitude. Chris was the first one to get suited out, the first one to finish warm-up drills, the first one to do whatever his coach wanted. Chris had no fear. He would take on a 200-pound defender—stick his face in a big lineman's gut and stay with him like a clinging vine. Despite his small physique, I never saw anyone run over Chris Mayo.

Derwin Williams was a perfect example of a kid developing late and why a coach should never give up on any player or discourage any youngster from playing football. What so many coaches don't understand is that some boys improve dramatically between their junior high years and the time they become a high school senior.

When Williams was in seventh grade, Brownwood fielded three seventh-grade teams with maybe twenty players on each team. Twelve-year-old Derwin wasn't much of an athlete. His coaches were so unimpressed that Williams never started a single game. As he moved up to the eighth- and ninth-grade squads, Derwin still didn't play much.

For sophomores and juniors, Brownwood fields two football teams. The best players participate on the JV. Players with less talent are relegated to the sophomore squad. As a tenth grader, Williams played on the sophomore team, but as the season progressed, he showed tremendous improvement. Against San Angelo in their last game of the regular season, Derwin was absolutely awesome.

At Brownwood, we initiated a policy of bringing several JV players up to the varsity during post-season playoffs. For the kids we

Derwin Williams—
two times first team all-state.
(*credit:* Brownwood Bulletin)

moved up, that was their biggest thrill of the season, and it provided a powerful incentive for the next year's JV players. I don't remember ever moving a player up from the sophomore squad before, but in November of 1976, on Coach Steve Boothe's recommendation, I brought Derwin Williams up to the varsity. It was one of the best coaching moves I ever made.

In 1977 and 1978, his junior and senior years, Derwin Williams started for the Lions on both offense and defense. He was the very first Brownwood player to be named first team all-state two years in a row.

◆　◆　◆

BAY CITY HAD BEATEN Gregory-Portland 28–27 on Friday evening to advance to the semifinal round. Their coaches and officials were in Austin on Saturday to observe our quarterfinal victory over Crosby. After the game we met to decide on home team and all the other points which have to be agreed on prior to a playoff game. As our meeting progressed, Bay City's superintendent kept leaving the room. While we coaches discussed game officials and possible playing sites, he'd leave for a few minutes and come back. I wondered about his strange behavior but assumed he was sneaking out for a quick smoke. When he left and came back a third time, a broad grin was tattooed across his face.

"Well, boys," the superintendent advised, "the dome is available!"

Bay City's superintendent figured he had pulled off a huge coup. Thinking we Brownwood coaches would leap at an opportunity to play in the Astrodome, he had been calling Houston. He was devastated when I wouldn't agree to his plan. Playing in the Astrodome would have been exciting, but Houston was an eight-hour drive from Brownwood—maybe nine hours for our band and drill team who rode on school buses. No way I intended to subject our loyal fans to that kind of ordeal. I told the superintendent we would flip him for home and home. If he wanted to play in Houston real bad, he could call the dome his home field. Warily, the superintendent inquired about the condition of Brownwood's football facility.

"To the best of my knowledge, it's the worst in Texas," I advised, telling a tiny white lie because I didn't want to flip and take a chance on playing in Houston.

Eventually, we decided to play our semifinal bash right there in the state capital at Memorial Stadium.

◆　◆　◆

THE UNDEFEATED BLACK CATS had size and speed at every position, and they specialized in big plays. Running backs, Gerry Flannel and Billy Booker, and alternate quarterback Greg Williams were their home run threats. For passing, the Royal and Gold relied on quarterback Barry Bell and ends, Wilson Gee and Robert Franklin. Prior to the game, Bay City was touted by many sportswriters as an equal to the '77 Dickinson club which beat Brownwood 40–28. Nevertheless, maroon faithful remained optimistic. Besides being the home of the Longhorns, Memorial Stadium was a favorite haunt for the Brownwood Lions. Three state trophies had been won there on previous visits.

Because of cold, miserable weather, only six thousand die-hard fans witnessed what I believe to be the greatest comeback in

Brownwood history. For darn sure it was the most exciting and unexpected.

Bay City received the opening kickoff and fumbled on the second play from scrimmage. Brownwood recovered and scored in eight plays, with Glen Coles snaking through for the final three yards. Our PAT went awry, making the score 6–0.

Brownwood held the lead for exactly fifty-five seconds. Bay City took our kickoff and marched seventy-three yards for a TD. Most of the damage was done by Cat running back Billy Booker who gained sixty-two yards on one dash then scored from the eight on the next play. Barry Bell missed on the extra point attempt, and the game was deadlocked at 6–6.

Brownwood bounced right back with the longest drive of the night, a 12-play, 83-yarder which featured the hard-nosed running of Coles and Mayo and the exceptional passing skills of Scott Lancaster. A 25-yard scoring strike to glue-fingered Derwin Williams put icing on our cake, but when we tried for two bonus points, we came up short.

The score remained at 12–6 until Bay City's Greg Williams picked off a tipped pass in the second period. Williams' interception launched a 37-yard Royal and Gold thrust for the go-ahead score. Bell's extra point attempt was good, and Bay City had the lead 13–12.

Later in the first half, Lion kicking specialist Mark Boyd got off a boomer to pin the Black Cats deep in their end of the field. Calling time-outs after every play to conserve the clock, Brownwood's defense stopped Bay City's running game cold, and the Cats were forced to punt.

During the week prior to our match with Bay City, our team had worked on a defense specifically designed to block punts. This was the opportunity we'd hoped for, and our scheme worked to perfection. Glen Coles, who was playing linebacker, leaped high over the head of Bay City fullback Billy Booker to get a hand on the kicked ball. Lion Greg Perkins recovered at the thirty, and with time running out, Scott Lancaster banged in a field goal on the last play of the half.

Midway through the third quarter, Mark Boyd nailed another long punt, forcing Bay City to take possession deep in their own territory again. Our defense blunted the Cats on three straight tries, and Bay City was obliged to punt with their backs to the wall one more time.

In our game film review, my coaches and I had noticed that Bay City center Jim Humphries always lifted the ball and moved it forward before he snapped it to his punter. We decided we could use this knowledge to our advantage, so on every punting situation, we stationed 210-pound noseguard Dan Daniell directly in front of Humphries. Daniell was to keep his fist on the ground in front of the football and give it a quick, backhanded knuckle-punch the instant the ball was moved. Our plan worked like a charm. Bay City's center sent the ball sailing over the punter's head, and it rolled through the end zone for a safety, increasing Brownwood's lead to 17–13.

Early in the fourth period, Bay City's offense got untracked, pushing eighty yards for their third touchdown. A successful two-point conversion made the score 21–17.

◆　◆　◆

BROWNWOOD'S QUARTERBACK Scott Lancaster wore jersey number *15*. Scott was thin and frail-looking. Standing only five-foot-eleven-inches beneath thick locks of sandy blond hair, he resembled a choir boy more than a football player. I once told a reporter, "If someone was out to shoot football players, Scott Lancaster wouldn't even be on their list."

Scott had a high, squeaky voice. If a person didn't know the slightly built young man real well, they would never guess he possessed a competitive heart and a poise way beyond his years. Lancaster wasn't the gung ho type. It was his cool confidence that cemented and motivated his team.

After Bay City scored their touchdown to pull ahead, Scott came to me and advised me not to worry. He assured me Brownwood

Scott Lancaster—quarterbacked 1978 state champions; 2nd team all-state. (credit: Brownwood Bulletin)

could score again, but when my quarterback re-entered the game, he ran an unusual quarterback keeper play and fumbled the football. Bay City recovered and immediately scored to go ahead 28–17.

Two members of the Bay City coaching staff that afternoon were ex-Howard Payne basketball players. At the time, they were employed as basketball coaches at Bay City High. The two Howard Payne exes were in the stadium press box feeding information to Black Cat football coaches when Bay City's head coach Ron Mills called up and told his coaches to wrap things up and come down to the sideline. Coach Mills said he wanted all the Bay City coaches on the field to shake hands with Coach Wood and Coach Southall—to congratulate us for a fine game.

"We'd better wait awhile," Eddie Nelson told the head coach. Eddie was the Howard Payne graduate who related this story to me. "I've watched Brownwood for a lot of years, and they never give up."

Coach Mills answered Eddie gruffly, "I said come on down! We're all going to line up in the center of the field and make Coach Wood and Coach Southall shake our hands and congratulate us!"

◆　◆　◆

WITH SEVEN MINUTES and seventeen seconds left on the clock, Scott Lancaster may have been the only person on Brownwood's side who was still confident. Before he went back in the game, Scott coolly informed me we would score twice and win. That's when the heart-stopping comeback began.

Lancaster engineered a 12-play, 74-yard drive, using a 23-yard, fourth and eighteen pass to Lion end Kevin Taylor to finish the job. A two-yard pass to Gerald James was good for the two-point conversion, and the gap was narrowed to 28–25.

Now our fate lay in the hands of Brownwood's defense, and my Gorillas were up to the task. Lion defenders dug in and forced another Bay City punt. Black Cat center Jim Humphries, who had been harassed all night by Dan Daniell, literally rolled the snap back to his punter Cliff Mullen. Mullen was under such severe pressure, he was fortunate to get off an eleven-yard shank which Kevin Taylor returned to Bay City's twenty-two.

My quarterback had promised me two scores, and he delivered with twenty-six seconds to spare. A seven-yard run by Chris Mayo and a sneak by Lancaster worked the ball to the eleven. Three plays later, Glen Coles scored on a two-yard stab. A circus-like catch by Coles tacked on another two when we went for the bonus points.

While our football team was locked in the do-or-die battle at Austin, Brownwood assistant coaches Wayne Rathke, Bob Agnew, Fred Gamble and Ronnie Fowlkes were in Wichita Falls scouting the Lubbock Estacado-Gainesville game. They were listening on the radio when Bay City went ahead of Brownwood 28–17. The Bay City scouts who were sharing the Wichita press facility began to razz our guys. In between the whooping, hollering and bragging, they even asked our coaches for their scouting notes.

That's about the time legendary ex-Wichita Falls coach Joe Golding stuck his head through the press box door. "You Brownwood fellows better keep a scouting and a writing," Golding told our coaches. "Ol' Babe has scored. He has the football, and he's on the move again."

Bay City mounted a furious last ditch attack after our kickoff, but their comeback died in the arms of Lion defender Billy Sawyer who intercepted a Barry Bell bomb with five seconds left. Every person in the stadium was totally exhausted when the final second ticked off the scoreboard clock.

Final score: Brownwood 33, Bay City 28.

At a Brownwood Chamber of Commerce luncheon the next week, I was invited to brief the board of directors on the current status of Lion football. President O.C. "Putter" Jarvis jokingly introduced me as, "a man who does a lot for football in Brownwood, but very little for the mental health of the community."

◆ ◆ ◆

OVER THE YEARS, Gainesville coach Jim Thomason and I had become good friends. We coached the 1977 Texas Oil Bowl all-stars together. The previous spring Thomason had invited me to speak at Gainesville's sports banquet. Thomason was an assistant coach at Dumas before he accepted his head coaching position at Gainesville High. Jim had done a fantastic job at Gainesville, winning eighty while losing only forty and tying two. Since 1974, Coach Thomason's football teams had made it to the state finals three times.

On Saturday, December 23, 1978, there was a two-hour lapse in our friendship. Thomason's Leopards were 13–1 when they clashed with my Lions at Irving's Texas Stadium before an audience of 13,446. At the time, it was the largest crowd to ever watch a AAA game.

Despite all the media hoopla, compared to our Bay City contest, the title game was almost anti-climactic. Our Maroons exploded for twenty-one points in the first half while our under-rated and undersized defense held the Leopards scoreless. Glen Coles scored the first two Lion touchdowns—one on a four-yard burst, the other on a 62-yard punt return. A 57-yard flea-flicker pass and run play, with Lancaster and Billy Sawyer teaming up, accounted for our third tally.

The second half belonged to Gainesville's offense, but a deter-mined maroon defense led by Glen West, Dan Daniell, Bill Wedeman, Greg Perkins and Craig Clements fought and scratched the Leopards for every inch gained. Gainesville fullback Charles Jackson scored with 1:08 left in the final stanza to make the score 21–12, but it was too little, too late. Billy Sawyer and Lupe Barrera eliminated all hope for the Red and White by breaking up Leopard quarterback Jeff Brown's pass for the two-point conversion.

Final score: Brownwood 21, Gainesville 12.

Brownwood's cast of heroes that Saturday afternoon would rival a John Wayne film festival. Our front line, which included Kevin Taylor, Craig Agnew, Todd Hewitt, Dan Spence, Chris Ellett and Shawn Hollingsworth, was nothing less than magnificent. On defense, Glen West, Bill Wedeman, Greg Perkins, Craig Clements, Kirk Chastain, Derwin Williams and Jeff Walker were absolutely superb. Billy Sawyer's classy, over-the-shoulder interception in the fourth quarter may have been the most vital play of the day. Mark Boyd's long punts, highlighted by a 51-yarder with 3:32 left, guar-anteed the Leopards always had plenty of artificial turf between them and the Brownwood goal line when they took possession.

Little Chris Mayo was the game's leading rusher with 64 yards on 19 carries, but during the game, Glen Coles became Brownwood's all time leading rusher with 1,494 yards. Coles lugged the ball 57 yards to eclipse the school record set by Gary Barron when Brownwood made its 1970 title run. Scott Lancaster completed 95 of 177 passes for 1,723 yards and 24 touchdowns to become Brownwood's second leading passer behind Jimmy Carmichael.

◆ ◆ ◆

ACCEDING TO A TRADITION established by previous Lion state champs, every coach, every school official, and every reporter who entered our dressing room received a victory baptism after the game. In spite of our differences, Brownwood school superintendent Howard Murchison was there to join in the happy celebration. As he emerged fully clothed and dripping wet from the showers, the superintendent surveyed our whooping tribe of young Lions and summed up the locker room situation.

"Absolute chaos," Murchison observed grimly, but a satisfied smile adorned his water-splashed face.

When things calmed down, Chris Mayo ambled over to speak to me. He had a sly grin on his face.

"Coach Wood, come over here. I want to show you something," Mayo said. We were using the Dallas Cowboys' dressing quarters. Chris walked across the room and stepped on the scales the Cowboys use. The scales showed Chris weighing only 128 pounds.

"There must be something wrong with these scales, Chris," I said. "Surely you weigh more than that." At Brownwood, we weighed our players at the beginning of the season and at mid-season. Both times Mayo had tipped the scales at more than 135 pounds.

"No sir. They're right on the money, Coach Wood. I've never weighed more than 130 pounds. Don't you remember when you weighed me in at Brownwood? I was wearing shorts with big pockets and a shirt that came down to my knees. I had my pockets filled with weights. I didn't want you to think I was too small to play."

CHAPTER EIGHTEEN

Two Decades of Winning
(1979–1981)

FOR MOST OF THE COUNTRY, 1979 was a year to forget. In March, a malfunction at the Three Mile Island nuclear plant near Harrisburg, Pennsylvania, scared the daylights out of every American citizen and prompted hundreds of protest demonstrations against building nuclear power plants. A movie, *The China Syndrome*, which depicted the shutdown of an unsafe nuclear reactor and starred Jack Lemmon, Jane Fonda and Michael Douglas, fanned the flames of unrest.

In April, the state's deadliest tornado ever struck Wichita Falls, killing forty-two, injuring seventeen hundred and forty and causing four hundred million dollars in property damage.

In July, Chrysler Corporation, the third largest U.S. automobile maker, admitted it was losing the battle with foreign competition and requested a one-billion-dollar loan from the federal government to prevent the company from going bankrupt.

In November, the unthinkable occurred. Iranian militants stormed the United States embassy in Tehran, seizing ninety hostages, including sixty-five Americans. The hostage crisis would last until January, 1981. Before the hostages were released, the whole world would suffer an oil shortage and our nation's status as a world leader would be greatly diminished.

For me, though, 1979 is a very special chapter in my book of memories. In February, the National High School Athletic Coaches Association named me High School Football Coach of the Year—an honor no other Texas coach had ever received. At their annual banquet held in June at Orlando, Florida, I received a plaque and a ruby-accented ring to commemorate the occasion.

For Coach Southall and me, that year was also extra special for another reason. It was a kind of milestone. It marked the beginning of our twentieth year of coaching the Lions. During almost two decades at Brownwood High, our football teams had won one hundred and ninety-four games, won or shared fourteen district titles, and captured six state championships. Other sports also fared well during our tenure. Our track team, which Kenneth West coached, had won more championships than the rest of our district combined, and no other school in our district had won more titles in either basketball or golf. Yes, Brownwood had a good run during our nineteen years of directing the show, and we sure weren't finished—not by a long shot.

1979

AS HAD BECOME OUR CUSTOM, we opened the '79 season by playing Cooper's Cougars at Abilene's Shotwell Stadium. Abilene Cooper was ranked number one in Class 4A. Sports gurus all across the state were warning Cooper opponents that this was the best Cougar club since Jack Mildren led Big Blue to the state finals in 1967. They'd get no argument from Brownwood players. The Cougars were every bit as good as the sportswriters suggested. Cougar quarterback Lanny Dycus piloted his team to four touchdowns in the first half. Two of Cooper's first half tallies were on short blasts by 225-pound fullback Terry Orr. Backup quarterback John Slaughter added another TD in the top of the third and two more early in the fourth.

Final score: Brownwood 14, Cooper 50.

Brownwood was also a pre-season favorite—picked number one in Class 3A by the Associated Press. The next weekend we invited DeSoto to play at Cen-Tex Stadium, and my Lions proved to five thousand fans the pollsters weren't wrong.

Lion Kirk Chastain intercepted an Eagle pass on the second snap of the game and ran it back for a touchdown, and whoosh, our Maroons were off and running.

My gorilla defense, led by Glen West, Greg Perkins, Wade Cottrell, Billy Taylor, Craig Clements, Denny Morris, Tony Wilde, and Chastain, harried and sacked three different Eagle quarterbacks as Brownwood blasted the Eagles 34–7.

Gaining momentum, we journeyed to Round Rock where,

despite eight penalties which cost us a hundred and eleven yards, Lion quarterback Kevin Smith was able to squeeze out four touch-downs—one in each quarter. Again, our defensive players were the heroes, tackling Dragon field general Von Breaux and two other quarterbacks behind the line of scrimmage five times, as we crushed Round Rock 29–0.

San Angelo proved to be much tougher than expected when we returned to Cen-Tex Stadium for what had become an annual knock-down, drag-out affair with the Lake View Chiefs. From start to finish the hard-charging blue and white warriors kept Lion QB Kevin Smith on the run and our passing attack bottled up. Brownwood's sledgehammer tailback Lupe Barrera carried the football 27 times for 104 yards, but it was a 28-yard field goal by Chief Derrick Rushing with 1:07 left in the first half that made the difference. Lake View edged Brownwood 3–0.

After our Maroons sailed past Bowie 27–0, we opened the District 11–AAA North Zone chute. The Lions came out strong, romping and stomping as they kicked Cleburne 35–0 and knocked off Everman 33–6. Brownwood High's win over Coach Lay Law's purple and gold Bulldogs was the two hundredth for Coach Southall and myself as BHS coaches.

Wading deeper into conference play, Brownwood sunk Granbury's Pirates 21–0, grounded Crowley's Eagles 28–7, then sacked up the North Zone title by hanging a 38–0 hickey on Stephenville.

◆　◆　◆

WACO'S CONNALLY HIGH was the 11–AAA South Zone champ. When Connally officials balked at flipping for home and home, we agreed to settle matters at Tarleton's Memorial Stadium in Stephenville. The underrated Cadets proved to be a hard night's work for our Lions.

For almost three quarters neither team was able to cross the other's goal line. A 33-yard field goal by Lion Mike Thomas and a twenty-yard three-pointer by Cadet Alan Griffin were the only scores. It was an over-the-shoulder interception by Lion Billy Sawyer that provided the momentum for victory.

Brownwood's scoring drive took ten downs, and we picked up an all-important penetration along the way. The clutch play came on third and thirteen when Kevin Smith passed to Kirk Chastain for seventeen at the Cadet five. From there, James Fikes ran for two, and after offsetting penalties erased another Fikes' gainer, Waco was flagged again for jumping offside. With the ball on the two, Chastain blasted through a crack at right guard for the TD. With ten minutes left, Mike Thomas tacked on the PAT, and although the Cadets mounted a furious last-minute comeback, our hard-headed Lions successfully defended the fort until the final second ticked away.

Final score: Brownwood 10, Waco Connally 3.

◆　◆　◆

BROWNWOOD WON STATE CHAMPIONSHIPS in 1960, 1965, 1967, 1969, 1970 and 1978. Most of the years in between, our football team was in the playoffs. Possibly the only negative aspect of producing so many winning football teams and participating in state playoff games, which extend past Thanksgiving into late December, is every weekend half the city's population is out of town. This puts a tremendous strain on local merchants who depend heavily on Christmas sales for their livelihood.

Many of our local merchants reached deep in their pockets to help us build the new football stadium, which was completed in 1972. J.R. Beadel, who owned twenty-one stores, two of which were in Brownwood, was one of our first and most generous contributors. After Brownwood beat Stephenville to capture the district championship, Mr. Beadel called me to complain.

"Coach Wood, you promised us if we'd build a new stadium, you'd hold all your playoff games here in Brownwood."

Actually, I hadn't made that promise. No way I could. The teams we met in the playoffs were just as anxious to play at home as we were, but most 3A stadiums were way too small to accommodate a playoff crowd. Even our brand-new stadium seated only eight thousand. Most playoff games were played at a neutral site with more seating capacity. To play at home often meant both schools received less from gate receipts and concessions.

J.R. was an elderly gentleman, but he had a mind like a steel trap. I wasn't sure whether he was serious or not, but I went to his office to visit with him anyway. A few days later, he set up a meeting with several other merchants. I told them my coaches and I would do everything possible to maintain the stadium and keep it in good condition. I also explained how playoff teams decide where to play their games and promised we would play in Brownwood on every possible occasion. My explanation seemed to satisfy the merchants.

When I discovered our bi-district opponent would be Austin's Westlake High, my conversation with Mr. Beadel and the other merchants was fresh on my mind. Austin was a two and a half hour drive from Brownwood, with no logical place to play in between. Although Brownwood had been suffering a terrible streak of bad luck when it came to guessing coin flips, I decided to insist on a home and home coin toss, and I won.

Our bi-district battle with Austin Westlake's Chaparrals was played at Brownwood's Cen-Tex Stadium. My team definitely needed the home field advantage. We also needed the talented toe of Mike Thomas, a magnificent performance by our defensive troops, and all the luck we could muster to eke out a 10–6 win.

◆　◆　◆

BEAUMONT HEBERT HIGH was our quarterfinal opponent. We didn't know much about the South Texas team except they had beaten highly-ranked Huntsville in bi-district, and they were supposed to be extremely fast. Our Maroons squared off against the Panthers on the familiar turf of Austin's Memorial Stadium.

Brownwood was leading 11–8 early in the third quarter, with possession of the football on Hebert's fifteen and threatening to increase the lead, when the roof caved in. On third down, Hebert safety Gerald Broussard stepped in front of a Tim Oehrlein pass at the two and raced ninety-eight yards for a touchdown.

Up until that point, the Lions had dominated the contest. When the game ended, Brownwood's defense had limited Beaumont to six first downs and 110 yards total offense.

Maroon defenders Glen West, Tony Wilde, Kirk Chastain, Craig Clements, Billy Taylor, Greg Perkins, Wade Cottrell, Kevin Smith, Greg Williams, Jack Lyle, and Billy Sawyer played the best game of their lives that day. For several seasons afterwards, Brownwood coaches used the Hebert game film to show upcoming Lions how great defense should be played.

Nonetheless, Broussard's interception ended our dream of a seventh state championship.

Final score: Brownwood 11, Hebert 15.

The following weekend, the Panthers lost 7–0 to Bay City in the semifinals.

1980

LIKE MOST OTHER YEARS, 1980 began with a lot of bowl games and plenty of sports. In the Sugar Bowl, Coach Paul Bryant's Alabama team beat Arkansas and was voted national champion. In late January, the Pittsburgh Steelers won their fourth Super Bowl in six years with a 31–29 victory over the Los Angeles Rams. In February, the United States hosted the Winter Olympic Games at Lake Placid, New York, and for two weeks, half the television sets in America were tuned to ABC. In March, Louisville defeated UCLA 59–54 to win their first NCAA basketball crown.

Sports were big that spring, but at the Palace Drug Store in Brownwood, the predominate topic of conversation was inflation, which had soared to more than twelve percent. About half the coffee drinkers blamed the Japanese who were buying up U.S. companies left and right. The other half blamed the Iranians who were still holding fifty-three American diplomats hostage. Almost everyone blamed President Jimmy Carter for the gas shortage, the high inflation, the outrageous interest rates, the Russian invasion of Afghanistan—the whole stinking mess.

When August rolled around, we Brownwood coaches were excited about the upcoming season, as usual. Our squad was heavy with talent. On offense, we had guys like quarterback Tim Oehrlein; running backs, Aundrey Henderson and Gene Gibson; wingback, Bill Donahoo; ends, Marcus Spearman and Jesse Smith; tackles, Frank Brister and Ronald Hickman; guards, Barry Steele and David Carroll; and center, Justin Stevens.

On defense, linebackers, Tony Wilde and Carl Burr; linemen, Mike Kinsey, Billy Taylor, Mike Davis, Jewell Brown, Denny Morris and Pat Mooney; and defensive backs, Greg Williams, Mark Campbell and Marvin Rathke reinforced our optimistic outlook.

To the dismay of maroon faithful, our season got off to a frustrating start. First, we suffered a tough-to-swallow 13–12 opening loss to Abilene Cooper. Brownwood was leading 12–6 with 6:40 left in the game when the Cougars began a 69-yard march toward our goal line. Cooper tied the score and kicked the game-winning extra point with only fifty-eight seconds remaining.

Next, we lost at home to arch-rival Breckenridge 21–7. The Bucks were no longer in our district, so the loss had no effect on our playoff hopes. Nevertheless, despite all the wins and all the success Brownwood's football program enjoyed during the sixties and seventies, Lion fans still remembered those embarrassing years of continuously losing to Breckenridge. Even today, Brownwood fans loathe the idea of losing to Breckenridge.

Reeling from back-to-back losses, our Maroons finally tasted victory in the third game of the season. Led by running backs Aundrey Henderson, Robert Garcia, Gene Gibson and Andy Atkins, and quarterback Tim Oehrlein, who passed for one hundred and fifty yards, Brownwood smothered San Angelo Central 37–6.

Our roller coaster non-conference schedule continued as Weatherford battled us to a 0–0 tie. Brownwood finally evened its season record at 2–2–1 when we plastered Azle's Hornets 41–7, but this was still the Lions' worst start since 1972.

◆ ◆ ◆

ACCORDING TO CALVIN FRYAR, it was a telephone call from Lawrence Elkins that triggered the stadium committee's decision to change the name of Cen-Tex Stadium. Elkins was a member of Brownwood's 1960 State Championship football team. Lawrence and his teammates were planning a reunion to celebrate the twentieth anniversary of winning that title.

On Saturday night, the evening after Brownwood opened 4–AAAA conference play with a 31–6 win over Crowley, Morris and Lorene Southall accompanied Katharine and me to the players' reunion held at Brownwood's Travelers Steak House. The 1960 Lions were now in their late thirties. Most of the men were married. Some even had kids in college.

It was a fun evening—an opportunity to reminisce, to renew long time friendships and retell old war stories. Morris, Lorene, Katharine and I sat at the head table, thoroughly enjoying ourselves while one former Lion after another paraded to the podium to offer light-hearted quips and poke fun at us. Morris and I had been on the griddle for almost an hour when Calvin Fryar strolled to the front of the room, took a position behind the microphone, and upstaged every speaker who had gone before.

Back in the fifties, Calvin was a star basketball player at BHS.

During his term as president of Brownwood's Chamber of Commerce, Calvin played a vital role in the construction of the new football stadium. Now, he was serving as president of the steering committee which managed the stadium.

"So many coaches are honored after they retire," Calvin told the audience of football players and wives, "but we felt it absolutely right that we salute Gordon Wood while he is active, because of his contributions to the community, as well as his ability to build character in our children. As of tonight, Cen-Tex Stadium will be called Gordon Wood Stadium. There's no doubt that Gordon Wood is the best football coach in the nation. His record proves it."

Fryar's unexpected announcement was greeted by a standing ovation. When the clapping died down, I climbed to my feet, stunned and overwhelmed. I brushed back tears forming in my eyes and tried to think of a way to express my gratitude. My voice quivered as I said, "Through the efforts of Coach Southall and the other coaches, you players and so many others, I've been able to win just about every award possible. But this is the greatest honor of all."

At the time I meant what I said. But now, recalling the contributions, the teamwork, the community effort it took to build that amazing football facility, I realize my words of appreciation were a miserable understatement. No award, no honor, no victory even comes close to meaning so much to me. To think my friends would name that great stadium after me fills my heart with indescribable pride.

◆　◆　◆

THE UNIVERSITY INTERSCHOLASTIC LEAGUE ushered in the eighties with a number of sweeping rule changes which affected more than eleven hundred and fifty Texas schools. Initially, the biggest change was a revamping of the class numbering system. Every classification was moved up an "A." Class 4A became Class 5A and so-on, with Class B eliminated. When the dust settled, there were still five major classifications, ranging from 5A for the largest high schools to 1A for the smallest.

Brownwood moved from Class 3A to Class 4A. Our district designation was changed from 11–AAA to 4–AAAA with six high schools competing—Cleburne, Crowley, Everman, Granbury, Stephenville, and Brownwood. Happily, there was no South Zone and no North Zone. Schools which won district championships would advance directly to a bi-district bout.

◆　◆　◆

BY MID-OCTOBER, Jimmy Carter and Ronald Reagan were locked in a neck-and-neck race for the presidency. Pollsters and oddsmakers claimed the heated contest was too close to call. As the two candidates stormed across the country with their last ditch campaign drives, my maroon crew began a campaign of their own— a campaign which would take Brownwood to the state playoffs for the fifth consecutive year.

On Friday, October 17, we began our crusade, traveling to Everman to wallop the unbeaten Bulldogs 32–0.

Seven days later my maroon comrades and I played our very first game at Gordon Wood Stadium. With a season record of 7–1 and no district losses, Stephenville was very much in the hunt for the District 4–AAAA title, and for three harum-scarum quarters, it appeared our football team might anoint the newly named facility with a loss. Then on the first play of the fourth quarter, with the score knotted at 7–7, Aundrey Henderson burst through a huge hole and ran fifteen yards for the tiebreaker. Henderson's TD jaunt seemed to deflate the pesky Yellowjackets. Before the game ended, my explosive Lions scored three more times.

Final score: Brownwood 34, Stephenville 7.

With heavyweights Everman and Stephenville out of the way, Brownwood only needed one more district victory to reach the playoffs. My Lions weren't satisfied with just making the playoffs. They insisted on roaring into the playoffs, tacking a 21–7 loss on lowly Cleburne and whipping up on Granbury 33–8.

◆　◆　◆

LONG TIME ADVERSARY and 3–AAAA champion Wichita Falls Hirschi was our bi-district foe. At our meeting in Brecken-ridge to decide playoff questions, we agreed to use Abilene's Shotwell Stadium as the setting for our shootout. Hirschi put on a rousing defensive show early in the game. Then a seventy-yard punt return by Greg Williams primed our maroon scoring machine. On Brownwood's next possession, Tim Oehrlein orchestrated a picture-perfect 71-yard touchdown march.

After the kickoff, Wichita shoved out to Brownwood's forty-five where our mule-stubborn defense set up a picket line and refused to yield. On fourth down, the Huskies gambled and failed to make a first down. That's when Oehrlein, who had been nursing a pinched nerve in his neck, slammed the door shut.

In six plays Tim took his team fifty-five yards, commencing the drive with a nineteen-yard pass to tight end Jesse Smith. Then, with time running out and no Brownwood time-outs left, Oehrlein arched a long bomb to wingback Bill Donahoo. Donahoo leaped over a Huskie defender, grabbed the football and fell to the ground at the two. Seconds later, Donahoo completed the mission by spearing a sideline bullet, barely touching down one foot before he ran out of bounds.

With a 20–0 halftime lead, our defense took over, and the outcome was never in doubt. Brownwood was leading 27–0 when I jerked the regulars and sent in our reserves to finish the game.

Final score: Brownwood 27, Hirschi 7.

◆　◆　◆

LUBBOCK ESTACADO came into our playoff game with a reputation as a big-play team. The mighty Matadors, who were now under the direction of Coach Louis Kelley, had eliminated state-ranked, unbeaten Andrews with two, late-in-the-game, come-from-behind touchdowns on Andrews' home field the previous weekend.

Our quarterfinal skirmish took place at the Mustang Bowl in Sweetwater, and for forty-eight minutes Brownwood's savage maroon defense totally dominated while our offense charged up and down the field. Brownwood had possession for fifty-four plays while Estacado was limited to only sixteen. The Lions racked up two hundred and forty-five total yards of offense compared to fifty-seven yards for the Mats. Brownwood made seventeen first downs. Lubbock recorded only four. Sound one-sided? It was. Lubbock scored two touchdowns. Brownwood never crossed Estacado's goal line.

With 3:06 left in the first half, the Mats' Kenneth Cade gathered in a Jimmy Morris punt at Lubbock's nine-yard line and snaked his way ninety-one yards for a TD. If that wasn't an indication of the bad luck in store for Brownwood, the conversion try was. The Mats lined up for a one-point kick, but they botched the snap. Mat quarterback Jerry Gray picked up the football, scrambled out of traffic and passed to Kelley McBride. Estacado wound up with two points instead of one.

Brownwood's final undoing came late in the third stanza when we fumbled at our own fifteen, and the Mats recovered. On their first play, Gray rolled out and ran in for the touchdown. Lion Mike Kinsey blocked the extra point, but the damage was done.

Final score: Brownwood 0, Estacado 14.

In the state semifinals the next weekend, the Matadors lost to Paris.

1981

SEVERAL WEEKS AFTER Ronald Reagan took the oath of office to become our fortieth president, Chuck Curtis took the head coaching post at Cleburne High School. Since his playing days at TCU, where he quarterbacked the Horned Frogs to a dramatic 28–27 victory over Syracuse in the 1957 Cotton Bowl, Coach Curtis had enjoyed an exceptional coaching career. In 1962, Chuck enhanced his winning reputation by guiding Jacksboro to the Class AA state title. Then he moved to Garland where he added two more state championships to his resume, becoming one of only four Texas high school coaches to win three consecutive state crowns.

Coach Curtis left the high school ranks to work as an offensive coordinator on SMU's coaching staff in 1965 and 1966. Although he did coach one year at Grand Prairie High in 1969, Chuck was essentially out of coaching from 1967 until 1979. In 1979, he returned to Jacksboro, the school where his coaching success began. In 1979 and 1980, he directed the Tigers to 4–6 and 7–2–2 seasons.

When Curtis accepted the Cleburne job, the announcement made headlines all across the country. Chuck Curtis was a fierce competitor. Very few Texas coaches commanded his national recognition or his winning reputation. Cleburne's hiring of Coach Curtis served notice on the rest of the conference. The Yellowjackets were tired of playing the role of doormat for District 4–AAAA. Cleburne was raising the bar of competition.

Of course, for any team to succeed in District 4–AAAA, they had to beat Brownwood. For the next three years, the heated rivalry between Cleburne and Brownwood would be the most talked about feud in the state. There would be no love lost between Chuck

Curtis and Gordon Wood. From the very first git-go we went after it tooth and nail.

◆　◆　◆

DURING THE SUMMER MONTHS I sometimes drank coffee with a group of businessmen and football fans at the Holiday Inn. One morning in mid-July, while our group was leaving the restaurant, Oneale Tabor and her husband Joe approached me. I knew Mrs. Tabor. She worked for the Brownwood I.S.D.

The Tabors told me they were concerned about their son's education. They lived in Blanket which is a small community ten miles east of Brownwood. Oneale and Joe were thinking about moving to Brownwood so their son Tyler could attend Brownwood High. Tyler wanted to go to college. The Tabors thought he'd be better prepared if he graduated from Brownwood High. Joe Tabor told me his son was a fairly good quarterback and wanted to know if I would give him a chance to play.

Brownwood already had two excellent quarterbacks on board, Jimmy Morris and Marvin Rathke. Morris and Rathke were both exceptional athletes, and they were familiar with our offense. I honestly couldn't see any way a new kid could come in and get much playing time.

"I suppose he can come out for the team, if that's what you want. I don't think he'll be able to play at quarterback. In fact, I doubt if he'll be able to start at any position. We're pretty solid this year," I told the Tabors.

Boy, was I wrong. Tyler Tabor turned out to be one of the best athletes who ever played for me.

In a pre-season scrimmage with Pat Culpepper's Midland High Bulldogs, Tabor showed me he had the ability to start at any number of positions. One play that particularly impressed me occurred late in the scrimmage game. Midland had a six-foot-eight end named Sloan, and he could really run. Sloan ran a down and out route. When Midland's quarterback lofted a long, high pass, the tall Bulldog end was wide open. He looked like he was on his way to a sure touchdown. Suddenly, Tyler Tabor came from out of nowhere, jumped real high and grabbed the football right out of the big end's hands. Tabor's slick maneuver was one of the greatest defensive plays I've ever seen. Right then and there, I knew Tyler would have no problem finding playing time on my team.

During the Midland scrimmage, we gave each of our three quarterbacks a chance to show their skill. Jimmy Morris performed admirably. Marvin Rathke played well, and despite his late start, Tabor also looked very good. However, after we reviewed the scrimmage film, my coaches and I decided to make Jimmy Morris our starting quarterback. Tabor would start at defensive safety. I called Tyler to my office to tell him of our decision. Here's what Tyler said:

"That's fine, Coach Wood. You gave me a fair chance. That's all I can ask for."

When I called Jimmy Morris to my office to inform him he had won the starting quarterback position, he wasn't exactly enthusiastic. Here's what he said:

"You know, Coach Wood. When I get in a tight spot, I tell myself, 'I'm not going to make a mistake. I'm not going to make a mistake.' Then sure enough, I make a mistake. Pressure doesn't seem to affect Tyler that way."

That afternoon as Coach Southall and I drove downtown to broadcast our daily radio show, I told Morris we had probably made a mistake. We had always judged our quarterbacks by their poise and confidence. Now, here we were with a kid who had all the poise and confidence in the world, and we were moving him to defense. And we were making a starter out of one who had very little poise or confidence.

We were still struggling with our decision when we played Abilene Cooper. In that game Tyler looked great. He moved the team on two long drives for two touchdowns. Jimmy Morris also played well in that game.

Little did we know that before the season was finished we would depend on junior Marvin Rathke, our third-string quarterback, to lead Brownwood to its seventh state championship.

◆　◆　◆

EARLY ON, COACHES SOUTHALL, West and I suspected 1981 might be a banner year. Our club was overloaded with talent at every position. Our offense line, which included ends, Jesse Smith and Kyle Story; tackles, Ronald Hickman and Russell

Sheffield; guards, Doug Wynn and Gordon Lee; and center, Bryan Driskill, averaged more than 200 pounds. Our lightning fast ball-carriers, Aundrey Henderson and Gene Gibson, were both returning starters. With sure-handed, hard blocking Chris Ellis at wingback and muscular sling-shot Tyler Tabor at quarterback, our backfield was the heaviest Brownwood had fielded since Morris and I took over in 1960.

Our defense also looked great—big and boot-tough. Jewell Brown and Mike Davis played the end positions. Mike Kinsey, Mike Watkins and Ronald Isom anchored the interior with line-backers, Kevin Howard, Kendal Nelson, and Scott Haynes, backing them up. Our secondary included head-hunting speedsters like Darrell Heald, Marvin Rathke and Jimmy Morris.

Brownwood's regular season kicked off in Abilene, and for the second consecutive season, we lost by one point. The game's final seconds were not for the faint of heart. Cooper scored on a 46-yard pass play with forty-one seconds left to snap a 7–7 tie and kicked the extra point to go up 14–7.

Stunned but not intimidated, Brownwood roared back, capitalizing on a fifty-yard kickoff return by Darrell Heald. On second down at the Cougar forty-one, Tyler Tabor rolled right, scrambled out of a jam and fired a long pass to Lion wingback Chris Ellis. Ellis fought off Cougar defender Roy Flores and raced in for the touchdown.

Every fan in the stadium was on his feet when, instead of kicking the PAT and settling for a tie, we went for two. To Brownwood boosters' dismay, almost certain victory turned into another disappointing defeat when Tyler Tabor was stopped a foot shy of the Cougars' goal line.

Final score: Brownwood 13, Cooper 14.

After the game a couple of sportswriters stopped me outside our dressing quarters and questioned my decision to go for two.

"Going for a tie in this game makes no sense whatsoever," I told the reporters. "I don't think anyone came here to see a tie."

◆　◆　◆

OVER THE LABOR DAY WEEKEND the installation of a brand-new scoreboard at Gordon Wood Stadium was completed. Donated by Brownwood's Nathan's Jewelers, the scoreboard was one of the biggest and most technically advanced in the state. It was even equipped with a timing devise for track meets. A few days after the scoreboard was ready, Brownwood played host to Breckenridge, and our Maroons lit it up like a Christmas tree. Avenging our 1980 upset loss, Brownwood mauled the Greenies 42–8.

Cranking up for conference play, we took on San Angelo Central. Brownwood scored with seventy seconds left in the game to win a 15–10 thriller over the Bobcats.

In our Weatherford game the next weekend, Brownwood was trailing 17–13 late in the fourth when Tyler Tabor backpedaled and fired a rocket to split end Kyle Story who was running wide open and full throttle downfield. Brownwood left the door slightly open when our two-point try failed, but thanks to the steady pass rush of Mike Kinsey and Gordon Lee, and alert secondary play by Marvin Rathke, the Kangaroos never came closer than sixty-five yards to our goal line in the final minutes.

Final score: Brownwood 19, Weatherford 17.

At home against Azle, our offense rushed for 346 yards and passed for 91 yards to overwhelm a spunky bunch of Hornets who arrived with a 3–1 record. A second quarter, fifty-yard field goal by Lion Jimmy Morris, the longest three-pointer in BHS history, totally crushed the spirit of the shell-shocked Hornets.

Final score: Brownwood 44, Azle 12.

◆　◆　◆

MY INITIAL CONFRONTATION with Chuck Curtis occurred about a week prior to our Cleburne game. Having beaten Crowley, Everman, and Stephenville in conference games, my Lions were 7–1 overall and 3–0 in district. Coach Curtis was doing the job he had been hired to do. His Yellowjackets were also undefeated in district play. Our upcoming encounter would most likely determine the district champ. The game was scheduled to take place in Brownwood.

Gordon Wood Stadium seats eight thousand fans with four thousand on each side of the playing field. Because the first row is elevated, every seat has a good view. Cleburne's stadium isn't nearly so user-friendly. Their visitors' side, which contains only about fifteen hundred seats, is particularly bad. The visitor bleachers begin at ground level, and fans in the lower sections have to strain to see the action on the field.

Besides being an outstanding football coach, Chuck Curtis possesses another unique talent—he can fill up a football stadium. Brownwood officials were expecting a sellout, but a phone call from Coach Curtis complicated matters. Curtis insisted Brownwood assign all the seats on the visitors' side to Cleburne—all four thousand seats. Even though Cleburne had the right to half the seats—UIL rules allow for such a request—no visiting school had ever required that many seats before.

Cleburne is one hundred and twenty miles from Brownwood, a two-hour drive on a narrow two-lane blacktop. Never in the history of our long series had four thousand Cleburne fans braved the long trek to support their Yellowjackets, but when BHS officials questioned Curtis, he stood his ground. Brownwood had no choice but to reluctantly comply.

As things turned out, Cleburne was unable to sell all the requested seats. Our championship-deciding contest, which Brownwood won 22–6, was played with more than a thousand empty seats—all on the visitors' side.

This may sound petty, but I vowed to get even the next year when Brownwood played at Cleburne. My plan was to turn the tables on Chuck, use the UIL rules to ask for half the best seats at Cleburne's stadium—half their home side seats. My plan of retaliation never got off the ground. Coach Curtis would have a much better idea.

◆ ◆ ◆

A FEW DAYS after our Cleburne game, Brownwood school superintendent Jim Lancaster called me to his office. When I arrived, he told me we had been ordered to appear before a meeting of District 4–AAAA members to answer allegations of illegal recruiting made by a Mr. Larry Young. Young claimed to be a Johnson County Constable. He had been hired to check on Brownwood High quarterback Tyler Tabor—to determine whether the Tabor family actually lived in Brownwood or if they maintained a residence in Blanket.

Constable Young swore in a letter addressed to the district committee that he had conclusive evidence the Tabors still lived in Blanket. If this was true, the district could declare Tyler Tabor ineligible and force Brownwood to forfeit all the games Tabor played in. If that happened, Cleburne would be crowned district champ and would represent the district in the state playoffs. Superintendent Lancaster showed me Young's letter, telling me he was humiliated by the situation. I grabbed the letter from Lancaster's hands, took one look and blew my stack. The letter was full of lies—several that could easily be repudiated.

Even before I left the superintendent's office, my mind shifted into high gear. A few telephone calls and a brief conversation with Oneale Tabor gave me all the ammunition I needed, but I did better than that. I drove to Blanket to see the house for myself. I talked with the next-door neighbors and with a man named Tyson, who owned the grocery store in Blanket. In short order, I had a response to all of Young's accusations. This is the information I presented to the district committee:

1. Young claimed there was a bicycle in the yard and this proved someone lived there—the bicycle had two flat tires and no chain.

2. Young claimed the electricity to the house was on—according to Texas Power and Light records, the electricity was cut off on July 30, 1981.

3. Young claimed the water to the house was on—according to city records, the water was turned off on September 21, 1981.

4. Young claimed the telephone was working—according to General Telephone records, the Tabor's Blanket telephone was disconnected July 17, 1981. Their Brownwood telephone was installed July 17, 1981.

I was truly worried about some of the statements Young claimed to have taken from Blanket residents, not because they were factual but because the people might be misinformed. However, every one of the Blanket people I talked with confirmed that Young had falsified their statements. Mr. Tyson, who owned the grocery store where the Tabors shopped, told me he hadn't seen the Tabors since midsummer. Every person I talked to said they'd be glad to go before the district committee and swear Mr. Young had lied about interviewing them.

When we appeared before the District 4–AAAA executive committee, I was first to speak. I began my defense by stating, "I believe Chuck Curtis and Cleburne superintendent Don Smith are behind Mister Young's allegations because they are the ones who would profit most."

After I presented my detailed response, proving beyond a shadow of a doubt that Larry Young lied, the committee dismissed the charges, and Brownwood was allowed to pursue the conference championship—with Tyler Tabor still on my team. After the meeting adjourned, two of the school superintendents on the committee told me privately that Chuck Curtis had called them prior to the hearing and tried to persuade them to vote Brownwood out of the district.

The following Friday, Brownwood wrapped up conference play with a 44–13 rout of Granbury, clinching a sixth straight district crown.

◆　◆　◆

AFTER THE GRANBURY GAME my coaches and I met with officials from Wichita Falls Hirschi, the winner of District 3–AAAA. When I tossed the coin to decide which team would choose the game site, I flipped the coin so high it bounced off the ceiling. Hirschi called tails, and they were right.

Our bi-district battle took place at Memorial Stadium in Wichita Falls. For both teams the contest was a frustrating experience. The crew of game officials came from Tyler, and they stayed busy, flagging Brownwood to the tune of 101 yards in penalties and the Huskies for 72. Brownwood was penalized thirteen times, and the Huskies turned down at least a half-dozen other calls.

Still, our maroon troops overcame the parade of yellow flags to score a touchdown and a field goal the first two times they had the football and added another TD on their last possession. That was all the cushion our stout-hearted defense needed.

Final score: Brownwood 17, Hirschi 0.

Our quarterfinal game was played at Snyder. Our opponent was Borger. For three quarters the Bulldogs hung tough, using stunts and overshifting to stifle our running game and shut down our passing attack. To counter their stunts, we decided to run right at Borger the second half, and it worked. By the end of the third quarter, Brownwood's huge offensive line had the Bulldogs on the ropes. Midway through the fourth, the red and white defenders were whipped. Lion fullback Gene Gibson gained seventy-seven of his ninety-eight rushing yards in the second half while his backfield partner Aundrey Henderson ran for forty-seven of his eighty-five yards.

Final score: Brownwood 21, Borger 0.

◆   ◆   ◆

COACH JAMES CAMERON and I enjoyed a close friendship which extended back to 1967 when his McKinney Lions played Brownwood in the state semifinals. Brownwood won that game, but Cameron's team gave us quite a scare.

After he left McKinney, James came to Brownwood to take an assistant coaching position at Howard Payne. A couple of seasons later he was promoted to head coach. From Howard Payne, James moved to San Angelo. Cameron was head football coach at Angelo State when friends in Rockwall enticed him to rejoin the high school coaching ranks.

During the week preceding our semifinal bout, the sports pages were full of stories praising Coach Cameron's undefeated Yellowjackets. In two playoff games, Rockwall had scored ninety-one points. In twelve games, the Yellowjackets had put an average of thirty-three points on the scoreboard. Their winning margin averaged twenty-four points.

One reporter used the game scores of our common opponent, Weatherford, to demonstrate Rockwall's superiority. Reasoning that Rockwall had breezed past Weatherford in their quarterfinal match 48–0 while Brownwood barely squeaked by the Kangaroos 19–17 in regular season, the writer theorized Rockwall was a 46-point favorite. He predicted the game would be a Rockwall blowout. When a sportswriter from the Dallas paper called to get my reaction, here's what I told him:

"I reckon a lot of people are saying Rockwall is better than we are. They do have a fine team, but I think by Saturday afternoon they'll know they've been in a football game."

Our semifinal skirmish took place at Baylor Stadium, and, oh, what a game it was—a spine-tingling struggle from start to finish.

◆   ◆   ◆

BEFORE THE GAME, our kids were wrapping up pre-game warm-ups, about to go to the locker room, when a huge fellow jogged down the stadium steps directly behind our bench. He was a giant of a man, perhaps six-foot-eight-inches tall and weighing 280 pounds. He stepped easily over the short wall which divided the bleachers from the playing field and grabbed a megaphone from one of Brownwood's cheerleaders. He pointed the megaphone toward our football team which was divided into three groups at the north end of the field.

"We beat Weatherford forty-eight to nothing! We beat Weatherford forty-eight to nothing! We beat Weatherford forty-eight to nothing!" the man screamed loudly. He paused to take a breath then started in again.

"We beat Weatherford forty-eight to nothing! We beat Weatherford forty-eight to nothing, and y'all remember it! We beat Weatherford forty-eight to nothing, and y'all remember it!" The man was still yelling wildly as my football team left the field.

To get to the dressing quarters at Baylor Stadium, you have to go up a long, dark tunnel. As our players negotiated through the tunnel, I was trying to think of some way I could use the crazy man's yelling to motivate my team. I was walking behind 200-pound Mike Kinsey, one of the most ferocious linebackers to ever wear a Brownwood uniform. Mike was terribly upset.

"Did y'all hear what that man said?" Mike yelled to his teammates. "That big guy's making fun of our team! He's making fun of our team!" By the time we reached the dressing room, Mike had worked himself into a rage.

Inside the dressing room, I let the players get a drink and use the bathroom before we congregated for our usual pre-game talk. I talked maybe five minutes before Mike Kinsey butted in.

"It's time to go, Coach! We gotta go!"

"No, we still have five minutes," I advised and continued to talk. I doubt if two minutes passed before Kinsey butted in again.

"Coach, it's time to go! Let's go!"

"No, Mike, we still have a couple of minutes," I told my anxious linebacker, but a minute later Kinsey butted in again.

"It's time, Coach! It's time!"

"No, Mike. Be patient. There's plenty of time," I said, but before I could recollect my thoughts, Kinsey had his teammates heading for the door.

"Come on, team! Let's go!" Kinsey bellowed, and all Coach Southall, Coach West and I could do was get out of the way. In all my years of coaching, I've never seen a football team so ready to play a football game.

◆ ◆ ◆

AFTER FLEET-FOOTED SENIOR Carnell Payton returned Rockwall's opening kickoff forty-five yards to the Yellowjacket forty-seven, Brownwood drew first blood. With Tyler Tabor calling the plays, the Lions needed only six downs to jump out to a 7–0 lead. The payoff came on Tabor's first and last pass of the day, a 29-yard beauty to tight end Jesse Smith. Smith ran under the ball, made a nifty over-the-shoulder catch at the five, and dashed into the end zone. When Jimmy Morris booted the extra point, only 2:41 had elapsed.

Our game that Saturday afternoon was played with a stiff breeze blowing in from the north end of the stadium. Midway through the first quarter, the wind gave the Orange and White a big break. After Rockwall stopped us in our territory, Jimmy Morris hung his punt in the wind, and the Yellowjackets took possession at Brownwood's thirty-five. On second and twelve, Rockwall quarterback Jerry Tidmore worked a screen pass to wingback Hayden Bookout. Sidestepping a diving Lion defender, Bookout exploded down the sideline for the TD. When Brad Lamberth kicked the point after, the game was tied at 7–7.

Our fired-up Maroons responded to the challenge by conjuring up their longest charge of the day—an 83-yarder which required only nine plays. Halfway to Rockwall's goal line, our starting quarterback Tyler Tabor was forced to leave the game with a damaged rotator cuff, and junior Marvin Rathke took command. Possibly unnerved by his unexpected role, Rathke fumbled the snap from center four plays later. Rathke recovered like a champ. He picked up the ball and fired a sideline shot to Jimmy Morris who left Yellowjacket defenders grabbing for air. Morris cut against the grain twice before he finished his 47-yard romp to the end zone. Right before the half, Rathke directed the Lions on another touchdown drive which allowed Brownwood to take a 19–7 lead to the dressing room.

With the wind to their backs, our Maroons were sailing along midway through the third quarter when Rockwall's Brad Lamberth intercepted Rathke's first pass of the second half and tight-roped thirty-seven yards to the Lion thirty-one. On the Yellowjackets' first play, Tidmore fired a perfect strike to tight end Alex Hoover who trotted in for the touchdown. On the extra point try, Lion end

Jewell Brown broke through to block Lamberth's kick, leaving the score at 19–13, but now the game was up for grabs again.

For the next fifteen minutes the two teams bludgeoned one another with neither able to get anything going. Every time our offense would get rolling, a turnover would stop us cold.

Late in the fourth period a great defensive play almost secured a Brownwood win. After our defense held the Orange and White on downs, Lion Bryan Driskill charged in to strip the football away from Yellowjacket punter Hayden Bookout. Maroon lineman Scott Haynes recovered at Rockwall's fifteen, and all Brownwood had to do was run the ball in for the game clincher. This was easier said than done. Brownwood moved the ball down to the three, but there an aroused Yellowjacket defense slammed the door shut on four straight plays, taking possession on their own one-yard line. Rockwall's brilliant goal line stand set the stage for a bell ringing finish.

With the stiff northerly breeze at their backs, Rockwall made good use of the wind advantage, driving out to mid-field before Bookout's punt put Brownwood deep in its own territory. Three stabs at the unyielding Yellowjacket defensive line gained only a few yards, and we were forced to punt. With 2:32 left in the game, Jimmy Morris got off a 45-yard, into-the-wind boomer to get his Lions out of a tough situation. Now, the game was in the hands of our grave digging defense, and they came through in the clutch.

Starting at his thirty-four, Rockwall quarterback Jerry Tidmore hit a couple of short passes, but our swarming defenders were in the Yellowjackets' backfield on every play. Rockwall's hopes finally died in the arms of BHS guard Mike Watkins who recovered Tidmore's fumble at the Lion forty-one.

Final score: Brownwood 19, Rockwall 13.

◆ ◆ ◆

BEFORE OUR SEMIFINAL PLAYOFF GAMES, the odds of Fort Bend Willowridge and Brownwood meeting to decide the State 4A champ was probably at least ten to one. Willowridge took on top-ranked defending champion Beaumont Hebert and barely survived 15–14. Brownwood, of course, beat heavily favored Rockwall. That set the stage for two underdogs to slug it out at Austin's Memorial Stadium, and for ten thousand screaming, wild-eyed football fans, it was definitely a Friday to remember. After the game, Brownwood sportswriter Bill Stovall would write that the most amazing thing about the exciting, down-to-the-wire shootout was there weren't ten thousand heart attacks before the last shot was fired.

◆　◆　◆

BECAUSE TYLER TABOR suffered a severe shoulder injury in the Rockwall game, no one expected him to be able to play in the championship game. During practice that week we alternated Tyler with Marvin Rathke at first-string quarterback. Not wanting to aggravate his bad shoulder, we didn't allow Tabor to throw a single pass.

Friday morning, as we were loading the team bus preparing to leave for Austin, Tyler walked past me. I asked him where he was headed.

"I'm going to the dressing room to get my equipment," Tabor replied.

A few minutes later Tyler reappeared carrying his football gear. He shoved his bag onto the bus and stepped over to talk.

"Am I gonna start today?" Tabor asked.

I considered his question for a few seconds. Actually, I hadn't made up my mind until that very moment.

"Tyler, if you don't break a leg between here and Austin, you'll be our starting quarterback," I declared, and it was one of the best decisions I ever made.

◆　◆　◆

FOR THE FIRST forty-three minutes the two ballclubs were exactly equal. Each team had scored in the second quarter, and the game was tied at 7–7. Then, late in the fourth quarter, Brownwood drove down to the Willowridge five-yard line and lost the ball on a fumble. Two plays later the Lions got the ball back, and this time they cashed in. Maroon fullback Gene Gibson crashed into the Eagles' end zone from the three. With five minutes left, Jimmy Morris kicked the extra point to make the score 14–7. For fans on Brownwood's side of the field, those final five heart-stopping minutes would seem like an eternity.

Willowridge received our kickoff and roared toward mid-field. Like a westbound freight train, the Eagles were chewing up yardage when Lion safetyman Chris Ellis threw the brakes on Willowridge's last ditch scoring thrust. Running neck and neck with a blue and silver wingback, Ellis outmaneuvered the Eagle receiver and intercepted a Tony Hubbard pass. Chris' great play should have settled matters, but our offense couldn't move the ball, and Brownwood was forced to punt.

When maroon defenders held the Eagles to three and out, Lion boosters heaved another deep sigh of relief, but again, they were premature in assuming Brownwood had won. The fireworks were just getting started. With 1:16 remaining, Willowridge punter Scott Zamora nailed a 54-yarder to pin the Lions on their own eight. Three stabs at a stubborn Eagle defense netted nine yards, and with the Eagles calling time-out after every play, only thirteen seconds ticked off the clock.

With 1:03 left, I called Tyler Tabor to the sideline and instructed him to have our punter Jimmy Morris take an intentional safety. Jimmy did that. He also wasted an additional eleven seconds before running out of the end zone.

That left the Eagles with fifty-two seconds to work their magic. Morris made the job even more difficult by thumping a 57-yard into-the-wind punt on the free kick. The Eagles went to work on their thirty-five. On second down, Eagle quarterback Tony Hubbard hit Ron Garner for twenty-five. Then, Hubbard passed out of bounds to stop the clock. On the next play, a fierce rush by Lion defensive end Jewell Brown forced Hubbard to throw the ball into the ground.

In the final seconds, I made one more gutsy move. I grabbed Tyler Tabor by the arm and sent him into the game to play free safety. Coach West objected, telling me Tabor had a bad shoulder and hadn't played a down of defense all season. I told Kenneth not to worry because Tyler was the best defensive back on our team.

It was Tabor who intercepted Hubbard's third-down pass to nail down the hard fought victory and Brownwood's record-breaking seventh state championship.

Final score: Brownwood 14, Willowridge 9.

After the game, heroes were plentiful in Brownwood's locker room—Jesse Smith, who caught four passes for sixty-eight yards; Kyle Story, who snagged two aerials for twenty-five yards; Aundrey Henderson, who led all rushers with ninety-eight yards on twenty-two carries; Gene Gibson, who caught one pass and ran for sixty-

two yards on twenty-one carries; Chris Ellis, whose key inter-
ception turned the tide in Brownwood's favor; linemen Ronald
Hickman, Doug Wynn and Gordon Lee, who matched the fierce
Eagle defense muscle for muscle; and defenders Jewell Brown,
Kendal Nelson, Mike Kinsey, Mike Watkins, Scott Haynes and
Mike Davis, who played the best game of their lives. And without
the long, booming punts of Jimmy Morris, Brownwood might not
have been in position to win.

During a brief interlude in the wild post game celebration, I
gathered my team around me and congratulated them for a great
win. "Look around you," I told my ecstatic young men. "The best
friends you will ever have are right here in this room. This is something no one can ever take away from you. You're champions!"

Coaches Wood, Southall and West savor Brownwood's record-breaking
seventh state football championship.
(credit: Brownwood Bulletin*)*

CHAPTER NINETEEN

Searching for a Fitting End

(1982–1984)

AFTER THE LIONS won the state championship in 1981, I began to seriously consider retirement. Katharine wanted me to quit. My wife loved the excitement, the games, and the kids as much as me. Since 1945, Katharine had only missed two of my football games— one in 1947, when Seminole played Pecos and she thought it was too far to drive with a baby, and one in 1971, when she was in Corpus Christi looking after a very sick daughter. But Katharine worried about my health.

Although my salary had increased dramatically, now up to thirty-one thousand a year, I had been paying teachers' retirement for forty-two years and social security for more than twenty. By my calculations, it was costing me about four thousand a year in take-home pay to continue coaching.

Still, it seemed like every time I'd get close to making the "Big R" decision, someone would call to say I'd been selected to receive another award or honored in some way, or some other neat thing would happen to convince me to keep going.

The previous spring, with a number of new faces on the school board, Howard Murchison's zany antics had finally caught up with him. Disgusted with his bizarre managerial style, the trustees bought out Howard's contract and hired James Lancaster to replace him as school superintendent.

In March, when my coaching contract came up for renewal, the school board rewarded me and my coaching staff with substantial raises and told me I could continue to coach for as long as I wanted.

1982

A DARK CLOUD was forming over the Lone Star State as Brownwood High launched two-a-day football workouts. A bill passed by Congress to deregulate the savings and loan industry put the state's boom-or-bust economy on a collision course with Texas bankers' loose lending policies.

The first indication of things to come was the failure of Abilene National Bank. Loan problems, caused by a recession in the oil industry, was the main culprit. In a legal maneuver that rankled every West Texan, Mercantile Texas Corporation of Dallas abruptly foreclosed on the assets of Abilene National, even though the bank's chairman, Don Earney, insisted his bank was in no danger of going under.

Abilene National's troubles were only the tip of the iceberg. Before the bleeding subsided, every major Texas banking institution would fall victim to the Reagan Administration's ludicrous monetary policies.

With returning starters Mike Davis, Marvin Rathke, Kendal Nelson, Carl Burr, Kevin Howard, Mike Watkins, Kyle Story, and Russell Sheffield back from our '81 team, we Brownwood coaches couldn't help but be optimistic about our prospects for the '82 season. Two-year starting tailback Aundrey Henderson had undergone knee surgery several weeks earlier, but Aundrey was recovering nicely. We expected him to be at full speed for our season opener.

Our biggest problem lay in replacing all-state quarterback Tyler Tabor. Marvin Rathke had shown lots of poise by stepping in at the end of last season when Tabor was injured. We were confident Marvin could do the job, but if he couldn't, we had David Pounds, a 144-pound junior who quarterbacked the JV in '81, waiting in the wings. Other players like tight end Tim Perkins, center Milton Talkington, guards H.W. McGowen and Shane Cockerham, linebacker Doug Howey and defensive halfback James Galloway added to our high expectations.

◆ ◆ ◆

DURING THE FIRST THREE DAYS of August practice, Lion squad members usually dressed only in shorts, shoulder pads and helmets. Traditionally, we concentrated mainly on conditioning exercises, blocking and tackling fundamentals, and on offensive and defensive assignments. In 1982, though, I was concerned about our kicking game. With all-state punter Jimmy Morris graduated and gone to play professional baseball, I was anxious to find a replacement.

The second item on my priority list was two-point conversions. Misfires on two-point plays had denied Brownwood victories over Abilene Cooper the two previous years. Losing to Cooper never seriously affected Brownwood's season, but since 1960, my Lion teams had lost only thirty-eight games—thirteen of those were to the Cougars. Those close losses to Cooper were like a burr under my saddle. I was determined not to lose by one point ever again.

Pre-season polls all across Texas were picking Brownwood as the top 4A football team in the state as Brownwood players replaced shorts with football pads and got down to serious business. After scrimmage games with Paris at Amon Carter Field in Fort Worth and with Abilene High at Gordon Wood Stadium, we Lion coaches found little reason to argue. Our defending state champions seemed up to the task of defending their number one ranking.

◆　◆　◆

WHEN BROWNWOOD KICKED OFF at Gordon Wood Stadium to open the 1982 football campaign, Coach Ray Overton's Cougars held a 13–6 edge in our long series. Brownwood had not beaten the Cougars since 1977. The Lions had never beaten Cooper in Brownwood. A five-foot-seven, fleet-footed kid named Aundrey Henderson changed all that. Early in the second quarter, two plays after Cooper had taken a 7–0 lead, Henderson bolted for a 72-yard TD. The Lions would never trail again.

An eighteen-yard pass from Rathke to split end Kyle Story gave Brownwood a 14–7 halftime advantage. A one-yard plunge by Lion fullback Ronald Isom in the fourth jacked that lead to 21–7, and our defense handled things from there. With Lion kicking specialist Raul Mosqueda nailing all three PATs, we never needed the tricky two-point conversion plays I had devised.

Final score: Brownwood 21, Cooper 14.

Before our Weatherford game, Coach Southall and I discussed giving more playing time to second-string quarterback David Pounds. Our starting field general Marvin Rathke also played safety on defense. We were worried going both ways might affect Rathke's stamina at the end of a tight game.

Pounds got his chance alright—a little earlier than expected. Rathke came to the sidelines nursing an upset stomach at the end of the first quarter, and we were left with no choice except to insert Pounds at quarterback.

On the first play of the second quarter, never having taken a snap in a varsity game, and with the score tied at 3–3, our untested junior signal caller exhibited the poise of a veteran. In his first three quarters at the helm, David directed his maroon team to forty-eight points.

Final score: Brownwood 51, Weatherford 15.

With two notches on their gun, our Lions may have been a bit overconfident when we boarded the bus for San Angelo to take on Jimmy Keeling's state-ranked, 5A Central High Bobcats. Maybe we should have guessed what kind of night it would be when the air-conditioning on our bus didn't work. By the time we changed busses and reloaded, the team was an hour late leaving Brownwood.

Still, it was a game Brownwood could have won, but Central played an almost flawless game—no turnovers, few penalties, and a ball-hogging Bobcat offense; combined with four maroon fumbles, the hill was just too big to climb.

Final score: Brownwood 7, San Angelo 21.

Because a number of schools had been added to the conference by the UIL's '82 realignment, District 4–AAAA was, once again, split into a North Zone and a South Zone. Brownwood opened South Zone play by taking our frustrations out on Granbury's Pirates 49–0. Then we thundered past Everman 42–0 and rolled over Joshua 51–0. That set the stage for a no-holds-barred tangle with Chuck Curtis and his Cleburne Yellowjackets.

Like Brownwood, the Yellowjackets owned a record of 5–1. No non-playoff 4A game in history ever attracted more media attention or received more pre-game hype. That's why I abandoned my "get-even-with-Chuck" plan and agreed to play the game on Saturday night at TCU's Amon Carter Field in Fort Worth. No Class 4A stadium in Texas was large enough to hold the anticipated crowd.

After his team beat Everman to remain undefeated in district, Coach Curtis told reporters, "Next year is here!" Cleburne hadn't beaten Brownwood since 1964, and the Lions hadn't lost a district game since 1975. That was the year Graham kicked a field goal with nine seconds left to pull out a 31–29 win. Every football fan in Texas was expecting a battle royal—and it was.

◆　◆　◆

NEWSPAPERS REPORTED the next day that an estimated crowd of twenty-seven thousand five hundred fans witnessed the Brownwood-Cleburne game, but attendance would have easily exceeded forty thousand had Fort Worth officials not bungled their job. For some reason and without the knowledge of either school, Forth Worth police set up barricades on streets leading into the stadium. They stopped cars and turned them away, telling people the game was a sellout and they couldn't get in.

For instance, my brother Dick and five other men drove all the way from Wichita Falls to attend the game. Police officers stopped Dick's car as he headed down University Drive and advised him to turn around and go back. The officers told my brother the stadium was full; there were no more seats available. Dick and his guests never made it to the game.

At Amon Carter Stadium, only one ticket window was open. An hour before game time the line to purchase tickets was three blocks long. Fortunately, most Brownwood and Cleburne supporters had purchased their tickets prior to the game, so they were able to get through the blockade. Midway through the second quarter, though, fans were still filtering into the stadium.

Cleburne scored first, using a 49-yard opening kickoff return by Robbie White to get them going. The Yellowjackets then drove thirty yards to score the only points of the first half—a thirty-six-yard field goal by Kyle Sims. Cleburne's halftime lead was 3–0.

Offensively, Brownwood played its most mistake-prone game of the season. Turnovers literally killed our chances. A fumble on the first play of the second half gave Cleburne possession in Lion territory, and the fired-up Yellowjackets took full advantage. In ten plays Cleburne rang Brownwood's bell for six more points, with fullback Peter Pope punching across from the two-inch line.

Up until the fourth quarter, Cleburne completely dominated the game, reeling off fifty-three plays to Brownwood's twenty-three. The final period, however, ushered in a whole new football game. Midway through the last stanza, Brownwood mounted a 71-yard drive which featured the running of Aundrey Henderson and Carl

Burr. A tipped pass, which Ronald Isom turned into a thirteen-yard gain, kept the drive alive. When Brownwood stalled out at the Yellowjacket nineteen, Raul Mosquedo booted a 28-yard field goal to make the score 9–3.

Cleburne took the kickoff and drove to mid-field where a defiant maroon defense drew the line and held. Just 5:16 remained when Lion safety James Galloway made a fair catch of Dwayne Grigg's 42-yard punt at Brownwood's two-yard line. (Note: When Galloway fielded the football that close to the goal line, James violated everything he had been taught by his coaches. At Brownwood, our punt receivers were instructed over and over to never ever field a punt inside our ten. But Galloway was a junior who didn't play a down of football as a sophomore. We recruited him off Coach Steve Boothe's basketball squad because of his speed and quickness. James had also never played in such a large stadium with twenty thousand people screaming their lungs out.)

With Marvin Rathke barking signals, our comeback drive began at the two. Along the way, Marvin rifled 26- and 13-yard completions to Burr, a 7-yarder to Kyle Story, and a 14-yarder to Henderson before arriving at Cleburne's twenty. After a clipping penalty pushed the ball back to the thirty-four, Rathke aimed a strike at Grant Wells who was running full throttle across the middle. Wells appeared to have Cleburne defender Rodney Fowler beaten, but Fowler made a game-saving decision and grabbed onto Wells. The resulting interference call moved the ball to the eight. On the next play we called a trap play over left tackle with Carl Burr carrying the football. As the play unfolded, Brownwood blockers Shane Cockerham and Russell Sheffield opened up a huge hole, and it looked like Burr could just walk through for the tying touchdown, but a Yellowjacket defender grabbed Carl's arm and jerked the ball loose. Cleburne linebacker Ken Cunningham fell on Burr's fumble, and Brownwood was done. Chuck Curtis had accomplished the job he had been hired to do. In the process, he left every person in Amon Carter Stadium exhausted and hoarse from yelling.

Final score: Brownwood 3, Cleburne 9.

◆　◆　◆

IN THE LOCKER ROOM after the game, I overheard one of my linemen jump on Carl Burr, the ballcarrier who fumbled at the goal line. The lineman was chastising Carl for losing the game. I raced across the room, grabbed the huge lineman by the arm and whirled him around to face me. I was so mad smoke was coming out my ears.

"That boy is your teammate! He didn't intend to fumble! If you say one more word to him about fumbling, your ass is gone! You'll never play another down of football for Brownwood High School!"

Every man in the locker room understood why I was so angry. Lion players were taught to support one another. If they didn't, they knew the consequences. At Brownwood High, we never blamed each other for a loss. Losing is hard, but when we did, we sucked it up and went on to the next game—together, as a team. We won together. We lost together. Every team member was expected to contribute to every win, and to accomplish that, we all had to believe in each other.

Controversy and self doubt can destroy a football team. Players must believe in one another and support one another. I insisted on it, and I never allowed a player to criticize another.

◆　◆　◆

IN SPITE OF OUR LOSS to league leading Cleburne, the Lions were still in control of their own destiny. Thanks to a change in the UIL '82 playoff format, two teams from each district could qualify for the state playoffs. So, as far as post-season play was concerned, Brownwood was still in the hunt. The trick now was to climb off the canvas and win the rest of our district games.

Here's the weird part. Now it was to our advantage for Cleburne to keep winning, thereby avoiding the possibility of the South Zone winding up in a three-way tie and the chance of Brownwood being eliminated by the toss of a coin.

Friday, October 22, was homecoming night, and the Lions treated Brownwood High exes to something extra special—a 41–0 rout of unbeaten Stephenville. By the time homecoming queen Barbara Latson was crowned at halftime, our Maroons were leading 27–0. The lopsided score doesn't really tell the whole story. At intermission, Brownwood was leading in first downs 12–1 and in total yards 307–8.

With their team goal of making playoffs now in sight, the Lions charged forward, picking up steam with every win. As the regular season wound down, Brownwood bowled over Mansfield

35–0, then reloaded and shot down Crowley's Eagles to secure a second place finish. A week later Brownwood completed 4–AAAA business, clinching a slot in the state playoffs by knocking off North Zone champ Fort Worth Brewer 41–0.

◆　◆　◆

FOR THE BI-DISTRICT ROUND, Brownwood drew a familiar old adversary—the Gainesville Leopards, who were now coached by Robert James. The Leopards had speed and experience at every skill position, with explosive one-thousand-yard rusher James Calhoun and cat-quick quarterback Terry Jackson shouldering much of the load. Their huge offensive line, which included 232-pound Spencer Leftwich, 217-pound Jeff Braden and 233-pound Dane Young, was heavily stocked with two-year starters.

Our playoff contest took place in Fort Worth. A stiff northerly wind affected our passing game, but six turnovers were the real reason for our downfall. With the wind at their back, Gainesville gained possession near the end of the first quarter and marched forty-five yards to the Lion goal line. Leopard running back James Calhoun capped the drive by rambling twenty-four yards on a cutback play.

On Brownwood's first play after the kickoff, Aundrey Henderson fumbled and Devron Overstreet recovered for the Leopards. When Tollie Royal crashed over from the one a few downs later, Gainesville had scored twice in a span of a hundred seconds. At halftime Brownwood was down 14–0, but even worse, we were trailing in penetrations 3–0.

James Galloway got our offense untracked when he took the second half kickoff and ran it back to Gainesville's thirty-one. Then with hard-running Carl Burr doing the dirty work, Brownwood needed only seven plays to power into the Leopard's end zone. Aundrey Henderson handled the chore by leaping over a sweating heap of humanity at the one.

Trailing 3–1 in penetrations, we decided to go for two, but Rathke was forced to hurry his swing pass to Galloway. The pass went awry, leaving the score at 14–6. It would stay that way until early in the fourth quarter when Brownwood held the Leopards on downs, took possession and drove sixty-five yards to Gainesville's fifteen. There, red and white linebacker Dane Young ended our threat with a second-down interception.

Still, our long drive gave us excellent field position, and when our defense turned back the Leopards, Gainesville punter Allen Bruce had to kick into the wind. The ball traveled only twenty-five yards. Brownwood took possession at the forty with 6:11 remaining.

On our first play from scrimmage, Burr burst through for ten yards, then Rathke hit Tim Perkins and Grant Wells with key passes as our Maroons worked the ball to the six. A short pass to Burr was rubbed out by an illegal use of hands penalty, but Brownwood got a break on the very next play. A roughing the passer flag moved the football back to the seven, and four plays later, with 2:13 left in the game, Henderson went over the top for the TD.

Our previous drive, which ended with an interception, had evened tie-breaker penetrations at 3–3. Brownwood was leading in first downs 13–8. A tie would send the Lions to the quarterfinals and extend Brownwood's bid for an eighth state championship. Since mid-August, I'd had a premonition our season might boil down to a two-point conversion. Our offense worked on two-point plays in every practice, but all those efforts went for naught. Marvin Rathke's pass was intercepted in the end zone, and a relieved Gainesville team was satisfied to run out the clock.

Final score: Brownwood 12, Gainesville 14.

A week later Gainesville lost to Lubbock Estacado 29–0 in the quarterfinals.

◆　◆　◆

FOR TEXAS POLITICIANS, surprise was the norm in 1982. Republican governor Bill Clements was supposed to be a shoo-in for re-election, and during the campaign, Clements spent more than thirteen million dollars to assure his return—almost double the amount spent by his Democrat opponent Mark White. However, a number of factors went against the Republican incumbent, including the state's sagging economy and an unemployment rate that jumped to eight percent in October. The result was an unexpected large voter turnout, and when the votes were counted after the November election, former Attorney General Mark White had defeated Bill Clements by more than two hundred thousand votes.

Searching for a Fitting End

After Governor White's inauguration in January of 1983, one of his first official acts was to appoint Dallas millionaire H. Ross Perot as chairman of a select committee to investigate public education in Texas schools. Perot was a hound for publicity, and he attracted national attention when he attacked extracurricular school activities. To the chagrin of Texas high school coaches, Perot zeroed in on sports, especially on football. He somehow sold the people of Texas that there was a conflict between academics and sports. Nothing could be further from the truth. In all my years of coaching, I never worked at a school where anyone except coaches pushed kids to do their school work.

During a special session in 1984, the Texas Legislature passed House Bill 72 which introduced the concept of no-pass, no-play. The law barred high school students from participating in any extracurricular activity if they received even one failing grade over a six-week period.

At many schools, particularly smaller high schools like Brownwood, the no-pass, no-play rule was the worst possible solution to academic problems, because the kids who needed help the most were the ones hurt the most. Instead of encouraging poor students to try harder, many times the strict rule caused us to lose them. When a player failed, we coaches were required to change the player's class schedule to exclude him from the sports program, and for six weeks, that student would be outside our control. For a young person, six weeks is a very long time.

At Brownwood, before Ross Perot interfered, we imposed a policy which required a player to pass four solid subjects in order to play. If a student was taking five courses, he could fail one and still be eligible. After Ross got his way, a student was forced to sit out a full six weeks if he failed any course. At many Texas high schools, House Bill 72 had a terrible negative impact. However, because we Brownwood coaches constantly monitored our players' grades, no-pass, no-play never had much effect on our sports program. The groups the new rules really hurt at BHS were the band and drill team.

The spring semester after Perot's law went into effect, Brownwood's band director Kirk Woolery stopped me in the hallway one afternoon.

"Coach Wood, there's something wrong here. Your teams didn't lose a single player this spring."

"That's right, not a single one," I responded.

"I don't understand. My band kids are just as smart as your football players."

"That's probably true. They may even be smarter."

"Well, what's the deal then. I've lost so many kids we can't hold a spring concert."

"It's real simple," I told the band director. "Your band kids haven't had their grades checked every week since they were in seventh grade. My coaches make sure our players know they're responsible for making passing grades. Our boys know they'll catch hell from us coaches if they don't pass."

What I told the band director was true. Our players not only knew they'd catch hell and not get to play; they understood we coaches backed up our resolve with swats. Every week, players brought us reports from their teachers. Any player who received a poor report paid dearly. Once a week, swats were administered by Brownwood coaches. We were careful not to hurt the boys, but I guarantee every kid who took a swat to the butt for bad grades or poor behavior thought twice before he repeated the offense.

Happily, the no-pass, no-play rule has been revised. Nowadays, players are only out for three weeks. During that time, they are allowed to remain in the sports program where coaches can watch their grades and help them get back on track.

Because of the no-pass, no-play law and changing disciplinary attitudes, swats disappeared at Brownwood High sometime during the mid-eighties. Nevertheless, I'm still convinced our method of constantly monitoring grades and punishing players who didn't measure up was superior to the way things are done today. To see my point, all you have to do is look at the quality of the young men who participated in our sports program and see how they turned out after they graduated from Brownwood High.

1983

MY STRAINED RELATIONSHIP with Cleburne coach Chuck Curtis sank to a new low in August of 1983. A few weeks before Brownwood began pre-season football practice, I was told Coach Curtis had recruited a football player named Trey McNeill. The previous fall, McNeill had been a star quarterback at Fort Worth Paschal High School. According to my sources, the boy had transferred from Paschal to Cleburne in January. This was perfectly legal. In 1981, the UIL revised its long standing, but controversial, one-year rule. For a high school athlete to play at another school, the new transfer rule only required written approval by the student's parents and by superintendents of the two schools involved.

I had no problem with the boy transferring to Cleburne High. What bothered me was—the kid was living at Chuck's home. I immediately reported the situation to our District 4–AAAA executive committee, and a three-man delegation made up of Mansfield superintendent Lee Pennington, Fort Worth athletic director Ronny White and Crowley superintendent Sidney Poynter was assigned to investigate.

After the delegation completed a preliminary investigation, a meeting was held at Granbury to hear arguments from both sides. The McNeills came to the meeting with three lawyers, and during the course of the meeting, they claimed their move to Cleburne was based on academic considerations. By transferring to Cleburne, McNeill's lawyers argued, Trey could graduate at mid-term and apply for medical school. Their point being that Cleburne High required only twenty credits to graduate, whereas Paschal required twenty-two.

The executive committee was not swayed by the early graduation argument. Ronny White questioned the timing of their move.

"If you were so concerned about early graduation, why was the first person you contacted in Cleburne a football coach?" White asked. "And why was the first document you had processed an athletic transfer form?"

At one point in the questioning, Sam McNeill, the father, was asked if he had registered to vote in Cleburne—registering to vote is one of the University Interscholastic League's requirements to establish residency. McNeill responded that, yes, he had registered to vote in Cleburne.

"When?" Superintendent Poynter asked, requiring a more specific answer.

"Day before yesterday," McNeill answered.

The meeting lasted for four long hours, but in the end, the conference decided the McNeill's had not established residency in Cleburne. The vote was 5–0, with Cleburne abstaining. Even though the committee elected not to rule on the recruiting issue, which might have included sanctions against Coach Curtis, the whole affair was embarrassing for everyone involved.

While the committee was in executive session discussing the pros and cons, Trey McNeill walked over to me and introduced himself.

"I've always wanted to shake hands with you, Coach Wood," Trey told me.

"I wish it could have been under different circumstances," I replied, accepting his firm handshake. Trey McNeill was a fine young man. It's a shame he had to get caught in the middle of his father's ambition and a coach's disregard for rules. Trey could have had a great senior year of football had the rules been observed. Instead, he watched the entire season from the sidelines.

◆　◆　◆

AS FOOTBALL PRACTICE BEGAN in August, Brownwood had some huge holes to fill. Every starting lineman on both offense and defense had been lost to graduation. Coaches Southall, West and I, along with our new helper Coach Rick Wilson, had some hard decisions to make. From a group which included Tommy Smith, Troy Carroll, Tim Heath, Erin Bird, Forrest Blanton, Fernando Mosqueda, Pat Cowan, and Thad Ellis, we had to cull out the best blockers.

Our task of finding people to lug the football was easier. Both David Pounds and Randy Oehrlein looked like they could get the signal calling job done, and with speedsters like James Galloway, Sky Sudderth, Ricky Henderson, Mark Ellis, Taylor Baker, Bryon Williams, Bryce Ratliff and Wes Denton to handoff to, our running game seemed unstoppable. Sure-handed receivers like Carter Sharpe, Chris Loudermilk and Chris Barton added to our offensive firepower.

On defense, we were counting on rock-ribbed guys like Artie Woodcox, Ruben Gonzales, Terry Schulze, Martin Vasquez, Ronald Isom, Rocky Allen, David Lancaster, Johnny Hillary and Kevin Boscamp to hold the line.

◆　◆　◆

RONALD REAGAN'S ELECTION seemed to usher in another era of change—change in economic policies, change in dress codes and change in lifestyle. A study done by a group of foot doctors revealed one in every ten women wore a size ten shoe or larger as a result of participation in dancing, aerobics and jogging.

By 1983, strange musical groups I'd never heard of like Air Supply, The Greg Kihn Band, Afrika Bambaataa, and Earth, Wind and Fire were recording the hit songs. I couldn't understand the words, so I quit listening to popular music. One pop singer named Madonna performed on stage wearing her underwear as outer-wear, and according to the Abilene newspaper, a skinny kid named Michael Jackson, who never played a down of football in his life, was the "top hero" of young Americans.

In Central Texas, thankfully, change came more slowly. Brownwood opened the football season in Abilene against Cooper's Cougars, and our Lions ran head on into a 208-pound Mack Truck named Allen Gunter. Gunter hammered my gorilla defense for 148 yards, ran for the game's only touchdown, and set up a Cougar field goal. Our only score came when Mark Ellis, a sophomore playing his first high school game, thumped a 27-yard three-pointer through the uprights four seconds before intermission.

Final score: Brownwood 3, Cooper 10.

In our second game, we fared much better. Our maroon offense put together drives of eighty-one and fifty-nine yards to wreck new Weatherford coach Steve Reid's home debut 14–7.

Faced with the king-sized task of playing 5A powerhouse San Angelo Central, we returned to the friendly confines of Gordon Wood Stadium. There, our young Lions gave everything they had for all forty-eight minutes, but the home field advantage made no difference. Our offense spent most of the night on the sidelines, as a bunch of ball-hogs dressed up like Bobcats rolled for five touch-downs to beat Brownwood 35–10.

From mid-September through mid-October, while Martina Navratilova was nailing down her first U.S. Open women's singles title and Australia II was outsailing U.S. yacht Liberty to end a string of 132 consecutive U.S. victories and capture the America's Cup, my sporadic young Lions were finding their sea legs. In a road engagement at Granbury, Brownwood opened zone play with a convincing 38–0 keeper.

Next, we traveled to Everman where we fell behind early and were forced to mount a 46-yard drive in the final quarter. Tailback James Galloway, who rushed for a career high 137 yards, delivered the knockout punch. With only 4:34 remaining on the clock, James burst in from the eleven for the go-ahead TD. Gordon's gorilla defenders took over from there.

Final score: Brownwood 27, Everman 22.

On the first Friday in October, Brownwood edged Joshua 27–17 to set up the most anticipated, most talked about high school game in the country.

Both Brownwood and Cleburne were undefeated in zone play. Cleburne was 6–0 overall and ranked third in the state, but it wasn't rankings or records which attracted all the attention. By then, the whole world knew Gordon Wood and Chuck Curtis had no love for each other.

After the residency decision went against Cleburne in mid-August, I became the target of several letters which were published in area newspapers. The letters accused me of hypocrisy, saying I was guilty of the same crime I had charged Coach Curtis with. The writers claimed I recruited Tyler Tabor out of Blanket High School to quarterback my Brownwood club to the state championship back in '81.

Of course, the allegations were completely false. I had proved that with my presentation to the District 4–AAAA investigation committee back in the fall of 1981. At first, I tried to ignore the renewed claims, but as time passed and the accusations persisted, I have to admit they got under my skin. While I had absolutely no proof Chuck Curtis was behind the letter writing attack on my integrity, I couldn't help but wonder.

◆　◆　◆

OUR 4–AAAA SHOWDOWN was played at Gordon Wood Stadium before a standing room only crowd, and despite the animosity between their head coaches, both teams played good clean football.

Steve Hafford had stepped in as Cleburne's quarterback after Paschal transfer Trey McNeill was ruled ineligible, and Hafford proved he was the right man for the job. Early in the first quarter Hafford handed the football to his 198-pound tailback Randall Scott. Scott blasted through our BHS picket line and darted sixty-five yards to give the Yellowjackets a 7–0 lead. A short time later, the Yellowjackets cashed in on Brent Jones' fingertip interception at Cleburne's forty-eight to increase their margin to 14–0. Then, in the final minutes of the first half, a jarring tackle applied by black and gold defender Randy Petty, separated Lion quarterback David Pounds from the football. James Jones recovered for Cleburne at Brownwood's twenty-two, and with fifty-eight seconds left, Hafford completed his only pass of the night—a scoring strike to Carlton Liggins. That made the score 21–0.

With Randall Scott and 205-pound pile driver fullback Charles Walker taking turns hammering at Brownwood's defense, Cleburne completely dominated the first half. During the halftime intermission, we made some defensive adjustments, and in the third period, our defensive crew held the Jackets to one first down while our offense rolled, scoring on their first two possessions.

After Martin Vasquez recovered a Cleburne fumble at the Jackets' forty-six, Brownwood went the distance in nine plays. Galloway did most of the damage, blasting for consecutive gains of fifteen, four, three, four, four, and four yards. Then Pounds took it in from the one. Kevin Boscamp tacked on the extra point, and the score was 21–7.

Following the kickoff, Brownwood's defense stopped the Jackets again, with Lion linebacker Ronald Isom corralling David Self for a two-yard loss on third and five at the Cleburne twenty-three. Following a 24-yard punt by Joe Chavez, the Lions got the ball back at the forty-seven. Four plays later Pounds hit Armando Salazar for a 26-yard touchdown. Salazar had been moved up from the JV two weeks earlier. This was his first reception as a varsity player. Boscamp missed on the extra point try, but with the gap narrowed to 21–13, victory was in sight.

Brownwood kicked off, and my gritty maroon Gorillas held Cleburne again. In order to have Chavez punt into the wind from his twenty-six, we used up two time-outs. That strategy backfired when the strong-legged kicker got off a 35-yarder, forcing Brownwood to start from the 39-yard line. Nevertheless, our Lions came out firing on all cylinders. Galloway ran for twelve. Pounds rifled a rocket to tight end Rocky Allen for a first down at Cleburne's thirty-five. A swing pass to Wes Denton gained six before Galloway carried the ball to the twenty-one on an end sweep. Then ever-present Yellowjacket Randall Scott threw a monkey-wrench in our plans. He intercepted a Pounds' pass at the one.

Cleburne's Joe Chavez had quit football during August two-a-days and didn't rejoin his teammates until mid-season. When the Jackets ran out of downs at the two, Joe made Coach Curtis and every Cleburne fan in the stadium glad he'd changed his mind about football. On fourth down, Chavez retreated to the back of the end zone, took the snap from center, and calmly booted a 55-yard punt which traveled to the Lion forty-three. Brownwood's desire seemed to die right there. We never made another first down.

Final score: Brownwood 13, Cleburne 27.

When Cleburne coach Chuck Curtis resigned in the spring of '84 to take the head coaching job at UT-Arlington, I can't say I was sorry. But now, looking back, I have to admit he always fielded competitive teams. Those times our football teams clashed in '81, '82 and '83 were three of the most exciting, most spine-tingling games Brownwood ever played outside the state playoffs.

◆ ◆ ◆

FOR A SECOND YEAR in a row, Lion boosters owed a debt of gratitude to El Campo football coach Buzzy Keith who conceived and promoted the runner-up proposal to the UIL. Thanks to Buzzy, the Lions still controlled their own destiny, and they headed down the home stretch with high hopes of making the state playoffs as the runner-up in District 4–AAAA.

Our Maroons assured their invitation to the party with wins over Stephenville, Mansfield and Crowley, but to reach the inner circle where the real fun was, members of District 4–AAAA had to get past the best teams in the other zone. That was often a tough chore, but my Lions got it done without much hassle, beating North Zone champion Fort Worth Riverside 28–7.

That win set up a bi-district bout with Coach Leo Brittain's Vernon Lions. Vernon boasted a season record of 8–0–2. In ten games, Coach Brittain's defense had given up only sixty-nine points, but two other items added to the pre-game hype. Vernon was Coach Southall's hometown, and Leo Brittain had coached the Graham team which beat Brownwood in 1975—the last year Brownwood's football troops failed to reach the playoffs.

◆ ◆ ◆

EVERY COACH AGONIZES over his losses, perhaps even more than he savors his wins. But some losses torture your soul. The losses which grieve a coach most are the games he should have won. My most bitter loss was our bi-district game against Vernon in 1983. The game was played on a Friday night at Abilene's Shotwell Stadium. The weather was cold, wet and windy—a horrible night for a football game.

Brownwood scored a touchdown in the second quarter via a short pass from David Pounds to Rocky Allen. Thanks to no fumbles, no interceptions, no penalties and gutty defensive play, our Maroons were leading 6–0 late in the game.

Vernon had an outstanding kicker named Chris Burns. During the second half, his long punts forced our offense to start from inside our twenty, three times. Less than five minutes were left on the clock when Burns got off another star scraper. The ball rolled dead at Brownwood's eight-yard line. After we took possession, our offense was unable to move. Rather than have our punter, Thad Ellis, kick from inside the end zone, we elected to take an intentional safety.

With 3:05 remaining, Brownwood was leading 6–2. Vernon had been going nowhere against our raging defense. So you'd think all Brownwood had to do was free kick and rely on my gorilla defense? Wrong! Here's why a coach's hair turns gray early.

Vernon received the free kick and ran the ball back to midfield. There, our defense drew a line and refused to budge. On third and long, Vernon quarterback Bill Owen lofted a poorly-thrown desperation pass in the direction of his right end Ron Johnson. Even though the throw was way off target and impossible to catch, Brownwood was flagged for pass interference. On the next play, Owen found halfback James Dixon open for a 49-yard touchdown, and Vernon went ahead 9–6.

On the kickoff, we dug ourselves another hole. Our receiver mishandled the ball at the right corner of the playing field and stepped on the sideline marker at the two-yard line. This meant my offense would have to drive ninety-eight yards to win the game. With time so short, that task seemed next to impossible. I sent in instructions to my quarterback David Pounds to take the snap, step back into the end zone, drop down on one knee and take another safety.

Now the Lions were down 11–6. What happened in the next sixty-one seconds will be talked about in Brownwood coffee shops for years to come.

Prior to the free kick, I notified the referees that we planned to kickoff out of a huddle. I explained that one of our players would put the ball on the kicking tee. The rest of the team would stay in a huddle. I advised the officials to get out of the way as soon as the whistle blew, because our players would break their huddle and rush the ball for an on-side kick.

Brownwood's unusual on-side free kick caught the V-Lion receiving team totally by surprise. A maroon-clad player recovered the football at the 32-yard line.

Still sixty-eight yards from the winning touchdown, and with only a minute remaining, a Brownwood comeback seemed next to impossible, but I had a plan. Before the game I had told the referees if Brownwood was behind late in the game, we might line up in an unorthodox passing formation I called the "Crazy Eight." After Brownwood gained possession of the football on the on-side kick, I informed the officials we would use the "Crazy Eight."

My "Crazy Eight" strategy worked like a charm. When the Lions broke from their huddle and lined up with maroon jerseys spread all across the football field, Vernon's defense was completely baffled. We had a tackle and end lined up wide left, three backs set out wide right and our right end lined up where the right tackle would normally be.

Pounds' first pass fell incomplete. Then he started clicking. On second down David faded back and hit Wes Denton for eight. His next pass was to Rocky Allen at mid-field. Brownwood had one time-out left. We burned it with seventeen seconds left on the clock.

During the time-out, I sent in halfback Chris Loudermilk to substitute for Rocky Allen at end. Loudermilk's instructions were to run twenty yards downfield and break across the middle. Chris was wide open when he made his cut, and Pounds' pass was right on the money. The play was good for thirty yards. Chris was pulled down at Vernon's twenty. When the game officials took a time-out to move the chains, the scoreboard showed one second left on the clock.

On the long pass play, Brownwood lineman Tim Heath suffered a broken ankle. We wanted to bring a stretcher on the field, but the officials were impatient. They probably thought Heath was faking an injury because they began yelling at BHS players to hurry up even before our young men reached the new line of scrimmage. Team managers Curtis Evans and Ricky Kelly and two of my assistant coaches were trying to carry our injured player off the field when one of the referees put his foot on the football, holding it down as he prepared to blow his whistle and begin play.

Because the official had his foot in the way, our center Thad Ellis was unable to get his hands around the ball. Ellis looked up at the referee and told him, "Ref, you gotta take your foot off the ball. Because the second you blow your whistle, I'm gonna snap it."

Now, Brownwood was back in our regular winged-T formation, with the quarterback taking the ball directly from the center. Pounds called a goal line passing play, and it worked perfectly. Chris Loudermilk caught the ball in the end zone for a touchdown.

The official who deprived our center of his position over the football rolled to the right and never stopped the play, never blew his whistle, or made any move to indicate Brownwood didn't get the snap off in time. All five officials signaled Loudermilk's catch a touchdown, and the stadium went wild. Brownwood players and fans went absolutely bonkers, hugging each other, rolling around in the grass. It's a wonder Chris Loudermilk didn't get hurt, with his teammates climbing all over him during the jubilant celebration.

I walked across the field to shake hands with Vernon coach Leo Brittain and sympathize with him for losing. We were still talking when this loony referee ran up to me.

"Don't worry about the extra point, Ref," I said, thinking he wanted to get my team back on the field for the extra point try. "We'll forego the kick."

"No, Coach, you didn't score."

"Whatta you mean I didn't score? You officials called a touchdown."

"Time ran out. Vernon won the game." As soon as he gave me the bad news, the official broke and ran for the field house, not bothering to explain.

At first I was stunned. Then I got mad. My temper was simmering when I approached the officials' dressing quarters. I intended to get an explanation. An Abilene policeman was guarding the door.

"You can't go in there, Coach," the policeman warned me.

"There's no doubt about me going in. You see those two men coming toward us? One man is Vernon's school superintendent. The other fellow is James Lancaster, Brownwood's superintendent.

This was our game. And I am going in. I won't create a problem, but I intend to get an explanation."

The police officer saw the determined look on my face and quickly stepped aside. Inside the room, the five game officials were hurriedly changing clothes.

"Now, one more time," I said, walking up to the official who made the call. "Tell me why Brownwood lost."

"Time ran out!" the man snapped. He was obviously intimidated by my question. He stood up, like he was preparing to leave.

"Wait just a minute! I want a better explanation than that!"

"Time ran out!" he repeated curtly, still not bothering to justify his call.

"How can that be? When you rolled to the right, you didn't blow your whistle. You didn't cross your arms to stop the play, and every official out there called it a touchdown." I turned to the other men who were in various states of dress.

"Did you hear a whistle?" I asked one of the other officials.

"No sir. It was too noisy."

I turned to another official. "Did you hear a whistle?"

"No sir. It was too noisy."

I asked every man in the room the same question. Each man gave me the same answer.

"Fellows," I said, my voice quivering with anger, "you can lie for this man, but you know and I know there was no whistle."

Every man there knew they had made a mistake, but they were covering up. They weren't necessarily lying, because no whistle was blown. I was mad as hell when I stormed out of the room. I was ready to fight, protest, see that justice was done. Then something happened to change my mind.

My four captains, Ronald Isom, Thomas Smith, David Pounds and James Galloway, were inside Vernon's dressing room, shaking hands with the Vernon players, congratulating them on a great game and telling them we'd be supporting them in the playoffs. It was a scene that warmed my heart. Sometimes it takes kids to show us grownups how to act.

The game films later showed every official signaling a touchdown. One Abilene television station put a timer on their video recording. The TV document showed our center snapped the football in four-tenths of a second. Our superintendent and many Brownwood fans wanted to protest to the UIL, but I resisted. Brownwood had enjoyed a great relationship with Vernon High School for so many years. I didn't want to spoil it over a football game. If my players could accept the loss gracefully, I thought I should too.

Final score: Brownwood 6, Vernon 11.

Several days later I telephoned Bailey Marshall to ask how the UIL would have ruled if Brownwood had protested. Marshall told me the league would never change an official's call.

"What about the game officials? Can they change their call after the game?" I asked, not letting the league president off the hook so easily.

"Don't ask me such hard questions," Bailey replied and hung up.

In their quarterfinal contest, Vernon lost to Lubbock Estacado 35–13.

1984

LIKE HIS FATHER, my son Jim decided to be a football coach. Jim attended Texas Tech where he played football as a "walk-on" for one semester. Then he transferred to McMurry University and played there for a couple of years. Even though his playing time was limited, he learned a lot about coaching and made excellent grades. His senior year, Jim decided to give up playing and concentrate on coaching. While he continued to attend classes at McMurry, he worked as an assistant football coach under Bill Anderson at Cisco Junior College. Bill was an assistant coach for me at Stamford back in the fifties. Coach Anderson is a terrific guy and a fine football coach. He and Jim got along great.

After he graduated from McMurry in 1981, Jim moved around for a few years, coaching at Elgin and Jacksonville. Jim met his wife Jan while he was still a student at McMurry, but they waited until she graduated from the University of Texas in 1982 to marry. In the spring of '83, Jim landed at Early High School as the Longhorns' head football coach. Early is located right on the outskirts of Brownwood. Katharine and I looked forward to seeing a lot more of our son and his wife.

His first season at Early High, Jim's Longhorn team only won three games. A limited talent pool forced Jim to start one freshman and three sophomores, but still, he did a fine job. During the '83 season, Jim's JV team didn't lose a single game. They even beat

Brownwood's JV. One superintendent in Jim's district told me, "It's all over. Once Jim Wood gets his system going, nobody will ever win this conference except Early."

◆ ◆ ◆

WHILE RONALD REAGAN was being renominated for president at the Republican convention held in Dallas, Brownwood High began August two-a-days in preparation for our '84 campaign. Line coaches Ken West and Rick Wilson were anticipating several real battles for starting offensive positions, but no matter who started, Tim Heath, Erin Bird, Artie Woodcox, Harold Isom, Blanton Dees, and Brant Horner were expected to see plenty of action.

Brownwood's backfield stable included Terry Carrathus, Mark Ellis, Byron Williams, Ricky Henderson, Chris Loudermilk, and quarterbacks Kevin Boscamp and Mike Norman. When it came to toting the football, every one was a real hoss.

On defense, Armando Salazar, Taylor Baker, Daniel Gonzales, Rocky Allen, Sky Sudderth, Carter Sharpe, David Lancaster, Fernando Mosqueda, Randy Oehrlein, Jason Cauble, Jackie Galloway and Robert Jackson looked rock solid.

With Bryan Hensley drawing placement duty and Joel Hoover handling the punts, we expected our kicking game to improve dramatically.

◆ ◆ ◆

AS ALWAYS, BROWNWOOD opened the season against Abilene Cooper. The Cougars were coached by Mike Garrison, a former Cooper assistant. Garrison was the Cougars' third head football coach in as many seasons, but Cooper's unstable coaching situation didn't help Brownwood much.

Bucking a stiff wind, Cooper took the opening kickoff and traveled seventy-six yards to take a 7–0 lead. As it turned out, that was all the points Abilene would need. Even though our defense held the Cougars' offense to only 136 more yards, a sputtering Lion offense and a self-destructing kicking game killed our chances. Brownwood never advanced the football past the Cougars' forty-yard line.

Final score: Brownwood 0, Cooper 17.

In our second game at Weatherford, our Maroons were trailing

7–3 late in the third quarter when Lion Terry Carrathus came to the rescue. Terry fielded a Kangaroo punt at the Brownwood nine and electrified the nearly full house with a breathtaking 91-yard return. With linebackers Daniel Gonzales, Armando Salazar, Carter Sharpe and Sky Sudderth in on almost every tackle, our defense took over from there.

Final score: Brownwood 10, Weatherford 7.

Playing in a light mist at Killeen's Buckley Stadium the next week, we weren't so fortunate. Brownwood's defense held the maroon and white 'Roos to 123 total yards, but our offense could only generate 116. Brownwood got a last chance to pull out a win when Sky Sudderth picked off a pass with 3:14 left. All hope died, however, when Jackie Galloway couldn't find the handle on junior quarterback Mike Norman's fourth-down desperation pass, and the game ended in a 0–0 draw.

Coaches Wood and West share a tense moment during the Killeen game.
(*credit:* Brownwood Bulletin)

◆　◆　◆

DURING THE WEEK prior to our conference opener with Coach Gerald Jack's Crowley Eagles, a department store chain announced plans to build a new discount store in Brownwood. According to the *Brownwood Bulletin*, the Bentonville, Arkansas-based chain currently operated 134 stores in Texas, and they liked the business climate in Brownwood. Naturally, my builder friend Herman Bennett would be the prime contractor. The fast-growing chain, which would eventually dominate retail sales and change buying habits of shoppers all across the country, was, of course, Wal-Mart.

In three games, Brownwood's anemic offense hadn't scored a single touchdown, but in a pre-game interview, Coach Jack told Brownwood sportswriter Bill Stovall he was worried. "Brownwood's offense is just waiting to explode," Jack proclaimed, and he was absolutely right.

*Coach Wood has a few choice words of advice for senior
quarterback Kevin Boscamp. (credit: Brownwood Bulletin)*

Quarterbacks Mike Norman and Kevin Boscamp combined to complete nine of ten passes for 188 yards with eight different receivers logging a catch. Eleven different maroon jerseys toted the football as Brownwood added another 223 yards rushing. The honor of scoring the season's first offensive touchdown, however, went to Todd Reeves, a junior fullback we had just promoted from the JV team.

Final score: Brownwood 47, Crowley 13.

Warming up for another head-knocking showdown with Cleburne, we journeyed to Joshua where our Lions put on a crackerjack performance for one and a half quarters, scoring four touchdowns to take a 27–0 lead. Then we suffered the embarrassment of giving up two TDs in the final seventy-two seconds of the first half to let the pesky Owls back in the game.

After intermission our Maroons regained their composure and salted the game away 37–14.

◆　◆　◆

WHEN CHUCK CURTIS put on his famous cowboy hat and rode off to UT-Arlington, Cleburne handed the reins to Chuck's assistant coach Jerry Cunningham. Cunningham inherited a mother lode of talent, from which he put together an awesome scoring machine. Cunningham's big gun was multi-talented Steve Hafford. In two years as the Jackets' field general, Hafford had completed forty-four of fifty-nine passes, winning eighteen games while losing only one. Cleburne's attack also featured 200-pound sledgehammer tailback Alvis Scott. Scott could run you ragged with his running and his pass-catches, then beat your brains out from his defensive linebacker position. Of course, to beat Cleburne's Black and Gold, you also had to stop Carlton Liggins, a 160-pound waterbug wing-back with 4.4 speed.

With the Gordon Wood-Chuck Curtis catalyst missing, pre-game media hype was much more reserved than in previous years. But for both Brownwood and Cleburne a win was still vitally important. Both teams were undefeated in district play, and with an improving, unbeaten Everman team still on the horizon, the loser could find himself sitting at home come playoff time.

Before the kickoff, every fan in Gordon Wood Stadium expected another rock-'em, sock-'em, last-man-standing brawl, but the anticipated rumble never materialized. Cleburne's tight end Al Smith and wingback Carlton Liggins roamed our secondary almost at will, and quarterback Steve Hafford's passes were usually right on target. By halftime, Cleburne was ahead 30–3, and the Yellowjackets wrapped up their third straight win over Brownwood, a feat no team except Abilene Cooper had ever accomplished.

Their 30–3 loss to Cleburne was also the Lions' most one-sided defeat since Burkburnett whipped an injury-riddled maroon squad in 1972.

◆　◆　◆

BROWNWOOD'S LOSS TO CLEBURNE left the Lions facing a tough assignment. In order to reach the playoffs, Brownwood had to win out. Taking a deep breath, our kids lowered their heads and went to work. We put the show on the road by walloping Stephenville 30–6 on a rain-swamped football field at Tarleton's Memorial Stadium. That set up a "must-win" encounter between Brownwood and unbeaten Everman. With Cleburne playing so well, the loser seemed certain to be eliminated from post-season play.

Everman was coached by Joel Edwards, a San Saba native and

a graduate of Howard Payne University. Coach Edwards' stingy defense was working on its fifth straight shutout when they arrived in Brownwood to take on the Lions, and for three and a half quarters, his purple and gold defenders made their coach proud.

With 6:30 left in the game, Brownwood had only crossed the mid-field stripe one time, and the Bulldogs were leading 14–0. That's when Lion barn-burner Terry Carrathus fielded an Everman punt, shifted into high gear, and blasted sixty-three yards for Brownwood's first points of the night.

After a knee injury at Stephenville ended starting quarterback Mike Norman's season, Brownwood was down to one quarterback—Kevin Boscamp. So we brought a kid named Mitch Moore up from the JV for insurance. Naturally, we hoped to give Moore some playing time—if we got a big lead. We never expected to put our whole season in Mitch's hands, but that's exactly what happened.

When Boscamp got hurt and couldn't go, we crossed our fingers and sent in a junior quarterback who had never played a

An anxious Mitch Moore gets encouragement from Lion coaches before he goes in to replace Kevin Boscamp at quarterback.
(credit: Brownwood Bulletin)

down of varsity football. In the next four minutes, Mitch Moore earned the admiration of every person in the stadium. Taking charge like an old pro, Moore completed three of four passes, one to Jason Cauble for thirty, one to Carter Sharpe for nine, and one to Todd Reeves for ten. After Reeves ran in for six points, Moore completed his comeback march by handing the ball to Jackie Galloway. Galloway smashed across for the two-point conversion, and with 2:16 remaining, Brownwood held a 15–14 lead.

In our district series with Everman, Brownwood had won six straight times. With their best chance in years to end that string, an unlikely hero stepped forward. Bulldog quarterback Jon Bural, who was averaging only sixty yards a game passing, came out firing. On the first play from scrimmage after the kickoff, Bural hooked up with L.C. Jackson on a fifty-yard bomb, moving the ball to Brownwood's thirty-three. Then, facing third and ten and under heavy pressure from maroon defender David Lancaster, Everman's senior quarterback speared Bradley Burney for a first down at the nineteen. After an incomplete pass, Bural called a quarterback sneak and ran the ball to the seven. With seventy-one seconds left, he hit tight end Broderick President for the game-winner.

Final score: Brownwood 15, Everman 20.

In the final weeks, after Ronald Reagan defeated Walter Mondale in the most one-sided election in U.S. history, Brownwood played out the '84 season, cruising by Mansfield 28–14 and whacking Granbury 28–15.

To everyone's surprise, Everman's Bulldogs pinned a 14–10 loss on undefeated Cleburne to capture Everman's first District 4–AAAA title and their first championship of any kind in twenty-two years. After his purple and gold team beat Cleburne, Everman coach Joel Edwards was a happy man.

"The old timers like to say a hungry dog hunts better," Edwards declared. "Well, we're pretty hungry. We've been after this for a long time."

Although North and South Zone alignments in District 4–AAAA disappeared prior to the '84 season, neither Everman nor Cleburne got very far in the playoffs. In bi-district play Everman lost to Fort Worth Brewer 15–14. Cleburne fell to Wichita Falls Hirschi 21–20.

◆   ◆   ◆

THE 1984-85 SCHOOL YEAR held serious disappointment for the Wood family. Over at Early High School, Jim found himself surrounded with controversy. Jim had heard several members of the basketball squad were smoking marijuana and called the boys involved to his office. When he confronted the players with the accusation, they each admitted their guilt and agreed to accept Jim's method of punishment.

Two of the kids were sons of school board members. One boy apparently had second thoughts. He went home and complained to his dad about being punished. The next day the father rushed into Jim's office.

"You don't understand, Coach," the man told Jim. "My son didn't admit to smoking marijuana." And despite Jim's lengthy explanation, the school board father would never believe his son did anything wrong.

As you might expect, the man's son was a big-time athlete. That, of course, was the major obstacle. When Jim resisted the father's demand to exempt his son from punishment, all hell broke loose. Before the marijuana incident was laid to rest, Jim became the object of unfounded parent grievances and school board accusations.

Since childhood, Jim has always been kind, sensitive and concerned. All the name calling and finger pointing nearly broke his heart. By mid-January, my son had all he could take. He resigned his job as head football coach.

That spring Jim decided to go back to college. He accepted a post as a graduate assistant for Coach John Payne at Abilene Christian University, but Jim's enthusiasm for coaching was never the same again.

The next summer Jim took a part time job selling insurance. He and Jan were expecting a baby, so Jim was hoping to earn a few extra dollars between the spring and summer semesters. Jim discovered he was really good at sales. In a matter of about six weeks, he earned more money than he made coaching for a whole football season.

Grandson Ty Wood came along in September. Jim was enrolled at ACU, studying hard and helping coach football, but one thing led to another, and before long Jim went to work for Payne-Webber as a stock broker. Two years later he switched to Merrill Lynch, but

Wood family get-together—Jim and his wife Jan, Gordon, Katharine, and Pat.
(credit: Wood Family Collection)

then the stock market went bust, and many of Jim's clients lost a lot of money. Seeing his customers and friends have their savings wiped out in the down market almost destroyed Jim. Jim quit eating. He lost weight. His health deteriorated. I truly thought my son might die from anxiety.

In the fall of 1988, Jim quit his job at Merrill Lynch and enrolled in law school at the University of Oklahoma. He graduated with honors in 1991. Deciding to specialize in courtroom law, Jim moved his family to Amarillo. In the beginning, neither Jim nor Jan nor Grandson Ty were too excited about living in Amarillo, but now they wouldn't leave. They like the town, love the people, and Jim has never been happier.

CHAPTER TWENTY

One Last Hurrah

(1985)

EVER SINCE BROWNWOOD won the state championship in 1981, I'd been promising assistant coach Kenneth West he would get my head football job when I retired. My promises were made in good faith. In '81, I truly never thought I would still be coaching after I turned seventy, but seems like every year something would come along to get my juices flowing, and I'd decide to go one more year. In 1983, I became the first active coach and only the second high school coach to be inducted into the prestigious Texas Sports Hall of Fame. In 1984, I was inducted into the Texas High School Hall of Fame at Waco, and following the 1984 football season, I was selected to coach the annual Oil Bowl game at Wichita Falls for a second time.

After the football season ended, Brownwood superintendent James Lancaster approached Coach West, asking if Kenneth might be interested in the high school principal's job. Royce Blackburn, who had been our principal for several years, was leaving. The school board was looking for someone to replace Royce.

Lancaster's job offer put Coach West in a real quandary. The principal's salary was too good to turn down, but in spite of the better pay, Kenneth wanted the head coaching position. He had waited patiently, without complaint, while I wavered back and forth about retiring.

Kenneth was also extremely loyal to me and to our sports program. Before he made a decision, Kenneth came to me, and we talked it over. I encouraged him to take the principal's job, telling him I had decided to coach another year. That made up his mind. That spring, Kenneth West assumed the vice-principal post at

Brownwood High, and in the fall of '85 after Royce Blackburn left, the man who had been my assistant coach for twenty-one years became my high school principal.

Kenneth's decision to accept the principal's job prompted several discussions about retiring between Coach Southall and myself. When I inquired if he would be interested in taking over as head coach when I left, Morris was very specific.

"Heck no! The minute I turn sixty-five, I'm retiring. I want to watch my son Si coach over at Angelo State, and I've got grandkids now. I intend to watch every down of every game they play, even if they're only playing flag football!"

1985

BECAUSE OF MY OIL BOWL commitment, my final season of coaching started early. On August 2, Katharine and I were on our way to Wichita Falls, looking forward to joining Texas coaches Marty Criswell of Denison and Joe Bob Tyler of Wichita Falls, when we heard the bad news. Delta Airlines jet L-1011 had crashed at Dallas-Fort Worth International Airport. One hundred and thirty-three passengers were killed in the worst air disaster in Texas history. For Texans and the whole nation, it was a sad day.

Despite the disheartening news, the Oil Bowl Classic was played the following Saturday. With running backs Ronnie Boyce and James Dixon from Vernon, Dudley McAfee from Wichita Falls, Dal Watson from Odessa Permian, and Chris Moore, son of Texas Tech coach Jerry Moore, our Texas all-star squad was loaded with backfield talent.

Adding to our firepower was Tom Enloe, a quarterback from Olney; Ray Crockett, a quarterback from Duncanville; Stan Stephens, a quarterback from Richland; and receiver-kick returner Tyrone Thurman of Midland Lee. Having sticky-fingered ends Fred Washington of Denison, Brent Parker of Decatur, and Mike Chisom of Vernon on the squad insured a successful Texas air show.

Before the game, Texas held a commanding 30–9–1 lead in the long series, but a fellow named Shell Henry from Picher, Oklahoma, hadn't paid attention. Not knowing Texas was supposed to win, Henry rushed for seventy-three yards and scored two touchdowns. Henry's second TD came with only 6:46 left to give Oklahoma a 13–12 lead, and it stood up.

◆ ◆ ◆

JOHN HARRIS, who operated the highly-regarded Harris Football Poll, was a former all-state basketball star at Brownwood High. However, when the *Texas Schoolboy Football Forecast* published his predictions for the '85 season, Harris had little empathy for his alma mater.

"Over a long period of years," Harris wrote, "the Lions have developed a fondness for winning not only district titles but state titles as well. Now, though, this legendary team has been caught by Cleburne, Everman, and more recently, Mansfield. All indications here reflect that the Lions cannot be motivated like they used to be."

Brownwood missed the playoffs in 1984, snapping a string of nine straight post-season appearances. Our '84 record of 6–3–1 was the Lions' worst since 1972, when we went 6–4. So what Harris actually meant was—we were complacent "fat cats" with an old coach who couldn't compete anymore. Well, we'd see about that. I posted the article on the locker room bulletin board where every Brownwood player could read it.

◆ ◆ ◆

TWO-A-DAY FOOTBALL PRACTICE unofficially commenced on Wednesday, August 7, with conditioning workouts under the direction of our seniors. The following Sunday, the Lions Mothers Club got everyone in the right mood by hosting their annual ice cream supper at PDQ Barbeque Park. On Monday, we coaches joined the party, issuing headgear, shoulder pads, shorts and cleats for limited contact drills.

With Kenneth West up to his ears in administrative duties, I invited Wayne Rathke to join Morris Southall, Rick Wilson and me on the varsity coaching staff. With only ten lettermen returning, we had a big rebuilding task to do.

Offensively, only tackle Erin Bird and all-district center Harold Isom were back, but Armando Salazar, Brian Dodds, Craig Comolli, Gunnar Giddens, and DeWayne Wood looked promising.

With quarterbacks Mike Norman and Mitch Moore directing the show, and lettermen running backs Todd Reeves, Jason Cauble and Mark Ellis to carry the football, our backfield looked unusually strong. Hard-running junior fullback Jim Slaton also looked good.

Defensively, I was expecting Kris Boyd, Cody Neal, Raymond Tijerina, Jimmy Shelton, Doug Hicks, David Jones, Carson Williams, Keith Cook, and Craig Jacobson to become my '85 Gorillas.

◆　◆　◆

BROWNWOOD KICKED OFF the football season in Abilene. As usual, our maroon troops were met head on by a revved-up pack of Cougars. But a funny thing happened during our visit to the Big Country—Brownwood won.

To the pleasant surprise of BHS partisans, the Lions outhit and outplayed Big Blue. On the fifth snap of the night, Lion quarterback Mitch Moore lofted a 28-yard scoring strike to Armando Salazar, and from that point, Brownwood dominated game action. Moore connected on ten of fourteen passes for 248 yards, hitting Salazar, Jason Cauble and Craig Comolli with scoring shots. Interceptions by Mike Norman and Carson Williams, and fumble recoveries by Raymond Tijerina, Kris Boyd and Jimmy Shelton helped shut down the pass-happy Cougars.

Final score: Brownwood 27, Cooper 14.

Brownwood's win over Abilene Cooper was only the eighth in the 23-game series.

The Lions played host to Weatherford the next week—on Friday the 13th. That was unlucky for the Kangaroos. With Mitch Moore completing eleven of eighteen passes, our offense exploded for 343 yards while a steel-belted maroon defense kept Coach Steve Reid's wishbone offense in a tight strait jacket.

Final score: Brownwood 21, Weatherford 6.

◆　◆　◆

AFTER OPENING THE SEASON with two consecutive victories, Lion boosters were in a party mood. Almost seven thousand fans packed into Gordon Wood Stadium to witness our Killeen game. Maroon faithful were hyped and anxious to celebrate Brownwood's third win in a row.

Leave it to a teenager to spoil all the fun. Up until the fourth quarter, Brownwood's swarming defense had stopped Coach Ricky Ray's Kangaroos on every possession. The score was tied at 0–0 when Killeen running back Mike Murphy took a pitchout, swept around the right side, broke a tackle at the line of scrimmage, cut back to his left, and hotfooted fifty-seven yards for the only touchdown of the game. Murphy had turned eighteen that day. He also turned out to be one of the biggest party poopers ever invited to Brown County.

In the closing minutes quarterback Mike Norman moved his Lion team from their own twenty to Killeen's twenty-three, but Brownwood hopes wilted when Mike's fourth-down pass slipped off the fingers of Armando Salazar.

Final score: Brownwood 0, Killeen 7.

◆ ◆ ◆

AFTER POSTING a 4–36 record from 1980–83, Crowley improved to 4–6 in 1984. As Brownwood prepared to face Coach Gerald Jack's team in 1985, the Eagles were unbeaten. Crowley was leading the district in scoring offense, defense against scoring, and total yards gained. Crowley running backs Barry Thomas and Scott Shafer were averaging 9.1 and 7.0 yards per carry. Eagle quarterback Charles Fisher had completed eight of fourteen passes for 214 yards and four touchdowns.

From start to finish, our battle with Crowley was a knucks-down matchup. Crowley got the first leg up by correctly calling the pre-game coin toss and electing to receive. Then a mix-up in mid-field decisions also gave the Eagles the wind advantage.

With a twenty mile per hour breeze at their backs, the Eagles took the opening kickoff and sailed down to Brownwood's seventeen where Gordon's Gorillas made their first big play of the evening. On fourth and one, Lion backup linebacker Fritz Speck met 202-pound Barry Thomas at the line of scrimmage and stopped him for no gain.

Brownwood took possession and picked up a first down before giving the ball back on a fumble at the thirty-three. This time the Eagles went all the way, scoring on a one-yard sneak by Charles Fisher.

In the second quarter, the wind table was turned, and Mitch Moore went to work. Sandwiching a sixteen-yard completion to Craig Comolli and an eighteen-yarder to Armando Salazar between his own runs of thirteen and fifteen yards, Moore guided the Lions to paydirt in four plays. Clay Childs nailed the PAT for the go-ahead point. For the remainder of the half, neither defense would yield, and Brownwood settled for a shaky 7–6 halftime lead.

On their first possession of the second half, Crowley drove down to Brownwood's thirty-one where Barry Thomas thumped through a three pointer, and Crowley fans began to smell an upset in the making.

Only nine minutes remained in the game when the Lions took possession at their own fourteen. Mitch Moore jump started our comeback drive with a twelve-yard strike to Craig Comolli then rolled out for a gain of nine. Backup quarterback Mike Norman came in to spell Moore and ran for another ten. After two stabs gained only two yards, we sent Moore back in to run a special play Coach Southall thought would work.

On third and eight, Jason Cauble took the ball on a reverse and bolted for thirty-two yards to Crowley's thirty-three. Six plays later, on fourth and one, Mark Ellis ran through a gaping hole in the left side of the line for the TD. On the two-point conversion, Moore called the identical play, and Ellis ran through untouched again.

With 3:50 remaining, Crowley had plenty of time for a comeback, but their dream of an upset perished in the arms of Lion defensive back Carson Williams who intercepted Fisher's desperation "Hail Mary" at Brownwood's thirty-five.

Final score: Brownwood 15, Crowley 10.

◆ ◆ ◆

NO MATTER HOW SWEET the victory, a football coach has little time to savor wins in the middle of football season. Next on our schedule was unbeaten Joshua. While Brownwood was fighting to pull out a win over Crowley, Coach Bob Brown's high flying Owls had stunned an undefeated Cleburne team 13–6.

Four games into the season, Everman's Bulldogs were also unbeaten. Granbury, Crowley, Cleburne and Brownwood each had only one loss. District 4–AAAA was shaping up to be a real dogfight.

Our game with Joshua was played in Brownwood. It was homecoming weekend. The Lions were a seven-point favorite. The stands were jam-packed with happy Brownwood High exes. By halftime when Homecoming Queen Shannon Burnett received her crown, Brownwood was leading 14–0, courtesy of a 69-yard bomb from Mike Norman to Craig Comolli and Clay Child's PAT with 2:09 left.

All night, though, the Lions were plagued with penalty flags. After Brownwood's punt coverage team pinned the Owls at their own twenty-three early in the third quarter, a fifteen-yard personal foul penalty moved the ball to the thirty-eight. From there, Joshua drove sixty-two yards for their first score. The key play in their drive was Owl halfback Craig Ray's 39-yard pass to Rick Van Weezel, which moved the football to the Lion nineteen. Two plays later quarterback Bill Payne scrambled to the ten where the Lions were penalized half the distance to the goal line. On the next play Payne hit blue and white end Joe Don Biggs in the end zone for the TD.

During the game, our Maroons were penalized eleven times. Every time Brownwood got the football, a penalty killed us. But to Joshua's credit, they played a near-perfect game. The Owls' only penalty was a harmless five-yard delay of game call while they let the clock wind down in the first half.

Joshua also made the big play when they needed it. Their game-winning drive began with four minutes left. The Owls pounded their way to Brownwood's twenty where our defense appeared to have them stopped. Then on third and eight, Joshua tried another Craig Ray halfback pass which had worked so well on their first touchdown drive, but this time the Owls didn't fool anyone.

Three Lion defenders were there, in position to knock down Ray's wobbly throw, but some nights you're gonna lose no matter how hard you try. Joe Don Biggs somehow came down with the football.

On the two-point conversion attempt, Biggs made another remarkable catch in heavy traffic to spoil Brownwood's homecoming party. The upstart Owls had accomplished the impossible. They had beaten 4–AAAA kingpins Cleburne and Brownwood on consecutive weekends.

Final score: Brownwood 14, Joshua 15.

Still reeling from our shocking loss to Joshua, we traveled to Cleburne the next weekend where Coach Jerry Cunningham and his Yellowjackets clubbed us with a controversial sucker-punch.

Midway through the fourth quarter, Yellowjacket tailback Alvis Scott took a short pass from quarterback Duff Cunningham, broke a couple of tackles, and raced seventy-five yards before Armando Salazar overhauled him at the Brownwood seven. On the next play Lion linebacker Fritz Speck nailed Scott for a six-yard loss, but Cleburne would not be denied. Halfback Donnie Kinner gained two up the middle then grabbed Cunningham's fourth-down pass for the TD. Don Elam tacked on the point after, and Cleburne took their first lead of the night 7–6.

Brownwood came roaring back, traversing the field with a 57-yard, ten-play drive which featured super-charged Lion Mark Ellis. Ellis had runs of nine and sixteen yards, and on a second and fourteen situation, he hauled in a nineteen-yard strike from Mike Norman to set up a first down at Cleburne's sixteen. There, the going got rough. It took four plays to score, with Ellis submarining for the final yard on fourth down. Norman's two-point pass to Comolli made it 14–7. That set the stage for a play which would fan the flames of Brownwood's on-going feud with Cleburne for years to come.

After the kickoff, Cleburne's quarterback fumbled on the first play from scrimmage, and BHS linebacker David Jones recovered at the Yellowjacket twenty-eight. However, two fumbled snaps, a delay penalty, and an aborted fake punt negated our short-lived advantage and allowed Cleburne to launch their last ditch, do-or-die drive.

Cunningham hit Matt McCarty with a 23-yard pass. Then Donnie Kinner ran for twenty to put the ball at the Lion twenty-five with 3:14 left in the game. That's where the controversial guard-around play took place.

What happened is this. Cleburne quarterback Duff Cunningham lined up behind center. The center snapped the football, but held onto the ball as the quarterback pulled away. While Cunningham sprinted toward the sideline, the center dropped down on both knees, still holding the football in his right hand and between his legs. Cleburne's left guard fell over the center's legs, concealing the ball from Brownwood players' and game officials' view. Then, while Brownwood's defensive unit chased after the Yellowjacket quarterback, the center handed the football to Cleburne's other guard Wade Daniel, and Daniel ran downfield for the touchdown.

The play was illegal for two reasons. First, Cleburne's quarterback never touched the football which is necessary to put the play in progress. Second, the center's knees were both on the ground, so even if the quarterback did touch the football, the ball was dead. The game officials didn't see it that way. They signaled a TD.

For the officials to allow the illegal guard-around play was bad enough, but the crowning blow came on the two-point conversion. Cleburne quarterback Duff Cunningham took the snap, found his receivers covered, and lit out for the right corner of the end zone. It was a foot race all the way, but Lion defender Jason Cauble was there to meet Cunningham head on when he tried to dive across the goal line. When the officials raised their hands to signal Cleburne had scored, not a person in the stands could believe their eyes. Cunningham and Cauble were lying there sprawled out at the goal line. The football was back at the two-yard line.

Final score: Brownwood 14, Cleburne 15.

In the locker room after the game every member of my team was upset and angry because of the sorry officiating. Morris Southall and his son Si were up in the press box when the controversial plays occurred. From their vantage point, they could see the game action very clearly. Both confirmed Cleburne's quarterback never touched the football on the guard-around play, and both believed the ballcarrier dropped the football at the two-yard line on the two-point conversion.

Jason Cauble, who made the tackle, was even more adamant. "No way he made those two points," Jason declared. "We kept him out!"

The next week a Brownwood dad told me this story about two Cleburne fans who were standing even with our goal line when Cunningham tried to dive across. After the officials signaled a score, one fan said to the other, "If you think Coach Wood is mad now, just wait until he sees the film on that call."

◆　◆　◆

IN ALMOST HALF A CENTURY of coaching football, a Gordon Wood-coached team had never made the state playoffs with two district losses. With my starting quarterback Mitch Moore injured and probably out for the season, it looked like my last year of coaching would end early.

Still, like Yogi Berra once said, "It's not over 'till it's over." We had so many great kids on that '85 team. Since they were seventh graders, we'd been telling them to never quit, never give up, no matter how bleak the circumstances. So, even though Brownwood only retained an outside chance of making the playoffs, there was no way Gordon Wood and his coaching staff could relax and play out the season.

Putting the two disheartening losses behind them, our Lions stayed in the 4–AAAA hunt by sneaking past Stephenville 14–12. Then they took on unbeaten Everman. The Bulldogs were in the midst of a 21-game regular season win-streak, and Brownwood was a ten-point underdog. The score was tied at 7–7 when Mike Norman lobbed a 56-yard scoring rocket to Craig Comolli, and Gordon's Gorillas never let Everman back in the game.

Final score: Brownwood 21, Everman 7.

Our triumph over Everman boosted the Lions to a 3–2 mark in district play, but Brownwood was still far behind front runners Everman, Cleburne and Joshua.

When I scanned the *Brownwood Bulletin* to check the standings, here's the way things looked:

District 4–AAAA Standings
(District Play)

	W	L	T
Everman	4	1	0
Cleburne	4	1	0
Joshua	3	1	1
Brownwood	3	2	0
Granbury	2	3	0
Stephenville	2	3	0
Crowley	1	4	0
Mansfield	0	4	1

Because Brownwood had lost to Cleburne and Joshua, a minor miracle would have to take place for the Lions to reach the playoffs. Cleburne would have to sweep its final two games against Everman and Stephenville. Everman would have to beat Joshua, and Brownwood would have to win its final two games. All that seemed a most unlikely scenario as the Lions prepared to face last place Mansfield, but all the pieces fell into place that Friday night.

While Brownwood was beating up Mansfield 27–7, Cleburne knocked off Everman 10–6, and Stephenville shaded Joshua 12–7. Amazingly, that left Cleburne atop the district standings and Brownwood and Everman tied with 4–2 records. Since Brownwood had beaten Everman, only the Granbury Pirates stood between the Lions and the state playoffs.

A couple of days before our Granbury game, a headline appeared in the sports section of the Hood County Newspaper. The headline read:

PIRATES MIGHT END GORDON WOOD'S CAREER.

My maroon gang took care of that business on Friday night. Brownwood buried the Pirates 31–0, and Gordon Wood was still coaching.

◆　◆　◆

WHEN THE EUPHORIA of reaching the playoffs wore off, we discovered our bi-district opponent would be 3–AAAA champ Mineral Wells. Coach Joe Cluley's red and black team had crushed Grapevine 38–10 on Friday night to run their season record to 11–0 and reach the playoffs for the first time since 1966. We decided to slug it out with the undefeated Rams at Tarleton's Memorial Stadium in Stephenville.

Brownwood scored first on an 84-yard punt return by Craig Jacobson. On the ensuing kickoff, Mineral Wells tied things up with a 94-yard return by Myron Thompson, and the race was on. By halftime, with running backs Mark Ellis and Jacobson charging through big holes, Brownwood had rolled for 237 yards and scored three more times, but Mineral Wells was right on our tail. The Rams had gained 185 yards and racked up two more TDs to keep the score close at 28–21.

After a scoreless third quarter, Mineral Wells knotted the score at 28–28 when quarterback Sean Fisher rifled a 28-yard touchdown strike to tailback Henry Anders.

Following the kickoff, our offense, which had been struggling in the second half, pieced together its best performance of the evening. Ellis carried four times for forty-eight yards, and Norman speared wingback Jason Cauble for a seven-yard gain. From there, Jacobson ran in standing up, and Clay Childs booted his fifth extra point of the game.

Our 35–28 lead held up until near the end of the game. With Brownwood defenders Erin Bird, Raymond Tijerina, DeWayne Wood, Kris Boyd, Doug Hicks and Jimmy Shelton hot on his trail, our defense kept Ram quarterback Sean Fisher boxed up until Mineral Wells took possession at their own thirty-eight with 2:27 remaining. There, Fisher directed a pressure-packed 62-yard march to the Lions' goal line. Twice, Brownwood's fierce pass rush forced Fisher out of the pocket, but each time he was able to shake loose and run for key first downs. With only forty-eight seconds left, Fisher skipped in from the three to pull his team within one point.

With the Rams leading 6–5 in penetrations, both schools' seasons came down to an extra point try. Ram kicking specialist Kim Chung would do the honors, and he hadn't missed all evening. Hoping to rattle the Ram's reliable kicker, we called time-out just as Chung was lining up to boot the tying point. The strategy worked. Three minutes later, Chung shanked his kick wide, and every emotionally-exhausted fan in Memorial Stadium collapsed to their seat.

Final score: Brownwood 35, Mineral Wells 34.

On Saturday morning, Superintendent Lancaster, Coach Southall and I drove to Sweetwater where we met with Lubbock Estacado officials and decided our quarterfinal game would be played at Sweetwater's Mustang Bowl. Shortly after we arrived back in Brownwood, which was sometime around noon, I returned a call from sportswriter Bill Stovall. Bill wanted to get my thoughts on the exciting finish at Friday night's game.

"I woke up eleven years older this morning," I told Stovall. "That was as great a game as I've seen. People who missed this one game missed the game of the century."

◆　◆　◆

BROWNWOOD'S HEART-IN-THE-THROAT VICTORY over Mineral Wells was my two hundred and fifty-seventh win at Brownwood High. It would also be my last.

At Sweetwater the next weekend, Lion sophomore Jason Allred took the unbeaten Matadors' opening kickoff and squirted for ninety-six magnificent yards to get his maroon team off to a great start, but after that, the game was all Estacado. With quarterback O.T. Thomas at the controls, the Mats drove for a touchdown on their second possession. By halftime the tough gang from Lubbock had rolled for fourteen first downs, 276 yards and a 17–7 lead.

Brownwood had several chances in the second half to stage a comeback, but on every occasion the Mats made the right play at the right time. When play ended, the Mats had racked up win number one hundred for Coach Louis Kelley. Kelley was in his eleventh season at the Lubbock school.

Final score: Brownwood 7, Estacado 29.

After the game, while our players showered and changed to their street clothes, I stood at the locker room entrance, savoring the moment and proudly surveying the young men who had worked so hard and come from so far back to reach the playoffs. As my players filed past to board the bus for home, I shook hands with each one.

Seniors on that '85 Lion squad included Jason Cauble, Casey Clark, Mitch Moore, Mike Norman, Keith Cook, Jimmy Shelton, Mark Ellis, Carson Williams, Todd Reeves, Amador Arriaga, Doug Hicks, Michael Lee, Fritz Speck, Harold Isom, Raymond Tijerina, Erin Bird, Cody Neal, Armando Salazar, Kris Boyd, Craig Comolli, Jeff Montgomery and Richard Roberts. To me, they'll always be extra special because they were my last.

CHAPTER TWENTY-ONE

So This is Retirement

IN POST GAME INTERVIEWS, Coach Southall didn't mince his words. Morris had a decisive answer for everyone who asked: "This was my last game!"

Me, I wasn't quite so sure. Brownwood had a lot of very good football players coming back. Although I couldn't imagine coaching without Morris by my side, I wanted to consider the situation for a few days, let the air clear before I definitely decided. Looking back, I think I was really hoping something would happen to convince me to continue coaching.

I didn't finally make up my mind until a week later. It was on Friday, December 13. Maybe that's some kind of omen. Anyway, that afternoon I met with my players and told them I was ninety-eight percent sure I wouldn't be back to coach the next year. I asked them to support whomever the school board selected as my replacement.

On Saturday morning, I held a news conference at Brownwood's Holiday Inn to announce my retirement. Present in the crowd of more than one hundred people were newspaper reporters, TV crews, school administrators, fellow coaches, present and former players, and a lot of close friends.

"If we had held this news conference yesterday morning," I told the audience, "I would be telling you I positively want to coach again. Actually, if I did what I want to, I'd go after Alonzo Stagg's record. That, I think, would be a real challenge."

When a reporter asked if I would be tempted to come out of retirement if someone broke my record, I laughed. "It won't be broken in my lifetime, but records are made to be broken. This one will be too, and I'd be as happy as I could be, if I were still alive to congratulate the man who did it."

I wrapped up my comments by answering a question about the rewards of coaching.

"If I had my life to live over, I guarantee I would be a football coach. It's the finest profession in the world. Coaching has been great to Gordon Wood. I've had a lifetime job doing work I would do for nothing, and I got paid for it. I have no regrets."

Later, when I met with School Superintendent James Lancaster, I promised to work with the school board to get the best football coach available. I told him I couldn't recommend any one coach on my staff for the head coaching job because they were all about equal as far as I was concerned. I promised to support any coach the trustees selected. I also promised I would never second guess the new coach and to do everything in my power to help him grow.

I knew I'd done the right thing, for me, for my family, but to tell the truth, quitting my job at Brownwood High was the hardest thing I've ever done.

◆　◆　◆

ONE THING I KNEW I wanted to do was spend more time on the golf course. So after I retired, I went out and bought the best golf cart I could find. I also wanted a better automobile, so after several days of shopping around, I selected an elegant, brand-new four-door sedan. I drove it home to get Katharine's approval.

"It's real nice," Katharine told me, even before she checked out the luxurious interior. "But I'll never ride in it."

"Why not? It's a great car," I declared, exasperated that Katharine wasn't bubbling over with excited anticipation, like myself.

"There are too many hungry people in this town for us to drive a car like that," Katharine stated coldly, and that was that. I returned the expensive new car to the dealer that same day.

◆　◆　◆

THE FIRST FEW YEARS, I played golf almost every day. When I wasn't hitting golf balls, I worked at my office. Herman Bennett's construction company occupies a building located on Fisk Street near downtown. Since my retirement, my builder friend has generously provided me with my own private office.

The day I announced my retirement I pledged to continue fighting for education reform and against the no-pass, no-play restrictions imposed by House Bill 72. Since I'm big on writing letters, I bombarded state legislators and Texas newspapers with my opinions and suggestions for changes. Whenever I was invited to speak at an athletic banquet or some civic meeting, I pushed for education improvement. In 1990, I formulated all my ideas, complaints and proposals into a fourteen-page paper entitled "Why is Education Failing in Texas." The article was published in *Texas Coach* magazine.

Three hip replacements and a triple bypass operation in 1990 finally convinced me to give up golf, so in 1992, I published my first book, *Gordon Wood's Game Plan to Winning Football.* In my book I outlined in detail the offensive and defensive strategies which worked so successfully for us at Brownwood High. Intermingled among tactics for winning football games were lots of tips for young coaches and stories about my unusual experiences during forty-plus years as a football coach.

Of course, the main passion is still football, for both myself and Morris Southall. We rarely miss a Brownwood High football game. Coach Southall works with longtime Lion play-by-play man Dallas Houston doing the radio broadcasts for station KBWD. Generally, I sit in the stadium press box where I can talk and visit with reporters and BHS coaches while we observe the action on the field. On Thursday afternoons during football season, Roger Sweeney and I do a twenty minute radio show on KBWD to discuss the upcoming game and talk football.

When the state playoffs begin in November, Morris and I might drive a hundred miles to see a game we're interested in—one where we know the coaches or think a team might use some new wrinkle.

Several years back, Coach Southall and I decided to drive to Waco to see a playoff game. We'd hardly passed Brownwood's city limits when it started to rain. By the time we reached Gatesville, the bottom dropped out. At one spot, storm water was over the highway, and we had to drive through water up to our hubcaps. Undaunted, we kept going, and when we reached Waco, we sat in a heavy downpour while we watched the game. Because of the harsh weather, Morris and I spent the night in a motel rather than drive back to Brownwood. The next morning we drove to Dallas and watched three more games at Texas Stadium.

These days we exercise better judgement, usually limiting our playoff excursions to weekends in Dallas. I call Bruce Hardy who runs the show at Texas Stadium. Bruce arranges for Morris and me to sit in the press box with Max Goldsmith and Neal Wilson. Max was the track coach at Andrews when we coached at Seminole. Neal was the head coach at Boswell-Saginaw when our teams played in the '77 semifinals. Nowadays, Neal is the athletic director for the Lewisville school district.

Some Saturdays, the first game kicks off at ten o'clock in the morning, and the last game ends around ten that night. Last year, Morris and I watched five different playoff games in one day.

◆　◆　◆

LATELY, I'VE FOCUSED my attention on a project called Gordon Wood's Hall of Champions. In the mid-nineties, Brownwood obtained a government grant to restore the old Santa Fe Depot. Renovation construction was completed in 1999, and the old railroad depot is now one of the most beautiful and most impressive structures in Brownwood. The large waiting and ticket sales area is now a ballroom/auditorium, suitable for weddings, civic meetings, and all sorts of public gatherings.

The freight shipping section is two-stories high. Brownwood's Chamber of Commerce occupies the lower floor. Our Hall of Champions Museum is planned for the second floor, and once it is finished, I believe it will become Brownwood's main tourist attraction. My longtime friend Bill Jamar serves as chairman of the Hall's Board of Directors. He and Stuart Coleman provide the financial backbone for the idea.

Each year, five individuals from the Central Texas area will be selected for induction. Our first inaugural class was named in October of 2000. The five men selected were Gus Snodgrass, former Brownwood High track coach; and Brownwood High athletes Tommy Vaughn, Class of 1936; Ray Masters, Class of 1953; Lawrence Elkins, Class of 1960; and Jimmy Carmichael, Class of 1969.

So This is Retirement

◆　◆　◆

AT NINE O'CLOCK every weekday morning and every afternoon at three o'clock, my Brownwood pals and I convene for coffee at the Dairy Maid on Coggin Avenue—to talk politics, football, gripe about the weather, and retell old stories. Our outspoken buddy John Arthur usually has some beef about local issues. Calvin Lee always seems to have some news flash about Texas A&M. Herman Bennett loves to ask questions he already knows the answers to. Tommy Butler is big on doodling, and he'll run through a couple of sheets of paper at every meeting.

Rounding out our coffee crew are John Arthur Thomason, Dr. Richard Jackson, Calvin Fryar, Ed "Beezer" Day, Nelson Turnbow, Groner Pitts, Kenneth West, and Morris Southall. Our twice-a-day gatherings last maybe twenty to thirty minutes, but we each truly enjoy the fellowship. Most of us are retired, so it gives us a good reason to climb out of bed and get going every morning.

◆　◆　◆

THERE ARE HUNDREDS of stories and thousands of close friends I haven't mentioned in this autobiography. That doesn't mean they are not important to Katharine and me, or that we've forgotten. What it means is—I've simply run out of space.

Looking back, I don't know where the time went. Seems like only yesterday I was a towheaded farm boy horsing around with my buddies Otis Crowell and Ed Cherry at Hardin-Simmons, worrying about my future and wondering if I'd ever amount to a hill of beans.

My heart swells with pride when I think of my two children. Both are college graduates. Pat works in San Antonio at Alamo Junior College where she's deeply involved in a government-funded program designed to help people get off welfare. Jim is a successful lawyer in Amarillo. Naturally, grandson Ty is the apple of my eye, but my latest pride and joy is granddaughter Erin Franklin Wood who was born last September.

If I had searched the world, I couldn't have found a more compatible mate than Katharine. She's a terrific mother, and she has allowed me complete freedom to pursue my football career. Katharine is the most caring and unselfish person I've ever known.

She's been beside me every step of the way, supporting me through thick and thin, through heart-stoppers and heart-breakers.

Nine state championships and three hundred and ninety-six victories. That's quite a record, and every win is a story in itself. Several Texas coaches: G.A. Moore, Jr. at Celina, Charlie Johnston at Childress, Tommy Watkins at Rowlett, Bob McQueen at Temple, and Monte Driskell at Groveton are within striking distance of breaking my record, and I hope one of them does. That's what records are for—to be broken. When some coach does pass me, I hope he'll feel as good about his career as I do.

If you like my story, call me and let me know. My home phone is 915-646-9421.

If you have a complaint, call John Carver in Dallas at 972-669-0707. John has agreed to take the blame for misspelled names, over-embellished stories, and my poor memory. You may want to read Carver's two sports novels, *Winning* and *Hardball Fever*. I hadn't met John when I read *Winning*, but I liked it so much I called him and asked him to help me write this story.

When you're at a football game, check the press box. You might find Morris Southall and me there. We'd love to say hi—but we can only talk between plays.

Author's Afterword

AS MY DAUGHTER Renee and I were putting the final touches on this book, a sportswriter from Abilene began to question Coach Wood about the number of victories listed on his resume. Subsequent investigation verified that there was indeed some substance to the sportswriter's challenge. As we go to press, that issue has not been completely resolved. For that reason, even though it messed up the perfect ending to an absolutely amazing story, I have deleted portions of Gordon Wood's autobiography which relate to the exact number of games he won and the boisterous celebrations thereof. It took some soul searching, because I would rather take a beating than spoil a good story, but I finally decided to leave it out. I'm just not a good enough writer to explain why all the applause took place at the wrong time.

When you consider everything he has accomplished, though, it really doesn't make one iota of difference whether Coach Wood won 405 or 396 or 394 games. He is still the winningest Texas football coach of all time. Whether it be a football game, a courtroom battle or a game of horseshoes, I would always choose to be on Gordon Wood's side. After all, he's the *Coach of the Century*.

—John Carver

Gordon Wood

Professional Achievements and Recognitions

Year	Awards and Honors

1956 Selected High School Football Coach of the Year by the Texas Sportswriters Association

1957 Selected to coach the Texas High School All-Star Game

1958 Coached the North Team to victory in the Texas High School North-South All-Star Football Game

1959 Served as President of the Texas High School Coaches Association

1967 Inducted into Texas High School Coaches Association Hall of Honor

1970 Selected High School Football Coach of the Year by the Texas Sportswriters Association

1972 Guest Coach (Summer Camp), Winnipeg Blue Bombers, Canadian League

1973 Guest Coach (Summer Camp), Winnipeg Blue Bombers, Canadian League

1974 Guest Coach (Summer Camp), Winnipeg Blue Bombers, Canadian League

1977 Coached the Texas High School All-Star Team to victory at the Oil Bowl against Oklahoma All-Star Team

1978 Selected High School Football Coach of the Year by the Texas Sportswriters Association

1985—Gordon and Katharine celebrate the official dedication of Gordon Wood Stadium.
(credit: Brown Bulletin)

1958–59 Board of Directors, Texas High School Coaches Association.
(courtesy Texas High School Coaches Association)

1979 Named National High School Football Coach of the Year by the National High School Athletic Coaches Association

Received Distinguished Alumni award, Hardin-Simmons University

Inducted into the National High School Athletic Coaches Association Hall of Fame

1980 Brownwood's Cen-Tex stadium renamed Gordon Wood Stadium

1981 Selected High School Football Coach of the Year by the Texas Sportswriters Association

1983 Inducted into the Texas High School Coaches Hall of Fame

Inducted into the Texas Sports Hall of Fame

Honored by the American Football Coaches Association

1984 Inducted into the National High School Hall of Fame

1985 Coached the Texas High School All-Star Team at the Oil Bowl Classic

1986 Touchdowner of the Year Award—Touchdown Club of Houston

1993 Named Co-Coach of Century—Gordon Wood and Paul Tyson—by *Tops in Texas*, a Martin Communications Publication

1996 Inducted into the Hardin-Simmons Sports Hall of Fame

1999 F.C.A. Lifetime Achievement—NCAA—Grant Teaff Award

Named Coach of the Century by the *Dallas Morning News*

Coach Wood has lectured at coaching clinics in 16 different states.
(credit: Wood Family Collection)

Gordon Wood's First Team All-State Players

Year	Player	Position
	Seminole	
1947	Val Joe Walker	Back
	Stamford	
1952	Charlie Davis	Guard
	Kenneth Lowe	Back
1953	Wayne Wash	Back
1954	Ernie Davis	Back
	Bob Harrison	Center
1955	Mike McClellan	Back
	Joe Wash	Tackle
1956	Mike McClellan	Back
	Dale Robinson	Tackle
	Royce West	Guard
	Brownwood	
1960	Lawrence Elkins	End
	Ronnie Moore	Tackle
1962	Wayne Garrett	Tackle
	Doug Young	Guard
1965	Jimmy Piper	Fullback
	Joe Shaw	Tackle
1966	Rollin Hunter	End
1967	Mike Fuller	Center, Def-Line
1968	Lane Bowen	End

1969	Jan Brown	Def-Back
	Jimmy Carmichael	Quarterback
	Tommy Roderick	Tackle
	Ricky Stokes	Linebacker
	Perry Young	End
1970	Gary Barron	Tailback
	Gene Day	Lineman
	Tommy George	Def-Back
	John Isom	Linebacker
	Garry Moore	Lineman
1971	Tammy Hollingshead	Def-Back
	Kurt Newton	Lineman
	Brian Pinto	Linebacker
1973	Gary George	Linebacker
	Don Wright	Center
1975	Harold Barnes	Lineman
1976	Doug Reid	Tackle
1977	Eddie Gill	Lineman
	Derwin Williams	Def-Back
1978	Craig Agnew	Tackle
	Kevin Taylor	End
	Derwin Williams	Def-Back
1979	Kirk Chastain	Def-End
	Bo Shero	Center
	Mike Thomas	Kicker
	Glen West	Linebacker
1980	Mike Kinsey	Def-Lineman
	Tony Wilde	Linebacker
1981	Jewel Brown	Def-End
	Mike Davis	Def-Lineman
	Mike Kinsey	Def-Lineman
	Jimmy Morris	Punter
	Marvin Rathke	Def-Back
	Jesse Smith	End
	Tyler Tabor	Quarterback
1982	Mike Davis	Def-Lineman
	Kendal Nelson	Linebacker
	Marvin Rathke	Def-Back

Gordon Wood's All-Time Football Squad

The Best Players of Five Decades

Offense

Ends:	Lawrence Elkins, Brownwood (1960)
	Perry Young, Brownwood (1968–69)
	Billy Sawyer, Brownwood (1978–79)
	Rocky Allen, Brownwood (1983–84)
Tackles:	J.T. Lyday, Roscoe (1945)
	Minor Nelson, Winters (1950)
	Joe Shaw, Brownwood (1963–65)
Guards:	Jerry Smith, Victoria (1958–59)
	Doug Young, Brownwood (1960–62)
Center:	Bob Harrison, Stamford (1952–54)
	Larry Sanders, Victoria (1958–59)
Quarterback:	Jimmy Carmichael, Brownwood (1967–69)
	Scott Lancaster, Brownwood (1976–78)
Running Backs:	Walter Maloney, Roscoe (1945)
	Mike McClellan, Stamford (1955–56)
Wingback:	Val Joe Walker, Seminole (1947)
Kicker:	Mike Thomas, Brownwood (1979)

Defense

Ends:	Keith Miles, Stamford (1952–53)
	Dallas Christian, Stamford (1954–56)
	Truman Childress, Stamford (1955–56)
	Bryan Allen, Brownwood (1975–76)

Tackles:	Royce West, Stamford (1954–55)
	Ronnie Moore, Brownwood (1960)
Guards:	Charlie Davis, Stamford (1951–52)
	Jerry Lloyd, Brownwood (1973–74)
	Mike Kinsey, Brownwood (1980–81)
Linebackers:	John Townsend, Rule (1941–42)
	Jimmy Piper, Brownwood (1963–65)
	Ricky Stokes, Brownwood (1967–69)
Halfbacks:	Vernon Townsend, Rule (1941–42)
	Terry Southall, Brownwood (1961–62)
Safety:	James Harris, Brownwood (1962–64)
Punter:	David Henley, Brownwood (1963–65)
	Si Southall, Brownwood (1966–67)
	Jerry Don Gleaton, Brownwood (1974–75)
	Jimmy Morris, Brownwood (1980–81)

Index

Index

Index

Index

Index